THE SETTING OF THE PEARL

THE
SETTING
OF THE
PEARL

Vienna Under Hitler

In my eyes Vienna is a pearl to which I will give a proper setting.
Adolf Hitler, Vienna, April 9, 1938

THOMAS WEYR

OXFORD
UNIVERSITY PRESS

2005

OXFORD
UNIVERSITY PRESS

Oxford University Press, Inc., publishes works that further
Oxford University's objective of excellence
in research, scholarship, and education.

Oxford   New York
Auckland   Cape Town   Dar es Salaam   Hong Kong   Karachi
Kuala Lumpur   Madrid   Melbourne   Mexico City   Nairobi
New Delhi   Shanghai   Taipei   Toronto

With offices in
Argentina   Austria   Brazil   Chile   Czech Republic   France   Greece
Guatemala   Hungary   Italy   Japan   Poland   Portugal   Singapore
South Korea   Switzerland   Thailand   Turkey   Ukraine   Vietnam

Copyright © 2005 by Thomas Weyr

Published by Oxford University Press, Inc.
198 Madison Avenue, New York, New York 10016
www.oup.com

Oxford is a registered trademark of Oxford University Press

Library of Congress Cataloging-in-Publication Data
Weyr, Thomas.
The setting of the pearl : Vienna under Hitler / by Thomas Weyr.
p.   cm.
ISBN-13: 978-0-19-514679-0
ISBN-10: 0-19-514679-4
1. Vienna (Austria)—History—1918.
2. World War, 1939–1945—Austria—Vienna.
3. National socialism—Austria—Vienna.
I. Title.
DB855.W463 2005
940.53'43613—dc 22   2004018295

1 3 5 7 9 8 6 4 2
Printed in the United States of America
on acid-free paper.

For my father, Siegfried Weyr,
who loved Vienna beyond reason,
for my Viennese daughter, Teodora Weyr,
who loved it almost as much,
and for my wife, Nancy Shuker,
without whom this book could not have been written.

Contents

Acknowledgments

It is customary to thank those who have helped an author in his research, but in Vienna the customary is not so easy to fulfill, largely because Viennese bureaucrats do not like to reveal much about the city's Nazi past.

I am especially grateful, therefore, to the handful of scholars, archivists and librarians who opened doors and archives.

Dr. Peter Malina, the recently retired head librarian of the Institute of Contemporary History at the University of Vienna, made available his archives, his library, his staff, and other facilities and resources in a most generous manner.

Frau Dr. Klaralinda Ma Kirchner of the Vienna city archive waved a magic wand to unlock diaries, letters, memorabilia, and other eye witness accounts of life in Vienna under Hitler. And she cut through a thicket of red tape with consummate skill.

Professor Dr. Wilhelm Mikoletzky, the director of the Austrian state archive, is committed to making public the Nazi record and he helped where he could.

Professor Dr. Wendelin Schmidt-Dengler, head of the German department at the University of Vienna and a renowned expert on Austrian literature, opened important doors and read parts of the manuscript for factual and other errors.

I am especially indebted to my friend Fritz Molden, a genuine—and rare—hero of the Austrian resistance, if heroism is defined as a willingness to risk one's life for an idea, in his case a free and independent Austria, for sharing his first-hand experiences, for his insight, and his introduction to fellow resistants who are still alive.

ACKNOWLEDGMENTS

Mrs. Rosl Merdinger, the managing director of the Austrian PEN, graciously allowed me access to her extensive private archives on the arts under Hitler and arranged introductions to other sources.

Finally I drew on the memories and reminiscences of friends and acquaintances—not all of which I could in the end use—and I am grateful to them all.

Preface

I was born in Vienna and consider it my home town. My family's roots, certainly, go deep. In 1529 my great, great-on-and-on-grandfather, Eck von Reischach, a sword for hire from Würtenberg in southern Germany, commanded a regiment of mercenaries that helped defend the city against the Turks. When the Turks smashed through the wall at the Carinthian gate, Eck threw his men at the advancing foe, drove them out, and closed the breach. A street in the Inner City is named for him; so am I—Eck is a diminutive of Hektor, my middle name.

Weyrgasse in the third district is named for my great-uncle, Rudolf von Weyr, a sculptor of note and talent whose statues litter the city—a martial fountain in the Hofburg, a frieze on the Burgtheater, two lions astride a bridge across the Danube canal, a relief of Charlemagne on the Peterskirche, and on and on. My name, therefore, is carved on most of the principal buildings of the city.

My grandfather, Eduard Weyr, was a captain in the Austrian cavalry who fought against Prussia in 1866 and bequeathed me an abiding hatred of all things Teutonic, despite my German grandmother, the Countess Marie von Reischach. Family legend, no doubt apocryphal, has it that Eduard, full of rage at the Prussians, took aim at Bismarck after the battle of Olmütz, but was pierced by a Prussian lancer before he could fire. In 1878 he rode into Bosnia-Herzegovina when the Austrians "liberated" that territory from the Turks.

When in the 1990s the AP was about to send my Vienna-born daughter Teodora to Sarajevo to cover the Bosnian war, I pointed out to her that we had, in effect, "been there and done that" and that she did not have to go.

My father, Siegfried Weyr, wrote a dozen books about Vienna and its twisted history, books that became classics of their genre because he saw the city's history with a painter's eye and a filmmaker's verve. Thirty-five years after he died Vienna's leading tabloid ran everything he ever wrote to considerable resonance.

My childhood in Vienna was as happy as that of an only child of intellectual parents steeped in the turmoil of the times could be, and in a house where Alfred Adler, the apostate Freud disciple and founder of Individual Psychology, was a frequent guest. At age nine I wanted to be a writer, a psychoanalyst, and to fight in Spain alongside La Passionara, ready to die on my feet rather than live on my knees.

At age eleven I was driven out of Vienna and spent the next ten years in London, Philadelphia, and New York. After the war I came back for another decade—stretched over fifteen years—to take a PhD at the university and to work for the United Press, ABC, and *Newsweek*. I left for good in 1963 to raise a family in New York but returned regularly to Vienna, where I maintained my parents' apartment, led a local life, and watched the city change around me, not always for the best but often enough.

Nevertheless, I am ambivalent about my hometown, not only because we were driven out—in truth we had a much easier time than most other refugees—but because the Vienna of my childhood had been so thoroughly destroyed, and I was so deeply disappointed upon my return, a disappointment that lingered into the years I spent researching this book. For the Viennese my roots simply did not matter.

"You're not Viennese," a bureaucrat at the state archives said while perusing my American passport that says I was born in Austria, "so you'll have to wait longer for the stuff you want." The fact that I spoke better and more cultivated German than he did—not hard given his rude dialect—only made matters worse.

They did for my father, too, who was just as disappointed even though he had insisted we come back and thus made of his American-educated son a trans-Atlantic man who was both at home and a stranger in Vienna and in New York.

My father escaped into the "lost Vienna" that had so deeply influenced global culture between Austria's defeat by Prussia in 1866 and Hitler's annexation of Austria, the Anschluss, in 1938. But the bitterness over the destruction of "his" Vienna remained until he died.

This book is about how Vienna was destroyed—by Hitler, to be sure, but also by itself. The image of howling Nazi mobs beating old Jews will not wash off history as easily as the political slogans Jews were forced to scrub off city walls with toothbrushes, no matter how much the Viennese proclaim their innocence and victimhood.

For in the end it was the Viennese themselves who opted for wealthy Prussian provincialism over cultural and intellectual excellence that might have restored the city's greatness. All that is left today are the monuments.

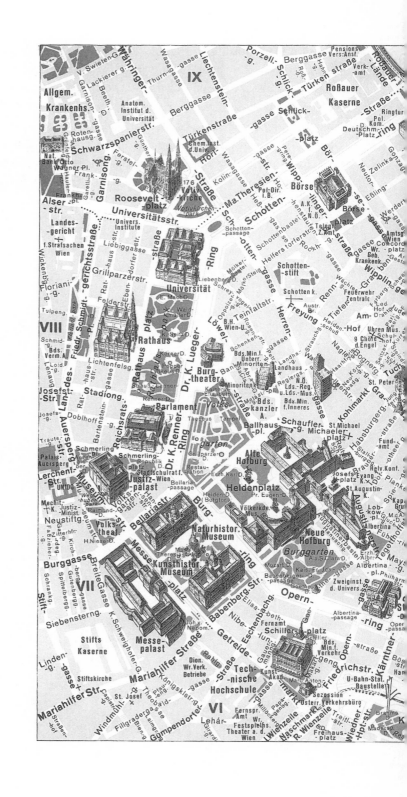

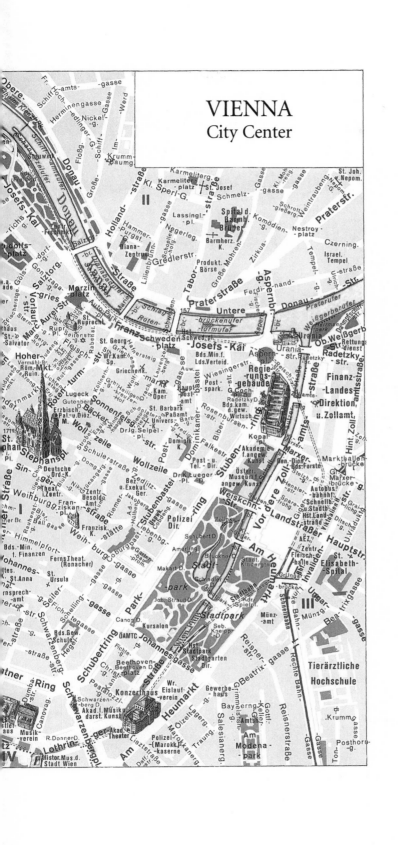

VIENNA
City Center

CHAPTER 1

Anschluss

From Berchtesgaden to the Heldenplatz:
February 12–March 15, 1938

At 8 A.M. on March 9, 1938, a Wednesday, Dr. Kurt von Schuschnigg, the forty-year old chancellor and virtual dictator of Austria, strode down the platform of Vienna's West Station and boarded the parlor car at the front of the D-121 express to Innsbruck, capital of his home province, the Tyrol.[1]

News photographs show him in his Ruritanian Fatherland Front uniform—belt tied around his overcoat and a leather strap across his shoulder, a feathered hat in one hand, and the inevitable Asta cigarette with red silk tip in the other.[2] He is smiling broadly, something the generally dour chancellor did rarely, but finally he had something to smile about. He was about to embark on his last—and in truth perhaps his first—real gamble.

He had been in power for almost four years in a country rent by civil war, shaken by a Nazi putsch that murdered his predecessor, and in desperate economic straits Schuschnigg's authoritarian regime could not set right. And he faced growing pressure from the Third Reich next door to conform to Nazi policy.

Less than a month before he had met Adolf Hitler at the Führer's mountain retreat in Berchtesgaden and been subject to a brutal verbal bludgeoning, unique in modern diplomatic history. Hitler told the chain-smoker he could not smoke, yelled at him throughout the morning, delivered ultimatum after ultimatum to the point where Schuschnigg

1

thought he would be arrested on the spot, and finally made him sign an agreement that was Austria's death warrant.

Hitler wasted no time with small talk. Schuschnigg had barely taken his seat and complemented the Führer on the imposing view from the Berghof's windows when Hitler interrupted to say they hadn't come here to talk about the view or the weather. And he soon demanded that "the persecution of National Socialists must end or I will make an end of it."[3] The string of accusations the Führer fired at the Austrian chancellor that morning included his failure to follow Germany out of the League of Nations—something, Schuschnigg pointed out, Austria could not do for financial reasons if nothing else—and his "ridiculous" fortification of the Austro-German frontier.

Patiently the Austrian chancellor tried to explain his actions but Hitler either didn't listen or interrupted with personal insults where "he played all the registers of emotion available to him."[4] After two hours they broke for lunch, with three German generals in attendance who clearly had no idea why they had been asked. The reason, though, was obvious: their presence was designed to lend weight to Hitler's threats to invade Austria.

Lunch was pleasant enough—at least in Schuschnigg's recollections; others who attended had a different impression—with Hitler talking about his preference for motorized vehicles on parades because horses tended to get out of hand, and his plans to build skyscrapers that would show Americans that Germans could build taller and more beautiful buildings than they could.

Austria's foreign minister, Dr. Guido Schmidt, remembered it somewhat differently. "Hitler led the conversation, noting that German mothers do not cry for their sons if they died for the Reich. He clearly wanted to show how fanatically the people were ready to do his bidding."[5]

After lunch Schuschnigg and his foreign minister were left alone for two hours, and the chancellor could finally light up one Asta after another. Then Joachim von Ribbentrop, the newly named German foreign minister, asked them into a small room where he showed them a two-page typewritten document, which, Ribbentrop said, was the most the Führer was willing to concede. The demands were harsh: Schuschnigg was to name Dr. Arthur Seyss-Inquart, a Viennese lawyer close to the Nazis but also a Schuschnigg friend, as minister of internal security in charge of the police; all National Socialists in prison were to be freed and a general amnesty issued; National Socialism could be practiced freely; economic affairs were to be placed under control of another Austrian Nazi; and one hundred German officers were to be assigned to the Austrian army.

Schuschnigg knew this was the end. Putting a Nazi in control of the police would make a mockery of Austrian independence, and allowing National Socialism to play an unfettered political role amounted to the same thing. But all the Austrian did was suggest minor changes—fifty instead of the one hundred officers (with fifty more to come later), and easing Nazi control of the economy. He refused demands that he replace his secretary of war and noted that his chief of staff, Field Marshall-Lieutenant Alfred Samsa, was about to retire and did not need to be removed. Samsa was one of the few Austrian generals eager to fight the Germans and was the author of a strategic plan to do so. This was not a man Hitler wanted in a potential enemy's cockpit.

After letting Schuschnigg wait a bit longer, Hitler called Schuschnigg back into his office where he ranted and raved and said that all his demands must be met within three days or else—the constitutional issues Schuschnigg had raised notwithstanding. Then Hitler called for Wilhelm Keitel, his top general, and asked Schuschnigg to wait outside. When Keitel walked into the room Hitler said, "please sit down. The chancellor wants to have a short meeting with Schmidt, his foreign minister. I don't have anything else."[6] It was simply another ploy to frighten the Austrians.

It succeeded. Schmidt, who had been talking amiably to the general, was surprised at the way his manner suddenly turned icy. In the end Schuschnigg signed the modified document, declined an invitation to supper, and returned to Austria.

Now Schuschnigg saw one slim chance. Days before he left for Innsbruck he had decided to order a snap plebiscite on Sunday, March 13, asking the Austrian people if they wanted a "free and German, independent and social, Christian and united Austria." A *yes* would be a vote to defy the Nazis; a *no* would invite Hitler to rule Austria. He would announce the referendum in a speech he was traveling to Innsbruck to make.

The plebiscite was a desperate gamble and Schuschnigg knew it. But he also knew that without it he could not fend off the Germans or try to rebuild some national consensus. He ruled a still bitter and divided nation, burdened by a killer unemployment rate and the legacy of both civil war and the murder of his predecessor, Engelbert Dollfuss.

3

Dollfuss had shut down Austria's parliamentary democracy in 1933 when the bitterly and closely divided legislature self-destructed in a bizarre drama that left it leaderless and unable to function. Months later he outlawed the NSDAP, the Nazi party, for a rampage of terror and death that included bombing Jewish-owned stores, blowing up telephone cells, and brawling in the streets. The Austrian Nazis had been a splinter group until Hitler became German chancellor—then its popularity began to surge. Next, in February 1934, Dollfuss destroyed the Social Democratic party in a bloody, four-day civil war. Believing the conflict had weakened Dollfuss, the now-illegal Nazis staged a failed putsch in July during which Dollfuss was shot and killed.

Schuschnigg had spent his entire term in office holding down the Left while grappling with the internal and external Nazi threat. As the train steamed across the length of Austria that March morning, he must have reviewed much of this history and thought of what was yet to come for his desperate country.

On Sunday, March 6, he had attended an Austrian matinee at the Theater in der Josefstadt, where actors read from works of Austrian writers—Franz Werfel, Stefan Zweig, Hermann Broch, and Guido Zernatto, a poet who was also a member of Schuschnigg's cabinet, all of them, as the theater's director Ernst Lothar would note, "emigrants of tomorrow"—and verses from Austria's classic nineteenth-century poet and playwright Franz Grillparzer ("they shall not have them, the green banks of the Danube"). Schuschnigg had risen in his box to lead thunderous applause. That night he had talked to Lothar until one in the morning about Jewish fears of the future and what could be done to still them. Lothar had suggested naming conductor Bruno Walter, a Jew, as head of the Vienna State Opera, and the chancellor had agreed. Then they had talked about Walter's interpretation of Anton Bruckner's symphonies.[7]

The chancellor's train arrived in Innsbruck at five o'clock that afternoon. Swinging the feathered hat that completed his semimartial outfit, he walked through the station and past waiting military formations. He began speaking at five minutes to seven and talked for an hour, mostly in his trademark singsong cadence, the clear sign of a poor orator, and mostly about his country's desperate economic situation and what he would do about it. Halfway through the speech Schuschnigg announced plans for the plebiscite and the reasons for it. In his peroration he exhorted his audience with the fighting words Andreas Hofer, the Tyrol's martyred hero, had used in his call to arms against Napoleon in 1809: in rough translation, "Man, it is time."

The American charge in Vienna, John Wiley, cabled to Secretary of State Cordell Hull that Schuschnigg had given an "impassioned" speech that showed "that the Government has not (as was feared) yielded to defeatism and that Schuschnigg is endeavoring to reassert his authority."[8]

The chancellor thought the element of surprise would help him win. The Austrian Nazis might get 30 percent of the vote, maybe less, and at the very outside 35 percent. A two-thirds majority would be a powerful deterrent, he was sure.

But so was Hitler. He had few illusions about winning such a plebiscite that gave him no time to mount his signature propaganda blitz, like the one that helped him become German chancellor in 1933. At first he refused to believe reports that Schuschnigg had pulled so daring a fast one—and he had received them hours before Schuschnigg went on the air. Despite tight security there had been leaks. A secretary who took notes at a crucial meeting the night before was an illegal Nazi and had slipped word to the party. In midmorning that Wednesday, March 9, a top Nazi, Friedl Rainer, called Wilhelm Keppler, an SS general, newly named state secretary in the foreign office, who had been Hitler's special representative for Austrian affairs since 1937.

Keppler had returned from Vienna to Berlin just two days earlier bringing cheerful tidings. Things were going well. The NSDAP was growing. The brown cloth used to make Nazi brown shirts for the SA (the Sturmabteilung) was in short supply, because so many new recruits were signing up to join the SA.[9] He would return to Vienna regularly and stoke the fires of opposition. Clearly, the gradual approach the German ambassador Franz von Papen championed would work best in bringing about some form of union between Austria and Germany. Hitler was satisfied.

Keppler listened to what Rainer had to say, but he was not persuaded. He called Seyss-Inquart, who had indeed been named Minister of the Interior as Hitler had demanded. Seyss was in a quandary. He had not taken part in the cabinet session the night before that approved the plebiscite, but the chancellor had briefed him privately later that evening; and Seyss had given his word of honor not to say anything to anyone before Schuschnigg's speech. So, in talking to Keppler, he was evasive but conceded that the situation had become serious.

Serious enough for Seyss to write a letter to Guido Zernatto, Secretary General of the Fatherland Front, the only legal political organization in Austria, and the man charged with carrying out the plebiscite. Seyss's letter raised constitutional and legal objections to the vote and set forth conditions that would let him—as minister of the interior and internal security—allow the vote to take place. The letter was carefully crafted—Seyss-Inquart, too, was a lawyer and a successful one at that—and designed to make holding the plebiscite more difficult without formally seeming to oppose it.

He gave a copy of the letter to Odilo Globocnik, a member of the new triumvirate from Carinthia (Austria's southernmost province) that had won the struggle to lead the still illegal Austrian Nazi party the month before. He was to fly to Berlin and give it to the Führer.

After hanging up with Seyss-Inquart, Keppler raced from the foreign office to the chancellery. But Hitler was skeptical and wouldn't believe the reports without more solid evidence. He put his personal pilot at Keppler's disposal and ordered him to fly back to Vienna at once.

Hermann Göring was lunching with former U.S. president Herbert Hoover, who was on a tour of Middle Europe (he had been to Vienna and Prague collecting honorary degrees[10]). Afterwards he planned to take Hoover to his villa, Karinhalle, outside Berlin of which he was immensely proud. Heinrich Himmler was on his way to Munich to make a beer-hall speech. Both men would play pivotal roles in the coming drama.

Late that afternoon Globocnik was taken to see Hitler. The Führer read Seyss-Inquart's letter. He was still not convinced. Globocnik asked to return to Vienna at once, but Hitler refused to let him go. He would spend the night; then "we will see."

Keppler landed at Vienna's Aspern airport in the early evening and went at once to the German legation in Metternichgasse, where he talked to Austrian Nazi leaders before Schuschnigg went on the air. The Austrian chancellor had not finished talking when Hitler called from Berlin. Keppler was to come back at once and report his findings. The Führer too had heard the speech, and now he realized the Austrians meant business.

Hitler flew into a titanic rage that shocked even his staff long used to his temper tantrums. He knew he had to stop the plebiscite, no matter what the cost. He knew he would lose, and a loss would damage his credibility abroad and dent the aura of invincibility he had built up over his five years in power. He didn't have much time to act—a little more than seventy-two hours before the Austrians were slated to go to the polls.

Schuschnigg's planning was already well advanced. On March 4, after days of toying with the idea, he had confided in Zernatto, Richard Schmitz, the mayor of Vienna, and several other close associates. Two days later he informed high officials in the Fatherland Front and told them to get the campaign rolling. On March 7 he told his finance minister to come up with 4 million schillings ($800,000) to finance the voting, and instructed his military attaché in Rome to tell Mussolini. (Il Duce thought dictators shouldn't risk free elections unless they were sure of 90-percent support; in his opinion Schuschnigg's guess of 65 percent was not enough). Even as Schuschnigg was speaking Zernatto had printing presses roll out ballots and other propaganda materials, and Fatherland Front trucks were on the streets before midnight to distribute them.

In Berlin, a perplexed and furious Hitler was uncertain on how best to proceed. Could he make Schuschnigg back down and cancel or postpone the plebiscite through diplomatic pressure alone? How effective were the Austrian Nazis? Could they seize power without overt, even military, help from the Reich? For hours Hitler pondered what to do next.

Colonel Alfred Jodl—then an aide to General Keitel (as a colonel general in 1945 Jodl would sign the instruments of surrender at Reims—wrote in his diary that the Führer had telephoned Göring about the Austrian situation and had ordered a number of top military leaders to return to Berlin. And, Jodl noted, the Führer had asked Edmund Glaise-Horstenau, a representative of the National Opposition in the Austrian cabinet who was in Germany on private business, to come to Berlin. Clearly, Hitler needed more information before he would decide what to do next.

In Innsbruck Schuschnigg walked to the castle above town for a supper of bacon, sausage, and red wine.[11] For once the generally introverted and formal chancellor was talkative and upbeat, still flushed from the ovation that had greeted his speech. Around nine o'clock he listened to a freshly cut record of his remarks—the speech had not been broadcast live and was just then going on the air. His train left the Tyrolean capital at 10:35 P.M. Schuschnigg went to sleep. The D-140 would arrive back at the West Station at 8:10 A.M. on Thursday, March 10.

By the time Schuschnigg returned home Keppler was already in a plane approaching Berlin—it was perhaps typical for the situation that the Nazis routinely flew back and forth and that Schuschnigg took the train. His predecessor had bought a DC-2 as the chancellery's courier plane, but the chancellor did not like to fly and had sold the aircraft in 1936.

Shortly after nine that morning Keppler was in the chancellery reporting to Hitler on the split in the Austrian Nazi party. The radicals around Rainer and Globocnik wanted armed action now because they knew they would lose the plebiscite. The moderates who followed Papen and Seyss-Inquart's line wanted to wait, confident that an evolutionary approach would bring Austria home to the Reich. Both thought the plebiscite was illegal and a breach of the Berchtesgaden agreement—an approach the German government would adopt in efforts to stop the vote.

As for the mood in Vienna, Keppler told the Führer, "it gave a really war-like impression." Trucks with armed men dumped leaflets on the pavement. More police than usual were in evidence and streets were alive with people. Demonstrations were held on street corners. This was not the kind of information Hitler wanted to hear. He called for the generals, at least those he could reach.

At 9:45 A.M. General of Artillery Wilhelm Keitel, in office as head of the newly formed Oberkommando der Wehrmacht or OKW (and as such a kind of chairman of the joint chiefs) for only a month, briefed Jodl on events of the past night; at ten o'clock he left the war ministry on Bendlerstrasse for the chancellery.

Hitler explained the seriousness of the Austrian situation and the need for action. Keitel remembered a plan hastily drafted in 1937 to counter a possible restoration of the Habsburgs and dubbed "Special Action Otto" for the pretender's first name. At 10:15 A.M. Jodl was told to bring the draft to the chancellery. It wasn't much, but at least it might be something to build on, no matter how inadequate; just how inadequate was explained to Hitler later that morning when his generals told him that nothing concrete about carrying out "Action Otto" had ever been prepared.

Hitler ordered them to come up with something, and to do it in a hurry. By 6:30 that evening they had cobbled up a battle plan. Three army corps including Blitzkrieg tactician General Heinz Guderian's Panzercorp were put together as the Eighth Army and placed under command of General Fedor von Bock. One division was ordered to move toward the Austrian frontier that night. Jodl noted in his diary[12] that

300 Ju-52 bombers were to be readied for a leaflet action across Austria, and four squadrons of fighter and battle planes prepared to support them.

Hitler's military option was fueled by telephone reports from Vienna during the day, which greatly exaggerated the situation. Rainer talked about the danger of imminent civil war, painting the situation in the darkest colors. Hitler instructed his charge in Vienna to protest against the plebiscite, which he did in a midmorning visit to foreign minister Schmidt, who was not unsympathetic but pointed out that the plebiscite was a domestic Austrian matter. The chargé demurred. The vote, he said delicately, might "touch Austro-German relations through the Berchtesgaden protocols." When former German ambassador Franz von Papen—he had been relieved only a couple of weeks ago—called Schmidt, he was told very much the same thing.

His envoys' reports did not improve Hitler's mood but did steel his determination to prepare for military action—both from the Reich and inside Austria.

Sometime after lunch Hitler called Globocnik into his office and told him to fly back to Vienna. He was to tell the Nazi party—still semiunderground because of its illegal status—to cut loose. Specific instructions on how to do it would follow in letters to Seyss-Inquart.

Sometime between eight and ten on the evening of March 10, the Führer met with Glaise-Horstenau for a second time, having spent two inconclusive hours with him the night before. Glaise would describe the German leader as "out of control." Hitler yelled and screamed: "do you want me to attack Austria with bombs and grenades?"[13] No matter what, he said, he was determined to invade on Saturday, March 12. And would Glaise-Horstenau take two letters to Vienna? One contained Hitler's demands and the draft of Seyss-Inquart's resignation statement as Interior Minister should Schuschnigg refuse them; the other the draft of a speech Seyss should broadcast following his resignation. Glaise, though a proponent of Anschluss, refused. Send a messenger boy, he told Hitler. Later he refused a request from Göring to take yet another message to Seyss—the draft of a telegram asking for German troops to help restore order. All three messages were sent by regular courier.

In Vienna, hopes in the Fatherland Front ran high. The papers were full of the plebiscite. Posters announcing the vote were plastered across the city and the "crooked cross" or "Krukenkreuz"—the symbol of Austro-Fascism, two Roman *I*s crossed—was stenciled on pavements, streets, and buildings. Leaflets were everywhere so that downtown side-walks seemed buried under snow as more paper fell from the sky. Leaf-lets, banners, and posters all bore the same text: "Yes! With Schuschnigg for a free Austria."

Ravag, the official radio, rebroadcast Schuschnigg's Innsbruck speech, dragged "voices from the people" in front of its microphones to drum up support, and played patriotic songs and marches. Columns of youth groups marched through the streets. Texts of official proclamations were couched in the tired rhetoric of the political Right: "We line up for a three day battle for the fatherland . . . a battle we must fight because the freedom and peace of our homeland demands it."

Crowds gathered outside the headquarters of the Fatherland Front at 4 Am Hof, a capacious square in the inner city, to cheer on patriotic efforts, while others crowded inside to drop their business cards in a silver dish, many with contributions attached. The head of the Kultusgemeinde, the umbrella organization for more than 400 Jewish groups including synagogues, prayer houses, schools, libraries, and kin-dergartens, ponied up 500,000 schillings ($100,000 at the high exchange rate of 5 schillings to the dollar) to help pay campaign costs. The next day they would add another 300,000 schillings.[14]

Nazis, too, were on the streets, as they had been for weeks. Nazi uni-versity students strolled arrogantly through downtown. Other columns marched to the German tourist office in the Hotel Bristol, across the street from the Opera where a large picture of the Führer hung in the window and was brightly lit at night.

As the afternoon wore on more and more workers joined the pro-Schuschnigg demonstrations; some even sported the three metal arrows—insignia of the outlawed Social-Democratic party—on their jacket lapels. Boxes of these insignias had been smuggled into Austria that morning from Socialist headquarters in Czechoslovakia.

Schuschnigg had realized a week ago that he would need labor sup-port if he were to win, and had begun hesitant talks with the outlawed party and its underground leadership. But he had never been comfort-able dealing with the Left, and his discomfort showed. Workers were split. Uniformly they hated the government for the repressive measures it had taken against them—executions, arrests, job loss—after the fierce and bloody civil war of 1934. Now they leaned to supporting the em-battled chancellor, but they had demands of their own—political legitimacy, a newspaper, pay for overtime, and restoration of other social benefits. But even with the threat of internal and external aggression, progress had been slow.

Finally, the Revolutionary Socialists, an underground group that had split from the Social Democrats and operated midway between them and the Communists, issued a manifesto urging workers to vote yes. The Communist party talked of arming workers and fighting the Nazis mano a mano. And on Thursday, March 10, a former imperial officer, who had fought with the socialists in the civil war, discussed the possibility of arming workers with city officials. Even without a formal agreement with the government, the Left was willing to fight together with Schuschnigg— at least against Hitler.

That willingness—and the various forms it took that day—was quickly communicated to Berlin. For Hitler it all smelled of "popular front" and was therefore more fodder for armed intervention.

That morning—March 10—Seyss-Inquart and Dr. Hugo Jury, a Nazi member of the "State Council," an advisory body to which he had been named after Berchtesgaden, came to see Zernatto. Dr. Jury was in high dudgeon as he let fly a series of charges that buttressed the "popular front" argument: two million leaflets with the socialist "Freedom" slogan and the three arrow insignia were in print. He pointed to the large number of demonstrating workers who carried red flags and greeted each other with a clenched fist, and charged that workers were being armed.

Zernatto pointed out that he had ordered the two million leaflets; that Nazi demonstrations, mostly manned by adolescents, had angered the workers; and that he had no evidence the other charges were true. He would write later[15] that he thought he had calmed his visitors and told Seyss that a meeting with Schuschnigg would be arranged later that day. He also checked with the authorities and determined that Jury's charges had been fabricated. He assumed, correctly, that they would nevertheless be sent to Berlin as fact.

After the meeting Seyss-Inquart wrote a second letter, this one addressed directly to Schuschnigg, repeating his demands for postponing the vote and even suggesting preparations for a regular election—or so Seyss-Inquart would tell the Nuremberg tribunal.[16] No copy of the second letter survived.

11

Schuschnigg meanwhile pored over both of Seyss's missives and together with Zernatto drew up a nine-point rebuttal that denied, among other things, that the vote was a violation of the Berchtesgaden agreement, that a *no* vote was tantamount to treason against the Austrian state, and he reiterated that the vote would be secret.

Schuschnigg then expanded on the nine points in a formal letter to Seyss-Inquart, which also urged him to keep Nazi terror in check because if he did not: "I will not be in a position to hold back the opposing forces." And he added, "I am at your disposal at any time."

They met early that evening, March 10. Seyss suggested that Schuschnigg add more National-Socialist ministers to the cabinet and in effect create a black-brown coalition, meaning a government composed of Fatherland Front and Nazi ministers. In that case, he said at Nuremberg, "I would ask the mass of Austrian National Socialists to take part in the plebiscite and vote yes." Schuschnigg seemed open to the idea of such a loose coalition, but refused to commit, "although time burned our finger nails."[17]

By the time Seyss left the chancellor's office Globocnik was back from Berlin with Hitler's directives. He had gone straight from the airport to the Hotel Regina, a broad-beamed building in the ninth district, which had served as a regular meeting place for the illegal Nazis and where the party's top leaders were meeting that night. Hitler's message was clear: the party was to be given a free hand and could move to seize power as it saw fit.

Meanwhile support for Schuschnigg was building on the street and off. The Jewish community had documented its fealty through large donations of money. That afternoon Cardinal Theodor Innitzer, the archbishop of Vienna and something of a pan-German, convoked a clerical conference that supported the plebiscite. So did the leaders of the much smaller Lutheran church.

As darkness fell streets were alive with people, and this time the Nazis seemed outmanned and outgunned. Columns of people marched from outlying districts to the inner city, and they came from all points of the political spectrum, legal and illegal. The Nazis, of course, were in force, but the Fatherland Front had more people out than in days past. Workers marched, so did monarchists. Clashes were frequent. The police, who had stood idly by and done little to restrain Nazi domination of the cityscape, began to play a more active role, blocking a Nazi attempt to push onto Kärntnerstrasse, Vienna's Fifth Avenue. On Schwarzenberg-platz, columns of Nazis and Fatherland Fronters seemed about to collide when police moved in to keep them apart.

By midnight it was clear that for the moment those who supported Schuschnigg were in control. Workers and people from all other walks of life marched shoulder-to-shoulder down the Graben, the wide street leading to the cathedral of St. Stephen. The Nazis were biding their time. Orders had gone out to prepare for action the next day.

Well before dawn on March 11 a cable arrived in the foreign office from the Austrian Consul General in Munich. It said "Leo Ready to Travel"—a prearranged code meaning the Wehrmacht was ready to roll across the Austrian frontier. The head of the German section called the foreign minister to tell him an invasion was imminent.

At 5:30 A.M. the head of the Vienna police woke Schuschnigg to tell him that the German frontier had been closed for the last hour, train traffic had been interrupted, and Austrian border guards had seen German troop movements. He also said that Dr. Jury had written a commentary in the "*Neuesten Wiener Nachrichten*," a newspaper with strong Nazi sympathies, bitterly criticizing the plebiscite as illegal and opening the way to "democracy and bolshevization." He suggested confiscating the edition, and Schuschnigg agreed. But publication of the commentary was not a good omen.

When the police chief had phoned Seyss-Inquart a half-hour earlier to ask whether the newspapers with Jury's article should be confiscated, Seyss had punted. Ask the chancellor, he said. He then took a walk to think things over and ended up at the local parish church in time for the six o'clock Mass. The parish priest remembered him sitting in his usual pew, head in his hands, clearly in great quandary.

On his way to the chancellery Schuschnigg told his driver to stop at St. Stephen's cathedral. A devout and observant Catholic, he went inside and said a short prayer before a portrait of the Virgin Mary, barely visible in the flickering candlelight. He looked at the group of older women around him praying to the Virgin and left, feeling stronger.[18] He would not enter the cathedral again for almost thirty years.

Before seven o'clock he bounded up the stairs to his office where the charwomen had not finished cleaning. The chief of the political section in the foreign office was instructed to make contact with the allied powers— Great Britain, France, and especially Italy. The head of the German section tried reaching the Western envoys in Vienna to inform them of the situation and to ask for help.

Shortly after eight Zernatto arrived at the chancellery. The two men had been briefed about Glaise-Horstenau's stormy meeting with the Führer and knew he was bringing a German ultimatum. They then went over the latest overnight reports:

- The SS had gathered forces in Burgenland province and planned to demonstrate.

- Border posts along the frontier with Bavaria reported the arrival of large German troop concentrations.

- Streets leading from Munich to the Austrian border were becoming clogged with troop transport.

- Austrian intelligence reported from Munich that schools were being used as barracks to house soldiers.

- Motorized transports had arrived in Passau, a German town on the Austrian border.

- SA and SS formations were gathering in Vienna and Lower Austria equipped with backpacks and supplies for an action of three to four days duration.

- Reports from all the provinces told of increasing tension with efforts to disrupt the plebiscite reported from parts of Upper Austria and Styria. Graz, the Styrian capital, was for all practical purposes already in Nazi hands.

- Fatherland Front propaganda was working, however, and technical preparations for the plebiscite were well under way.

Schuschnigg told Zernatto that internal security was in hand, despite nationwide Nazi disruption. He also saw German troop movements as an attempt to intimidate the Austrian government and not as a signal of imminent invasion. Hitler couldn't afford the international condemnation that would follow military action, Schuschnigg believed. Still, he wanted to talk to Seyss but the Interior Minister was nowhere to be found.

At eight he drove to the West station to meet Glaise-Horstenau who, he thought, was coming by train. Then his chauffeur took him to Aspern where Glaise's plane had just touched down. Hitler's letters had been sent ahead by courier and were already at the German legation; only after they were retrieved did the two Austrian ministers read them.

Hitler demanded that Schuschnigg postpone the plebiscite for several weeks and guarantee carrying out the elections in an orderly manner. If Schuschnigg refused, Austrian Nazis would take to the streets, Germany would consider military action, and both Seyss-Inquart and Glaise-Horstenau would resign. The letter also included the text of the telegram Seyss was to send to Berlin asking for German troops to restore order. Schuschnigg was given until noon to fulfill these conditions.

Somewhere around 9:30 that morning the two ministers arrived at the Ballhausplatz, site of the chancellery since Metternicht's day. For two hours the two men explained Hitler's position. Glaise-Horstenau urged Schuschnigg to cancel the plebiscite, which, he said, he had always opposed. Since only half an hour was left at the end of the meeting before Hitler's ultimatum would have expired, Seyss on his own authority extended it by two hours.

Out on the city streets that bright and sunny March morning enthusiasm for the plebiscite seemed to be mounting. Columns of trucks filled with cheering men and women wearing red-white-red insignias rumbled through the streets. G. E. R. Gedye, then a correspondent for the *New York Times* and author of an eyewitness account, *Fallen Bastions*, published less than a year later and still one of the most-often cited sources for the color of the Anschluss, wrote that "patriotic enthusiasm had risen to a pitch far above that even of the day before. The motor columns were greeted everywhere with waving handkerchiefs, cheers and shouts of encouragement. Today there were many more three-Arrow men on the streets; Socialists and Clericals greeted one another as allies. Unity was in the air at last—and victory."

The Left thought so, too. The Revolutionary Socialists had agreed on a text of a leaflet—"Workers, comrades . . . down with Hitler fascism! Freedom!"[19] —and it was being distributed on city streets that morning. The Communists issued an appeal to their membership to vote yes and to do so without conditions. The Socialists were still negotiating and had met that morning with a government minister who exuded optimism, if not much else. The Socialist leadership was sitting around in the Café Meteor in the third district waiting for something to happen.

15

About the same time Eugen Lennhoff, editor of the tabloid "*Telegraf*,"[20] bumped into a top Schuschnigg aide on Kärntnerstrasse who told him that the plebiscite was on schedule. Militia would keep order.

But Gedye noted a missing element—the Nazis. The real ones weren't out on the streets, no storm troopers, few swastikas. "The real Nazis have gone to ground and I don't like it," Gedye said to a friend over lunch.

Back at his office Lennhoff found more disturbing news bulletins coming in from Berlin allegedly from the German radio's Vienna correspondents. Among them were these:

Seyss-Inquart and Glaise-Horstenau knew nothing about the plebiscite and had not been informed. Kärntnerstrasse was in the hands of a Communist mob, and Communists were calling for a general strike. German nationals were being grossly mistreated. The Czechs were supplying the red mob in Vienna with artillery, and finally this warning: "Schuschnigg's acts may have catastrophic results." Shortly after noon the Germans claimed that serious labor disturbances had broken out, blood was flowing in streams, and Schuschnigg was no longer in control of the situation.

Lennhoff had his reporters check the alleged news. They found that everything the Germans put on the air was pure invention except for Schuschnigg's strength on the streets. But propaganda minister Paul Joseph Goebbels's purpose was clear enough—setting up the framework for military intervention.

After leaving the chancellery, the two Nazi-leaning ministers met with local party leaders and decided to follow up the face-to-face meeting with another letter summarizing —and expanding upon— the demands they had made that morning. Zernatto would claim that the new letter changed everything and that it had "the character of an ultimatum."

It demanded cancellation of the plebiscite and proposed a more formal election in four weeks time with rules laid down by the Nazis. In case Schuschnigg refused, Seyss and Glaise would resign and decline all responsibility for the consequences. They are clear enough, Zernatto noted: Nazis on the street, armed clashes, arrests, bloodshed, armed intervention from the Third Reich. [21]

Schuschnigg then came up with three alternatives:

Reject the ultimatum and terminate the Berchtesgaden agreement.

Accept the Nazi demands. That would mean Schuschnigg's resignation and formation of a new cabinet.

Compromise by accepting all the demands except postponement of the date of the plebiscite.

He chose compromise just as Seyss and Glaise walked back into the chancellery on Ballhausplatz, across the square from the old imperial palace. They had grabbed a quick lunch at the Café Herrnhof, a literary hangout on Herrngasse, a block up the street. The café was empty, except for a couple of writers and a literary agent. "Things must be getting serious," the waiter murmured to the trio. "All Seyss ordered was soup."[22]

Zernatto and Schmidt were sent to meet with the "nationals" waiting in the cabinet room. The government ministers presented the chancellor's counterproposal and sweetened it with an offer for Seyss to become vice-chancellor. Seyss was clearly tempted but said he had been instructed to make a "take it or leave it" offer.

In Berlin at one o'clock Hitler formally signed "order number one" authorizing armed intervention if the Austrians did not meet his conditions. He had also drafted a letter to Mussolini explaining his actions and asking for his support. At lunch Hitler handed the letter to his envoy to Rome, Prince Philip of Hesse, and told him to fly back to Rome at once. After lunch the group moved to the smoking room (a name it had acquired during Bismarck's time) and waited for news from Vienna. There was one complication: the phone in the smoking room didn't work, meaning that whoever wanted to talk to Vienna had to walk over to the chancellery's central telephone exchange.

Back in Vienna, there was mounting chaos in the chancellery as more and more people crowded the building, and discussions moved from room to room and across the public hallways. A coatrack in one corner was close to collapse, and Zernatto wondered how anyone would ever find his garment again.

Schuschnigg sat in his office pondering his next move. He knew from aides that the police were unreliable. Too many National Socialists had been restored to office in the wake of Berchtesgaden, and too many Nazis had been in the police even before then. For now, the police president had told him, law and order could be maintained. But he did not know for how much longer. Schuschnigg could count on the army, but could he commit his soldiers to battle against Germans? He feared not. After the Dollfuss murder he was convinced of two things—no second 1866, and no civil war. And he had not changed his mind since then.

The year 1866 was critical for those Austrians who thought of themselves as Germans. After he won the Austro-Prussian war, Bismarck pushed Austria out of the League of German states—which it had led since Napoleon's fall—and thus put Prussia in a position to form the German empire. Austria was left out in the cold. At Nuremberg Seyss-Inquart remembered that as a young officer in the Austro-Hungarian army he had been very impressed by President Woodrow Wilson's call for self-determination, but he realized that it meant dissolution of the Habsburg monarchy and a return of "the German hereditary lands into the union of the Reich from which they had been expelled fifty years ago, namely in 1866. This is important."

Schuschnigg too thought of himself as a German—and as a better German than those in the Reich because he and the Austrians were one with the holy Roman and apostolic Church. But as a German, how could he shed German blood? He had said as much in a speech on February 24: "We don't want to conjure up the spirits of 1866 but to think instead that for a generation the interest of 120 million people—two-thirds of them German—had been welded together." And he cited the emperor Franz Josef's proudest boast "I am a German prince." Austria, Schuschnigg said, "stands and falls with its German mission."

Gordon Brook-Shepherd speculated in his book[23] about the Anschluss that Schuschnigg would have ordered his army to fight anybody else—Hungarians, Czechs, Yugoslavs, even his protectors, the Italians—but never the Germans, and that his emotions had already determined what his mind would later decide. Always a tortured decision maker, he finally thought it best to cancel the plebiscite and told President Miklas so. He was, however, not yet ready to resign; he realized that having gone much farther than he vowed to go in his February 24 speech, when he had said of Berchtesgaden "this far, and not a step farther," he would eventually have little choice.

He returned to the four ministers—Zernatto, Schmidt, Seyss, and Glaise—who had still not reached agreement and after some hesitation told them he had decided to cancel the vote, at least for now. Glaise thought the worst was over, but in fact it was yet to come.

At 2:45 P.M. Seyss-Inquart was on the phone with Göring. It was the beginning of history's first coup by telephone. For the rest of the day Göring would dictate the flow of events with a phone in his hand. The records survived the war, and allied soldiers found the stenographic transcripts of the conversations in the charred ruins of the Berlin chancellery in 1945.[24]

Göring wanted to know if Seyss had resigned—or had anything else to report. Seyss told him that the chancellor had cancelled the plebiscite and "thus put us in a very difficult situation" because of the extensive security measures he had imposed including an 8 P.M. curfew. Göring was not impressed.

"The measures Chancellor Schuschnigg has taken cannot suffice in any form. I see the cancellation of the plebiscite only as a postponement but not as a change in the current situation." Göring then left to discuss events with the Führer. Later, he would testify at Nuremberg that "at that moment I had the intuitive feeling that the situation had begun to slide and that now, finally, the long desired possibility existed to carry out a complete and clear-cut solution, and that from that moment on I would have to shoulder total responsibility for everything because it was not so much the Führer but I who had to dictate the pace and to go beyond the Führer's doubts to bring matters to a decision."

Clearly, he saw a chance to annex Austria outright, now, that day, and not bother with any more "peaceful" overtures that still danced in Hitler's mind. For the last twenty-four hours the Führer had been intent on only one thing—stopping the Austrian plebiscite. Göring realized that Hitler was not yet ready to take the next step and needed a strong push to do so. Göring was more than willing to give him that push and in doing so take charge of the situation.

He knew that Seyss-Inquart wanted a National Socialist Austria, but one that would retain some semblance of sovereignty and independence. He thought a stronger man than Keppler was needed on the ground to achieve German aims and told Hitler to send one. But Hitler stuck with the tried and true.

Keppler was told to fly back to Vienna and to insist on Schuschnigg's resignation because he had broken the Berchtesgaden agreement and therefore a new government was needed. Göring even gave him a list of men he wanted in the new cabinet.

Shortly after three that afternoon Göring was back on the phone with Seyss. He did not mince words or use diplomatic niceties. He wanted action and he wanted it now:

"We demand that the national ministers in Austria resign at once and insist that the chancellor do so as well. If within the hour you have not sent us an answer, we will assume that you are no longer in a position to telephone. That would mean you have resigned. I further demand that in that case you send the telegram we have discussed to the Führer, (asking the Germans for military help.) And of course Schuschnigg's resignation must be followed by your appointment as chancellor"—thus going a little further than Hitler had himself, but by now Göring clearly was in charge.

Visibly upset, Seyss came back from the phone and read Göring's message to the others from a piece of paper in his hand. It included an ultimatum: if German conditions were not met, the Wehrmacht would invade starting at 7:30 P.M. Seyss did not relish giving Schuschnigg that message, but both Schmidt and Zernatto insisted that he do so. Seyss shrugged his shoulders and said "I'm nothing but history's telephone girl. I only have to bring the news and don't have any influence to change it."

Memories of what happened next vary, with various participants remembering events differently.

Zernatto said Seyss-Inquart went into the chancellor's office alone and gave him Göring's note to read. Schuschnigg went pale and said "such a decision goes beyond my competence. I'll have to discuss it with the federal president." Seyss left the room after several minutes with tears in his eyes.

Glaise-Horstenau backed the story. "Seyss-Inquart asked me to go into the chancellor's office with him," he testified at Nuremberg. "But I declined for reasons of tact. Seyss-Inquart went in alone and when he came out told me regretfully that 'we are going to have to take in the Nazis and I want to form an umbrella organization including Catholics and those similarly inclined' and he said he would demand from Hitler a five-year hold still agreement."

Other versions have it that Seyss and Glaise entered the office together. Schuschnigg remembered that Seyss read Göring's ultimatum from his notes.[25] "A moment of silence followed. Then I picked up the phone and asked for a line to Rome, Palazzo Venezia [Mussolini's office]. The three of us stepped up to one of the tall windows flanking my office. I don't know what the two gentlemen were looking at. I stared in the void for a moment and said, 'what is your personal opinion?' Seyss is so upset he cannot speak. There are tears in his eyes. Glaise is no less shaken; finally he said 'one doesn't know if one can go on under these circumstances as an honorable man.' Seyss does not contradict him." (An hour later Glaise would say of Schuschnigg, "Oh he's a corpse.")

As Keppler's plane taxied down the runway at Berlin's Tempelhof airport—it was around 3:30 P.M.—Schuschnigg was in Miklas's office to tender his own and his cabinet's resignation. He had gone through his options time after time and rejected them all. It was clear in midafternoon that Austria could expect no help from the Western powers. France, which might have acted, did not have a government, its cabinet having fallen on March 10. In London, Chamberlain was having tea with von Ribbentrop and thought Austrian entreaties for help an intrusion. Lord Halifax, the foreign secretary, did promise a diplomatic demarche in Berlin, a step hardly likely to change Hitler's mind. Mussolini was simply unavailable on the phone and clearly would not again march his troops up to the Brenner Pass.

At home things were, if anything, worse. The provinces were in open revolt. The loyalty and reliability of the police were uncertain. Parts of the army would have to be used to put down riots and other disturbances. Troops to fight the Germans were scattered across the country. It would take hours to bring them to the frontier and counter an invasion. Besides, they only had enough ammunition for two days. Under the circumstances resistance seemed hopeless. All it would mean was the death of thousands in a useless struggle. Or so Schuschnigg thought. Others thought differently, and the debate about whether Austria could or should have resisted has never been resolved, although in fact—and with hindsight—resistance would have been far more effective than Schuschnigg believed, given the logistical problems the Wehrmacht encountered rumbling on to Vienna without any resistance at all.

Miklas, however, refused to budge. He would not accept Schuschnigg's resignation. He had been president—a ceremonial head-of-state office with some clear powers including naming the chancellor and his cabinet—for ten years. He had once taught history and, staunch Catholic that he was, had fathered fourteen children. Short, squat, on the dumpy side, he was anything but a heroic figure. But he was a patriot and in the end would prove to be Austria's last one. He told Schuschnigg to think it over and not wilt in the face of German ultimata.

While Schuschnigg was talking to Miklas, Seyss was back on the phone with Berlin. The conversation with Göring around 4 P.M. was short. Seyss said Schuschnigg was resigning. Had he been appointed chancellor, Göring wanted to know. Seyss said he would know by 5 P.M., to which

21

Göring replied "I declare categorically that in addition to Schuschnigg's resignation this (your nomination) is an unconditional demand."

Unconditional it may have been, but it took another nine hours before it was finally met.

It is unclear just when that afternoon Schuschnigg finally persuaded Miklas to let him resign, probably some time before five. But the president refused—as categorically as Göring had demanded—to name Seyss-Inquart as chancellor. What was more, he told Schuschnigg to stay in office as caretaker until a new chancellor could be found.

Meanwhile Globocnik left the chancellery—in the mounting chaos, people wandered in and out almost at will even though the battalion of guards had mounted machine guns to protect the exits—and drove to the German legation. At 5 P.M. he called Göring and explained that Schuschnigg couldn't complete the technical details of dissolution until 5:30. Göring extended the deadline to 7:30 but said he wanted to know what was going on. "Did Seyss tell you that he is chancellor?"

At this point Globocnik decided to lie in hopes of winning time. Yes, he told Göring, Seyss was chancellor and the transfer of power had been completed. He tried to delay formation of the cabinet to sometime shortly after nine, but Göring insisted on 7:30. The conversation meandered and became repetitive, but then Göring made another demand that showed how shrewdly he had assessed the situation: "Pay attention, all the press people, they all have to go and our people get in there."

He was probably talking about the government press office and the need to get the Nazi message out to the world from day one. But the subtext was broader: Vienna, the "lost Vienna," was a Jewish town and most of the owners, editors, writers, and reporters of the city's twenty-two newspapers were Jews. They would have to be removed as quickly as possible.

Through late afternoon the Fatherland Front and its allies continued to dominate the streets. Trucks full of members of Catholic youth groups—the Austro-Fascists were as zealous as the Nazis in forming organizations to defend faith and fatherland—roamed through the streets dumping still more leaflets. Loudspeakers continued to broadcast election propaganda. Sound trucks blared the same message. And the Nazis had still not hit the pavements, held back in their redoubts by the Nazi leadership and still uncertain of how the political crisis would play out. The leadership of the left had moved to a downtown wine hall and continued to wait.

Around 5 P.M. the loudspeakers stopped broadcasting election propaganda, and as the light faded the twilight men emerged—the Nazis, the true Nazis, not their noisy hangers-on—and began to dominate the streets. The square outside the Opera and the German travel office (with Hitler's picture in the window) began to fill up with demonstrators, and most of them were now Nazis. A pile of flowers had grown up around the Führer's portrait. At six o'clock the radio announced that the plebiscite had been postponed.

At 5:20 Göring had talked to his Austrian brother-in-law who was slated to take the Justice portfolio in the new Nazi government. Göring rattled off some more names of people he wanted in the cabinet and then said, "And one more thing I forgot. Disarm the reds who were armed yesterday, and do it ruthlessly. That's obvious. And have him (Seyss) call me. Here's the number 12 52 24."

Seyss was on the phone six minutes later to tell a perplexed Göring that he had not been named chancellor although Miklas had accepted Schuschnigg's resignation. The president was looking for somebody else to become chancellor, preferably somebody with the guts to fight. Even worse, Miklas had refused to receive Globocnik and a Nazi delegation who wanted him to name Seyss.

Göring ordered Seyss to take the German military attaché, Lieutenant General Muff, to see the president and tell him that if he still refused, German troops would invade across the whole frontier. The cabinet had better be in place by 7:30 or else. And—oh yes, one other thing—put the party on the street "in all its formations, SA, SS, everybody." And Göring added, "if Miklas didn't get it in four hours, he'll now have to get it in four minutes."

But Miklas didn't get it, not in four minutes, and not in four hours, despite Göring's increasingly frantic and blustery phone calls. The president did receive General Muff and Keppler, whose plane had touched down only a short while ago, and in so many words told them to bugger off—in polite Viennese of course. Göring kept threatening to invade; Miklas refused to believe him. He offered the job to a former chancellor who turned him down. The army chief of staff said he was too old, and besides he wasn't a politician. Schuschnigg, as caretaker chancellor, gave orders that the army was not to resist the invading Germans.

He, Schuschnigg, now thought appointing Seyss-Inquart was the only way out and told Miklas so. Still the president refused, saying bitterly, "so in this decisive hour you are leaving me all alone."

Schuschnigg then decided on a farewell radio speech. The clock ticked toward 7:30. He made a few notes and went into his office where technicians had set up a microphone. At 7:47 he was on the air.

Listening to that speech sixty-odd years later, when the emotion and the drama of the moment have long since drained away, it seems an odd, unfeeling address, totally lacking what passion he had managed to convey in parliament in February and in Innsbruck only forty-eight hours ago. He spoke for about ten minutes in the cultivated High German of the Austrian intelligentsia recounting the events of the day. He hit consonants hard—the "*k*" in "Volk," the double "*t*" in "hatte"—and swallowed the vowels. The singsong that marked his oratory pushed his voice up at the end of each sentence—long, complicated sentences, rich with subsidiary clauses. He spoke slowly.

The German government had issued an ultimatum ordering President Miklas to name their choice of chancellor—Schuschnigg did not mention Seyss-Inquart—and have him form a new government, otherwise invasion would follow. Then Schuschnigg said: "I declare before the world that news disseminated in Austria that worker disturbances have taken place, that rivers of blood had flowed, that the government was no longer in control of events were fabricated from A to Z. The federal president has asked me to tell the Austrian people that we are yielding to force."

In the next sentence Schuschnigg would express his own and his country's tragedy: "We have, because even in this solemn hour we are not willing to spill GERMAN blood, ordered our army, in case an invasion is carried out, to pull back without any substantial resistance ..."— here Schuschnigg corrected himself to say "without resistance" and to "await the decisions of the next few hours."

And then he ended the speech with a sentence that again paid fealty to his Teutonic passion: "So in this hour I take my leave of the Austrian people with a GERMAN word and a heartfelt wish: God protect Austria. (Gott schütze Österreich)"

Accounts vary of what happened when he stopped speaking, and the recording does not contain the aftermath. Gedye wrote that those in the room repeated one word over and over "Österreich, Österreich," (Austria, Austria) like a song of doom. Another writer claims that Keppler and Seyss-Inquart (both of whom looked a little bit like Conrad Veit in

Casablanca but not as handsome) began to sing "Deutschland, Deutschland über alles" when a savvy engineer switched to a recording of Haydn's "Emperor" String Quartet, the music for both the German national anthem and the two Austrian hymns—the *"Gott Erhalte"* ("God save the Emperor") and the Dollfuss-era hymn *Sei gesegnet über alles, Heimaterde wunderhold*" ("Be blessed above all other things, earth of my homeland wonder to behold").

In a house on Osterleitnergasse in the posh nineteenth district, thirteen-year-old Fritz Molden saw his father, Ernst, deputy editor of Vienna's most important newspaper, *Die Neue Freie Presse*, cry for the first time in his life. His father had stayed home longer than usual to listen to the speech before going back to the office to close the morning edition. He got back late to his desk and, before he could finish up, was told to surrender his office to a young German. Then he was arrested. "They let him go a couple of weeks later," remembered Molden, who became one of the few genuine heroes of the Austrian Resistance and a newspaper and book publisher of note after the war.[26]

Chas Kelfeit, a Jew who owned a store on Glockengasse in the second district, had just sat down to dinner when Schuschnigg spoke. When he had finished with the words "God protect Austria" Kelfeit would write, "the tears rolled down my cheeks. Without eating a bite of the food in front of us we went to bed. My six-year-old son asked, 'Papa, why are you crying and why aren't we eating.' All night long we could hear the terrible noise in the streets with the shouts of *Sieg Heil* and *Jude verrecke* (Jew die) growing louder and louder."[27]

Gerhard Bronner, a fifteen-year-old Jew from the proletarian tenth district, had spent the day in euphoria. "You have to remember what it was like," he recalled, "we were so sure we would win and Austria would remain free. Schuschnigg would have gotten 85 percent, maybe even 90 percent." Bronner, who would become Vienna's leading cabaret star after the war, listened to the speech at a sausage stand. "When I got home my father said, 'it's all over.'"[28]

Fifteen-year-old Felix Fuchs had spent the day on Fatherland Front trucks distributing leaflets. He wore the gray uniform of one of the Catholic youth organizations. His truck got back to the youth group's headquarters around 6 P.M., and he listened to the speech there. Before Schuschnigg was finished, Fuchs's father arrived, threw an overcoat over his son so nobody would see his Catholic uniform, and took him home.[29]

"We ate with the radio on, and suddenly the music was interrupted for a short speech by Schuschnigg," Lore Segal wrote in her memoir *Other People's Houses*. "Then they played the Austrian national anthem for the last time. *Sei gesegnet ohne ende, Österreich, mein Vaterland* (Be blessed without end, Austria my fatherland).

'They're playing it slower than usual,' Tante Trude said. 'Franzi, don't you think they are playing it slower than usual?'

'They're probably using the record they always used,' my mother said.

'How can you say so, Franzi, and you a musician. Listen, Hansi! Igo! Don't you agree with me, they are playing it slower than usual?'

'Trude you are a silly cow,' my mother said. 'Don't you understand what has happened to us?'

'What has happened?' I asked."

Thirteen-year-old Inge Santner watched her father cry uncontrollably as Schuschnigg spoke. "He wasn't particularly political," the future Vienna correspondent of the German newsmagazine *Der Spiegel*, recalled. "But he was absolutely sure that once the Germans invaded Austria another world war was inevitable."

Sometime after 9 P.M. the phone rang at Hungerberggasse 13 in Grinzing where my family lived. My father picked up the receiver. "No," he said, "Tommy can't come out now. He's asleep." And hung up. The caller had been the leader of my scout troop. We had no idea that the Austrian scouts were Nazis. My mother, suddenly aware that "they" considered her a Jew, sat in bed crying. She had been baptized a Protestant but, for the Nazis, that didn't matter.

With Göring's "shackles off" order the SS and the SA swarmed through the city, and the heavily Nazi-infiltrated police moved to consolidate the Nazi grab for power. Ten minutes after Schuschnigg's speech Gedye was in a cab driving down Renngasse when he encountered a Fatherland Front group, still in blissful ignorance of what had happened, marching down the street, banners flying, distributing leaflets. As they passed a police station a dozen officers ran out to stop them. The leader was asked to step forward and then, "without a word the inspector drew his truncheon and hit him full across the face. As the man dropped, his face streaming with blood and writhing in agony, the whole mob of police traitors, with screams of *Heil Hitler* charged into the procession of men, women and children . . . who scattered terror stricken under the hail of truncheon blows."[30]

The mob on Schwarzenbergplatz carried Nazi flags; a speaker snarled that Schuschnigg and his Jewish-Catholic pack of traitors would pay. SS and SA who had been in hiding on the Kohlmarkt all afternoon began moving toward the chancellery where a crowd of thousands had gathered.

Gedye, the German playwright Carl Zuckmayer, and the Austrian writer Stefan Zweig have left surprisingly similar descriptions of the mood and temper of the moment. Gedye wrote:

> As I crossed the Graben, the Brown flood was sweeping through the streets. It was an indescribable witches' Sabbath—storm troopers, lots of them barely out of the school-room, with cartridge-belts and carbines, the only other evidence of authority being swastika brassards, were marching side by side with police turncoats, men and women shrieking or crying hysterically the name of their leader, embracing the police and dragging them along in the swirling stream of humanity, motor lorries filled with storm-troopers clutching their long-concealed weapons, hooting furiously, trying to make themselves heard above the din, men and women leaping, shouting and dancing in the light of the smoking torches which soon began to make their appearance with a pandemonium of sound— down with Jews! *Heil Hitler! Heil Hitler! Sieg Heil!* Hang Schuschnigg.[31]

"That evening all hell broke loose," Zuckmayer wrote in his memoirs.

> The underworld had opened its gates and let loose its lowest, vilest, most un-clean spirits. The city changed into a nightmare painting of Hieronymus Bosch: evil spirits and half demons seemed to crawl out of the filth and from swampy holes in the earth. The air was filled with unceasing, yelling, wild, hysterical screaming from male and female gullets that screeched for days and nights on end. And all men lost their faces, resembled distorted grimaces: some in fear, others in lies, and others in wild, hate-filled triumph. . . . What was unleashed here was the revolt of envy, grudge, bitterness, blind and evil vindictiveness— and all other voices were condemned to silence . . . a blind fury of destruction and hatred was directed at everything that nature or spirit ennobled. It was the witches' Sabbath of the rabble and the burial of all human dignity.[32]

"The mask was off," Zweig wrote in his memoir, *The World of Yesterday*.

> Now there was no longer mere robbery and theft, but every private lust for revenge was given free rein. University professors were obliged to scrub the streets with their naked hands, pious white-bearded Jews were dragged into the synagogue by hooting youths and forced to do knee-exercises and to shout *Heil Hitler*. All the sickly, unclean fantasies of hate that had been conceived in many orgiastic nights

found raging expression in bright daylight. Breaking into homes and tearing earrings from trembling women may well have happened hundreds of years ago...;
what was new, however, was the shameless delight in public tortures, in spiritual
martyrization, in the refinement of humiliation.[33]

At 7:30 that evening, Zernatto, himself an Austrian poet of note, thought
much the same thing. "I'm going abroad," he told a colleague and left the
chancellery without hat and coat although it had become cold and windy
with rain threatening. He went home, told his wife to pack her jewelry,
grabbed a few clothes, and hurried her into his waiting Austro-Daimler
limousine. He told his driver to head for Bratislava across the Czech border fifty kilometers away. When he got to the Hotel Carlton he ordered the
driver and his military aide to return to Vienna, believing that they had no
reason to leave the country. Both were subsequently arrested.[34]

At 8:20 P.M. Seyss-Inquart went on the air declaring that although the
government had resigned, he was still minister of the interior and in
charge of keeping public order. He called on all Austrians to maintain
discipline and warned that public demonstrations must be orderly. SA
and SS formations would help make sure they were.

The Nazis had already surrounded the radio station; shortly thereaf-
ter one of their own technicians sat in the Ravag CEO's chair. The Austro-
Fascists had burned as many of their records as they could before leaving
their headquarters in Am Hof. An hour later a Nazi mob stormed the
empty building and broke the Krukenkreuz above it into pieces.

Pandemonium raged in the chancellery. Schuschnigg noted young
men with Prussian crewcuts, smooth suits, and sneering faces move
through the corridors. He thought that although the mob might not
have stormed the chancellery, the Gestapo was already here. Keppler and
Muff made repeated forays into Miklas's office. Göring kept calling with
new instructions, new demands, new threats. Miklas refused to cave. The
mob outside grew louder.

"You're the minister of the interior," one frustrated Schuschnigg loy-
alist told Seyss, "Do something." Seyss shrugged. "I can't. I haven't been
appointed." Miklas's secretary told the commander of the guards to take
action. The colonel shrugged. Nobody had given him orders to shoot
and without them he wouldn't. The standoff at the chancellery continued, but not in the rest of the city.

Government offices fell like ninepins, finally even city hall. Mayor
Schmitz had counseled resistance to the last. But at 11:15, rifle-toting

Nazis arrived in trucks. Nazi flags already hung from the parapets. The gunmen forced their way inside, disarmed the city guards, and arrested the mayor.[35]

In the chancellery the chaotic drama was drawing to a close. Isolated, embattled, and alone, Miklas was under relentless pressure to name Seyss-Inquart chancellor, both from the Nazis and the Austro-Fascists who had made up the basis of his political support. Seyss made and discarded cabinet lists, accepting many of the names Göring had suggested, rejecting others. Sometime after 9 P.M. he had asked Miklas to appoint him, explaining he would follow moderate policies and that he did not expect immediate Anschluss. Miklas again said no.

But his position was crumbling fast. Ravag refused to broadcast an item about Seyss's refusal to ask Berlin for help, which Miklas had wanted on the air. And the Nazis were growing impatient. At 11:14 they aired a bulletin that Seyss was chancellor. Miklas held out for another forty-five minutes. Then, at midnight, he called Seyss into his office. At 12:30 A.M. Miklas approved the cabinet list, which included Glaise-Horstenau as vice-chancellor, and said he would swear in the new government the next morning.

Outside the mob was in control. Young Nazis had swarmed up the façade of the chancellery and fastened Nazi flags. A light rain had begun to fall. Torches gleamed in the night. At 1:08 A.M. Major Hubert Klausner, head of the Nazi party—now legal—stepped onto the balcony to announce "with deep emotion in this festive hour that Austria is free, that Austria is national socialist. . . . A new government has been formed." Then Seyss-Inquart led his cabinet onto the balcony to acknowledge the cheers of the crowd.

What to do with Schuschnigg? Seyss suggested that he hurry him to the Hungarian legation on Bankgasse, a hop and a skip from the back entrance of the Ballhausplatz. Schuschnigg refused. He would leave the way he came in, by the front door. Seyss drove him home and assured him that nothing would happen to him—another empty Nazi promise.

Fritz Bock, a young member of the Fatherland Front propaganda team and a vice-chancellor in a postwar cabinet, would note that Schuschnigg had made one major mistake—instead of "fight and run" he had opted to "surrender and stay," thus doing Austria no good whatsoever.

Thousands of others tried to run but were not as lucky as Guido Zernatto. The night train to Prague left the East Station at 11:15, but by nine o'clock the platform was jammed with people looking to escape. They stormed the cars, and there were so many of them that a second train had to be brought into the station to handle the overflow.

The Nazis were already in place. SS men, half in uniform and half still in civilian clothes, swarmed through the train searching, demanding papers, stealing jewels, money, and anything else that struck their fancy. Some passengers were taken off the train before it left the station. Finally the engine got up steam and began to puff out across Vienna and into the open country. Twenty minutes later the train stopped. Torches and lanterns lit up the night sky. More storm troopers climbed onto the train and forced the engineer to take it back to Vienna. Once returned to the East station, passengers were searched again. More valuables were stolen, more people taken off and imprisoned.

Finally, the train started out again and this time made it to the Czech border. Passengers passed the Austrian customs officials still on duty and walked over to the desks manned by the Czechs. But Czech authorities, uncertain if the Germans would attack them now and not in six months, had issued orders shortly after 9 P.M. not to admit anyone without a Czech visa. Passengers were herded into a waiting room and put on the next train back to Vienna.

In Vienna that night, the first Jewish store windows were broken and the first apartments searched. The Nazis had lists of the prominent and the wealthy, but they also broke into the homes of the poor. Some of the Nazis were cynical and polite, others brutal and destructive. The first Jews were dragged out onto the streets to begin cleaning Fatherland Front propaganda slogans from sidewalks and house walls under the jeering taunts of the triumphant mob.

Tchaikovsky's *Eugene Onegin* was playing at the Opera. After the intermission standees began to stream into newly empty seats up front and in boxes. Jews, who traditionally made up at least a third of Viennese theater audiences, had heard about Schuschnigg's speech during the break and left the Opera house, hoping to escape from the mob that still milled out front.

In Berlin, Hitler confirmed his decision to march into Austria and decided to follow his troops into his homeland—he was born in Braunau in Upper Austria close to the German border—the next morning. But the situation remained dicey. True, he was sure the Western powers would not intervene, but he had not heard back from Mussolini, and Seyss-

Inquart still had not sent the telegram asking for German help. Somewhere around 9:30 Keppler called from Vienna to say that Seyss had agreed to send the cable, although in fact Seyss had not. Hitler was vastly relieved, but the foreign office went ahead and had it forged anyway and entered into its records—a wise move for the Reich's government as it turned out. The final piece of good news that evening came at 10:25 when Prince Phillip of Hesse called from Rome. Il Duce was agreeable to the Anschluss and sent Hitler his warmest greetings.

Hitler went to bed. He planned an early start, flying from Berlin to Munich and then following his troops by car.

The newsreel German cameramen put together about the Anschluss opens with a stark shot in predawn darkness as Wehrmacht and Austrian soldiers remove the barriers at the Kufstein crossing point. In a haunting shot the face of an Austrian officer is shown, still in the imperial uniform with medals on his chest, saluting as the German soldiers march by. His face is solemn, not the trace of a smile under his mustache.

In Munich, Heinrich Himmler prepared to fly to Vienna with a large staff to take over law enforcement Nazi style. At 2:30 A.M. on Saturday, March 12, three Ju-52s rolled down the runway with Himmler, SD Chief Reinhard Heyrdrich, police general Kurt Daluege, and twenty-seven heavily armed SS storm troopers aboard. The planes flew without lights and maintained radio silence throughout. They landed at Aspern airport outside Vienna at 4:30 A.M., and storm troopers jumped out of the planes, machine pistols at the ready to secure the airfield.

There was little to secure. The Nazis were solidly entrenched and their leaders, most of them SS members, had gathered at the airfield to greet their new boss. Himmler was unmoved by the display. The Austrian Nazis had been a bickering lot, unable to put a coherent team together, and he did not trust them to carry out his kind of law and order. It was a measure of his contempt that he left Globocnik and Rainer at the airport to find their way back to Vienna while his motorcade roared into the city.

Hitler landed in Munich punctually at 10:10 A.M. where his motorcade was ready to take him to Eighth Army headquarters in Mühldorf. He planned to lunch in the village, cross the Austrian border near his home town of Braunau around 4 P.M., and then proceed to Linz.

At the Ballhausplatz the exhausted members of the new cabinet—few can have grabbed more than a couple of hours sleep—met at 9 A.M. and were formally sworn into office by President Miklas. At 11:30 the "council of ministers"—the formal name for the cabinet—met for the first time. The session lasted forty-five minutes and, although Seyss-Inquart no longer believed he could worm five years of independence out of Hitler, the business discussed was that of a government with longer-term plans and aims.

The new cabinet declared a bank holiday and stiffened foreign exchange regulations in order to prevent capital flight. It extended an investment incentive law and scrapped legislation allowing forced auctions of debt-ridden farms.

When the Wehrmacht crossed the border, motorcycle riders were warned to wear goggles lest the flowers the population tossed at them hurt their eyes. And indeed it proved to be a campaign of blossoms, not bullets. The crowds lining the streets through which Hitler's cavalcade traveled were six deep. Cheers were deafening, progress slow. The motorcade would not reach Linz until 7:45 P.M.

After the cabinet meeting Seyss-Inquart decided to fly to Linz to greet the Führer in person. He took one look at the mob already assembled on the provincial city's main square and told the local chief of security, "This is awful, we're sliding into the Anschluss with full sails." The local official replied "did you expect anything else given your policies?"

The frenzy of the crowd gave Hitler pause. Unlike Göring he had not been convinced that immediate annexation made much sense. But as he sat in his suite at the Hotel Weinzinger reviewing the out-of-control passion of the crowds that had greeted him, he began to change his mind. In Berlin the ministry of the interior had been working on the draft of a law for a "personal" union between Germany and Austria, with Hitler combining the functions of both head of the Reich and Austrian president. Details were deliberately left vague. Now the Führer wanted to go farther.

Wilhelm Stuckart, a state secretary in the ministry of interior, was ordered to bring the draft to Linz where on Sunday morning, March 13, he banged out two new drafts on a portable typewriter and, once Hitler had approved them, flew to Vienna to show them to Keppler and Seyss-Inquart, who had returned from Linz very late the night before. After lunch Hitler met with a group of local Nazis and told them that a new law would be promulgated that day and that the first article would say "Austria is a province of the German Reich."

At five o'clock Seyss-Inquart convened the second and final meeting of his cabinet. It lasted five minutes, enough time to approve the legislation, which now only needed Miklas's signature to become law. Miklas refused to sign on constitutional grounds but agreed to transfer his powers to the chancellor; when Seyss signed, Austria formally became a province of the German Reich. The law also called for a plebiscite on April 10 to approve the new status.

But the street had already approved it. The victorious Nazis wasted no time making their power felt. Jews were the most public target. Wherever SS, SA, and Hitler Youth found Jews they made them take part in so-called "scrubbing parties." Taunting mobs surrounded the Jews, many of them old and feeble, men and women alike, and they hurled insult and invective, most commonly that the Führer had finally found work Jews could do. "We thank our Führer. He has created work for Jews," mobs howled. Jews were made to do calisthenics until the older ones dropped. The Schadenfreude was palpable in faces twisted into masks of hate and in the body language of contempt. Finally, at last, the Jews were getting what they deserved.

Jewish stores were broken into and robbed while the police stood benignly to one side. Apparel and delicatessen shops were preferred targets of opportunity for the largely adolescent mobs. The SS "secured" the synagogue in Seittenstettengasse in the inner city. It would be the only one to survive the rampage of Kristallnacht eight months later.

The Nazis had prepared well. Schools were closed that Saturday— Viennese children normally attended schools Saturday morning, as they still do today. "Provisional commissioners"—a term applied to the thieves, after the fact, in order to give them some official status—took over an array of institutions with a first wave of random and chaotic Aryanization or nazification just hours before Hitler crossed the frontier.

That Sunday morning at 9 A.M. Baldur von Schirach, the Reich youth leader, already thirty-one and a bit too old for that job, climbed down from a first-class carriage at the West station. Some 4,000 youngsters, many still wearing the uniform of the Catholic youth organizations and many others imported from the provinces, had gathered to greet him.

He made a typically sloppy and sentimental speech, the kind that had already become his trademark, praising the courage and fortitude Austrian youth had shown and saying he was bringing greetings from 7 million boys and girls "who belong to Adolf Hitler and are eager to share your joy."

All morning long Himmler's SS and local Nazis—working from an Austrian police list that had fallen into their hands—rounded up political suspects and brought them to the police prison on the Rossauer Lände, a gingerbread architectural concoction built along the Danube Canal. Among those taken was the police officer who had commanded the security detail at the opera not twenty-four hours before. Two socialists who would become president and minister of the interior in the second republic, Dr. Adolf Schärf and Oskar Helmer, were taken from a police jail to the Rossauer Lände; one of the prisoners even agreed to pay for the cab.

In Linz, Hitler drove to Leonding to visit the graves of his parents. Again the streets were lined with cheering crowds. He entered the cemetery alone except for his photographer, who was to record the scene.

Back at the Hotel Weinzinger, Josef Bürckel, destined to be Hitler's point man in Vienna, hired young Helmut Sündermann, who worked for press chief Otto Dietrich, as his spokesman. He showed Sündermann a document with Hitler's signature appointing Bürckel as provisional leader of the NSDAP in Austria, and charging him with reorganizing the party and preparing the April 10 plebiscite.

Bürckel planned to begin work right away and left for Vienna that afternoon. Seyss-Inquart may still have been chancellor that morning, but it was clear from the outset that Bürckel would be the man in charge in Vienna.

Meanwhile the army had run into logistical problems. Elements of Guderian's panzer corps had reached the city and some ordnance had come in by train, but the bulk of the Eighth Army was stuck en route, suffering from lack of fuel, poor roads, crowds, and bad planning. Fedor von Bock knew his army was not ready for battle, and he must have thanked God that he did not have to face one.

The logistical nightmare is the most convincing evidence that—had the Austrians implemented the Jansa plan, which called for falling back to the Enns River and fighting from a strategically superior position that even unquestioned German domination of the air could not have soon unsettled—they could have resisted for a couple of weeks, and in so doing changed the outlook of the Western powers and perhaps even Mussolini.

Sunday night, March 13, Hitler sat around the hotel talking to Seyss, Keppler, and Stuckart about party and economic matters. He set a new exchange rate for schillings and marks, and told Seyss the Austrian party might keep a semblance of independence. Then he too signed the draft law. Austria had ceased to exist as a separate state.

Hitler's motorcade left Linz shortly before noon on Monday the 14th for the 120-mile trip to Vienna. The writers at the *Neue Freie Presse* pulled out all stops: "Before the shadows of the evening sank over Vienna, when the wind died down and the many flags fell silent in festive rigidity, the great hour became reality and the Führer of the united German people entered the capital of the Ostmark."[36]

Hitler stood in the front seat of his six-wheeled Mercedes—the cars had been built as all-terrain vehicles but had proved too heavy for cross-country traffic and been commandeered for parade purposes[37]—his arm stretched stiffly in the German salute for brief moments and then lifted at the elbow in the jerky motion Charlie Chaplin would capture with such deadly accuracy in *The Great Dictator*.

As Hitler passed by, men and women hung out of every window and massed on the roofs of houses. The streets were packed. Church bells pealed. The SS men on the running boards of the cars looked worriedly around for possible assassins. But flowers were the only missiles. Films show Hitler with an almost sappy grin on his face, less triumph than disbelief that he had returned in triumph to this city where he had been a poverty-stricken young man more than a quarter of a century before. His car pulled up in front of the Hotel Imperial. He could have stayed in one of the Habsburg palaces but, according to one account, picked the Imperial because he once had a job there shoveling snow in winter while the aristocracy swept inside for gala dinners.

At seven o'clock Hitler stepped onto the balcony outside his suite to deliver a brief address. He sounded tired and his usual élan was missing. "Whatever may come," he told the huge crowd, "the German Reich, as it stands today, will never be torn apart again. No peril, no threat, and no act of violence can break this our oath. Thus say all Germans from Königsberg to Cologne, from Hamburg to Vienna."

Then Hitler went to bed. It took police a while to disperse the crowd, somehow disappointed in this brief encounter after three days of waiting to "see our Führer." And what days they had been. It was only Monday night, but the ebullient Schuschnigg of Friday morning was already a distant memory—both for the bullies and their victims.

Austrian Nazis had gone berserk. Looting, mayhem, violence, beatings, even murder became so common that they became too much for officials from the Reich who saw Austria as a source of wealth and raw materials needed to speed Hitler's military buildup, not as an oriental bazaar to be looted. Bürckel readied demands that the violence stop, going so far as to charge that Communists dressed in Nazi uniforms had been the perpetrators and that those caught would be severely punished. But in the chaos of Anschluss this was only rhetoric that took another week to turn into consistent action.

Hitler's speech at 11 A.M. on Tuesday, March 15, on the Heldenplatz was the high point of the celebration; when it came to writing about it Nazi rhetoric was solidly in place:[38]

> The city of Vienna, the southernmost metropolis of the German Reich, today prepared a magnificent reception for the Führer and Reich Chancellor on the Heldenplatz. Many hundreds of thousands were on their way to hear him. Streets are dipped in a frenzy of color. The Heldenplatz could not hold the masses.
>
> A few minutes before eleven the Führer's car drives slowly along the roadway cleared for him. He stands tall in the car to greet the enraptured masses. *Sieg Heil* shouts storm across the square, many thousands of arms are raised in the German salute. . . .[39]

In the room of the Neue Hofburg—the palace Emperor Franz Josef had begun building in 1887 and completed in 1913—behind the balcony overlooking the square, the announcer asked Hitler how he should present Seyss-Inquart, who was to introduce the Führer. "Announce that the Reichsstatthalter (the Reich commissioner) in Austria Seyss-Inquart will speak."

Seyss was properly obsequious:

> My Führer. As the last highest agent of the federal state of Austria I report to the Führer and Reich Chancellor the completion of the lawful decree according to the will of the German people and of its Führer. Austria is a province of the German Reich. . . . The Ostmark has returned home. . . . My Führer! Wherever the road leads we will follow! *Heil* my Führer.[40]

Hitler savored the moment as he strode to the microphone amid the deafening cheers of the crowed. Staring him in the face was a swastika flag draped around the rump of Prince Eugene's horse—one of two equestrian statues on the Heldenplatz.

"Germans! Men and Women. . . .The oldest eastern mark of the German people from here on will become the youngest bastion of the German nation and with it of the German Reich. For centuries . . . the storms from the East broke against the borders of the old Reich. For centuries to come they will again be an iron guarantee for the security and freedom of the German Reich."

And he ended his speech with a sentence that entered the history books of familiar quotations:

"In this hour I can report to the German people the greatest accomplishment of my life, as Führer and Chancellor of the German nation and the Reich, I can announce before history the entry of my homeland into the German Reich."

His voice had reached a crescendo, typical of his oratorical style, that called for slow beginnings and a gradual, step-by-step increase in volume and emotion. The crowd exploded when he intoned "before history" and for minutes would not let him continue.

"Germany and its new limb, the National Socialist Party and the armed forces of our Reich: *Sieg Heil.*"

The ovation was endless. As German cameras panned across the crowd they picked out faces in sheer ecstasy, women who seemed almost orgasmic, men at the edge of bearable emotion. Planes thundered overhead. The cameras caught the silhouette of some flying close to the bare trees, many thick with young people who had climbed into their branches.

After a brief stop back at the hotel, Hitler returned to the Heldenplatz at 1:30 P.M. to review a massive military parade that featured tanks, mobile artillery, truckloads of troops, marching infantry, and 400 planes flying overhead. Despite this panoply of power Hitler reportedly was furious at the performance of his armies, and it was a signal of his displeasure that he left Vienna soon after the parade was over. His plane landed in Munich shortly after 7 P.M. He had spent barely twenty-four hours in Vienna, and only seventy-two hours had passed since his car had crossed into Austria on Saturday afternoon.

Die Neue Freie Presse would write that "Vienna had not seen such a day in the memory of man" and waxed ecstatic over what the future would bring for the city—the second capital of the Reich once again confronted with world politics from which it had been excluded since 1918.[41]

What vain hopes they would prove.

CHAPTER 2

The State Nobody Wanted

From St. Germain to Berchtesgaden:
October 16, 1918–February 11, 1938

The destruction of Austria-Hungary at the end of the Great War laid the groundwork for the first Austrian republic's sudden collapse in 1938. The shockwaves of the 1918 upheaval were too great, too sudden, and too harrowing to be fully absorbed, and they reverberated through the twenty years that "the state nobody wanted" managed to survive.

Consider Vienna's position in mid-1918: It was still the capital of an empire of 55 million people that stretched from the Alps in the West and the Dalmatian coast and Trieste in the South, to Krakow and the Duchy of Auschwitz in the North and to Tarnopol and Czernowitz along the Russian border in the East. The empire had an army in the field of several million men that had fought the enemy to a standstill along a front that ran from Bulgaria to Belgrade and to the Isonzo river in Italy. A centralized and seasoned bureaucracy administered the vast lands of the Habsburg realm that covered a dozen nationalities—Italians, Slovenes, Czechs, Slovaks, Bosnians, Germans, Ukrainians, and Poles. While the Hungarian half of the empire was largely autonomous in ruling Croatia, Slovakia, and a large swatch of Romania and Transylvania, Vienna dictated defense, foreign, and fiscal policy.

As late as January 1918, when President Woodrow Wilson issued his famous Fourteen Points, destruction of Austria-Hungary was not among allied war aims. Indeed, point ten, as American leaflets dropped across the Western front noted, said "the peoples of Austria-Hungary, whose place among other nations we wish to assure, should be given the earliest opportunity for autonomous development."

But as the military situation of the central powers deteriorated in the summer months, so did allied willingness to adhere to point ten; when on October 16 the unhappy, tubercular, and indecisive young Emperor Charles—then thirty-one years old—issued a proclamation turning the monarchy into a group of federal states and giving autonomous rights to its diverse peoples, it was too late, a point the American secretary of state, Robert Lansing, made three days later. On October 19 he sent a note to Vienna, via the Swedish prime minister, saying the president was no longer in a position to accept the autonomy of these peoples as a basis for peace and that the peoples themselves would have to make that determination.[1] Austria-Hungary's fate, and that of the Habsburg dynasty, was sealed.

Signals of destruction had been flying for months. The number of deserters rose dramatically with armed so-called "green" units hiding in forests behind the front ready to shoot it out with the army's much feared "field gendarmes." The Bulgarian front had collapsed in the middle of September, and on September 26 Thomas Masaryk and Eduard Benes had proclaimed the independent Czechoslovak republic from their exile in Paris. On October 6, Croats, Serbs, and Slovenes met in Zagreb to found a "national council" as a first step toward creation of a southern Slav kingdom without ties to the House of Habsburg.[2]

In Vienna, on October 21, the German-speaking members of the "Reichsrat"—the imperial parliament—met to constitute themselves as the "provisional national assembly" of German Austria and issued a manifesto: "The German people in Austria are determined to decide their future themselves, to form the independent state of German-Austria, and to regulate that state's relations with other countries through freely reached agreements."[3] On October 30 the provisional assembly picked a Social Democrat, forty-eight-year-old Karl Renner, as "state chancellor" of the new country and Karl Seitz, another Social Democrat and a future mayor of Vienna, as provisional president. Both men would play pivotal roles in the first republic, with Renner reprising his role as head of government and head of state after World War II.

THE STATE NOBODY WANTED

Outside, Vienna was seething. Mobs took to the streets, clogging inner-city thoroughfares. They demanded "action" from the barely formed government, action to stop the war, of course, but also to end the misery it had caused. Hunger was rampant. Ration cards entitled individuals to two pounds of potatoes per week, only on October 30 the city had no potatoes. The fat ration was cut from forty grams a week to twenty grams. Men tramping through the wet streets still wore shoes, but soles were of paper, not leather.

Industrial workers demonstrated for higher wages and better living conditions. Soldiers tore insignia off their own collars and off any officers they met. The walking wounded wanted better care. Prisoners of war returned from Russia shouted revolutionary Soviet slogans. Bedlam was everywhere as law and order collapsed with no force available to restore it.

The next day, October 31, the provisional government was forced to act. Dr. Julius Deutsch, who ten days earlier had been named minister of war, demanded approval for turning the army—at least that part willing to follow the new regime's orders—into a "people's militia." It was badly needed, and not only to maintain order in the streets: the imperial army was beginning to disband, the exemplary discipline the multinational force had displayed through four years of war unraveling in the inevitability of defeat. Hungarians started to shoot their way home from the Italian front, and, when the imperial forces laid down their arms on November 3, a week before their hardier German allies, it seemed that everybody was coming through Vienna. The soldiers would have to be disarmed and transport found to send them home. (The guns they left behind would form an arsenal for the private political armies that marred the republic's first fifteen years of life.)

Even more ominous, the far left was girding for action. Intellectuals plotted in suburban beer halls to take power in the new state, while increasingly radicalized industrial workers marched through the streets to demonstrate their might. Leaders—they would organize themselves as the Austrian Communist party on November 3—told Deutsch they wanted permission to form the "Red Guards," a typically Austrian request. What other revolutionaries would ask for a government imprimatur to rebel? Deutsch agreed and began to seed the new organization with trusted Social Democrats who would keep him apprised of what the Communists plotted.

Meanwhile, the imperial government continued to function in pow-erless and parallel lockstep with the republican regime. Indeed, on Oc-tober 27 a new—and the last—Habsburg cabinet took office. It lasted only for a few days, time enough for the prime minister to receive the first minister of Czechoslovakia in Vienna with the words "your Excel-lency, I have the pleasure of receiving you as the new ambassador of the Czechoslovak state," to which the new envoy replied "Prime Minister, the pleasure is all mine."[4] Austria-Hungary, it seemed, would go down not with a bang nor a whimper, but with the unfazed *politesse des rois.*

A week after the empire stopped fighting so did the emperor. On November 11, 1918, Charles withdrew from "further participation in government affairs."[5] He did not, however, abdicate (a legal distinction monarchists would use later to challenge the legitimacy of the first Aus-trian republic). Still, his removal paved the way for proclamation of the republic of "German-Austria" on November 12, 1918, hours after the Na-tional Assembly had approved the necessary legislative framework that included two key provisions: Article one stated that "German-Austria is a democratic republic with all power flowing from the people." Article two said "German-Austria is a constituent part of the German Republic." (Emperor Wilhelm II had crossed the Dutch border on November 9, 1918, and the same day German Social Democrats proclaimed a German Re-public in Berlin. They had acted in haste to prevent the Communists from turning Germany into a Soviet state.) Only one man voted against article two—Wilhelm Miklas, the Austrian president in 1938 who would resist German demands for Anschluss on March 11 until the bitter end.

Still, it was not an easy birth. Even as Renner and his government moved to the steps of parliament in the afternoon of November 12 to announce advent of the new nation, the Communists attempted a putsch. Tens of thousands had gathered on the Ringstrasse below to watch the hoisting of the new red-white-red Austrian flag—legend has it that dur-ing the Crusades Duke Leopold V's white tunic and breeches had turned blood red after a day of slaughter on the walls of a Saracen town, but that his white belt had been untouched[6]—and the taking down of the black and yellow Habsburg banner.

The Red Guards had marched downtown together with the workers, but unlike the others the Communists were heavily armed. They took up positions on the ramp leading to the main gate and when the new flag began to rise they stormed forward, tore out the white strip, and hoisted a red banner. The mob cheered. The red flag was as much a Social-Democratic icon as a Communist one. One of the Communist leaders began to read the proclamation of a workers and peasants state on the Soviet model. The crowd cheered and began to sing revolutionary songs; then it started to disband. In the confusion the Red Guards tried to break down the doors of parliament and seize power.

Glass shattered. The first shots fell. Panic gripped the mob, which began to flood away from parliament and run down the Ring. Firing increased as the Red Guards thought a cameraman, getting ready to film the scene from the top of the building, was drawing up a cannon. In the melee two people were killed and forty-five were wounded. Now the Red Guards lost their nerve. Had they broken down the door and hanged the cabinet, as one of them urged, Vienna would have been in Communist hands. They didn't because the lieutenant in charge of the guard unit failed to give the order to do so, thus saving the republic from being stillborn.

But the aborted putsch was only one obstacle of many the new state faced. To begin with, nobody knew exactly what geographic boundaries the new country would have. In its proclamation of German-Austria the assembly had laid claim to sovereignty over "all the German territories, and in particular the Sudetenland." But Austria had not existed as a separate entity since 1867 when the double monarchy was formed, and the German-speakers—some 10 million in all—had more local than dynastic roots. They lived in Vienna and in the provinces of Upper and Lower Austria that together had been the core of the "Eastern Marches" around the turn of the first millennium when the Margraves of Babenberg ruled; in the former dukedoms of Carinthia and Styria; in the "princely earldom" of Tyrol (the Earl of the Tyrol—one of the Emperor Franz Josef's many titles, he was also Duke of Auschwitz and King of Jerusalem—had the rank of prince); in the archbishopric of Salzburg; in western Hungary; and in the Sudetenland—patches of German-speaking lands spread across Bohemia.

Even if borders could be drawn around so amorphous a geography, this stretch of land, those who lived in it were convinced, could never be economically viable. Vienna, and the Alpine and Danube regions, had drawn wheat and milk from Hungary, pork from Croatia, coal from Moravia and Silesia, and goods from overseas via the port of Trieste, not to mention beer from Bohemia.[7] Clearly, the only way to retain the protection of great power status was to take all 10 million of these German-speakers into the German Reich, as article two of the independence law had demanded. But that would prove easier said than done.

Revolution had inflamed Germany with the political tides flowing sharply to the left. Neighboring Bavaria was particularly hard-hit with Munich shaken by Far Left violence. Hungary was rocked by revolution, and in both states Communist dictatorships seized power, albeit briefly, in the spring of 1919. For Austria's Social Democrats the danger from the Left, therefore, seemed greater than that from the Right, especially given the growing impact of the Russian revolution on middle European politics.

In the midst of uncertainty, elections were held on February 19, 1919. The Social Democrats emerged with 72 seats, the Christian Socials won 69, the Greater Germans 23. Another six seats went to splinter groups. The vote would signal the deep split within the state that has not healed to this day. With very few exceptions the two major parties have kept that rough balance, even if from election to election a few seats shifted one way or the other.

The Social Democrats had expected to do much better, and now faced a "bourgeois" majority, which led them to agree to a coalition with the Christian Socials. But the Social Democrats kept the reins of power— Renner remained chancellor and Deutsch secretary of war. Dr. Otto Bauer, the party's intellectual mainspring and most brilliant orator, took over the foreign office. On the right Joseph Schumpeter—the future Harvard economist and economic guru of the American Right—served as Christian Social minister of finance. Six women were elected to parliament, the first time ever.

Austria-Hungary did not have much of a democratic political tradition. The three major parties had been in existence for less than forty years. Universal suffrage as the West knew it was not introduced until 1907, and the first parliament elected with something close to a popular mandate took office in 1908. By the time the republican parliament met in 1919 it could look back on a bare decade of history.[8]

Both Christian Socials and Social Democrats were products of ferment in the late 1880s and early '90s, and both were the first political parties that appealed to important segments of the "masses." The pan-Germans had been around for a little longer but had never made it as a mass party.

The Christian Socials were founded in 1889 by, among others, Dr. Karl Lueger, mayor of Vienna for more than a decade beginning in 1897, and idol of the "little people"—artisans, shopkeepers, the disaffected lower clergy, and, in time, the business community. The party's ideology was based on Pope Leo XIII's famous encyclical "*Rerum Novarum*" in which the pope pleaded for better treatment of the working class lest in its despair it fall prey to Marxist rhetoric. Lueger's voter appeal, however, was based not only on social justice but on anti-Semitism, in its modern form a largely Viennese invention.

The Social Democrats took shape around the same time under the leadership of Victor Adler, a bold socialist thinker and friend of Leon Trotsky during his Vienna years. Their target was the industrial proletariat, and their ideology was based on democratic Marxism—meaning rule of the proletariat through democratic, not dictatorial means. They quickly won the loyalty of industrial workers and attracted many of the "best and the brightest" among Jewish intellectuals.

The Greater Germans, finally, had their roots in the politics of one man—Georg von Schönerer, who hated the Catholic Church, the Habsburg dynasty, and the Jews, and saw in the Prussian house of Hohenzollern the repository of Teutonic virtue. Schönerer's anti-Semitism was virulent, targeted, and in the end violent. His speeches attacking Jews thundered through the Reichsrat with a vituperative rhetoric that made liberals shudder. He had disciples and great influence but failed to build a modern party by reaching out to the masses. Still, his poisonous rhetoric lingered, deeply influencing Hitler during his Vienna years.

By the time the first republic was founded, however, the pan-Germans had lost Schönerer's fire and brimstone. They still favored union with Germany and hated the Jews but because in the 1920s the party was an amalgam of several pan-German groups, it lacked a clear focus and was able to attract only disaffected voters—jobless bureaucrats and cashiered army officers, for example. As a result the pan-Germans never grew beyond a balance of power role, often broke apart, and reappeared in different guises.

On March 23, 1919, the emperor Charles and his family boarded the old imperial train for a forty-two hour journey across Austria into Swiss exile. Before crossing the border at Feldkirch Charles took back everything he had decreed since October 16, denied the legality of the republic, and charged that the elections in February had been rigged. The new government responded by confiscating Habsburg property. Most of it still has not been returned.

With Soviet governments in power in April in Budapest and Munich, Vienna clearly was the next target. On April 17th Austrian Communists tried again. Massive demonstrations gathered around parliament. Emissaries entered the building to demand an increase in bread rations and more financial aid for the unemployed. Renner professed sympathy and promised that once Austria signed a peace treaty with the allies new food shipments would reach the starving country. Outside the mob grew unruly. Rocks were thrown, windows smashed, and burning oil-soaked rags tossed into the building. Police and firefighters intervened. When the riot was over, five policemen were dead but no civilians had been killed. Again, the Communists had been stopped—but now the Right was furious. It demanded cleansing of Communist influence from the People's Militia, something Deutsch was more than willing to do.

But whatever he did was not enough for the Right. The Communist surge in 1919 left deep scars. Men like Monsignor Ignaz Seipel, chancellor for most of the 1920s, saw their major task in stopping the "red flood." For Seipel it did not matter that the Social Democrats were committed to democratic change. He saw them as part of the left-wing enemy that had to be destroyed to save the new country, and while he was in power he would lay the groundwork for that destruction.

On May 12, 1919, Karl Renner and Otto Bauer left Vienna to lead the Austrian delegation for peace talks in St. Germain. If the Austrians hoped for negotiations they were deeply disappointed. The allies handed them a 300-page treaty draft, which blamed Vienna for every wrong the empire had committed. Terms were draconian. The Sudetenland plus parts of Lower Austria would go to Czechoslovakia, the South Tyrol to Italy, and southern Styria to Yugoslavia. The fate of Carinthia, which the new Yugoslavia had invaded on May 10, would be settled later. Economic reparations were harsh; military conscription was banned. The nation's army would be limited to 30,000 men. And finally, union with Germany— *Anschluss*—was strictly forbidden.

Why the Austrians—and the Germans—had expected otherwise is hard to grasp, except for the fact that they believed in Wilson's Fourteen Points and their stress on self-determination. Surely, they thought, if Austrians and Germans wanted to unite, a natural combine given language and cultural ties, the allies would not object. They did, however, feeling they had not fought a desperate war to defeat Germany only to have it grow in size, population, and resources. Bauer had gone so far as to meet his German colleague, Count Ulrich von Brockdorff-Rantzau, in Weimar from February 27 to March 2, 1919, and draw up secret protocols for the union. Austria would join the Reich as an independent part of the federal state. The president would spend part of each year in Vienna, and parliament would meet there at least once a year, in effect making the city the second capital.[9] The Viennese would nourish a similar hope when Hitler marched into the city in 1938. Both hopes, of course, were dashed.

The treaty was signed on September 10, 1919, and about the only thing the Austrians got was agreement on a plebiscite to determine Carinthia's future, and, in 1920, the return of German-speaking Hungary, the Burgenland.[10] The Austrians won the plebiscite in Carinthia but return of the Burgenland took another year—and weeks of fighting as Hungarians battled for the province despite the allied ukase.

With the treaty signed, the Communist threat contained, the borders more or less determined, and union with Germany outlawed, the government buckled down to dealing with the domestic problems of the new country. The Social Democrats wrote a constitution that gave Austria a start as a modern state based on parliamentary democracy in which political parties would rule. The adopted new social legislation included an eight-hour workday, stiffer child labor laws, and compulsory health, injury, and unemployment insurance.

The coalition broke up on June 10, 1920, in a fairly routine dispute over the people's militia. But the real reason was the deepening split between Left and Right—Social Democrats on the one side and Christian Socials and pan-Germans in uneasy alliance on the other. The Right chafed under its lack of armed might since the militia was controlled by Social Democrats. The Left feared that continued coalition with the bourgeoisie would alienate its base among industrial workers, especially if the Christian Socials refused to go along with Social Democratic social reform programs. The Right did just that.

New elections were held in October and the Social Democrats were badly beaten, losing 10 seats for a total of 62, while the Christian Socials captured 79, not enough to govern alone but enough for an easy majority with 26 Greater Germans. Things didn't become any easier for the new chancellor, Christian Social Max Mayr, however. A tattered economy, rising inflation, food shortages, failure to obtain allied credits, and the outcome of unofficial—and meaningless—plebiscites in Tyrol and Salzburg in the spring of 1921 that saw 99-percent voter support for Anschluss with Germany, helped topple Mayr in June 1921.

He was succeeded by Johannes Schober, Vienna's police chief, a tough law-and-order man who was close to the pan-Germans but was considered nonpartisan. Monsignor Seipel backed Schober because Seipel was not yet ready to assume power. He wanted Schober to do more of the dirty work. Schober did. He presided over the return of Burgenland, developed ties to Italy, the one country that even then seemed willing to help Austria out of its diplomatic isolation, and negotiated a substantial Czech loan.

Schober fell in the spring of 1922, and Seipel formed his first government. Four months later he signed three agreements with the League of Nations in Geneva that gave Austria a basis for economic development—a new currency that would end hyperinflation. In June one Swiss frank was worth 3,141 crowns, in August it had nearly quadrupled to 12,218 crowns. Printing presses could barely keep up with demand for banknotes. The price the League charged for the bailout? Agreement to hold off Anschluss for twenty years.

Introduction of the new currency—the schilling was worth 10,000 old crowns—would also provide the basis for as much political stability as a country rent in two by conflicting ideologies could manage. For the next decade the so-called bourgeois bloc—Christian Socials and various stripes of pan-Germans and peasant parties—scratched together enough votes at election time to stay in power on the national level.

When Seipel became chancellor the Social Democrats had already lost control of the army, but the Christian Socials had not yet cemented their hold, something they would achieve over the next few years and thus turn the army into a political instrument rather than an organ of national unity. In the meantime private armies began to proliferate on both sides of the ideological divide. Seipel had begun to build a home militia in early 1920 when he sought Hungarian money to arm irregular troops. These home guards began to form across the Austrian provinces as early as 1919 to fight against Yugoslavia in Carinthia, to guard against expected Communist attacks from neighboring Bavaria, and to protect farms from marauding former soldiers in the Tyrol and Salzburg. They even stopped poachers and other miscreants at princely estates, as did twenty-year-old Ernst Rüdiger, Prince von Starhemberg, a future vice-chancellor and major player in the rough-and-tumble politics of the first republic. There were plenty of guns left over from the war so that arsenals were not a problem. Nor did the Social Democrats stand idly by. Although their official paramilitary organization—*der Republikanische Schutzbund* (the Republican Guards)—was not launched until 1923, Social Democrats, too, began to arm workers. The stage for bloody conflict a dozen years later was being set.

Out of power in the national government, the Social Democrats concentrated on their main bastion—the city of Vienna. Under Mayor Lueger the Christian Socials had carried out social reforms and launched a program of infrastructure development. But after Lueger died in 1910, the Social Democrats began to surge and in 1919 won a thumping majority and the mayor's office, which they have held ever since except for the eleven years of Austro-Fascist and Nazi rule.

When they arrived they found a city in chaos. "Its buildings and streets were dilapidated, half the tramways were dismantled and the other half almost useless, its population was half starved, tens of thousands were unemployed, and the Treasury was nearly empty," Julius Braunthal, the most innovative media mind the party had in the twenties and thirties, wrote. Municipal workers "had to be paid in installments: the municipality was on the verge of bankruptcy. Vienna appeared to be a dying city beyond help."[11]

Housing was the most pressing and important issue. If the city was badly housed before the war, it was worse now. One lavatory and one water faucet to a floor often had to serve thirty or forty people. "No new houses had been built for nine years, and the old ones had not been repaired. Vienna was infested with vermin." The Social Democrats moved quickly, vigorously, and innovatively to ameliorate the situation, launching an unprecedented new housing program that in fifteen years built 65,000 new apartments and changed the face of the city.

The architecture was new and bold—huge blocks of apartment buildings designed with a modernist flair that gave facades a mostly plain surface softened by arches, balconies, triangular windows, and by the bold use of color. The Karl Marx Hof, the largest single project with 1,600 units, was painted in rust, blue, and yellow. Only about 30 percent of the land was used for actual building; the rest was reserved for squares and greeneries that often featured open-air sculpture. "Every housing block contained a nursery, a health care department and a library, shower-baths, common kitchens, and laundries electrically equipped with washing, drying, and ironing apparatus," Braunthal wrote. At least one room of each apartment received sunlight, and most apartments had access to balconies.

The bankrupt city raised the money through a series of special taxes and other innovative financial devices that hit homeowners and those who lived in large apartments the hardest. Graduated taxes were imposed on entertainment, domestic employees, carriages, and automobiles. Rents were low to allow workers to move in—the projects clearly were designed to keep the proletariat loyal to the Social Democrats and in this they succeeded. Postwar inflation coupled with stringent rent-control laws slashed housing costs from one-third of average incomes before the war to 8 percent.

Social welfare was built from the ground up: counseling services for pregnant women and young mothers; a network of daycare centers that operated from seven in the morning to six in the evening; dental clinics and regular medical examinations for school children; a free lunch program; summer camps for 25,000 children; special help for the hard-to-educate. The city undertook a save-the-children campaign. Since the war, child mortality had doubled. Only a handful of almost 200,000 children given medical examinations were found not to be undernourished.

Childcare began before birth. Prenatal clinics were established. Hospitals had to provide facilities for married and unmarried mothers. The city gave each newborn child a complete baby outfit. Mothers had access to free medical treatment and several weeks of postnatal leave, revolutionary for the 1920s. Every district had a birth-control clinic, and the city launched an antivenereal disease campaign.

Polluting steam engines were taken off the elevated lines and replaced by electric trains. Trolleys were modernized, buses put into service on new lines. Badly lit streets were brightened by 20,000 electric lamps. Garbage trucks making regular pickups spearheaded modern urban sanitation. Alfred Adler opened a child guidance clinic in 1921, and, a decade later, personally ran a network of thirty such clinics. For Social Democrats, education of the proletariat was more important and more urgent than establishing its dictatorship. Adult schools that offered courses in everything from anthropology to zoology sprouted in working-class neighborhoods. Workers, depicted in the bourgeois press as drunkards and loafers, now spent their evenings in class.

The Austro-Marxists who ran the party developed an ideological platform in the twenties that posed serious competition to Communist orthodoxy as an ideological alternative for the Left. Its leaders were high-carat intellectuals, international in scope and interest, sharp-tongued, democratic, forward-looking, mostly Jewish, with a clear-cut political vision and the power of language to articulate it. They believed in the truths of Marx and Engels yet had little faith in Leninist theory and far less in Stalinist practice. They made Austro-Marxism a socialist doctrine that served as an alternative to Communist ideology, and one that other socialist parties could embrace. Their voice in the councils of the Socialist International was ringing and respected.

The social psychologist Marie Jahoda, one of Vienna's many gifts to Anglo-Saxon culture, wrote that social democracy in the Vienna of the twenties had reached its social, intellectual, and cultural high point. "Despite economic crisis, inflation, and unemployment this mass movement, based on the tenets of Austro-Marxism, was filled with a spirit of life, which I believe had no parallel in the twentieth century. It believed in the possibility of a humanistic, democratic socialism whose victory would be achieved without violence through democratic elections. . . ."[12]

Outside Vienna and in the sprawling apartments of the city's bourgeoisie these advances were not much appreciated. "Red Vienna" became the enemy that had to be defeated, and Social Democrats had to be kept out of the national government at all costs.

In the October 1923 election Seipel succeeded. He did not win the majority he had hoped for, but the pan-Germans, with a shrunken total of 10 seats, gave him the margin he needed. The Social Democrats had rebounded, however, adding 6 seats for a total of 68 versus 82 for Seipel. The chancellor resigned on November 8, 1924, over a dispute with the provincial governors. Two years later Seipel was back. His successor had soothed the governors and brought the budget close enough to balance to satisfy League of Nations conditions for the currency loan. But unemployment rose dangerously on his watch; pessimism spread, and as it did demands for Anschluss spiked. It was enough to topple him.

Seipel faced regular elections six months later, in April 1927, running on a "unity list" with the pan-Germans. Again Seipel hoped for a majority but instead lost nine seats and had to depend on the support of all the minor parties to gain a parliamentary majority. The Social Democrats won 42.3 percent of the vote and seventy-one seats, their highest total yet but short of that elusive majority. Still, the Left was encouraged. The political tides seemed to be running its way at last, but events outside of parliament were not.

Private armies had grown on both sides but the *Heimwehr* or home guard, now the single largest such grouping, was growing faster and arming more heavily. Bloody clashes between the two sides grew more frequent, as did the bitterness on both sides of the ideological divide.

Some three months before the 1927 election, on January 30, a clash in a village in Burgenland set the stage for the demise of democracy in Austria. Local republican guards beat up a delegation of old "front fighters" come from Vienna for a demonstration. When the guards marched back through the village in triumph, three local front fighters opened fire from a bedroom window in the village inn. An old man, a cripple, and an eight-year-old child were killed. The murderers were finally put on trial months later, and on July 14 a Viennese court acquitted them.

Now the workers marched in anger. On July 15 they sacked and burned the palace of justice next to parliament in downtown Vienna. Police armed with carbines were called out and, when the mob refused to disperse and continued to throw cobble stones, opened fire, killing ninety-four workers.[13] The party called a general strike. It was complete and shut down the city. But it did not move Seipel's government and was called off after four days.

The events, Braunthal wrote, "broke the spell of the invincibility of the Social Democratic party. And as the Republic was wanted by none but the Social Democrats, the counterrevolutionaries now knew that it would be possible to smash it by smashing the Social Democrats; what was required was merely the audacity and the recklessness."

Seipel, who henceforth was known as "the prelate without mercy" among the Left, had that in spades. He relied more and more on the Heimwehr to discourage and frighten the Social Democrats. Politically he set the switches in the direction of the corporate state along the lines of Mussolini's model in Italy. It would take the Christian Socials another seven years—two years after he died—to complete the journey.

The Social Democrats, meanwhile, did their utmost to stop the Christian Socials by maintaining the momentum they had gained in 1927.

The Social Democrats realized earlier than other political parties—in Austria and elsewhere in middle Europe—that innovative media was the most effective way of reaching voters. Julius Braunthal was the innovator. He launched a successful tabloid, "*Das Kleine Blatt*" (the little paper) squarely aimed at the lower class, Right and Left, that deftly mixed tabloid fare—sex, murder, mayhem—with clever calls for social action. It caught on at once and proved a good vote-catching vehicle. So did the *Kuckuck* (*The Cuckoo*) a pioneering picture weekly that used dramatic photo montage covers to attract readers, ran intelligent editorials and news stories on current politics, and covered the lifestyle of the times in dramatic pictures that ran from what the modern baby wore to the sly sex appeal of scantily clad female athletes caught in the beams of the setting sun. (My father was its first and only editor.)

The Social Democrats used film as a propaganda medium and showed their works at cinemas owned by KIBA, a socialist organization. A feature with an English title, *Mr. Pim's Trip to Europe*, made a clever pitch for votes. It had a story line—an American newspaper publisher comes to Vienna where his daughter is involved with a Social Democrat. The father gets the lowdown on Vienna from the editor of a reactionary paper, who tells his American colleague how great things were before the Social Democrats took over city hall. The film counterpointed his words with clips of social squalor and misery. His daughter's social democratic boyfriend then takes him on a tour of Red Vienna and shows him the new city's achievements—the apartment blocks, the kindergartens, the greenery, the clinics. In one of them the father is saved after suffering a severe injury in a traffic accident. The father is convinced and gives the young couple his blessing. Then the pitch is made: vote for the Social Democrats. The silent film was shot Russian-style, with Pudovkin and Eisenstein's influence clear in almost every frame.

The new Social Democratic appeal scared the Right. In 1930 Seyss-Inquart, then a leading member of the German Club, a pan-German association with strong Nazi leanings, gave a prescient speech in which he suggested that a Marxist majority was possible at the next election, in which case "it was questionable whether the men now constitutionally in power could marshal the amount of determination needed to meet the danger with the constitutional means at their disposal." If they could not, he added, civil war was possible. So was fascism. In May 1930 members of the Heimwehr met in Korneuburg north of Vienna to take an oath that said in part: "We grasp at the power over the State. We reject democracy and parliament. We stand for the principles of the Leadership State."[14] This oath was almost identical to the dogma of Italian fascism.

Seipel had stepped down for a second time on April 3, 1929, his coalition in fragments.[15] The small parties split, and finding a majority grew harder and harder. Over the next three years, five chancellors tried to grapple with growing economic and political problems. In 1930 one of them called a snap election, fearful that Nazi successes in Germany—where the party won six million votes and 106 seats in the Reichstag—would be repeated in Austria and that the Social Democrats would win a majority. The outcome was a disaster for both major parties. The Social Democrats gained a seat, now 72, but lost 20,000 votes. The Christian Socials dropped to 66 seats and lost 187,000 votes. The Heimwehr set itself up as a political party and won 8 seats. The Nazis got 100,000 votes but, given Austria's complicated electoral math, not a single deputy.

The impact of the Wall Street crash in 1929 did not reach Austria until 1931 when the country tried to find protection in a customs union with the Weimar republic. The allies said no. Months later the Creditanstalt, Austria's largest bank, crashed, scaring even the British. The governor of the Bank of England worried that "Southeast Europe is in flames. The Creditanstalt has closed its counters."[16] In the fall of 1931 the last democratic chancellor of the republic faced an armed insurrection in Styria. It was put down, but it demonstrated how shaky the republic's institutions were.

These institutions would be destroyed by the next man through the revolving door—Dr. Engelbert Dollfuss, minister of agriculture in the outgoing cabinet. The new chancellor was thirty-nine-years-old and stood just under five feet, a height that earned him the sobriquet of "Millimetternich." He would prove to be the most dynamic, controversial, and tragic figure of the first Austrian republic. He came from dirt-poor peasants in Lower Austria and managed to get an education at a seminary, thinking he wanted to be a priest. In 1914 he switched to law and, after Sarajevo, fought in Italy where he earned a fistful of decorations for bravery. He made a career as an agrarian reformer, had a short spell running the railroads, and in 1931 entered the cabinet.

He took office after local elections on April 24, 1932, had given the Social Democrats close to a two-thirds majority in Vienna's city hall and the Nazis fifteen city councilmen—the first time they had won any elective office in Vienna. While the election did not affect the makeup of parliament, it did influence the votes of the minor parties on which Dollfuss would have to depend. They were now even less willing to support the Christian Socials than they had been over the last three years.

It took Dollfuss ten days to form a cabinet in May, and he nearly fell on August 3 when the pan-Germans asked for a vote of no-confidence. With former chancellor Seipel ill and away from parliament, Dollfuss would have lost by one vote. Fortuitously Seipel died that very day, and someone was appointed to take his seat, thus saving the new chancellor's hide. Social Democrats demanded dissolution of parliament and new elections. Dollfuss knew he could not afford them because had the people gone to the polls the Right would have continued to splinter, the Nazis would have entered parliament in disturbing numbers, and the Social Democrats would have won an even larger share of the popular vote and perhaps a parliamentary majority. Dollfuss began to look for other ways to survive and pondered the elimination of parliament.

In March 1933 he found his opportunity during another one of those cliff-hanger votes that had become the country's daily political diet. All three presidents of parliament (roles akin to speaker and his two deputies in British or American legislatures; Renner was the speaker) resigned in order to vote (theirs were nonvoting positions), and Dollfuss decreed that parliament had voted itself out of existence. He put police on the steps of parliament to make his point. On March 31, 1933, he outlawed the Schutzbund, the Social Democratic militia, also known as the Republican Guards. For the next eleven months he used wartime legislation passed in 1917—the "Economic Empowering Law" that had never been repealed—to rule by decree. That allowed him to ban the Nazi party, which that spring had unleashed a campaign of terror across Vienna, bombing Jewish stores, and blowing up telephone booths. Unfazed, the Nazis went underground. Hitler retaliated by imposing a thousand-mark tax on German tourists visiting Austria. The revenue-producing tourist industry, heavily dependent on German visitors, was decimated.

The Schutzbund, too, went underground, at least partway. Police scoured the city for their weapons and confiscated as many as they could find. Many of the paramilitary group's leaders were arrested. In Vienna the party leadership began to fall apart. Otto Bauer may have used his oratory as an ideological sword, but like most intellectuals he wilted in the face of brute force; by early 1934 it became clear that the Heimwehr and the government were ready to use guns to put down the Social Democrats.

When police and detectives raided a workers' club in Linz in the early hours of February 12, the workers picked up guns and fired back. The civil war was on. It lasted four bloody days, with most of the fighting in Vienna. The Socialists called a general strike but coordination was poor and was only partly effective. When the Heimwehr failed to put down the insurrection, Dollfuss moved up army troops and field guns. Howitzers bombarded workers' housing projects like the Karl Marx Hof, never mind that women and children lived in them. Workers fired back with guns they had cemented in the walls of their housing complexes, forcing the army to move in building by building. On February 16 workers hoisted a white flag above the Karl Marx Hof.

Official figures put the number of dead at 239 and 718 wounded but, Braunthal argued, the real figures were never established and were probably much higher. Nine Socialists were hanged, one carried to the gallows on a stretcher with his bowels torn open. Bauer and most of the party's top leadership including Braunthal fled to Brünn in Czechoslovakia where they set up a party in exile and later went on to Paris and London. In Vienna, Renner and the last Socialist mayor of the city, Karl Seitz, were arrested.

Dollfuss did not have much time to savor his triumph—little more than five months, months marred by a new wave of Nazi terror financed and abetted by the Third Reich. Railroad stations were blown up, rails uprooted, phone lines cut, and power stations bombed. Police seized vast arms caches, which had been smuggled across the German frontier. Nazi planes violated Austrian air space to drop leaflets urging citizens to refuse paying taxes and to withdraw money from banks. Alfred Frauenfeld, the illegal Nazi Gauleiter in Austria who had fled to Munich, made incendiary radio broadcasts inciting the people to rise and murder the chancellor. Even as he spoke, a Nazi plot began to take shape.[17]

On July 25 some 154 members of an underground SS regiment, the SS Standarte 89, led by Friedolin Glass (who would become Bürckel's propaganda chief in 1939) along with a thug by the name of Otto Planetta as trigger man, shot their way into the chancellery, trapped Dollfuss in one of the ornate rooms, and shot him dead as he was trying to escape. Murder was not the object, however. The SS wanted to capture the little chancellor, force him to announce his resignation on the radio, and nominate a Nazi to succeed him. Once Planetta fired, however, the plot collapsed, even though the Nazis had occupied the radio station and proclaimed the Austrian ambassador in Rome as the new chancellor. By the time they did President Miklas had named Kurt von Schuschnigg, the minister of justice and of education, as acting chancellor and army tanks surrounded the chancellery. Hours later the plotters surrendered. But it took another five days of often-bloody fighting across the country to finally put down the Nazi putsch.

Mussolini sent Italian troops up to the Brenner Pass to stop any German effort to support the plotters with armed force, a move that put the Austrian government more deeply in his debt than it was already. On July 31 Planetta and six of his cohorts were hanged. Thousands of other Nazis ended up in the Wöllersdorf detention camp where they joined Social Democrats arrested after the civil war, and the first tentative bonds between the two were knotted. The bonds were never tight, but the fact that they existed at all made it easier for the Nazis after the Anschluss.

President Miklas formally named Schuschnigg as chancellor on July 29 and the thirty-six-year-old lawyer was left to grapple with the inheritance Dollfuss had bequeathed him—a political structure based on the corporative state, organized to represent the interests of different social groups like business, labor, the farmers, and the church—in other words, the corporations. The only legal political organization was the Fatherland Front through which all decisions were filtered first. A new authoritarian constitution, adopted in May 1934, anchored the system firmly into law. A preamble made its purpose clear: "In the name of God Almighty, from whom all justice derives, the Austrian people receives this Constitution for a Christian, German and Federal State on a Corporative basis."[18] Law flowed from God, not from the people, as the republican constitution of 1920 had decreed (and which a 1929 constitutional "update" had reaffirmed), and Austria was no longer a republic, but a "federal state." At last, Seipel's dream had been fulfilled.

The Nazis had been defeated, at least for now. Hitler had dropped those responsible for the failed putsch and claimed the Reich had played no part in it—a blatant lie, but good enough to give Austria some temporary breathing room from Nazi intrigues. The Social Democrats had been eliminated as an active political force. Red Vienna was gone. The corporative state rested on the twin pillars of a newly renascent Catholic Church, and the bayonets of the army and the Heimwehr. Dollfuss was an ardent Catholic, and now the Church assumed a much more important role in political life than it had in the twenties.

But while political opposition had been outlawed, it seethed underground where social-democratic resentment grew and the illegal Nazi party flourished. As the economy worsened and unemployment skyrocketed, their party membership expanded dramatically, far more so than the Social Democrats. The newly unemployed—dismissed bureaucrats, students who couldn't find jobs, shopkeepers who lost their businesses, and other members of the disgruntled lower middle class—all flocked to the NSDAP. The Social Democrats had reached their natural limits under democracy and were hard put to add to their membership. Moreover, the party split soon after the civil war with the "Revolutionary Socialists" looking for overt action against the Austro-Fascist state, while the party leadership in Brünn counseled restraint and faith in the imminent collapse of an impossible regime. The country was thus effectively split into three hostile camps where nobody could find a majority to support any one of them.

Schuschnigg would serve as chancellor for exactly three years, seven months, and eleven days, and not one of them was free of turmoil. He was a compromise candidate, chosen by President Miklas to avoid naming one of the Heimwehr leaders, Major Emil Fey or Prince Stahremberg. Fey, vice-chancellor in Dollfuss's first cabinet, was suspected of complicity in the chancellor's murder, enough to rule him out (even though he was never convicted), and he remained as head of the Heimwehr and a member of Schuschnigg's cabinet. Stahremberg, who had succeeded Fey as vice-chancellor on May 1, was seen as too unstable and unfocused. None of the three, Schuschnigg included, had Dollfuss's charisma, passion, and political savvy, and none of them, therefore, was a man for this season.

Schuschnigg was the product of elite Jesuit schooling, an introverted intellectual, the son of an imperial general, and heir to the imperial bureaucracy's unbending arrogance. Born in the South Tyrol in 1897 he left Stella Matutina, the Jesuit college in Vorarlberg, imbued with a sense of Teutonic mission and Wagnerian grandeur, but also with strong loyalty to the House of Habsburg. Barely eighteen years old he won a commission and, like Dollfuss, fought bravely on the Italian front. Elected to parliament at the age of thirty, he soon joined the cabinet and became one of Dollfuss's closest associates.

He was not a likable man and had few friends. He lacked the popular touch. His speeches were often cold and stilted. He had great personal courage but little vision beyond maintaining the authoritarian state he had inherited and cementing the hold of his burning Catholic faith on the country. He closed city birth-control clinics. Vending machines selling condoms in public toilets were removed. "Theater, film and literature were harnessed to the chariot of the Catholic Church.... The smallest piece of work undertaken by government or municipality required the solemn blessing of a priest," Gedye wrote. Vienna's large agnostic population did not relish the new rules.[19]

Nor could Schuschnigg bring himself to make peace with the Social Democrats, something Dollfuss had seemed ready to do when he was assassinated. So he had to take on Hitler, the underground Austrian Nazis, and their "national" allies—men like Seyss-Inquart and Glaise-Horstenau—alone. Hitler had toned down his public support of Austria's Nazis, but he had not given up his campaign to undermine his homeland and eventually incorporate it into the Reich—a campaign he had announced brazenly in his book, *Mein Kampf* (My Battle).

On July 27, with Dollfuss not yet buried, the Führer asked Franz von Papen, his former vice-chancellor, to go to Vienna as minister and repair the Nazi image, which the murder had badly damaged. Papen agreed but told Hitler to halt the violence and keep the party underground for the time being. Papen favored Anschluss but on an evolutionary model. He arrived in Vienna on August 15, 1934, and was given an icy reception, far icier than he had imagined. When he arrived at the Ballhausplatz, the Austrians had put Dollfuss's death mask on a pedestal so that the German envoy could not miss seeing it. Papen was too shrewd to be discouraged. He worked quietly behind the scenes and within a year had become a player in Austrian politics, able to talk to Schuschnigg at a Vienna Philharmonic concert about concluding a normalization agreement with the Reich.

The chancellor was willing, even eager, to do so, but he first had to resolve other domestic and foreign policy issues. Despite the demise of democracy Schuschnigg headed an uneasy coalition between his increasingly religious Christian Socials and the now openly fascist Heimwehr, which had little use for the chancellor's Catholic fervor. Moreover, power in the ruling Fatherland Front was reversed—Starhemberg was Front leader and Schuschnigg his deputy. Fey still led the Heimwehr and remained a member of the cabinet. On October 17, 1935, Schuschnigg maneuvered to fasten his hold on power. He fired Fey from the cabinet and from his Heimwehr position. Starhemberg acquiesced. Heimwehr demands for a putsch got nowhere.

Events abroad complicated Schuschnigg's position. He had spent his first year in office cultivating ties with Mussolini, since Italy was the guarantor of Austrian independence and the political model for his corporative state. He also had to keep the League of Nations happy to assure continued financial support. When Mussolini invaded Ethiopia in October 1935 Austria faced a dilemma: It could not support League of Nations sanctions against Italy and had to risk the League's disdain. It didn't help matters that Mussolini's tanks and airplanes needed six months to defeat Emperor Haile Selassie's ill-equipped army, nor did Hitler's military occupation of the Rhineland in 1936, which the Allies accepted without opposition. Relations with the Reich remained rocky, even though the illegal Austrian Nazi party's political structure had been decimated by repeated police crackdowns in the wake of the Dollfuss murder.

Also, the economic situation had worsened, tanking badly as 1935 turned into 1936. Industrial output fell below that of the 1920s. Unemployment rose to 415,000, higher than in 1933. A quarter of the jobless received no unemployment benefits. The tourist industry was in tatters thanks to Hitler's thousand-mark tourist tax. Since 1930 exports had dropped by 50 percent. And the sour economy benefited the Nazis as more and more of the newly unemployed joined the Nazi underground to replace those leaders Schuschnigg had jailed. Police reports confirmed the trend. Jobless intellectuals and disgruntled officers made up the party leadership, and they itched for action.

Before Schuschnigg could agree to begin talks to normalize Austria's relations with the Reich, he had to remove the biggest obstacle in his own coalition—Prince Starhemberg. Although the prince was an unrepentant fascist who had no use for democracy, he was also a bitter opponent of Hitler and the Nazis. Schuschnigg and the prince clashed in May 1936. and Starhemberg quit with the words "if you think you can go ahead without me, just try."[20] Schuschnigg did just that. He added leadership of the Fatherland Front to his chancellor's portfolio and on July 11, 1936, signed the pact with Germany.

Now, Hitler formally recognized Austrian independence. He also agreed that National Socialism in Austria was an internal affair, and he lifted the thousand-mark tourist tax. In return Austria agreed not to oppose German foreign policy, to take two representatives of the "National Opposition" into the cabinet—he picked Glaise-Horstenau as minister without portfolio and Guido Schmidt as foreign minister—to free most of the arrested illegals, and to refrain from criticizing the Reich in the media.

The quid pro quo, however, was not as clean as it seemed. Hitler had already promised to recognize Austrian independence in a 1935 speech. The German government had pledged noninterference in domestic affairs, but the NSDAP had not and saw the agreement as a green light to push ahead. With generous resources coming from the German party and new manpower provided by those Schuschnigg had freed, the Nazis quickly became louder and more active, belying their illegal status. On July 29, 1936, they turned the festive departure of the Austrian Olympic team for Berlin into a Nazi demonstration, bringing in 30,000 followers to disrupt ceremonies on Vienna's Heldenplatz.

They wasted no time rebuilding the party structure destroyed after the failed putsch. New cadres of SA, SS, and Hitler Youth were put in place, as were political leaders down to precinct levels. Lists of candidates to take over key posts in government, education, and the cultural establishment were drawn up. By 1938 something close to a Nazi shadow government was in place.

More seriously, the Italian alliance began to fray. After Göring visited Mussolini early in 1937 to explain that the Reich needed Austria's economic resources—timber, gold, coal, iron and other ores, oil, hydroelectric power—for its military buildup and sooner or later would have to take them, Mussolini began telling Schuschnigg to shore up his ties to the Reich and to hint that next time his divisions would not help out. A year after the July 11 agreement all the advantages Austria may have won from it had evaporated.

Things went from bad to worse. In November 1937 Hitler laid out his plans for war. Integration of Austria and the Sudetenland headed the list of conquests. Papen began pushing plans for a customs and currency union. He also wanted greater military cooperation, especially in counterintelligence.

On the ground in Austria rank-and-file Nazis became more belligerent, looking for action now, rather than following an evolutionary course. The party may still have been illegal, but its membership did not act that way. Illegal Hitler Youth clashed with Schuschnigg's Austro-Fascist youth groups. After-school fist fights became a daily occurrence.

"In those days Austria was a country totally torn apart," Fritz Molden wrote. "Ten-year-old boys beat each other bloody because of political differences. Not a week passed in our fourth-grade class without pitched battles between Nazis and Schuschnigg supporters."[21]

In January 1938 Viennese police found in the desk of a Nazi official plans for an "action program for 1938," calling for overthrow of the government. The number of Nazis arrested skyrocketed, again filling jails.

On February 4 Hitler shook up his cabinet, firing his defense and foreign ministers, the chief of the Wehrmacht, and a number of key ambassadors including—to Papen's total amazement—Papen himself. Papen, who had been working on a Schuschnigg-Hitler meeting to iron out differences over the 1936 accords, hopped the next train to Berchtesgaden and persuaded the Führer to issue an invitation.

Two days later he was back in Vienna as a special envoy. It took him a week to work over Schuschnigg, promising that Hitler would make no additional demands and would reaffirm the 1936 agreement. Duped, the Austrian chancellor agreed to attend what would become his greatest personal humiliation—and the destruction of the country he led.

CHAPTER 3

Bürckel Takes Charge

From Plebiscite to Peace at Easter:
March 15–April 25, 1938

On Sunday March 13 Josef Bürckel, the Gauleiter of the Pfalz and the Saarland, arrived in Vienna to begin work as Hitler's Austrian paladin—the man charged with leading and reforming the Austrian Nazi party, carrying out the plebiscite, and later, with integrating Austria into the Greater German Reich.

Bürckel came to the job with impeccable credentials. A party member since the 1920s, he became Gauleiter of the Pfalz and in 1935 brought the Saarland, a German province under League of Nations mandate, back to the Reich with 90.5 percent of the vote. He was an excellent organizer and something of a shirtsleeve brute, a quality still treasured in the Reich.[1]

On the morning of March 14 his newly minted press chief, Helmut Sündermann, arrived at the Hotel Regina, where Bürckel had set up temporary headquarters, to find his boss in shirtsleeves already hard at work with a staff of cronies he had flown in from the Pfalz. They had only four weeks to prepare and carry out the kind of election campaign that had taken months in the Saarland.[2]

The first order of business was finding larger headquarter space for his team than the Regina provided. Bürckel settled on the Austrian parliament on the Ring. He needed a well-lighted building, he explained, because people work twice as fast in them, and he expected his staff to work double time. He also found a more congenial hotel, Meissl & Schadn on Kärntnerstrasse, long favored by Nazi dignitaries.

From day one Bürckel was out to deliver a thumping majority on April 10 in elections that even the "Ausland"—that amorphous group of nations whose opinions mattered to Germany from Scandinavia to Spain and the United States—would perceive as "honest." The press, he knew, was key, and he pushed hard to develop a uniform line at home and to sell it as the real goods abroad, using the foreign outlets as his channel. On March 17 he told a Swedish newspaper that the plebiscite would follow the Saarland pattern, that voting would be secret, that voters could say yes or no, and that no multiple voting—possible under the Schuschnigg plan, he claimed—would be permitted. He couldn't predict the outcome but expected "an overwhelming victory."

The next day Bürckel wrote Hitler pledging to win "unanimous consent" of the Austrian people provided he was given a free hand. He would have to exclude the local Nazis until after the election. They lacked organization and personnel and had failed to stop certain "excesses" committed immediately after the Anschluss. He had restored order with a "firm hand" but required operational authority without interference from other Nazi bureaucrats. He also needed more seasoned propagandists to advise party officials and control the media.[3]

Vienna was already swarming with Germans. John Wiley, the U.S. chargé, had cabled Cordell Hull after midnight on Sunday, March 13 that representatives from every conceivable German office "except the fire department" were in the city.[4] Ribbentrop arrived on March 14 and the next morning took control of the foreign office. Police and government officials took solemn oaths of fealty to the Führer and the Reich. Himmler stayed in Vienna to supervise German police who had come to take over key positions in the public safety apparatus. Austrian army units were quickly integrated into the Wehrmacht. And on Wednesday, March 16, an SS lieutenant named Adolf Eichmann arrived in the city to set up the local SD Section II-112, charged with supervising Jewish organizations.[5]

Reporters, writers, and editors had been shipped in by the carload. Some had arrived before Schuschnigg resigned. They not only took over local media but prepared the launch of the Vienna edition of the *Völkische Beobachter* (*VB*), the party newspaper. It hit the streets on March 15 when Hitler was still in the city.

The next day the *VB* and other newspapers printed directives about the plebiscite including a preliminary text of the ballot: "Do you adhere to our Führer Adolf Hitler and thus to the reunion of Austria with the

German Reich, which was carried out on March 13, 1938?" On Thursday the 17th they published Bürckel's proclamation—"to all Austrians, German men and women"—in which he outlined the task the Führer had given him: "to help you Austrians prepare for your great historic day. My task is not hard because in your hearts you are all Germans. And the question the Führer poses is none other than that: are you a German?"

But technical management of the elections was anything but easy.[6] Schuschnigg's voting lists were out of date because they were based on 1932 data, the last time Austrians had voted. Moreover, they contained the names of Jews and those of Jewish descent. Bürckel solved that problem by sending everybody on his lists voting cards with instructions for Jews to return them on the pain of severe punishment. Aryans were to keep them for election day.

Jews, supporters of the Schuschnigg government and other "undesirables" were declared ineligible to vote—in Vienna the number of ineligibles totaled 230,000, or 18 percent of the population. That left Bürckel with two major targets in his propaganda gun sights: the church and the workers.

The archbishop of Vienna, Theodor Cardinal Innitzer, proved an easy prey.[7] He had published an appeal in a Catholic daily on Sunday, March 13, asking the faithful to thank God for the bloodless revolution and to pray "for Austria's happy future." On the 14th all the church bells of the city had tolled a welcome for Hitler's arrival. In addition, Innitzer had been in touch with Franz von Papen, the former German ambassador in Austria, about a possible meeting with Hitler.

During the military parade on the Heldenplatz on Tuesday, March 15, Papen suggested that Hitler see the cardinal that afternoon. "Austria is a Catholic country. If we treat the church here the way we did at home the joy over the Anschluss will lessen markedly," Papen would write in his reminiscences.[8] In Germany, where about half the population was Catholic, Hitler had clashed with the Church, and Catholic-Nazi relations were badly frayed. Hitler accepted Papen's suggestion and that afternoon, Innitzer and his secretary drove up to the Hotel Imperial. The guards presented arms, but the crowd of mostly Hitler Youth yelled "to Dachau, to Dachau" as the cardinal got out of his car, an early signal of the deep-seated anticlericalism among Austria's Nazis. The meeting with Hitler lasted fifteen minutes. Innitzer worried about maintaining the

Concordat—the agreement the Vatican had concluded with major Catholic states including Germany and Austria—that assured the Church of clearly defined rights and privileges. Hitler showed some charm and told the cardinal "if the Church were loyal to the state, it would not be sorry." Innitzer left deeply satisfied, barely aware of the crowd that spat at him as he entered his car.

The next day Innitzer issued a pastoral letter telling the clergy to stay out of politics and urging Catholics to support the new regime. When the media failed to pay attention to his letter he complained to Bürckel, who responded almost immediately with the draft of a declaration he wanted the bishops to sign. Austria's bishops, the document said, had a duty to pray for Nazi goals, to vote yes in the plebiscite, and to remind the faithful of "what they owed the people." Clearly, the declaration had been prepared well in advance.

Innitzer summoned a council of the Austrian bishops who in principle were willing to accept the draft after making minor changes. Given Hitler's promises, a recommendation to vote yes wasn't much of a sacrifice. Besides, pushing a no vote would have little impact given the reality of Anschluss. The draft was kicked back and forth a few times, but the main thrust remained the same: vote yes on April 10.

The first signs of Vatican displeasure came from the papal nuncio in Vienna, Monsignor Cicognani, who wanted key changes—the Nazis should promise not to tamper with the rights of God and of the Church. On March 19 Innitzer and the archbishop of Salzburg, Sigismund Waitz, again met Bürckel's emissaries and the new wording they wanted was put into the document.

Finally on Monday, March 21, Bürckel received the bishops, told them he'd have to think over the new language because he wanted to avoid any impression of coercion or barter, and asked them to trust him; if they did all differences would be ironed out. Waitz and Innitzer believed that Bürckel was sincere, and they even agreed to include an old cliché used so often in the past—"Give God what is God's and Caesar what is Caesar's."

Then Innitzer committed a major blunder. He signed the covering letter of the final draft, which was to be read from every pulpit in Austria on March 27, with a handwritten *Heil Hitler.* The next day the signature was on the front page of the *VB* and plastered on every leaflet and outdoor poster. It was indeed a Nazi coup, and the Vatican saw it for what it was—a disaster. It was only the first.

The second followed quickly—an Innitzer letter to Bürckel denying that the declaration had been prompted by a meeting between the papal nuncio and Ribbentrop in Berlin. Instead, "it was a spontaneous reaction . . . and should be seen only as an act of faith and an expression of the common voice of our German blood."

That was too much for the Vatican, already enraged by the original declaration, which the *Osservatore Romano* had characterized as "unauthorized" and issued without Vatican approbation. The Vatican's secretary of state, Eugenio Cardinal Pacelli—less than a year away from being installed as Pope Pius XII—ordered Innitzer to Rome; he arrived there on April 5. How much hell Pacelli gave him is a matter of dispute, but he did force Innitzer to sign an addendum to the original declaration, which made the text far less yielding to Nazi demands than the original had been.

In Pacelli's version the declaration did not approve "what was not and is not reconcilable with the Laws of God, with the freedom and the rights of the Catholic Church," nor can it be seen by the German government or the Nazi party "as a duty of conscience nor must it be used for propaganda purposes."

Back in Vienna Innitzer faced new fire from the Nazis. Hitler's reaction to the Vatican statement was frosty. He told the cardinal that he could include nothing positive about his relationship with the Church in the major election speech he planned to deliver on April 9.

Bürckel had first used the "God and Caesar" simile in an election speech on March 24. Good will on both sides, he said, would be a blessing for the people. And two days later Göring pledged, "We don't want to annihilate any church nor destroy any faith or religion."[9] For most Catholic voters this was enough.

Labor would require more skillful handling because Bürckel saw the workers, who still adhered to the old socialist party, as the key to the election. For the next four weeks he launched an unprecedented drive to win their hearts and minds, drawing on every big Nazi gun to get his prolabor message across.

His very first speech in Vienna, on March 21, was directed to them. "You former Communists and Social Democrats are not bad people," he told a group of workers off on a tour of the Reich he had arranged. "No one who has German blood in his veins is that. Good people can defend a bad cause."[10]

Even those workers not thrilled about Anschluss were impressed that a "socialist workers" party tried so hard to win their votes. Venues chosen for campaign demonstrations such as the cavernous garage of a bread factory in the tenth district, a working-class neighborhood, reflected that eagerness. Picking these sites, the *VB* wrote, was part of a "commitment" the Gauleiter had made to help meet his biggest challenge—bringing the city's workers into the National Socialist fold.

The election campaign in the Ostmark would be unlike any the people of Austria had ever seen, the *VB* continued. (The use of Ostmark and Austria in one sentence was designed to ease transition from one term to the other.) "This is not an old style campaign in which dozens of political parties fight each other; it is a campaign focused on only one question: 'Do you embrace your German people?'"

The *VB* story fitted Goebbels's meticulous campaign. On March 19 he issued ten pages of detailed instructions to the party apparatus that covered everything: personnel, assemblies, demonstrations, speakers— who was to say what where—text and illustration on posters, leaflets, brochures, a special sixteen-page illustrated election newspaper with a print run of 30 million copies, and a special four-page supplement to appear in 20 million copies of the *VB*. Two films were to be produced, one devoted to the constructive achievement of the Nazi party, the other to the leadership of the Third Reich, and would be shown during the last two weeks of the campaign in every German cinema. A million leaflets would be printed for Austria, with 290,000 destined for Vienna. Different posters with different campaign slogans were to be displayed across the city every day. The text of one of them proclaimed, "Hatred and disunity were the result of the agitation by Jewish criminals and their helpers. The Führer has destroyed them and welded the German people into solid unity."[11]

Preparations for Bürckel's kickoff speech on March 24 had all the razzle-dazzle the Nazis had spent years perfecting. Outside the "Konzerthaus," the city's largest concert hall, the "formations"—SS, SA, HJ, police—began marching hours before the start. Inside every seat was filled. Flags and insignia hung from the walls. A German army band played the "Radetzky March," the old Austrian battle hymn by Johann Strauss the elder, which imperial army bands had played in the 1866 war against Prussia. No matter: the Nazi crowd cheered wildly.

On stage the labor imagery was carefully crafted, with workers straight from the factory floor wearing work jackets and blue overalls placed next to Nazi dignitaries like Seyss-Inquart in their black SS uniforms. Fanfares opened the proceedings as Bürckel, dressed as always in a "simple" brown shirt, mounted the podium. Although much of his long and dreary speech was devoted to what he had accomplished in the Saar, he hit both his socialist and anti-Semitic messages hard:

"In our state nobody can be a National Socialist who is not also a Socialist. If National Socialism is to guarantee the maintenance of community, then socialism is the means for that maintenance."

As for Jews, the city had too many of them; too many doctors and lawyers, too few Aryan stores. They would have to go. "Every system has the Jews it deserves and every people deserves as much Jewish freedom as it allows."

He would restore the balance among Jews and Aryans but in an orderly—"under all circumstances orderly"—and in an all-the-more-thorough fashion. Jewish property was an asset to be husbanded, not wasted through random plundering.[12]

Two days later Hermann Göring came to town to stress the same thing: the Jewish economy would be transferred to the Reich "in accordance with our laws." He was scheduled first among the major electoral guns for good reasons. He had big plans for economic development, which he unfurled in the cavernous "Nordwestbahnhalle" of the abandoned northwest railroad station. He was greeted with "thunderous cheers" from tens of thousands gathered inside and outside the station. "The surge of *Sieg Heils* seemed to have no end," the *Neue Freie Presse* said.

Neither did Göring's speech. It droned on for two-and-a-half hours and it is doubtful that all those who listened found it, as the *Neue Freie Presse*(*NFP*) did, "the greatest and most impressive speech Göring had ever given." But his list of promises was impressive.

The Nazis would eliminate unemployment—all of it. Building of homes and factories would accelerate with a thousand new construction jobs opening up the very next week. Austria's mineral resources would be exploited more quickly. The Alpine Montan, one of Austria's largest manufacturing companies, would double production. The chemical industry would expand to include coal liquefaction for fuel production. A factory to manufacture artificial fibers would be built, as would several "mighty" hydroelectric power plants. Timber and farming would receive generous subsidies. The giant Hermann Göring steel and iron works would be built near Linz instead of in Franconia. Construction would begin in the next few weeks on the Salzburg-Linz and Passau-Linz Autobahns.[13]

On March 29 the media prepared the public for the next Nazi howitzer, Paul Joseph Goebbels, who, the *VB* said, was widely known in Germany as "der Doktor," a clear reference to his academic attainment since he was the only top Nazi with a university degree. He was to have spoken from the same balcony as Hitler on the Heldenplatz, but an "overstrained" voice and rough weather forced him to switch to the Nordwestbahnhalle. He delivered a pedestrian speech short on content but long on enflaming listener emotions and here Goebbels was a master. He could make language sing in a peculiar music all his own, a uniqueness reflected in editorial comment: it was much less about what he said than how he said it, and how his listeners perceived his words.

The *NFP*'s commentator was far more thoughtful than most Nazi bloviators. Germany had no rhetorical tradition, he said, to match that of England under Pitt and Fox, and many had made this trait a virtue, cultivating suspicion of those who used language well. Hitler and the Nazis, however, had made oratory into a sword that could win elections. Goebbels had been sarcastic, bold in attack and joyful in combat. He had moved easily from ridicule to irony to radiant commitment. The audience had followed him all the way and proved how the distance between Berlin and Vienna shrank "once the arch of German unity stretched from Berlin to Vienna."[14]

The point was prescient. Berlin and Vienna had been political and cultural rivals for a century. Now Berlin's political dominance seemed assured but it would be challenged by Vienna's cultural aspirations and by Hitler's on-and-off support for them, a reflection of his ambivalence about a city he both hated and admired.

From the day Seyss-Inquart named him mayor, Hermann Neubacher had talked about turning Vienna into "the Hamburg of the East." Building a mighty harbor on the Danube would make the city not only the transit hub for shipping from the Black Sea to the North Sea via the Danube but also the focus of a planned network of inland waterways. It would become the gateway to the Balkans and beyond, and the East would be expanded to the Southeast reaching to Greece and Turkey. "We've already started to make preparations for this project," Neubacher told workers at the Leopoldauer gas works on March 31. He promised to expand the gas and electricity works to construct new exhibition and conference centers that could stand comparison with cities of "the first rank the world over." And he pledged to improve city schools. Workers cheered loudest, however, when he greeted socialist workers laid off, under Schuschnigg's watch, who had been given the city hall jobs of dismissed Jews.[15]

With the plebiscite only ten days away Bürckel picked up the pace, as one Nazi dignitary followed another on podiums across the city—from factories to concert halls. Reich minister Hans Frank spoke about German law to a select group of dignitaries in the old Palace of Justice and to a crowd of 15,000 at the Engelmann Arena.

Youth leader Baldur von Schirach spoke in industrial Wiener Neustadt and at Vienna's city hall. Economics minister Walther Funk spoke to business groups. Both dripped pathos and kitsch. Funk talked about how the suffering of Austrian Nazis had been a dagger in the Führer's heart. Schirach said the numbers, which he did not cite, tell it all: Austria was a dying, starving, joyless country before the Anschluss, now it was already booming. On April 7 Hitler's deputy, Rudolf Hess, arrived to speak to workers in a city garage. Even committed Marxists and Communists, he said, would become supporters of NS teachings, converted "not by our words but our deeds."

Hitler himself arrived in Austria on April 3 to begin a triumphant tour of the country, which was to culminate on April 9 with the proclamation at noon of the Greater German Reich from the balcony of city hall, and in the Führer's speech that night in the Nordwestbahnhalle.

Displaying the party's political stars across the city, however, was only part of the drive to roll up a huge majority. Goebbels gathered endorsements for the Anschluss from the stars of stage and screen that were no different from American hucksters using the star power to sell deodorants or detergent. "We want to be a single folk of brothers" one ad proclaimed, while in another Oscar-winner and *Blue Angel* star Emil Jannings expressed the "thanks of all German artists" to Hitler for creating Greater Germany and renewing German culture. "Therefore—with a moving heart, our yes."

On April 3 the Nazis landed their biggest domestic fish—Karl Renner, socialist leader, first chancellor of the republic, and Austrian negotiator at Saint-Germain. "I will vote yes," Renner told the *Neues Wiener Tagblatt*.

His "yes" was the result of lengthy negotiations between Bürckel's men and the socialist underground. (Renner would claim after the war he had tried to save socialist lives, but, in reality, he had been a champion of Anschluss since the end of the Great War.)

Bürckel quickly created a seamless organization that reached down to every city, town, and village precinct across the country. And the precinct leaders knew their future depended on the size of the "yes" vote they turned out. They had help; Bürckel produced something for every voting bloc—from clothing and food for those who were no longer eligible for public assistance to cheap credits for farmers and free vacation trips to the old Reich for students and members of the Hitler Youth. The Gauleiter of Hamburg brought twenty-six wagonloads of food, clothing, and shoes to alleviate "hunger and despair" in Vienna.

Election rallies were held in every town and village. Leni Riefenstahl's Nuremberg party film, *Triumph of the Will*, played in seventeen cinemas in Vienna alone. A film short in which a friendly policeman explains to a would-be woman voter where to go and what to do in order to vote yes (the film did not consider a no option) was also shown and could be rented for home use. Bürckel had money for everything he wanted to do—at a rough estimate more than $150 million in 2004 money.

Vienna became one gigantic election theater. Trams were sheathed in red buntings with swastikas in front and on top, and election placards were plastered on the side of cars featuring Hitler's picture and slogans like "Adolf Hitler creates Work and Bread." Party headquarters in individual districts were emblazoned with banners and slogans. In the Leopoldstadt, the old Jewish quarter, Nazi flags hung from every window, and streamers proclaimed "we remain true to the honor of our blood and give our voice to Adolf Hitler." A huge, freestanding poster covered the base of the cathedral spire of St. Stephen with a heroic couple, a fighting eagle at their back, pointing at a man-sized *Ja* (yes). On the Freyung outside the Scottish church a tiny tobacconist was draped in placards extolling "*Ja*."

At exactly 11:00 A.M. on Saturday, April 9, Hitler's special "green" train chugged into the West Station. The roof of the platform had been painted silver, and a deep red velvet carpet ran along the ground. Flowers and green plants completed the "tasteful" decoration of the arrival hall where top Nazi dignitaries, including Hess, Goebbels, and Himmler as well as Bürckel and Seyss-Inquart, waited to greet the Führer.

It was the beginning of the final push, a day of pomp and circumstance that inevitably was the high point of the aesthetic politics the Nazis loved—the Hollywood climax of the hero, triumphant in a rush of martial music. For the theater-loving Viennese it was a new experience. It was not that they were averse to street theater, but theirs was more nuanced and played in a lower, more subtle key, more Papa Haydn than Richard Wagner.

The Führer walked past the honor guard and got into his Mercedes limousine. The motorcade pulled into Mariahilferstrasse, Vienna's main shopping street. Every building was thick with flags and banners. Thousands lined the street and hung from every window and from rooftops, quite a change, the *VB* noted, from three weeks ago when this had been the most "Jew-infested" commercial thoroughfare with closed windows bare of flags and bunting, "a sign for those in the know that the international opposition of the Hebrew faith against the empire of the Germans lives here. Today Vienna is again a German city."

The motorcade turned left on the Ring. As it approached the Burgtheater, fanfares of trumpets announced the Führer's arrival. The vehicles turned left again down the short and broad avenue that led to the capacious square in front of city hall, now "proudly" renamed "Adolf Hitler Platz." Three columns of cars drove slowly past the crowds; Hitler stood straight in the lead limousine, hands clutching the wind shield rather than raised in salute.

When he entered the festival hall, the chorus of the Vienna State Opera, stashed in the gallery upstairs, struck up "Wachet auf," from Wagner's *Meistersinger.* As the music faded a jackbooted mayor Neubacher greeted the equally jackbooted Führer (indeed the only dignitary without jackboots was little Dr. Goebbels whose long coat hid his shoes) with a speech so fulsome that even Hitler winced:

> My Führer, this city belongs to you. . . . We ask you, my Führer, to take this city under your tender and careful hand. Let it bloom anew before the nation and the peoples of the world. Be its master builder. Love and gratitude strike from this city like a flame that no darkness, no storm can ever extinguish. In this holy hour time stands still. We feel the wind of great history. We pray: Almighty, lead us. Germany, Germany take us to your holy heart.[16]

Hitler's reply was much cooler and more distant:

> Mr. Mayor, rest assured that in my eyes this city is a pearl. I will give it a setting that is worthy of this pearl and place it in the care of the whole German

Reich and the German people.... Tomorrow, this city, and that is my conviction, will pronounce its *Ja*....

As the clock ticked toward noon Goebbels and Hitler moved to the balcony outside the festival hall.

> Heavy, silken, purple cloth flutters from the balcony below the city hall tower. A golden swastika is on it and nothing else. The hand of the clock reaches twelve. The noon hour has arrived. Dr. Goebbels steps onto the balcony and announces: "Germans. I proclaim the day of the Greater German Reich. Up flags." Sirens howl. Flags rise on their masts. And the hundreds of thousand stand there with heads bared. Their silence is prayer. If we were asked to shout our joy out loud we could not. The tears running down the cheeks tell our creator infinitely more than storms of joy could say.[17]

Minutes after Goebbels's announcement hundreds of homing pigeons rose into the Vienna sky—in all 30,000 of them would carry announcement of the Greater German Reich's creation into every corner of the country.

Millions, the *VB* claimed, were on their feet at 7 P.M. streaming toward the Prater amusement park and the surrounding areas to hear the Führer's Nordwestbahnhalle speech on loudspeakers. The pageantry was a shade richer than the Nazi norm but the template was the same: floor-length flags, bunting, platforms wrapped in red cloth, microphones on the lectern, honor guards from the "formations," and bands hoisted above the entrance arch to play martial and patriotic music. Banks of giant searchlights illuminated the hall, picking out the gold insignia against a white background and the purple canopy above the hall.

The speech clocked in at eighty-one minutes and was not one of Hitler's better efforts, as the often hesitant applause that can be heard on the recording attests. His voice was low, steady, even flat, as he began speaking. He sounded reasonable, conciliatory, as he tried to persuade those who had not been converted to join his side. He had kind words for his critics. And he clearly felt sorry for himself, not surprising since he was talking in the city of his failed youth, as the historian Gerhard Botz points out.[18]

"Never in my life have I had a fair opponent," he said, his voice dropping into pathos. His enemies had not allowed him to speak out, they had jailed him. He had been a nameless, unknown soldier. Much of what he said was stale formula: Germany's humiliation in World War I for which he, a simple soldier, bore no responsibility; the failure of political parties and parliamentary democracy to solve Germany's postwar problems; the achievements of the Nazi party during its five years in office. These were the elements of his standard stump speech, and they lacked the passion they might once have had when still fresh.

"I stand here because I believe that I can do more than Herr Schuschnigg," Hitler said, finally hitting his stride. His voice had begun to rise as he picked up the tempo and neared a crescendo. Applause followed, and his remarks about Schuschnigg drew prolonged volleys of *Sieg Heils*.

"To say this is no presumption. If I were not convinced of it I would not stand here, and Germany would not stand where it stands now. I have proved that I can do more than the dwarfs who ruined this country. I don't know if anyone will remember them in a hundred years; but my name will remain as one of the great sons of this land." The applause was now frenetic, so loud and sustained that for the first time in the speech he could not continue.

"I believe that it was God's will to send a boy from here into the Reich, to raise him to be the leader of the nation so as to enable him to bring back his homeland into the Reich. Otherwise one would have to doubt God's providence." Hitler had begun to shout, his voice cracking as he spoke, given respite only by the chants of the crowd—"We thank our Führer."

The Führer was now close to tears. "I believed in Germany at the time of its deepest humiliation," he shouted, and called upon all Germans to do likewise by voting yes the next day. And he closed with "tomorrow let every German recognize the hour. Germany. *Sieg Heil*."[19]

Every church bell in the city began to ring. Searchlights built a cathedral of light above the tower of St. Stephen. Across Austria fires were lit on mountain tops and fireworks brightened the night sky. At 10:06 P.M., the *VB* reported, Hitler's special train pulled out of the North Station for Berlin, where he arrived the next day to cast his ballot at the capital's Anhalter railroad station.

In Vienna all the dignitaries voted early. Seyss-Inquart, dressed in civilian clothes, a tight suit over a yellow sweater, crossed the *Ja* circle and handed his ballot across an open table, eschewing the closed voting booth and setting an example for others. You could vote in secret, but why bother when, of course, you were for Anschluss.

Bürckel drove up to his polling place in an open car, signing autographs as he pushed his way inside. Cardinal Innitzer arrived at eight o'clock sharp and lined up behind other voters. Once recognized he was quickly taken inside, where he too pushed an open ballot across the table.

Another demonstration started at nine that night in the Konzerthaus, with an open radio line to Berlin so that Bürckel could relay results in Austria directly to the Führer. At 11:15 he did. Some 99.7 percent of all Austrians who voted, voted yes. "I am so happy," Hitler said, "This is the proudest hour of my life."

Bürckel had invited twenty-five foreign journalists to visit polling places at random and to certify that it was a fair vote, which they did. In fact, it was anything but. Knocking 18 percent of eligible voters off the rolls in Vienna alone gave the Nazis an unfair head start. The opposition had no voice, so that all anyone heard or read was the drum beat of Nazi propaganda.

Secrecy was a farce. Few Austrians went into voting booths. My father, no hero, tried but was told, "Why bother. You're for the Anschluss," so he circled his *Ja*. The Nazis let it be known via the popular grapevine that they were keeping tabs on *Nein* voters, that everybody who went into a booth would have his name put on a list.

Most historians believe that a majority of Austrians in fact favored Anschluss on April 10, whereas at least 65 to 70 percent would have backed Schuschnigg on March 13. Why? Historians tend to credit a blend of events. Schuschnigg's support may have been broad but it was not deep. Much of it must have been burned away by the surge of hope for better times that accompanied Hitler's arrival. The grinding economic hardships played a role, but so did the fact that tens of thousands had already found new jobs.

The surge in new employment was part of Bürckel's election strategy, of course, but it was also based on more solid ground—the growing labor needs in the Reich where the armaments industry was expanding rapidly, and on the vast new projects in Austria that Göring had outlined in his March election speech.

But Viennese cynicism also played a role—a lust for advantage and personal aggrandizement, a coldness of character hidden behind the facade of waltzes and wine so often presented to the world. These traits were cut open for all to see in the plays of Ödon von Horvath, a young playwright killed in 1938 by a falling tree branch in Paris, especially in one work titled *Tales from the Vienna Woods* that shows a group of lower-middle-class Viennese at their most vicious and cruel. Schuschnigg summed it up shortly before the scheduled March 13 vote; he reportedly said that 25 percent of the people backed the Nazis, another 25 percent were for him, and "the rest ran after the rabbit."

My father's friend Beppo Kalmar saw the benign side of the conundrum and Gerhard Bronner the more brutal, but both of their experiences were illustrative of the mood. A couple of weeks after the Anschluss, Beppo met a friend on the street who said to him, "Beppo, I'm so ashamed I could flush myself down the toilet, but would you come into this doorway so no one will see me talking to a Jew."

"One day I met one of my friends who had demonstrated with me against Hitler," Bronner recalled. "He wore the uniform of the Hitler Youth and wanted to walk past me without saying hello. I stopped him and said, 'how come you're suddenly with the HJ?' 'You have to go with the times,' he replied condescendingly. 'A lot has changed these days, or haven't you noticed?' 'Sure,' I replied shyly, 'but just a few weeks ago you demonstrated with me against Hitler.' My fellow fighter was not at all embarrassed. He looked me straight in the eye and said, 'One more slander like that and I'll smash your face in.'"[20]

Bronner had already been beaten—not in the face but in the kidney—by a marauding band of Hitler Youth who caught him and a friend as they walked through side streets in Simmering in order to avoid just such an encounter. Among those who beat him were former schoolmates. Across the street a policeman watched and refused to help, but at least Bronner survived.

Not everybody was as lucky. On March 15 a car drove up to Jakob Futterweit's jewelry store at Reindorfgasse 42. Four SA men got out and told the owner to close his store and give them the key. Futterweit's brother had been blown to bits in 1933 when two young "illegals" threw a bomb through his store window. "Isn't it enough that you killed my brother," Jakob yelled. Unimpressed, the brown shirts tied his hands behind his back and dragged him into the car. The next day they called his wife to tell her that her husband had thrown himself out the window. In fact, his body had been riddled with bullets.[21] But suicide was often a plausible explanation. The number of Jews (and Austro-Fascists) who killed themselves in the days following Anschluss showed a remarkable spike. Reliable numbers are hard to come by, but records kept by the IKG (*israelitische Kultusgemeinde*, the city's leading Jewish organization) showed that 160 Jews had taken their own life in March and April, a substantially higher number than the historic average. Some were famous, others not. The bulk came from the professions—doctors, lawyers, teachers, accountants, businessmen, government officials, shop owners.

Thus on March 16, Major Emil Fey and Dr. Egon Friedell killed themselves. Fey, a former vice-chancellor and Heimwehr leader who had been in the chancellery when Dollfuss was murdered, shot himself, his wife, and his son. Apparently he feared the Nazis would put him on trial for Dollfuss's murder. Friedell jumped out the window of his flat, convinced the two storm troopers he saw enter his building had come to arrest him.

Friedell was the most famous Jewish suicide. He was an intellectual polymath whose range reached from acting on the stage to writing *A Cultural History of the Modern Age*, a seminal book of the 1930s that even the Nazis admired because it was antimaterialistic and therefore anti-Marxist. A few days before the Anschluss playwright Karl Zuckmayer had gone out drinking with Friedell, who asked him: "What will you do when the Nazis come?" Zuckmayer said he'd head for the frontier. "He shook his head," Zuckmayer wrote in his memoirs "'I won't go,' he said in a tone at once obstinate and frightened. 'What would I do in another country? I'd only be a beggar and cut a ridiculous figure.'"[22]

There were others who killed themselves that day—a widowed mother and her young doctor son, for example. The son had been fired from his hospital job that night and despaired of ever finding work again. He gave himself and his mother lethal injections.

The owner of a large furniture warehouse was dragged into the street, made to kiss the pavement, beaten and abused in other ways. Afterwards, he turned on the gas in his kitchen, killing himself, his wife, his daughter, his son-in-law, and his granddaughter. All five were buried together.

In his March 29 speech Goebbels had joked that the number of suicides hadn't really gone up; whereas in the past Germans had killed themselves, now it was Jews and the result was a suicidal wash. But it was no joke. In the first weeks after the Anschluss the *Neue Freie Presse* carried numerous death notices of what were clearly suicides. Many who did not kill themselves must have wondered sometimes why they had not—Jews . . . and sometimes Aryans.

On Saturday, March 19, an Aryan woman left a Jewish store just as several SA men strolled by. They hung a placard around her neck that proclaimed "this Aryan swine buys from Jews" (in German the slogan rhymed: *dieses arische Schwein kauft bei Juden ein*) and made her sit in the store windows for two hours. While tears ran down her cheeks, hundreds gathered to jeer and to spit in the woman's face.

An SA man prevented a customer from entering the shop Bronner's mother owned. She said she was picking up some shirts. He accompanied her inside but told her not to bother paying for the merchandise. "She thanked *him*, not my mother," Bronner recalled.

The horror stories had no end. On Monday morning, March 14, four SS and SA men barged into Otto Schneider's apartment with drawn guns. They dragged his elderly parents out of bed, took money and valuables, and made the family go downstairs to their shop where the Nazis distributed the money to waiting employees as a "victory bonus."[23]

A troop of SA walked into the Kaffeehaus (Café) Kühn on Taborstrasse in the Leopoldstadt to make sure the Jewish establishment did not serve any Aryan guests. Then they took the owner aside, beat him, made him lie down on the floor, and forced him to drink the content of the spittoons. He spent two weeks in a hospital.

For eight days the SA drove trucks to the front door of the Schiffmann department store and systematically loaded every piece of merchandise onto the trucks. Hundreds came every day to watch and yell *Sieg Heil* and *Heil Hitler*. When the store was empty they closed it and arrested the owners, the four Schiffmann brothers, and sent them to Dachau with the first transport on April 1.

E. H. Kampelmacher, a seventeen-year-old preparing his "Matura" (graduation from the Gymnasium), kept a diary. On March 20 he saw a howling mob surrounding several Jews lying on the ground. "Some were older women," he reported.

"The beast in man has awoken," he wrote, "finally the day has come when human beings can unleash their sadistic lust on fellow humans".... [24]

Indeed, the days after the Anschluss had all the attributes of a medieval pogrom. It is unclear how many people were arrested and detained in the first few weeks. Initial estimates were as high as 70,000, a number that still shows up in some of the literature, but 20,000 is now a more accepted figure.

Perhaps the randomness of the assaults accounts for fluctuating estimates. Clearly, coming to power at last had unleashed all the bloodlust Austrian Nazis had accumulated during their years underground. Torturing Jews, physically and psychologically, became a public spectacle, as Austrian Nazis were no longer constrained by the more verbal than physical anti-Semitism that had been the Austrian norm.

The day after Adolf Eichmann arrived in Vienna he took part in an SS raid on the headquarters of the leading Jewish organization, the IKG, in Seitenstettengasse.[25] When the SS found records of IKG contributions to Schuschnigg's plebiscite campaign, they demanded payment of an "equivalent" sum—RM 500,000. They shut down the offices until payment was made and arrested Desider Friedman, the president, and Josef Löwenherz, the managing director. That left the head rabbi of Vienna, Dr. I. Taglicht, and the IKG secretary, Emil Engel, to raise the money. (Taglicht was a tough bird—when made to scrub the streets he remarked "I am cleaning God's earth.") Engel promptly assessed every tax-paying member of the IKG an extra 50 percent, while Taglicht made timely payment a "religious duty."

On April 23 a satisfied Eichmann wrote to Berlin that he had already raised RM 200,000 and freed Dr. Löwenherz to work out an "action program" for the IKG and other Jewish organizations, including the personnel needed to run them. And he noted laconically that Engel would have to keep raising more money.

Eichmann was not yet in charge. He had ideas on what to do about the Jews but was not in a position to implement them. Policy was in flux with different centers of authority in Vienna and Berlin competing for jurisdiction in Jewish affairs. Dr. Leo Lauterbach, a London-based Zionist official, said the situation in Vienna was "characterized by confusion, uncertainty, and a state of flux," which made determination of official policy toward the Jews almost impossible.

But Lauterbach had a good sense for what would happen, and his prognosis was eerily close to Eichmann's ultimate design. Whatever policy toward Jews the Nazis would adopt in Austria, he wrote after returning to London from a tour of Germany and Austria in the spring of 1938, would be "essentially different from that adopted in Germany and may aim at complete annihilation of Austrian Jewry. To all appearances it is intended to eliminate them from economic life, to deprive them of all their financial resources, and to compel them either to starve or to leave the country without means."[26]

By the end of April Eichmann was in effective control of all Jewish organizations in Vienna, and he was ready to roll out plans for Jewish emigration that would push the largest possible number of Jews out of Austria at the highest possible per capita cost to them. In other words Jews would have to pay substantial amounts of money and assets to leave the country. This was exactly what Göring, desperately anxious to halt the mindless plundering of Jewish property, wanted.

Vienna's theaters were another early target. On the evening of March 11 actor Fred Hennings, a committed "illegal" Nazi who had joined the party in the early thirties, walked into the Burgtheater—the oldest and most prestigious in the German-speaking world—and for the first time bellowed "*Heil Hitler.*" Then he went to a nearby wine cellar with two colleagues who shared his Nazi sympathies—Ulrich Bettac and Eduard Volters—to talk strategy. Despite their party membership all three were concerned about their theater's continued artistic viability. They knew what had happened to the quality of performances at the Dresden State Theater when a barber had become director in 1933, and they were determined to avoid a repetition in Vienna by taking charge before somebody far less qualified took over.

That night Hennings persuaded Hubert Klausner, head of the Austrian party, to make him political leader of the Burgtheater and give him the appointment in writing. Hennings was sure he could now prevent the worst. He was wrong. When he returned to the theater the next morning he found that writer Mirko Jelusich had fired the director, Hermann Röbbeling, and had taken over the Burg at the instigation of the illegal NS cultural organization, which months before the Anschluss had slotted tested Nazis to assume command of theaters, museums, and other institutions. Hennings would find his political mandate almost meaningless.

Jelusich set briskly to work to clean up the theater. He fired Jews and "other undesirables," and purged the Burg and its satellite, the Akademietheater, of plays deemed unsuitable—not easy, given the number of Jewish works in the repertory. He had to close the second house for ten days before reopening with a weak French farce, and to postpone a new production of *Julius Caesar* at the Burg. He might have done better to postpone it longer. Goebbels attended the opening and made it clear his would be the first and last word in Viennese theater. He banned Raul Aslan, a theater divinity, from appearing in a Reich theater-week production slated for June because he thought his Marc Anthony was a "tearful old woman."[27]

After the curtain came down on *Eugene Onegin* on Friday, March 11, the State Opera remained closed for "unknown" reasons until March 17, when a "festive" performance of Beethoven's *Fidelio* ushered in the new era. "Radiant light filled the hall," the *Neues Wiener Tagblatt* reported. "Many officers sat in the orchestra and in the boxes. The "Deutschland" and the "Horst Wessel Lied" were played. The public listened standing up, hands raised in the Hitler salute." Clearly, ideology would come first, with art a distant second.

About a week after the Anschluss two Nazi actors showed up in the office of Josefstadt director Ernst Lothar and told him they were taking over. The first order of business: dropping Carl Zuckmayer's play *Bellmann* from the repertory because the playwright was partly Jewish. Lothar pointed out that he was a full Jew and planned to resign. He would have to stay to manage the transition, they said, and promised nothing would happen to him. Lothar sacrificed most of his assets to obtain passports and other exit documents. He paid one last visit to "his" theater where a play was in rehearsal. Two of his actors came over to say hello and good-bye when the stage manager's cutting voice called out, "Please do not disturb the rehearsal."

When Lothar returned home he found the two Nazi actors in his living room, this time in jackboots and brown shirts. They had heard rumors that he planned to leave and would take "decisive measures" to stop him. Lothar denied the rumors but said that a director who is ordered off his own stage by an underling isn't much use to anyone. "You're the director," one of them said, "and you're responsible for the operating costs. I've told you and now you know. Cut out and you'll go to a concentration camp. *Heil Hitler.*" The actors left, but so did Lothar. Thanks to friends and family connection he ended up in the United States.[28]

The Nazis quickly closed half the city's theaters, most of them for good, others for the time being. Theaters went dark repeatedly for election speeches and other "events." Closures were one way to buy time in which to change a theatrical culture, but they also so disrupted theatrical life that six weeks after Anschluss, Vienna faced a full-blown theatrical crisis. A third of the audience—the Jews—was gone, and repertories were stripped of Jewish plays. On April 15 Vienna's vice-mayor Hanns

Blaschke, in charge of culture, urged the Viennese "to bridge the difficult transition from the degenerate stage of the past to the theater of the people" by attending more plays. The appeal didn't help. Theaters remained empty. The Josefstadt closed a month early for the summer to cut losses. It would take massive subsidies from Berlin to end the crisis.[29]

Education was attacked with equal vigor. An underground NS teachers' organization helped target Jewish and Catholic teachers, principals, and educational bureaucrats. Many were ousted even before schools reopened a week after Anschluss—thirty-four school principals in Vienna alone were dismissed before the end of March. Those who remained took the obligatory oath to the Nazi state by March 20.[30]

When schools reopened on March 21 chaos reigned. The HJ was everywhere. Instruction was constantly interrupted by marches, demonstrations, lectures, and a general sense of uproar in a new age. Even the ministry of education recognized reality. It noted that regular classes could not be held in the weeks ahead and eased up on end-of-the-year examinations. On April 2 schools were closed again because many were to be used as polling places. Easter vacation followed; when schools reopened on April 20, half the day was devoted to celebrating Hitler's birthday.

My school, the Döblinger Gymnasium, was not untypical. The day I came back to school every teacher in my class—except for Professor Oskar Weidinger, my Latin and homeroom teacher—showed up with a big, round, party membership insignia on his lapel. Weidinger wore a simple silver swastika.

The music teacher came into class with the party insignia on his tan gabardine suit and handed out sheet music and text for Nazi songs. History lessons changed focus from the past to the here and now. Classes started with *Heil Hitler* salutes. Upper-school boys ran around in HJ uniforms—white shirts, dark shorts, white stockings, a belt clipped across the shoulders—and quickly began to set the tone for school activities and even classroom behavior. Our class "captain" was removed because he insisted on the Austrian command, "*Habt Acht*" ("Take Care") instead of the German "*Achtung*" ("Attention") when a professor entered the room.

My class—as did most of the city's secondary schools—had a large percentage of full, half, and quarter Jews, fifteen out of forty-five children, one-third and thus more than the average 20 percent, reflecting Döbling's status as a posh suburb. At first they—we—were left in relative peace, perhaps a little isolated. But on April 28, about 90 of the 106 or so Jews and those of Jewish descent in the school were called into the gym and told they would be leaving for an all Jewish school. When they returned to our classroom a sorrowful Weidinger told them to take their books and leave. The moment was solemn. Most of the boys stared at their desks. Since I was a Catholic half-Jew I was allowed to stay.

Wilhelm Stern was put in a special class for Jews that started fifteen minutes later than the one for Aryans. "We had to enter the building through a special door and use separate toilets. A couple of classmates told us they were ashamed. But one boy spat in my face and called me a Jewish pig. Understandable. He used to copy my math and Latin homework."[31]

The situation at institutes of higher learning was worse. Most Jewish students were banned from taking their year-end exams. New Jewish students would not be allowed to register, and the number of Jews allowed to continue studying was reduced to 2 percent of the total. Whereas 11,000 students had attended the University of Vienna in March, the number quickly fell to 5,000.

Fritz Knoll, a noted botanist, was named acting rector on March 15, after the incumbent declared that a party member should lead the university.[32] On March 19 reliable party hacks were named deans of the various faculties. The number and quality of teachers plummeted. Tenured professors at the law school dropped from seventeen to seven, and all of Austria's seven Nobel Prize-winners in the sciences left or were dismissed.

The Nazis kicked out eighteen members of the Institute for Mathematics and Theoretical Physics at the University of Vienna, the majority of them Jews. The Vienna Psychoanalytic Society had fifty official members. All but three, including Sigmund Freud, left. Another fifty social scientists including Paul Lazarsfeld and Ernst Dichter—the father of "advertising psychology"—went into exile. The entire Institute of Radium Research was banned from the Austrian Academy of Sciences. Nazis were named to head the academy of Fine Arts and of the Applied Arts.[33]

The celebration of Hitler's forty-ninth birthday on April 20—the first one held in his homeland—marked the end of six weeks of "Sturm und Drang" and the beginning of what Goebbels called the "Easter Silence"— a period of quiet and reflection after the ardor of the election campaign.

Vienna celebrated the birthday with a military parade that drew thousands and thousands of people to the Ring and the inner city after factories and offices shut down at noon. As the *Völkische Beobachter* noted, not even "an icy northwest wind that whipped through the streets could dampen the enthusiasm of the people."[34]

Three days later, on April 23, Hitler appointed Bürckel as "Reich Commissioner for the reunification of Austria with the German Reich," gave him full authority "for the governmental, economic, and cultural reintegration of Austria into the German Reich." Bürckel now reported directly to Hitler.[35]

Bürckel had already begun planning Austria's future. He would carve the country into seven Reichsgaue—administrative units of party rule in the "*Altreich*," (or the Old Reich, a distinction used often in the early years of Nazi rule)—and thus deepen the split among the Alpine provinces, the Danube region, and Vienna. And he wanted to give Reichsgau administrators both party and governmental responsibility, akin to those he had as boss of the Saarland.

As Gauleiter or party head of the Pfalz, on the other hand, Bürckel ran only the party; Munich handled governmental affairs. Under his plan the head of the Ostmark Gaue—and Vienna would be one of them—would be both Gauleiter and Reichsstatthalter, a sort of expanded governor-like office. Eventually the Austrian experiment could be transferred to the Reich, thus breaking the power of the Reich government over local affairs and cementing party primacy.

The plan was leaked on April 4, and Seyss-Inquart was not happy. He was ambitious. He had enjoyed being chancellor. He still hoped Austria could be semi-independent on the Bavarian model. But that wasn't in the cards he held, and he didn't know how to play the few trumps he had—notably that Hitler and Himmler liked him personally. Had he shown any sign of competing in the Darwinian struggle the Führer liked to see among his subordinates, he might have done better. Seyss-Inquart was too indecisive, too intellectual, too thin-skinned to stand up to Bürckel, a seasoned, tough, bureaucratic infighter who took on all comers he could beat and flattered those he couldn't beat, like Hermann Göring.

Himmler gave Seyss-Inquart a general's rank in the SS, which allowed the tall and lanky lawyer to cut a more dashing figure in his tailored black uniform than did the squat, beer-bellied Bürckel in his brown shirt.

But that only made him an extra on the political stage, someone brought front and center when the image makers needed him. Hitler wrote him a letter to put salve on his wound. Bürckel would stay only for a year to integrate Austria into the Reich, and Seyss would help him introduce German law into the Ostmark. At the end of the year Seyss would join the Reich's cabinet "so that you can continue to work on Austria's behalf."[36]

At Nuremberg Seyss-Inquart testified that "more and more Bürckel took over. He got the party and with it the politics including press, propaganda, and the Jewish question. . . . I did not report to him personally but in all matters of reunification I was bound by his directives. . . . I was left with the administration. His decisions were based on political considerations and not on objective criteria. His planning reflected a lack of knowledge about the Austrian situation."

Maybe so. But Bürckel wasn't interested in Austria. He saw the provincial government as a nuisance and couldn't wait to get rid of it. Seyss tried to fight him but was no match for the brawler—no matter how hard he tried or how many legalistic letters he wrote to Bürckel, Himmler, and Göring explaining his positions and his hopes. The switches had been set in the opposite direction. Austria was finished.

CHAPTER 4

To Kristallnacht

May 1–November 14, 1938

In the Red Vienna of the twenties and early thirties, the First of May was the great holiday of the working class, when labor took to the streets and turned the city into a gigantic festival. Columns of workers led by streetcar conductors in red and blue uniforms marched down the main arteries that led to the inner city, red banners flying overhead. Streetcars were decorated with red flags. Crowds lined the Ringstrasse to cheer the marchers and jammed the square in front of city hall to listen to Mayor Karl Seitz and party boss Otto Bauer declaim the tenets of Austro-Marxism: revolution and democracy were compatible; workers could have both.

The Austro-Fascists didn't know what to do with the holiday, and it became a lackluster event. The Nazis, however, restored it to new glory. "Our Best First of May—Vienna in Smiling Festive Joy," the *VB* headlined its account of "the national holiday of the German people." How different from the past when Marxist machine guns, or the forced marches of the Fatherland Front that resembled a "first class funeral," set the tone! No more. The city was sheathed in festive decorations—from Maypoles to flag-decked windows—while German army bands oompahed through working-class districts starting at 7 A.M.

By eleven the Heldenplatz was jammed with crowds strung out along the Ring and its side streets to the Votivkirche. Loudspeakers were set up at every street corner for Hitler's speech from Berlin. "And now the men and women hear the voice they have learned to love," the announcer said, "the voice of the first worker of our Reich."

The celebration fell into the period of Easter Silence that Bürckel extended to May 10, explaining that he needed the extra time to reorganize the party and handle administrative changes, meaning that he had to keep the restless "old fighters" in check.[1] On May 6 he published "an open word" to the illegals that dashed the hopes of many.[2] No matter how much they had done for the cause, only the able and qualified would get leadership positions—those, for example, who could deal with the flood of new laws and regulations that began to pour from Bürckel's office, and were all dutifully published in the *VB*.

Some were significant, others were not—decrees about protecting the uniforms, the insignia, and the seal of the Reich, for example. More substantively, the four-year economic plan was promulgated in Austria on March 19, an economic development plan issued on the 23rd, and price increases banned on the 29th. By May 1 all judiciary facilities had been turned into Reich institutions.

Politically Bürckel was busy pushing plans Hitler had approved for reorganizing Austria into seven Reichsgaue and thus setting the stage for obliterating Austria as a geographic, economic, and political entity, and he was winning his battle with other German bureaucrats to control the breakup process. Despite party opposition he settled on Globocnik, a Carinthian without a Vienna base and most likely to do his bidding, as the former capital's Gauleiter.

Creation of the new "Reichsgaue" completed the first chapter of the Anschluss and the beginning of a new life for Ostmark Germans in the Third Reich, the *NWT* wrote on June 5. The economy was switching into high gear. Unemployment had continued to drop rapidly, in part a function of shifting Austrian labor into factories in the Altreich, but also a result of the booming German economy's spillover into Austria. Vienna was back playing the big power game even though it was no longer a capital.

It would have an even brighter future as a hub of trade and culture with the Balkans—what Mayor Neubacher had called "the Hamburg of the Southeast." Port facilities and warehouses would be built.[3] By 1943 completion of the Rhine-Main-Danube canal would allow ships up to 1,200 tons to sail from the Black Sea to the Ruhr. Finishing industries could process raw materials coming in from the Southeast on the spot. Fashion and tourism would boom.

City planners plotted the setting Hitler wanted to give the city. One such plan—one of many—called for extending the Ringstrasse at both ends of the circular boulevard as "festival avenues" across the Danube Canal to the Danube.[4] Party buildings would line the new streets with a central railroad station at its core, while a wedding-cake monument, reminiscent of Victor Emmanuel's in Rome, would dominate the Danube Canal side of the inner city at the cost of razing two Gothic churches. Mercifully, it was never implemented.

One of Bürckel's first and most intractable problems was holding the wage–price line, a problem complicated by Hitler's agreement on March 13 to peg the mark–schilling exchange rate at 1.50 schillings to the mark instead of 2 to 1, more in line with the official pre-Anschluss exchange rate of 2.17 schillings to RM 1.[5] (The move was more political than economic because it protected the "little man's" savings and provided extra capital for industry. But it made prices—and with them wages—more difficult to control.)

On May 27 Bürckel demanded an immediate halt in the spiral of both: "This is my last warning. Under no circumstances may anything be done about wages." And he promised to close stores that had violated price guidelines and send owners to concentration camps. His "watchdogs" would exercise strict controls.[6] It was a good idea in theory, and no doubt some Aryan price gougers did end up in Dachau but not enough to make much of a difference.

Merchants were not the only ones to hurt the Ostmark's economy. The so-called "provisional commissioners" did far more damage and they would be Bürckel's next target. The commissioners had taken advantage of the post-Anschluss chaos to seize Jewish homes and businesses at will, a process known as "Aryanization." The plunder had begun before the first German soldier crossed the old Austrian frontier and had gone unchecked for several weeks, with party members and their protégés as well as "ordinary" Aryans taking part. Mostly, they were incompetent people with little knowledge of the businesses they had taken over, and consequently too many firms were being run into the ground.

By the time Bürckel had the reins of power firmly in hand in Vienna, it was too late to redress the situation. As he wrote to Göring on April 29, 1938, efforts to undo what had been done could have led to "serious riots which could have damaged the governance of law and the reputation of the Reich in middle Europe."[7] Instead, he had decided to anchor the commissioner system into law with some supervision of their activities to avoid random and destructive seizures. But more than stopgap measures were needed if Jewish assets were to be acquired in an orderly and profitable fashion. It would not be easy. Many of the Aryanizing "commissioners" had long records as illegal Nazis working underground for the party at considerable personal risk and financial damage. They wanted easy money as compensation, and initially they had real support within the Austrian party. Even economic advisor Walter Rafelsberger felt they were owed something. Bürckel and Göring did not.

Göring, who was in charge of the German economy through the four-year plan to build up the Reich's military strength, started his "transfer-the-wealth" campaign with an order, issued on April 26, to catalog the assets of Austrian Jews. Every Jew with property worth more than RM 5,000 was obligated to report that fact to the authorities. Data was gathered on some 33,000 Jewish-owned companies, most of them small and many barely solvent. It was used by "The Office for Regulating Jewish Property" (Vermögensverkehrsstelle or VVsT), which Bürckel had set up on May 18 with Rafelsberger in charge, to prepare for the transfer of profitable firms to Aryan control, or the liquidation of mostly "mom-and-pop" shops—Jewish or Aryan—that no longer made economic sense; the former through so-called "silent boycotts" in which Aryans were actively discouraged from patronizing the shops.

Once a Jewish company had registered with VVsT the owner would be "allowed" to put his business up for legal "Aryanization," meaning for sale at a price far below its real value. VVsT would handle every aspect of the Aryanization process—from appointing trustees, executors, and others to run Jewish businesses to assessing their value, approving sales contracts, and setting the price to be paid for them. Jews, desperate to leave the country, clamored to sell out, no matter how ridiculous the price.

The VVsT set two prices on each business, both far below their actual value. The first was the price VVsT paid the Jewish owner, usually minus taxes and other duties. The second was the price the buyer paid. VVsT pocketed the difference and put it in a special fund that would lend money to qualified buyers (they did not have to be party members), support the Jewish proletariat, and help speed Jewish emigration.

Large companies with capital in excess of RM 100,000 and a 1937 turnover of upward of half a million marks were taken over by the Austrian control bank, which, in turn, sold them to other banks and enterprises, many from the Altreich. Jewish owners, whether their businesses were large or small, did not see much of the meager sales price. Funds were put into blocked accounts that paid minimal interest and limited the amount Jews could take out to cover the bare essentials and eventual emigration costs.

But the new rules did not at once settle the problem of what to do with the roughly 25,000 provisional commissioners who had appropriated everything from cinemas to little street-corner kiosks selling tobacco and newspapers. The commissioners had to go—too much was at stake. (Confiscated Jewish wealth would be estimated at RM 2.3 billion[8]). On July 2 Bürckel announced that he was scrapping the whole commissioner system as of August 1, and said a dozen miscreants who had confused "mine and yours" had already "moved their activities to Dachau." Rafelsberger gave the departing commissioners until August 15 to submit their reports. Understandably, this left some 25,000 Nazi provisionals angry and embittered, robbed of their hopes for easy money and their sense of entitlement. Still, Bürckel's reforms made economic sense. Vienna needed to consolidate businesses to catch up with global economic development.

An inventory of Aryanized businesses shows just how broadly the city's economy was affected. Half of Vienna's apothecaries were Aryanized by September—eighty-two stores in all—while seventy-four Jewish cinemas, again half the total, were seized. The city's cafes were an early target, as more than twenty changed hands in the same time frame. Knize, an elegant men's shop that for decades had a store on Fifty-fifth Street in Manhattan, was part of the haul among fashion, jewelry, confectionary, and carpeting stores. Jewish shareholders in leading hotels like the Imperial, Hitler's Vienna home, were forced to sell their stakes.[9]

Jews were frequently caught in bureaucratic cross fire. Kurt Steinitz, a wealthy jeweler, had moved money and precious stones to Switzerland but failed to declare his foreign assets. He was denounced and forced to admit he had broken the law. He brought his valuables back and deposited them with the Reichsbank. The Gestapo gave him until August 17, 1938, to leave, but he couldn't make a move because the local Vienna finance office and the VVsT couldn't agree on dividing Steinitz's domestic assets. Repeatedly arrested, Steinitz was finally able to buy his way out in 1939.[10]

Wilhelm Frankl was not as lucky. He had extensive real estate holdings, which the Nazis seized in June after forcing his wife to have a court declare him mentally incompetent to manage them. Subsequently the family was sent to a concentration camp. The property was placed under a curator and sold. Although the Frankls survived, they never got anything back.

Arnold Eisler, a lawyer with offices in the eighth district, was imprisoned in March and released at the end of June. He liquidated all his assets to meet his "legal obligations" and had to borrow RM 1,100 to pay off his maid before finally fleeing to New York in August. Dr. Adolf Schärf, a prominent socialist who served as vice-chancellor and president of the Second Republic, Aryanized his office, meaning he simply took over the Jewish lawyer's practice and made it his own. It was never returned.[11]

In mid-June Goebbels staged the annual Reich Theater Festival Week in Vienna in an effort to bolster the city's flagging performing arts, and to explain to the Viennese the role of the arts in the National Socialist state. The festival, the *NFP* said, would be "a political program for the arts and a symbol of cultural politics" and bring the city's theatrical tradition into the dramatic culture of the Reich.

The arts in the Third Reich mattered in ways they did not—and do not—in most Western democracies. Goebbels saw all art as a way to exert political control and impose Nazi doctrine. And he knew that Vienna could best be harnessed through the arts. No great admirer of the city—indeed he often shared Hitler's disgust with the population—he nevertheless did what was needed to keep the performing arts solvent—and in line with party decrees.

The festival was carefully scripted. Sessions of the Reich's "cultural chambers"—organizations to which all artists, writers, and creative people in general had to belong in order to work—were interspersed with opera and theater performances by groups from Berlin and Vienna.

Goebbels attended the opening performance of *Der Rosenkavalier*, but the real kickoff came with the "great programmatic speech"—as the *VB* would call it—he delivered from the podium of the Opera house the next afternoon—with the Philharmonic playing Händel as background music.

"When the Nazi revolution swept across Austria and Vienna, hundreds of Jewish artists alien to our race disappeared from the city's stages and with them what had been praised as art in Vienna." So did the Jewish public. As for the general population, they had not attended for lack of money and interest. So theaters were empty and "a crisis of immeasurable dimensions threatened."

But the Reich would be "a warm-hearted protector and supporter" of Vienna's theaters and assure a "new blossoming of artistic life" so that the city could "once again live up to its German mission" and do it without censorship. "We haven't handcuffed the arts but have freed art from the handcuffs of non-art. . . . It is our cultural political mission to lead the theater," giving it shape, form, and purpose. But Goebbels conceded that "our young poets write too much history and not enough drama. And I know that for many of them enthusiasm is greater than technical know-how. They lack the experience and the stage craft to give life to the greatness of their story."[12]

This was an extraordinary concession for someone like Goebbels to make. But he was too intelligent, too clear-sighted, too sure of what he wanted, to fool himself. He knew how many ideologically pure plays were built on empty bombast.

That night, June 13, 1938, a Berlin production of *Hamlet* opened at the Burg to critical hosannas—or rather to the jubilation of art "observers," since Goebbels had banned all art criticism as counterproductive—with the *VB* "observer" analyzing the text by that "greatest of Germanic stage geniuses," and yes, he meant Shakespeare!

The day after the *Hamlet* performance Kajetan Mühlmann, the state secretary in charge of the arts, sat on the terrace of the Café Landtmann with the director of that production, Lothar Müthel. Would he be interested in the director's job at the Burg? Jelusich had proved a flop and Mühlmann felt heat from Berlin to make a change. Müthel was both overjoyed and flabbergasted. In Berlin such serious conversations were not held in cafés. He accepted the offer—a big plus for the Burg.[13]

On April 26 the *Völkische Beobachter* published a blueprint for a Vienna without Jews. Headlined "How will we get rid of the Jews? No single action, no violence—but systematic economic eradication," the story said that by 1942 "the Jewish element in Vienna must be eradicated. No store, no business may be under Jewish ownership, no Jew may have the opportunity to earn money, and . . . nothing may remain to remind us that once upon a time in this city Germans were reduced to scraps from the table of rich Jewish gluttons." The popular Viennese attitude of kicking out Jews and keeping their assets was understandable, but untenable. The Viennese had better remember that Germany was a state governed by laws. "In our Reich nothing happens without a legal base. Nobody has the right to take unilateral action to solve the Jewish question. Pogroms will not be tolerated."

Then the *VB* got down to brass tacks: Nobody would be allowed to make a living in the arts whose heredity was not impeccable. Jews would be banned from organizations for doctors, lawyers, and pharmacists. The civil service would remove all Jews, half and quarter Jews, and all those related to Jews by marriage. Jews would be booted out of the private sector. Jewish property would be expropriated over time. Existing businesses would be shrunk through denial of raw materials and customers. Jews would have only one way out—emigration. And they would not be permitted—as was the case in the Altreich—to take assets with them.

It was a program tailor-made for Adolf Eichmann, who had already begun implementing it by the time the *VB* story was published. On May 8 he wrote to Berlin: "I've asked the Kultusgemeinde [the Jewish community known as IKG] to make sure that 20,000 Jewish emigrants without means leave between April 1, 1938 and May 1, 1939. The preparatory work has already begun. Bürckel will deal with Aryanization, Jews in the economy etc. The more difficult business of getting the Jews to emigrate is the task of the SD."[14]

Dr. Josef Löwenherz, the IKG's managing director would emerge as Eichmann's closest (albeit involuntary) Jewish collaborator. He drafted a plan for the organizational structure of Jewish life in Vienna and fleshed out Eichmann's proposals for Jewish emigration. Eichmann liked Löwenherz's work and on May 2 had him reopen the IKG office, which soon had a staff of 400.

In a matter of weeks 50,000 Jews had registered with the IKG, which processed some 3,000 people a day despite formidable bureaucratic obstacles. Jews needed a wad of documents before they could even apply for a passport and the various offices involved were often at odds with each other. Taxes were a major issue. Jews had to pay an array of duties and penalties beginning with a "Reich flight tax," as well as all other taxes they may have owed—or been told they owed—for income, property, or simply for being Jewish.

In June Chaskel Futterweit, fresh out of a week's imprisonment, had the promise of an American visa but no passport—and a Gestapo deadline of September 10 to leave Vienna.[15] He first went to the finance ministry to prove that he did not owe inheritance and building taxes and other local fees. Futterweit stood in line with thousands of others for eleven hours, just to get a printed form to be filled out and returned the next day. He started his second vigil on line at 4 A.M. and reached the front of the line at noon. He was given another appointment in six weeks. Meanwhile he had to get other certification. From his district board he needed confirmation that he did not owe rental tax, a door tax, a welfare tax, and a dog tax. He had to stand in line at the local tax office all night with proof that he did not owe income, commercial, turnover, and pension taxes. (Futterweit owned a business). One official said he owed RM 1,560 in back income taxes. When Futterweit protested that six weeks ago he had only owed RM 960, and produced an official paper saying so, the official only said, "If you don't pay at once, it's Dachau."

Gerhard Bronner decided to emigrate in early May. Not only had he been beaten by Hitler Youth and threatened by a former friend, he had also lost his job at a department store. His mother's shop was going nowhere. His father, an illegal Social Democrat, was already in Dachau. "So I decided to emigrate. That meant getting a passport."

It also meant clearance from the tax office. "So I went to the regional finance office to get the declaration. When I got there I found about 2,000 people waiting." Some eighty hours later the fifteen-year-old Bronner finally stood before the responsible official. He wanted to see Bronner's tax return. The boy explained that fifteen-year-olds did not have to pay taxes. Well, what about his father's return? Nope. He was in Dachau. "Well then there is nothing we can do. You'll have to wait until he's released. Next." In despair Bronner said "but I don't know when he'll come out. How am I supposed to live till then?" The official looked at him kindly and said "nobody told you that you had to live. . . ." That tore it. Bronner fled to Czechoslovakia and then to Israel.

Such stories convinced Löwenherz—and Eichmann—that there had to be a better and quicker way to get Vienna's Jews out of the Reich. After the failure of the Evian conference, organized by the U.S. and other possible havens to help German Jews escape, Löwenherz suggested establishment of a central emigration organization in Vienna that would be able to shorten the bureaucratic process and cut through red tape. Eichmann loved the idea, and Bürckel cleared it with Berlin. The office was set up on August 20 to raise foreign exchange (the American Joint Distribution Committee provided $4.5 million by the end of the year), supervise retraining centers (the IKG had already begun training white collar workers as lathe operators, carpenters, and machinists), work with travel agencies and shipping companies to speed Jewish exodus, and issue bureaucratic guidelines.

The concept was simple: put all the needed offices under one roof, limit them to Jews (in other offices Jews were dealt with only after all the Aryans had finished their business), and thus handle emigration formalities on an assembly line basis. A man could start at one counter in the morning and leave the last one that evening, stripped of all his assets but with most of the needed papers in his hand. By September 30 Eichmann reported that he had processed 38,000 Jews in six weeks and estimated that the total was closer to 50,000 if illegal emigrants were included. In fact, he was bragging—the actual number was closer to 10,000.[16]

The new procedures did not ease Jewish life. Harassment was constant. Not all theft went through channels—Aryans grabbed thirty Jewish-owned stands on the Naschmarkt, the city's major produce and specialty food market, without following regulations. Jews were dragged into court on clearly trumped-up charges ranging from embezzlement to sexual harassment, and each case was lovingly detailed in the *VB*. Indeed the paper ran a flood of stories about what Jews had done under the Schuschnigg era and how they were now being punished. It was a steady, soft drumfire of hate that stirred an already heated popular anti-Semitism even more— and laid the groundwork for worse excesses to come.

On May 15 the *VB* began a series about "theater Jews" headlined "Sexual Blackmail Protected by Law—What Schuschnigg Allowed his Theater Jews to do." The stories dealt with such vile insinuations as Jews piling up debt while ruining one theater after another, and fornicating with blonde Aryan girls desperate to get on stage and willing to do anything the Jew asked them to do. One Jewish theater director, the *VB* claimed, kept four luxury apartments in which he held weekly orgies, which "only the sick brain of a Jew could invent and about which we could not possibly write."

No aspect of Jewish life was spared. Jail sentences were handed down indiscriminately for everything from selling goods below list price to sleeping with Aryans even if the sex was consensual. Dachau was used as a threat, but few Jews were actually sent there, according to *VB* accounts. The impression these stories left was one of Nazi tolerance for crimes that should have been punished much more severely. And, of course, they were in fact, but in the early months of Nazi rule, their propaganda was more interested in vilifying Jews and then exhibiting Third Reich generosity than in dealing with so-called crimes.

A far more ominous ruling was handed down by a district court in August—Jews could be evicted from rent-controlled apartments simply because they were Jews.[17] Johanna Grünbaum lived in a building with sixteen apartments, four occupied by Jews, the rest by Aryans. The owner charged in her suit that the apartment had gone to seed, that it was a site for Communist activities, and that the tenant was a Jew. Grünbaum conceded she was Jewish but denied the other two charges. That was enough, the court ruled. The presence of a Jew in a house that was three-quarters Aryan disrupted the Aryan community in it. Grünbaum was given two weeks to vacate.

The court's reasoning was indeed more tortuous than that, but the media recognized the ruling as a landmark. Both the *VB* and the *NWT* headlined their stories "No Rent Control Protection for Jews." Not that it made much difference, given how many Jews had been driven out of their homes, but it did root expropriation in a court ruling and thus provided the legal authority it had lacked. As the *VB* kept pointing out, the Reich was a country governed by law.

On August 2 the Nazis fanned Viennese anti-Semitism anew with the opening of a touring exhibit entitled "The Eternal Jew" at the Nordwestbahnhalle. Long swastika banners framed the facade, while in the facade's middle hung a huge portrait depicting the face of evil—a man with a long, flowing, black beard dressed in a black cap and a billowing black caftan, a whip in his left hand. He had large hooded eyes, thick lips, and a long curved nose that hung close to his mouth. Some 350,000 attended the exhibit, which, the *VB* reported, showed just what the Jews were— slimy cheats and swindlers, Communists, and thieves.[18]

By the end of summer Bürckel was established as Austria's de facto Nazi viceroy. An August 31 speech summed up what Bürckel had achieved already and what still needed to be done: unify the German and Austrian legal systems without destroying the "healthy" part of Austrian law, push economic integration, and keep reducing unemployment rolls, which were already down to a quarter of what they had been.[19] He denied that Jews and Catholics were being terrorized but said the Jewish question would have to be solved in accord with German law. Nor would anything happen to the Church so long as it stuck to religion and left education to the state. But true harmony among state, party, and faith could exist only if the Church agreed that "we Germans hold our people and our Germany above all other things in the world."

The Church did not agree, and as a result church-state relations had deteriorated from their high in March. After his frosty meeting with Hitler on April 9, Innitzer wrote to Cardinal Eugenio Pacelli, the Vatican secretary of state, that he remained hopeful. Pacelli replied on April 30, 1938, that he did not share Innitzer's optimism. Things were not going well and Pacelli did not expect them to improve. He noted that Innitzer's cable on Hitler's birthday—the Führer sent a hand-written reply—had not helped the situation. And the secretary of state pointed out that Bürckel had not kept his promise to meet again with the Austrian bishops. Dutifully Innitzer arranged a session on May 30, 1938.

Bürckel gave Innitzer fifteen minutes. He rejected Church complaints of harassment, said he could have won without their votes, accused the bishops of opposing the regime, and said the pope's closing of Vatican museums during Hitler's visit to Rome was an insult. Still, the cardinal did not think all bridges had been burned, and, with the help of Catholics around Seyss-Inquart, negotiations on some more permanent church-state arrangement continued over the summer. The Nazis wanted formal support from the Church and a pledge that they would stay out of politics and away from education. When they didn't respond appropriately, the Nazis moved to shut down Catholic institutions, not only Catholic primary and secondary schools but also the theological faculties in Innsbruck and Salzburg. Catholic lay associations had to surrender their funds. Nazi commissars took over Catholic hospitals and even seized monasteries for party purposes.

The final straw was a decree giving the *doctor*, not the priest, the right to determine when patients would be given extreme unction. On August 19 the bishops broke off the talks.[20] Bürckel's aides who dealt with religion were concerned enough to urge him to put his prestige on the line and continue talking. He did, but clearly his August 31 speech did not help, so that for the next month neither side showed much give. The church-state explosion would come in October.

As summer approached daily life began to change. Step by step Jewish activities were circumscribed. City swimming pools were closed to Jews; the private establishment in Grinzing that I frequented had a sign saying that Jews were unwelcome. As a half-Jew I ignored it. Parks were closed to Jews, not all of them at once but one park after another, each closure in a different part of the city. Parades and demonstrations became a constant. Police, SS, brown shirts, Hitler Youth (HJ), and the Wehrmacht began to dominate the cityscape. In the orchard behind our house German soldiers set up antiaircraft batteries. The soldiers were friendly. One sergeant sat me in a swivel seat and showed me how to spin the huge gun around and where the firing pin was—exciting for a ten-year-old.

Soon after the Anschluss my mother lost her job as a school doctor. In August she got her severance pay, RM 386. My father was fired from the Vorwärts publishing house. He sued for breach of contract and won. My mother had only one aim: to get her and me out of the country as quickly as possible, with or without my father. My uncle, a counselor at the Polish embassy in London, began working on getting us British visas.

One afternoon my friend Peter Schwarz, like me a half-Jew, came home from school on the streetcar and noticed a group of Hitler Youth pointing at him from the second car. As the #38 curved into the Grinzing station, Peter jumped from the platform—it was open in those days— flung his school bag into a corner behind him, and told his pursuers to come on. They did—one by one. He fought with the courage of despair. When he knocked down the second boy, the others—there were five of them—fled.

Late that summer my parents had a dinner party for eight or ten people. Maria Plobner, an old friend, was among the guests. As an only child I was used to sitting with adults and adding my tuppence to an evening's conversation. I made a few disparaging remarks about the Nazis. Suddenly I saw my father's face go white. He took a sip of water. He scrambled up from the table and motioned for me to go with him to the bathroom.

"Don't ever say such things in front of Maria again," he said. The man she was sleeping with, he explained—and I barely knew what that meant—was a honcho in the SA. One careless word from her and we would all end up in Dachau.

My father's words struck me with deep fear and a kind of arrogant pride, that I, a child of ten, could have brought us all so close to the edge of destruction.

Three months after the Anschluss the Sudeten crisis began to hit Viennese headlines with horror stories of how the Czechs were persecuting Germans. In late May the *VB* talked about Czech officials as "slave overseers" and charged "red hordes" with strip-searching German men. Personal attacks on Czech President Eduard Benes mounted. The cause of an independent Slovakia was championed. Headlines grew harsher: "The distorted face of Prague's hate." "Dastardly orgy of insult by Czech yellow press."

By mid-September headlines began to make the Viennese uneasy. The talk now was of war, something that those Viennese with close ties to Sudetenländers found unthinkable. But as British Prime Minister Neville Chamberlain shuttled back and forth to Germany in September trying to reach an accommodation with Hitler, Vienna's concern mounted. The Führer's "I will march at the head of my people as their first soldier" didn't help.[21] (19)

On Tuesday, September 27, Bürckel and Globocnik called for a mass demonstration on the Heldenplatz, which 100,000 attended to listen to martial speeches and to swear renewed allegiance—"Führer command, we will follow." Banners hoisted above the square proclaimed "down with Benes, the lying dog."[22]

When Hitler agreed to the four-power conference in Munich among Great Britain, France, Italy, and Germany that sold out Czechoslovakia and guaranteed, in Chamberlain's words, "peace in our time," the relief across the city was palpable, palpable enough to ease the coming showdown with the Catholic Church.

On September 8 Bürckel wrote to Innitzer suggesting yet another effort to reach a peace agreement between church and state. Innitzer's reply was frosty. Bürckel had done nothing to halt antichurch measures—for example, closing down a Catholic organization, which was really a papal prerogative. "Promises were made that no one thought to keep. Our declaration of March 18 was only used as electoral propaganda, a strange reward for our good will and trust."[23]

The next day Innitzer told the faithful pretty much the same thing: "They gave us soothing words and in the end nothing was kept . . . do not lose courage but remain faithful. Don't let them take your trust."[24] Comprehensive negotiations with Bürckel for an overall settlement were clearly at an end.

Traditionally a rosary service was scheduled at the cathedral to mark the beginning of the new school year. This year, however, was dicey and Innitzer knew it, but after some internal debate the church staff decided to risk it. Word was put out in whispers. An announcement was made at a cathedral Mass on September 19. Some 200 posters were printed and sent to local parishes. Catholic youngsters went house to house on their bicycles to give others the message—come to St. Stephen's on October 7 at 8 P.M. The church expected 2,500 at most. In fact almost 9,000 came.

"More than ever in this difficult time we want to commit to our faith, to Christ, our Führer and master, our king, and to his church," the archbishop began. "Faith is not given to everyone, but . . . it is something you will not surrender. . . . I have confidence in you. My heart is filled with gratitude and satisfaction that you have come today in such great numbers. . . . "

When he was finished the congregation moved outside to accompany Innitzer across Stephansplatz to the episcopal palace. Mocking Nazi slogans the youngsters chanted "We thank our bishop" and "we want to see our bishop." Innitzer appeared briefly and then withdrew. Some would claim the crowd had chanted "Austria, Austria," and shouted "Christ is our Führer" and "Innitzer command, we will obey." A few hundred hastily gathered Hitler Youth appeared singing the Horst Wessel song but they were drowned out by such well-known hymns as "Lift up our hearts to God."

For Bürckel the demonstration had put church-state talks into the ash can. He was furious that thousands had mocked Hitler and sworn allegiance to their bishop. Worse, Innitzer had put Christ above the Führer. The next night Bürckel unleashed the Hitler Youth. Glass shattered as the HJ tossed rocks at windows. Battering rams thudded against the palace gates. Innitzer's secretary called the police, who promised to come but didn't for forty minutes—the police chief sat in a nearby café, clock in hand to wait out the riot. Doors splintered and the young Nazis swarmed into the palace. Upstairs a young priest shoved the cardinal behind an iron gate and brought resident nuns to safety.

Elsewhere in the palace rampaging youths destroyed everything they could find. They ripped brass carpet holders from the staircase and used them to smash tables, chairs, and other furnishings. They slashed paintings on the walls, broke chandeliers, mirrors, the glass doors of bookcases, and especially every cross they could find. They dragged one priest to a window and threatened to throw him out, but the prelate tore loose and escaped just as the police came. Another priest was not as lucky. The marauders tossed him to the street, and he broke both his thighbones.

Rioters smashed 1,200 windowpanes, stole all the cardinal's garments, a pair of red shoes, a bishop's miter, a golden fountain pen, a box of cigars, two rings, and the bishop's cross. They swiped Charlemagne's sword from the winter garden of the cathedral museum and damaged a Gothic glass pane. The archbishop's rooms were devastated. The next day the Gestapo sealed the palace—no one was allowed to leave or enter, except Innitzer who was permitted to read Mass at St. Stephen's.[25]

The riot received scant media attention, but the grapevine spread the news quickly and thousands marched past the scarred palace that Sunday in a show of silent support. Three days later Globocnik delivered a scathing speech, laced with heavy-handed sarcasm, that blamed the cardinal for what happened, but he promised to replace the broken glass (he never did) so the prelate would not freeze in the winter. The *VB* gave the speech front-page coverage and used it as a jumping-off point to attack Innitzer as the embodiment of "political Catholicism" out to confront the NS regime.

The next day, Thursday, October 11, Bürckel gave what many called his worst demagogic speech ever before an anticlerical mob of 200,000 on the Heldenplatz. He downplayed the sack of the palace, calling it a prank, but promised it would be investigated. Then he whaled into the "political clergy" who had lost their influence and were out to regain it by inciting the people against the regime, and he warned that "the NS state will not tolerate political opposition under any circumstances." Anyone, Bürckel went on, who took to the streets could only demonstrate *for* the state, not against it.[26]

The mob loved every word, often interrupting the speech with cheers. Afterwards as many as a 100,000 people marched past the palace shouting epithets and insults at the walls of the darkened building. This time there was no violence. Bürckel had surrounded the palace with SS and SA formations.

Reaction abroad was different. Switzerland's *Neue Zürcher Zeitung* called the speech "the worst oratorical demonstration yet to come out of the Third Reich. Chopped up sentences and chopped up thoughts, grammatically wrong, badly constructed, often incoherent, were all underscored, rather than hidden, by the roaring applause of the fanatical mob." Church-state negotiations were over; so were hopes for peaceful coexistence between the two.

In Vienna the media continued their anticlerical drumfire for another two weeks and then leveled off—reportedly because Seyss-Inquart had warned Hitler that the anticlerical campaign would backfire in so Catholic a country.

Even while the battle with the church dominated headlines, the pace of anti-Jewish activities had begun to pick up. It was a clear prelude to Kristallnacht, the savage pogrom now only weeks away. In early September the Nazis used a blackout exercise to beat and plunder any Jews they found on the streets. The Rothschild hospital on the Gürtel, the second circular boulevard that girds the city, was so jammed that patients were placed in corridors and even in the garden.

The old Jewish quarter, Leopoldstadt, was next. Troops of HJ swept through the streets in mid-October. They gutted six prayer houses, burned books, and set fires large enough to call out the fire department. A day later SA men in uniform blew up the ark of the covenant in one temple, set Torah rolls on fire, and stole silver and money. On October 16 the largest temple in the city was set ablaze and suffered heavy fire damage. A Jewish school was damaged, and vandals threatened to kill the principal's wife if she called for help.

On October 14 Göring convened a meeting of economic experts in Berlin to discuss Hitler's new armaments program that called for vast new spending.[27] More foreign exchange was needed. The Austrian dowry of 400 million schillings in gold and currency ($90 million) had already been used; so had all Jewish assets seized in Austria to date. More money would have to be squeezed from Jews. Three weeks later, on November 7, 1938, Herschel Grynszpan, a seventeen-year-old German-Polish Jew who lived in Paris gave the Nazis an opportunity. He shot Ernst vom Rath, a third secretary at the German embassy in Paris. Rath died on November 9, the anniversary of Hitler's failed 1923 Munich beer hall putsch.

The Nazis had used the two days before Rath died to demonize the Jews and their global conspiracy, thus stoking the fires of anti-Semitism. The tone of the polemics grew shriller, and the call for action that would explode into Kristallnacht was hard to miss. On November 8 the *VB* ran a story that in retrospect was a clear blueprint for mayhem: a tour of Vienna's twenty-one synagogues and seventy-one prayer houses. The precise location of two synagogues was given and the pictures of two rabbis printed.[28]

On November 9, news of Rath's death reached Hitler around 9 P.M. when he sat with an assembly of "old fighters" in Munich.[29] He held a brief, intense conversation with Goebbels and then left. Moments later Goebbels was on his feet to deliver a vitriolic anti-Semitic speech that laid out a program of party action to support "spontaneous" outbreaks against Jews.

The first teletype arrived in Vienna around 11 P.M. notifying local party and Gestapo functionaries to start rounding up Jews, preferably mon-eyed Jews, and to burn and sack synagogues and other Jewish houses of worship. Strike commandos from the 11th and 89th "Standarte" (SS regiments) were to hit the streets at 4 A.M.; local police had been instructed at 4:15 to intervene *only* in criminal cases. The definition of criminal was, of course, left vague. Few of the SS had bothered to don civilian clothes.[30]

Hand grenades were thrown into synagogues, and prayer houses with what was left sacked and set on fire. Some forty to fifty houses of worship were completely destroyed. Only the central temple in Seitenstetten-gasse was not burned; not only was it wedged in among other houses in a narrow street where flames could not be contained, but the building housed the Kultusgemeinde (IKG) and other Jewish offices. Instead, the SS set to work with axes to destroy synagogue furnishings. "You've got to admit that was the least that could have happened," Eichmann told the IKG secretary Emil Engel.[31]

Throughout the day SS detachments (the Sturms) reported back to headquarters on their activities. One particular detachment, Sturm 4/11, reported that they had destroyed four synagogues, and ransacked and robbed 100 Jewish homes. "Several Jews were injured and the furniture smashed," the report said.[32]

Rudolf Unger, the leader of Sturm 1/11, had received his orders at about an hour after midnight and by 6 A.M. had completed destruction of a temple in the Josefstadt. Unger's group moved on to gut a prayer house, search numerous Jewish apartments, and confiscate money and other valuables. Fifteen Jews were arrested. Hauptsturmführer Kowarik's unit gutted four temples and "completely destroyed" another. They seized a silver chalice and "various writings." Obersturmführer Riegler reported that three detachments of Standarte 89 had destroyed fourteen synagogues and prayer houses, took part in blowing up the two ceremonial halls at the Central Cemetery and removing their contents so that "burials could not be carried out." Report after report noted how happy the population had been that at last authorities were showing a firm hand in dealing with Jews.[33]

Before the day was done 4,083 businesses were plundered, destroyed, and shut down. Only in rare cases did the SS or the SD intervene and then only when locals threatened to destroy such records as the Gestapo wanted. Estimates of the number of arrests vary, but the best guess puts them at 6,800; 4,600 sent to Dachau, 27 Jews killed, and 88 seriously injured. In the inner city some 1,950 apartments were sacked, and the Jews who lived in them kicked out.[34]

Plunderers stole everything they could carry with them—fur coats, money, securities, silver, gold, carpets, stamp collections, cameras, radios, bed linens, suits, dresses, and jewelry. Some of the jewels went to prostitutes who wore them on the street to solicit customers. SS and SD officers described the destruction in some apartments as "senseless." Simply reciting the statistics of Nazi mayhem and brutality during Kristallnacht does not give the flavor of actual suffering, nor does it measure the terror among Vienna's Jews as the full horror began to sink in.

Twelve-year-old Renate Jeschaunig-Rosner walked to her Jewish school across the Canal from her inner-city home. "When I came to the bridge I saw a truck parked on the other side. The SA were loading Jews of all ages, children, young women, old men. I started to cry but was so bewildered that I couldn't run away. An SA man came up to me, boxed my ears, and told me to turn around and run away. I was so shocked I cried even harder and he hit me again and whispered 'for God's sake turn around and run home as fast as you can, otherwise you are going to be on that truck, too.' When I got home my mother was in tears because the Gestapo had arrested my father."

The father of a friend suffered a worse fate. "When I went back to school after November 10 my friend Eva Gottesmann had a dead face.

This was the first time in my life that I saw dead eyes in a living person. During the night of November 9th her father had hanged himself from the window in the bedroom and Eva saw him hanging there." [35]

Seventeen-year-old Reinhard Eckfeld's odyssey began in the morning of November 10 and ended at 3:30 A.M. the following day. The SS had grabbed him near his aunt's house in Döbling during a roundup of local Jews. The group was marched to the nearest police station where they were interrogated and made to wait all day as more and more Jews were brought in, all carrying tales of their arrests—from homes, streetcars, businesses, and even out of their beds—and their mistreatment. Darkness fell. Lights were turned on. At 9:30 P.M. a hulking SS man strode in and began beating Jews and making them do knee bends.

At 10:15 they were loaded onto a truck and driven downtown to a police riding academy. They had to run across a ninety-foot courtyard lined with SS who beat and kicked the men. "I was beaten on the arms which I had raised to protect my head and my glasses, and on my back. I couldn't see where the blows were coming from. When I got to the middle of the courtyard I was suddenly hit hard across the nose which started to bleed."

They were driven into a riding hall with a sandy floor about 100 yards long and 35 feet high with windows close to the ceiling. Floor-length swastika flags framed a picture of Hitler. As Eckfeld stood in line he noticed that blood from his nose had soaked through two of his handkerchiefs, but he was not the worst: everywhere he looked he saw bruised and beaten men with bumps and swellings and split lips. He figured that about 2,000 people were in the hall with more arriving every minute. Old men collapsed around him and the SS let them lie in the sand. At 2:30 A.M. men over sixty and under eighteen were called up front. At 3:30 the gates opened and the Jews were told to run as fast as they could. Stragglers would be brought back. Eckfeld took off like a hare and stopped running only when he was a mile away. He walked home. Months later he managed to emigrate to Australia. [36]

E. H. Kampelmacher's father was arrested on the morning of November 10. "My mother tosses and turns on her bed in despair and I see before me the Jewish people under the torment of its oppressors," he would write in his diary. "And suddenly a rage rises up in me, an untamable fury, and I swear revenge, revenge for my father, for the thousands of brothers who were being dragged into prison that day. November 10. A pogrom has broken over German Jews. A pogrom that can only take place in a country without culture, a country where beasts command. November 10, day of horror we will never forget. What will remain with us as long as we live and as long as our children can tell their children is our hatred of Germany and its sadistic beasts."[37]

Days after this blood orgy even some of the participants had second thoughts. On November 21, SS Hauptsturmführer Trittner wrote that an impartial observer had to conclude that this was no spontaneous eruption of popular fury but a carefully scripted exercise. Although people who had watched Nazi brutality had applauded, others had been stung by the spectacle.[38]

A November 12 meeting of the Vienna Gau chamber for economic affairs gave an even harsher assessment: "There was only one opinion among the participants: rejection and shock at scandalous scenes that heavily damaged the prestige of party and Reich. Pogroms and vandalism are not ways to solve the Jewish question. Rape, robbery, and plunder have only produced horror and loathing."[39]

As a propaganda and PR effort the pogrom was a disaster, for all the gloss Goebbels tried to give it when he called off the wolves on November 11, a call not much heeded—Bürckel had to put an SA regiment on the streets to avoid further outbreaks—and the situation in Vienna did not return to normal until the weekend. But it served other, more important purposes: a speedier eradication of Jewish influence from the economy, and a surge in Jewish emigration.

Also on November 12, 1938, Göring convened a meeting in Berlin of economic experts, police, and propaganda—Goebbels and Heydrich were present—to discuss the Jewish question, specifically how to squeeze more money out of the Jewish community. Dr. Hans Fischbök, a member of the provincial Austrian government, suggested confiscating all Jewish-owned apartment buildings in Vienna, valued at RM 500 million, and seizure of all Jewish stocks and bonds, estimated at RM 266 million. Economics minister Funk put the sum for the Reich as a whole at half a billion marks. Göring was euphoric.

Toward the end of the meeting Göring turned to Bürckel and asked what he thought would happen if the Reich imposed RM 1 billion in punitive damages on the Jewish community, with Jews paying 25 percent of their net worth into the "reparation" fund. Bürckel said the

Viennese would cheer. Göring then sighed and said "I wouldn't want to be a Jew in Germany today."[40]

In the nine-and-a-half months between the Anschluss and the end of 1938, some 79,000 Jews had left Austria. My mother and I were among them. On a gray November day I said good-bye to the city where I was born. I took the bus up to the Kahlenberg, the most prominent of a chain of hills that are part of the Vienna Woods. The bus was empty, the driver friendly. "You won't see much today," he said. When we got to the top he told me he would wait for me and to take my time. He was right. I couldn't see much: the tip of the Steffel (the tower of St. Stephen's Cathedral) in the distance, the Danube on the left where the clouds had opened for a moment, the vineyards that crawled along the mountainside, bare and empty. I walked back to the bus, close to tears. I was going to live in London and I knew three phrases of English—please, thank you, and how do you do. The bus drove back down to Grinzing, and I walked on home.

My father took us to the West station where we boarded the train for London. It was about a week before Kristallnacht. He had not gotten a British visa. We did not know when we would see him again. We stood at the window and waved. I saw his jaw muscles move and his cheeks twitch. His eyes were wet. He was desperately trying not to cry, but not succeeding very well. The train puffed out of the station.

A week after we left my father went to Switzerland. Three days later the Gestapo came to the house looking for him. Winning a court case against a Nazi-run company was not a good idea in the Third Reich, not even for an Aryan. It took him nine months to join us in England, and he made it in August 1939, weeks before the outbreak of war.

CHAPTER 5

The Lost City

Vienna's Golden Autumn:
1867–1938

Most historians see Kristallnacht not as "a turning point in the tragedy of Austrian Jewry, but an organic continuation of the preceding developments, another peak in the persecution of the Jews by Austrian Nazism," as Herbert Rosenkranz wrote in *The Jews of Austria*.[1] But this misses the deeper significance of the pogrom: more than any other single event Kristallnacht buried the "lost Vienna" that flourished through the decline and fall of the monarchy and the brief life of the first republic.

It could be argued, as this author does, that this lost Vienna left a more lasting mark on history than did the 500 years that preceded Austria's defeat at Königsgrätz in 1866. During those centuries Vienna rose to become the hub of an empire that spanned half the globe—that of Charles V. The city was the western bulwark that twice repulsed the tide of Islam, in 1529 and 1683. Finally, after Napoleon's fall, Vienna swung the baton as conductor of the concert of Europe.

But Vienna's political clout began to fade when Bismarck ousted Austria from leadership of the German Federation following Prussia's victory in 1866, a process that the formation of the Austro-Hungarian double monarchy in 1867 only accelerated. Budapest now ruled over vast tracts of the empire including Croatia, Transylvania, the Banat, and the Hungarian regions of Slovakia. Hungary was largely independent,

108

with the emperor of Austria—as king of Hungary—the major link between the two countries. In the Austrian half of the realm, the question of nationality rights grew more virulent as Czechs, Italians, Slovaks, and southern Slavs sought more freedoms and greater representation. Discontent seethed across the regions. Politics were in chaos. The dynasty ruled with a tempered despotism increasingly under challenge. But, paradoxically perhaps, Vienna prospered in the turmoil—economically, socially, scientifically, culturally, and intellectually—and expanded from a conservative, catholic, and baroque city into the cradle of modernism, a trailblazer for the twentieth century. And that lost Vienna, grafted onto the tradition-encrusted city, was largely a Jewish creation. A new constitution adopted in December 1867 gave Jews if not full, then at least adequate, civil rights, which the liberal policies that dominated government activities for two decades protected and allowed to thrive.

Legend has it that the first Jews arrived in Vienna with the Romans and that Jews had been in and out of Vienna ever since, never very many of them but enough to leave a mark. Historically their presence was first recorded in customs documents issued in the early 900s when Austria was the Holy Roman Empire's "Eastern Marches" cited so often in Hitler's rhetoric. Around 1190 a man named Schlom was master of the mint for Duke Leopold V, charged with finding silver for coinage. His job became redundant, however, when silver collected to ransom Richard I, "the Lionhearted," flooded the country. Schlom owned real estate in Vienna, including a vineyard, and he built a synagogue. In 1196, in a macabre foreshadowing, crusaders passing through Vienna to the Holy Land murdered him and fifteen members of his family.[2]

By 1200 a small Jewish community had been established in Vienna. In the ensuing centuries, Jews were driven out twice and lived for the most part under tight restrictions. By the middle of the nineteenth century the city's 2,000 Jews began to push for emancipation; in 1848 Jewish intellectuals played a leading role in the revolution that changed the face of Europe, if not that of the Habsburg dynasty. (Their sudden visibility was one reason the Nazis took so skeptical a view of that landmark event.)

For the next twenty years the city's Jewish population grew, and so did demands for greater equality. In 1860 the 6,200 Jews made up 2.2 percent of the population. Ten years later, with emancipation a fact, their number had grown to more than 40,000, 6.6 percent of the total. By

1880 their number had swelled to 72,600 or more than 10 percent, a ratio that held until 1938. By 1910, 175,000 Jews lived in the city. With such a rapidly growing population Jews moved into hitherto Christian preserves—medicine, law, journalism, the arts, the university, and retail trade—and expanded their foothold in the traditionally Jewish enterprises of finance, banking, tobacco, and big business. Jews, for example, were intimately involved in development of the empire's rail network—and in the inevitable scandals that accompanied rail construction across the industrial world.[3] The grain, textile, and antique trades also were under solid Jewish control.

Jews had been allowed to study medicine in Vienna since 1782, when Joseph II issued a limited "tolerance" edict, and in 1869 some 275 doctors were Jews. In the 1887–88 school year, the number of Jews studying medicine in Vienna totaled 1,546 or 61 percent. Overall, more than half of the city's doctors were Jews, and they made major contributions to Vienna's growing international reputation as a focal point of medical science.

Law had moved more slowly. But soon after Jews were allowed into the profession, Vienna had 33 Jewish attorneys and in 1869 almost 100 law clerks. By the 1880s more than half of Vienna's lawyers—394 out of 681—were Jews, a ratio that held in the 1890s with one major difference—among 360 apprentice lawyers 310 were Jews.

Jewish dominance in the media was almost complete. True, *Die Presse*, founded in 1848, was started by a Christian but Jews helped manage it. The paper went out of business soon after Jews launched the *Neue Freie Presse* in 1864, and it became the leading newspaper of the empire with a reach far beyond its borders. Theodor Herzl was only one among many who made the paper sparkle with wit and insight. A string of other Jewish newspapers followed, which expanded the media's reach across all segments of the population. In his book, *The Jews of Vienna*, Hans Tietze, a noted Jewish art historian, wrote that their intellectual ability and business acumen, as well as corruption and lack of character, "could express themselves to the fullest" in journalism. Growth of the city's press "was a Jewish achievement. They made and steered public opinion during the liberal era."

In the cultural arena Jews first entered the performing arts: on the stages of the Burgtheater and the Opera and in the concert halls Jewish actors, singers, and musical virtuosi added a Jewish note to performances delicately attuned to local tastes, which they managed subtly to change. In the 1870s and early eighties Jewish painters and writers stuck to the conventions of the times.

But newly rich Jews moved quickly into patronage of the arts, while their wives launched themselves into Viennese society through creation of literary and other salons that drew the best and the brightest from the art world. Some of that day's leading society women made a cult of the aging dramatist Franz Grillparzer, already a monument of Austrian literature, and later they did the same for Johannes Brahms. They thus helped provide a fitting frame for the enormous changes shaking an expanding city whose population grew and changed with the inflows of the upwardly mobile—and those who hoped to become so—from all the corners of the empire, Jews and non-Jews. (At one point more than a third of the city's workers spoke Czech as a first language.[4])

Greater creativity began to mark the Jewish contribution to the arts in the 1880s, paradoxically just as modern anti-Semitism began to sprout in Vienna, triggered by rising resentment at Jewish success and at the role Jews played in shaping the new city. By the 1890s a surge of innovation in everything from art and architecture to philosophy, psychology, and science began to sweep the city and broadly influence the rest of the world. And most of the sweeping—albeit not all—was done by Jews. Looking back, Sigmund Freud clearly had the greatest influence of any Viennese on the intellectual development of the twentieth century. But his importance was never fully recognized in Vienna, which in his day showed little interest in psychoanalysis. Indeed, for decades Freud was a target of attack and derision, often from other Jews like the satirist Karl Kraus who called psychoanalysts "psychoanals" when he fired at Freud in his hugely influential weekly journal, *Die Fackel* (The Torch).

The movement itself split often, with Carl Jung and Alfred Adler the leading apostates. Adler's *Individual Psychology* had greater influence on Vienna's socialist city administration in the twenties than Freud's writings ever did. Also in the 1920s Karl and Charlotte Bühler built an imposing school of their own in experimental and child psychology whose influence would reach deeply into the Anglo-Saxon cultures, as would Melanie Klein, who pioneered play therapy for children, broke with Freud, and moved to England where her therapeutic approach reached audiences it never had in Vienna or in Berlin.

Ernst Mach put his marker on physics, philosophy, and psychology beginning in the 1860s when he discovered Mach's bands—the human eye's tendency "to see bright or dark bands near the boundaries between areas of sharply differing illumination."[5] Later he developed optical and photographic techniques for measurement of sound waves, and to this day his theories are applied to the design of airplanes. He influenced philosophy through "rigorous criteria of verifiability," which held that "no statement in natural science is admissible unless it is empirically provable"—a position that influenced Einstein. His rejection of metaphysics, derived from the Irish philosopher-bishop George Berkeley, led him to repudiate the concept of a self-contained ego as a "useless hypothesis," an approach that appealed to the Viennese mind and especially to fin-de siècle writers.[6]

His theory of *Empiriokritizismus* (empiric criticism) later gave rise to "such divergent schools as those of positivism, materialism, and even phenomenology" and influenced Ludwig Wittgenstein, Karl Popper, and the logical positivists around Moritz Schlick.[7] Wittgenstein wrote his major early work, the *Tractatus Logico-Philosphicus*, during World War I where he served as a highly decorated Austrian officer on several fronts. It was published in German in 1921 and in English in 1922, and his ultimate reputation was made in the English-speaking world, as were those of so many others. Yet he wrote in German and his roots were in Vienna's Jewish culture, even though, like many other Jews, his family had assimilated and adopted a veneer of Christianity. His father was an immensely wealthy steel magnate whose house became a focal point for the arts and sciences.

Jews were less visible in the development of modern architecture, design, and painting but did provide cultural soil that nourished all three. They were the audience the arts needed to flourish and the buyers of creative works whose money kept artists and designers financially afloat. August Lederer, a Jewish industrialist, for example, had the largest private collection of Klimt paintings, while another Jew, Fritz Wärndorfer, was the most important financier of the "Wiener Werkstätte," a factory of lifestyles that churned out furniture and furnishings from Thonet's bentwood chairs to cupboards, chests of drawers, crockery, and silverware.

Christians like Otto Wagner spearheaded a revolution in building that drew in non-Jews like Josef Hoffmann, Adolf Loos, and, later, Walter Gropius and Richard Neutra. They built houses that broke with the ornate past, used decoration sparingly but with greater effect, and introduced a cleaner, sparser look to the downtown cityscape and to the private houses they built—and did it long before that style took root anywhere else.

Gustav Klimt, Egon Schiele, and Oskar Kokoschka, Aryans all, gave the city a new artistic edge, and the shift from the hidebound and traditional "Künstlerhaus" to the "Secession"—a building that combined simplicity with a Klimtian sense of ravishing decoration—provided new visual excitement for which Jews were the most appreciative audience, and their loveliest women were often models for such artists as Klimt. Once Klimt climbed into the city's society "salons" he met "beautiful young women, mostly of Jewish origin, and began to paint them—the proud Adele Bloch-Bauer or the young Margaret Wittgenstein, whose families were not only rich, but had progressive artistic taste."[8] Her brother, the philosopher Ludwig Wittgenstein, designed a modern villa for her, using the architecture of the times as his model.

In literature Arthur Schnitzler, a Jew, put Freud's insights on stage and into novels that retain their potency to this day. He was a literary pioneer; in his novella *Leutnant Gustl* he invented the interior monologue long before James Joyce used it in *Ulysses*. He wrote critically and perceptively about Vienna's bourgeois society. He recognized the city's nascent anti-Semitism far sooner than anyone else—reflecting that recognition in such plays as *Professor Bernhardi* and in *Leutnant Gustl* as well—and certainly took it more seriously than those Jews who were hell-bent on assimilation into Viennese society. The latter were concerned, of course, but many Jews had come to Vienna from regions where pogroms were real, where fire and sword dealt out cutting punishment, and for them life in the city was sweet—full of opportunity and the freedom to write, think, and say what they wanted, the occasional imposition of imperial censorship notwithstanding.

Hugo von Hoffmansthal, a man of Jewish descent (his ancestor Isak Löw Hoffmann was a silk merchant from Moravia who became a force in finance) and of considerable wealth, was best known abroad as Richard Strauss's major librettist—*Der Rosenkavalier, Die Frau ohne Schatten, Ariadne auf Naxos*—but he also wrote a clutch of plays that gave some larger sense to the decay of the empire in which he lived, and he was a lyric poet of exceptional power. His early verses were printed in literary journals under the pen name of Loris; when the teenager showed up at

113

the Café Grienstiedl, a literary hangout, the literary pope of the moment, Hermann Bahr, was stunned that anyone so young could write so well and so perceptively.

Two Jews would dominate music: Gustav Mahler, whose work is both culmination of everything that went before him and two steps beyond it, and Arnold Schönberg, who blazed the trail of the truly new music. The conventional, somewhat hidebound, non-Jewish Viennese audiences disdained them both, even though Mahler scaled the high walls of official anti-Semitism to run the Vienna State Opera for a decade. Leonard Bernstein observed that Mahler wrote a Jewish vernacular riven with guilt for his shame at being Jewish. Hilde Spiel, analyzing that analysis in her book *Vienna's Golden Autumn* (from which the subtitle for this chapter is taken) chastises Bernstein for his lack of understanding of middle Europe and argues that Mahler was an amalgam of Jewish, Slav, Viennese, German, and "purely Christian elements. The complexity of them all makes him an Austrian composer." Perhaps so, but Mahler wrote of himself that "I am trice homeless: as a native of Bohemia in Austria, as an Austrian among Germans, as a Jew throughout the world." And Bernstein understood the *genius locii* well enough that in 1968 he could bully the Vienna Philharmonic into playing Mahler's music—specifically his Ninth Symphony—because not only was it great but it was their own. Indeed, as Katja Schmidt wrote, concertgoers "learned to understand Mahler through Bernstein and to value his music. So, quite unexpectedly, Bernstein had introduced a Mahler renaissance. In the final analysis Bernstein could win Vienna for Mahler."[9]

Arnold Schönberg, however, was not merely an Austrian composer, despite the debt he owed Brahms and Mahler in his early works. Certainly he was Viennese but more clearly of that "lost Vienna" then under construction. Once Schönberg left tonality in 1907 he met unprecedented hostility: at the first performance of his Quartet in F sharp minor, one music critic in the audience called out "Stop it," Alma Mahler would recall, and when he did the audience began "a whistling and yelling such as I never heard before or since." Mahler himself got into a fight with a heckler whom his father-in-law managed to push out of the hall, telling him "Calm down, I hiss at Mahler too." When Schönberg's Chamber Symphony was played at the Musikverein, members of the audience noisily shoved back their chairs and left in droves. Mahler rose in his box and told the mob to shut up. At the end he stood and applauded until the last heckler had gone.[10] Six years later Schönberg conducted a concert of his own music and that of his disciples Anton von Webern and Alban Berg, which was met with jeers and catcalls and led to fist fights in the galleries. Listeners demanded that all three composers be put in a loony bin! By then Schönberg had moved to Berlin and turned down an offer of a full professorship at the Vienna academy of music. "I cannot live in Vienna . . . ," he wrote, "I would not last two years." But he did indeed come home and in 1919 founded a society for playing the new music, even achieving a degree of success in the postwar republic that had eluded him in the empire. Still, in 1925 he left for Berlin, with the founding of the second Viennese school of music on the credit side of his ledger. By 1934 he was in the United States, where he died in 1951.

In politics Vienna's Jews had a free ride into the late 1880s. Liberals had assumed power precisely because Austria had lost the Prussian war, and there was no one else untainted by defeat and past failure who could take over. They survived the economic crash of 1873, which might have shaken the foundations of a more coherent state, but not the rise of anti-Semitism under Schönerer and the emergence of the mass parties—the Christian Socials and the Social Democrats. By the 1890s the liberal era was over. Schönerer's virulent rhetoric had helped create modern anti-Semitism and made it respectable among the middle and upper middle classes. Karl Lueger's election as mayor in 1895—Emperor Franz Josef, disgusted at Lueger's demagogic anti-Semitism, refused to certify his election until 1897—allowed lower-middle-class resentment at Jewish successes to spill over. The Social Democrats, finally, drew Jews away from liberal government and liberal causes, as did Theodor Herzl's Zionism. Both movements would attract Jews who poured into the city before and during the war from the empire's eastern provinces, much to the chagrin of Jews who went all out on assimilation. The immigrants were poor; they did not bathe much; they clustered in the Leopoldstadt ghetto—and they influenced the look of the city.

One example: Around 1910 my father took the entrance exam to the Vienna Academy of Fine Arts. Next to him sat a man who clearly had neither bathed nor shaved recently and who wore the caftanlike cloak popular among eastern Jews. My father assumed he was one of them. But he was not. His name was Adolf Hitler. My father passed. Hitler flunked.

A second example from the other side of my family: In the mid-1860s my great-grandfather Moses Merdinger, a successful merchant in Czernowitz, a city now in Ukraine, decided that his two sons should go the assimilation route. He would send both of them to Vienna to study—my grandfather became an engineer, my great-uncle a doctor. Both bathed regularly and wore meticulous clothes and thus reflected the assimilationist side of Vienna's Jews. But since one could never be too sure, Moses bet on two horses—his sons were baptized into the Christian faith *and* registered with the Jewish Kultusgemeinde. How was Moses to know that seventy-five years later only the Kultusgemeinde would count and that one of his grandsons would die in Auschwitz as a result?

But the politics of the new century, which saw assimilationist Jews caught between rising anti-Semitism on the Right and the anticapitalism of the Left with the further pull exercised by Zionism, did not stop the growth of that lost Vienna in which they played so large a part. Intermarriage grew more common, and as it did more Aryans were drawn into the web of the new city: when, in 1938, Göring spoke of 300,000 Jews in Vienna, he had more accurate numbers than the Kultusgemeinde, which stuck to religious rolls of about 175,000. Indeed it can be argued that another 100,000 Aryans moved in and out of this city-within-a-city, the Vienna that was truly a city on the hill, with its population of 400,000, almost a quarter of the 1.8 million who lived here in 1938.

That lost Vienna had survived the collapse of 1918 in better shape than the rest of the city. The Social Democrats picked up on its cultural tradition and strove to make it available to the working class. Anton von Webern took over the symphony concerts for workers that had been established in 1905 and a workers' choir formed by the typographers' union. Fragments of Alban Berg's opera *Wozzek* were played at workers' concerts (but not at the Opera until 1930; the work had its premiere in Berlin in 1925). Atonal work spread with composers like Hanns Eisler following Schönberg's footsteps. In the late twenties Ernst Krenek wrote a jazz opera called *Jonny Spielt Auf* (*Johnny Strikes Up the Band*), a good decade before *Porgy and Bess*.

This is not to suggest, however, that popular taste had changed as well. Most Viennese audiences remained conservative and opted for the classics or for rich and syrupy neo-romanticism like Erich Wolfgang Korngold's *The Dead City*. That Korngold ended up writing treacly music for Hollywood films was a natural progression. The modern tradi-

116

tion that Vienna at large *was* willing to accept was the music of Richard Strauss, whose works dominated the State Opera's repertoire.

In literature, Schnitzler, Hoffmansthal, and Karl Kraus continued to dominate the 1920s, even though all three were aging and showing their fatigue. Robert Musil, an Aryan, and Hermann Broch, a Jew, would bring a new, more robust sensibility. Musil's gargantuan and finally unfinished novel, *The Man Without Qualities*, is often ranked among modern masterpieces, even in the English-speaking world. Broch's trilogy *The Sleepwalkers* (*Die Schlafwandler*) and *The Death of Virgil* examined the decay and death of societies with psychoanalytic precision and Kafkaesque prescience. (Kafka was Czech, not Viennese, but much of his nightmare vision was rooted in the horror of the imperial bureaucracy).

Josef Roth began writing a series of books about the decay of empire that culminated in the *Radetzky March*, a brilliant dirge about the dying monarchy. Egon Friedell worked on his mammoth cultural history that became something of an intellectual bible. Stefan Zweig won international renown with novels and essays whose quality did not match that of his contemporaries but whose sales dwarfed theirs. Franz Werfel moved to Vienna from Prague, as did Leo Perutz and other Czech writers—and Kafka died in a sanatorium just outside Vienna in 1924. Hilde Spiel argues that Prague writers did not belong in rational, sophisticated Vienna because the brooding Czech capital's mysticism—it is, after all, the home of the Golem—did not fit the Viennese mold. But she ignores the impact their presence had on the city's cultural ferment.

Indeed, historian Norbert Leser argues that not since Renaissance Florence had so much talent, so much intellectual vigor, such strong disputation, and so great a landscape of the mind been mapped anywhere else. Between the wars the city's intellectual reach was literally all-encompassing—sociology, philosophy, the natural sciences, economics, psychology, politics, mathematics, the arts; everything was under challenge, everything had to be proven, demonstrated, shown to be true, no matter how new or how old.[11]

For many the collapse of the dynasty meant a new freedom, the end of a tired tyranny that allowed what had been thought and done for decades past to flower as never before. For others it meant a new exploration of the past, of what the monarchy had been—and what it had not been. In short, the contradictions that had long marked life in Vienna grew in size and importance as modernism battled nostalgia—both for the multinational empire and for the pan-German ideal. In the twenties and early thirties modernism was still in the intellectual ascendancy, at least in Vienna, even if the country at large looked with fear and skepticism at what was being done and thought there.

Psychoanalysis, as the most famous intellectual "product" of the lost Vienna, suddenly found itself in the midst of a global postwar boom that even the ranks of its domestic opponents—and they included not only the Christian Right but much of the Social Democracy—could not ignore. Freud was never made a full professor at the University of Vienna but was named an associate professor. On his sixty-eighth birthday in 1924 Freud was named an honorary citizen of Vienna, and when he turned seventy the mayor of Vienna visited Freud's home at Berggasse 19 to offer his congratulations in person.

The grudging laurels bestowed on the movement's founder were clearly a response to its growing worldwide influence.[12] After the war, Americans led a foreign invasion of people anxious to learn more about psychoanalysis, to be treated by Freud if possible, by his disciples if not. A publishing house was founded in 1919 and a central archive for psychoanalytic literature created in 1921 under the leadership of Theodor Reik. In 1922 a psychoanalytic clinic opened that looked for promising patients and possible therapists among the poor and disadvantaged whom it agreed to treat for free. Guidelines for psychoanalytic training were laid down in 1925 that went far beyond learning analysis. The push to allow therapists without medical degrees to enter the profession broadened, with Freud himself saying he didn't want medicine to swallow psychoanalysis.

Freud's own output in the 1920s and '30s helped boost the growth and popularity of psychoanalysis abroad and of Vienna's role as center of the movement. Freud himself was not totally happy about foreign adulation, fearing—rightly it would turn out—that its popularization would water down his doctrine's essence and lead to misinterpretation and ultimately opposition.

Marie Jahoda and her then husband, Paul Lazarsfeld, used Freudian concepts in their pioneering research in sociology and social psychology, probing the impact of prolonged unemployment in an industrial community on behavior and attitudes of the affected men and women. Their study, *Die Arbeitslosen von Marienthal* (The Unemployed of Marienthal), was published in 1933 and is still considered something of a landmark in its use of subjective and objective criteria, psychological insights, and statistical methodology.[13] Jahoda, a committed follower of Austro-Marxism, credits Otto Bauer with providing the impetus for the research, a signal for how far and how deeply the party wanted to probe the problems of working-class life.

Jahoda and Lazarsfeld represent something of a link between the psychoanalytic approach and the more experimental psychology of Karl and Charlotte Bühler. Both were already recognized in their field when they were called to Vienna in 1923 to launch an institute of psychology at the university. They brought new insight and broader international scope to their work, a scope that widened as their own reputation grew and more foreigners came to study with them. As with Freud, the largest number of their foreign students came from the United States, and these Americans brought with them the eagerness for greater application of psychology to society at large, thus fertilizing the work of Viennese researchers. For Lazarsfeld it was a first introduction to the concept of market research on which he built much of his own work, first in Vienna and after 1933 in the United States where he won a major reputation as a media and public opinion analyst.

In the natural sciences, radium research built on the foundations of an institute established in 1910, which after the war developed a range of scientific and commercial uses of radium that included measurement and tracking of chemical elements. Physicist Lise Meitner may have made her reputation in Berlin and in the United States, but she got her degree in Vienna (which never offered her a chair). Hans Thirring and Erwin Schrödinger did advanced work in theoretical physics and both were friends—if not collaborators—of Albert Einstein. Thirring is credited with contributions to the theory of relativity, while Schrödinger built his reputation on wave mechanics and atomic theory, work for which he received a Nobel Prize. Viennese scientists pioneered development of physical chemistry and were active in polymer research. Biology, genetics, geology, paleontology, and mathematics were all areas where scientists who lived and worked in Vienna made major contributions. All this intellectual activity was achieved with little government or corporate support. Franz Josef was an ignorant, narrow-minded bureaucrat who paid little attention to the sciences. The Prussian debacle should have taught him better. An Austrian officer tried to persuade him in the 1850s to invest in the breech rifle and thus equip his army with faster-loading guns. The emperor turned him down. The postwar government lacked money and interest.

Natural scientists took part in the philosophical controversy that surrounded the Vienna circle of logical positivism, a school that fertilized much modern philosophy in the Europe and America of the thirties and forties. Moritz Schlick was the pivotal figure around whom the circle turned.[14] Born of Protestant parents in Berlin, he was offered the chair for natural philosophy in Vienna in 1922, and here he began regular meetings with students outside the classroom. The Vienna circle drew widely from other intellectual disciplines: Otto Neurath brought sociological insight and a Marxian outlook. Mathematicians and logicians like Kurt Gödel and Hans Hahn argued from different perspectives. Rudolf Carnap, like Schlick a physicist as well as a philosopher, insisted on formulating philosophical problems in terms of natural science. Wittgenstein, at the time teaching in the Austrian countryside, was a brooding and hovering presence with the circle parsing his *Tractatus Logico-philosophicus* literally sentence by sentence. Karl Popper operated on the fringes, often in outright opposition, an opposition that grew much fiercer once he arrived in England after World War II.

Much of the discussion was arcane and beyond the ken even of ordinary intellectuals, and while the circle did not outlive Schlick—he was murdered by a disgruntled student on the steps of Vienna University in 1936—the influence of its members drove deeply into the English and American academic establishments. Wittgenstein and Popper were dominant in shaping British thought in Cambridge and London. Carnap taught at the University of Chicago, Princeton, and UCLA. Gödel became something of an American cult figure half a century later with publication of Douglas Hofstadter's *Gödel, Escher, Bach*. Friedrich von Hayek and Joseph Schumpeter deeply influenced the American economic outlook. The list of innovative Viennese thinkers is indeed a long one.

But perhaps as important as the stars and the innovators was the audience for their thoughts and insights. Vienna had a substantial public even for the avant-garde and the unconventional. Adler attracted bookkeepers and secretaries from insurance companies to his table at a café on the Danube Canal. Jews bought Schiele's pictures and listened to Berg and Krenek's music when it was performed. They made sure that intellectual activity was not carried out in an academic vacuum, even if the forum was a couple of tables in a smoky café.

"The ease with which we absorbed Vienna's intellectual ferment without worrying too much about the contradictions among the various scientific directions was characteristic for the period," Marie Jahoda wrote. "Everything was interesting and worth knowing. We all knew about the Vienna circle even if I only absorbed it by osmosis—a then widely practiced method for acquiring ideas. . . . Otto Neurath allowed me to participate in a seminar that attempted to translate Freud's *Massenpsychologie und Ich-Analyse* (*Group Psychology and the Analysis of the Ego*) into a positivist vocabulary. Needless to say the attempt failed."[15]

When Red Vienna fell in 1934, the lost Vienna did not. If anything it had become a center for German Jews and others opposed to Nazism who flocked there after Hitler seized power, at least culturally supporting Schuschnigg's claim of Austria as the second and better German state. But as Karl Kraus noted in a famous quip, the rats were boarding a sinking ship. Names that mattered to the culture of middle Europe in the thirties added some of the glitter lost in the civil war—the playwright Karl Zuckmayer, the poet Walter Mehring, the satirist Kurt Tucholsky, to cite a few. Even Bertold Brecht lived in Vienna for a time. Political cabaret blossomed, as it always does in authoritarian states that view them as steam valves for popular discontent and crack down on them only often enough to sharpen the cabarets' political edge.

Vienna, under Schuschnigg, was still a pleasant place to live for most people not involved in political confrontation, and that included the bulk of the Jewish population. True, most of the social achievements had been dismantled. The Fatherland Front did not build new housing or expand the social welfare net. Indeed, it allowed gaping holes to develop as it failed to master the economic crisis or reduce the swollen jobless rolls. Government muzzled the press. Censorship was enforced. In a famous scene in Franz Theodor Csokor's play *November 3, 1918*, the censors insisted on cutting one line—a group of officers are burying their colonel who has committed suicide, and as each one steps up to throw a shovelful of earth on his grave he says "earth from Hungary," "earth from Slovenia," "Czech earth"; the Jewish surgeon says simply "earth from Austria." It was 1937 and Jews were not supposed to be the only Austrian patriots, especially at a time when Jews were encountering a new form of exclusion. Few were allowed to make films, for example, since Austria's market was Germany and the Hitler regime would not buy movies with Jewish talent.

And increasingly the rats began to leave the sinking ship, many of the most talented for economic reasons. Members of the intelligentsia received tempting offers from the United States. Alfred Adler began lecturing regularly at the Long Island College of Medicine in 1932 and spent only his summers in Vienna. Members of the Vienna Circle accepted other assignments from American schools. In 1937 Karl Popper left to teach at the University of New Zealand. Wittgenstein had long since gone to Cambridge. The Vienna circle imploded when Schlick was murdered in 1936. Young writers like Hilde Spiel found the atmosphere in the city too oppressive and emigrated. Freud endured and as long as he did, Vienna continued to matter. But the lost Vienna died on Kristallnacht, never to matter again.

CHAPTER 6

From Kristallnacht to the Outbreak of War

November 15, 1938–September 1, 1939

After Kristallnacht life changed in both subtle and raw ways for many individual Jews, some of whom had not as yet been uprooted.

"Now all of a sudden you realized, through abuse and humiliation, that you have become a different person," Hans Kann—he would become a renowned concert pianist—remembered "At school students pointed at us, and in our building other tenants wouldn't speak to us."[1]

Reinhold Eckfeld's nose was swollen for a week after he had been beaten on November 10, "but the terror stuck in my bones for weeks. I began to look into emigration because November 10 made it clear I would have to leave."[2]

Michael Kehlmann, a successful stage and television director after the war, lost his home in a posh villa in Sievering—the price of springing his father from jail. A high Nazi official coveted the house, had him arrested, and freed him on condition of selling him the house cheaply.[3]

Desperate Jews began to write Bürckel for help, missives that ended up in the dead-letter file. One anonymous letter pleaded in the most hopeless and demeaning terms for the freedom of Dr. Guido Goldschmidt, a fifty-seven-year-old pediatrician sent to Dachau during Kristallnacht. Goldschmidt had won the gold medal for bravery in World War I and had an affidavit from someone in the United States assuring

123

him of an American visa. Could Bürckel please free him? A stamp on the letter says "to the archives."

In other letters a tailor asked for permission to continue practicing his craft, noting that he had fought for four years in the Great War and been repeatedly decorated. A widow who ran a small business out of her living room fixing torn ties for fifty pfennigs each, pleaded to be allowed to continue doing so. A well-to-do lawyer, booted out of his apartment on Kristallnacht with all his valuables inside, asked that it be unsealed. A half-blind sixty-six-year-old man who could not "move without help" asked to be allowed back in his apartment. A seventy-three-year-old woman was given notice to vacate an apartment where she had lived for thirty-eight years. Would Bürckel help? Emma Riha's Aryan husband had divorced her in April 1938 and left her with a fifteen-year-old daughter. The husband agreed to provide for both, but she needed permission to remain in Vienna, explaining she had no relatives abroad. If she could not stay she felt she would have to kill herself and her daughter.[4]

The flood of Jewish letters, signed and unsigned, continued well into 1939. They were all pointless.

Jews were forbidden to attend theaters, cinemas, dance halls, art galleries and other places of amusement. Goebbels said in a speech in mid-November, "It is a desecration of our German artistic life to expect Germans to sit next to a Jew in a theater or a movie house."[5] Jews were banned from higher education. All Jewish bookstores were closed. Anti-Jewish polemics in the media grew even harsher.

"The Jewish problem is no longer an issue for the German people but for the whole world," the *Neue Freie Presse* (*NFP*) editorialized. "Germany has made known its iron determination to exclude Jewry from its public, economic and private life."[6] So, then, did other countries. Belgium put Jewish immigrants into concentration camps. Poland wouldn't accept its own Jewish citizens. Holland resisted settling Jews in their overseas colonies. Latin America, Australia, and South Africa wouldn't accept them. And Palestine had been a fiasco.

"People who pity the Jews still don't understand what the Jew is," Dr. Robert Ley, head of the DAF (the German Labor Front) said in Vienna several days after Kristallnacht. "To allow Jews to continue living in the German body politic and to have pity with them means having pity with tuberculosis bacteria. Pity is the greatest danger facing the German people."[7]

For the Nazis, the weeks that followed Kristallnacht were a period of consolidating their power and normalizing their rule. Creation of "Greater Vienna" was formalized on October 15 through incorporation of ninety-seven surrounding communities that increased the geographic size fourfold and added more than 200,000 to the population.[8] Plans for the "Hamburg of the Southeast" were taking concrete form, at least on paper: expanded harbor installations on the Danube, new processing industries, generous housing, new defense construction, exploitation of an expanded industrial potential from chemicals to textiles. The *NFP* already saw Vienna as middleman for a burgeoning trade with India.[9]

The "first Vienna arbitration"—a meeting held in the Belvedere Palace among Germany, Italy, Hungary, and rump Czechoslovakia to decide a territorial dispute, was hailed as giving Vienna a new foreign policy role. It was small political beer but the pomp and circumstance allowed the Viennese to dream of past glories.[10]

Heinz Hilpert, the new director of the Theater in der Josefstadt and director of two other theaters in Berlin, gave a pre-Christmas interview in which he addressed the touchy topic of Berlin and Vienna and the cultural roles each was to play in the Third Reich. The idea, as he saw it, was that the theaters in the two cities would fertilize each other. "I came here to be a servant of Viennese culture, not to create anything *Berlinerish* (Berlinish)." And he would stage two Viennese comedies in Berlin because German drama lacked humor.[11]

Hilpert's remarks mattered because the only thing Hitler and Goebbels took seriously about Vienna was its cultural tradition, not the propaganda about the Hamburg of the Southeast. But since both men were ambivalent about the role they would allow Vienna to play, a consistent cultural policy toward the city never emerged, at least not beyond the strictures the party would periodically impose—like the occasional refusal to stage a controversial play.

In the eight months of Nazi rule the economy had clearly improved. Holiday sales were brisk and New Year's Eve was a blast. Cafés and restaurants in the inner city were booked solid and stayed open till four in the morning. Streetcars ran till five. Champagne was everywhere; even cafés in the outlying districts had laid in a good supply. Pricier restaurants like Sacher's and the Three Hussars featured champagne suppers. The opera was sold out for Strauss's *Fledermaus*, a New Year's Eve tradition, but there was a slight change: Alfred Jerger sang Frosch, the jailer, instead of Szöke Szakall. The Hungarian Jew was in Hollywood. Indeed, it was the first New Year's Eve without the Jews who had once dominated the entertainment business. KdF (Kraft durch Freude) staged a "people's festival" at the Hofburg where "even simple day laborers" could come and celebrate.[12]

On January 23 1939, the city was shocked by the sudden and unexplained death of Mathias "paper man" Sindelar, Austria's greatest soccer star. The center forward had played in three World Cups and after the Anschluss had powered an Austrian team to a 2–zip thrashing of the Germans. Every newspaper but one vied for total coverage. The *VB* ran a story two days after Sindelar's death, and did not play the story again until after his funeral—coverage that fueled the later rumor mill.

The facts, as reported in the media: He was found dead on the floor of Camilla Castagnola's apartment. The woman was sprawled unconscious on a chair. A half-empty liquor bottle and two glasses stood on the table. She never recovered consciousness and died twenty-four hours later. Police suspected gas but couldn't prove it. When they still hadn't come up with a plausible explanation two days later, the city buzzed with rumors of murder or suicide, rumors media accounts (that he probably died of carbon monoxide poisoning) could not put down. When doctors finally confirmed that diagnosis it was too late to put the rumor genie back in the bottle.[13]

A favorite story: Castagnola had poisoned Sindelar because he had refused to marry her. Another—and one that stuck—was that Sindelar had killed himself because of a Jewish wife or mistress—and *that* story has become embedded in global soccer lore. Click an Internet search engine today to look for Mathias Sindelar and you will get, as fact, that he committed suicide after his Jewish wife died. The true fact is he never had a wife, Jewish or otherwise, and that after 1938 he took over a Jewish café. Nevertheless mystery clung to his death, and in legend Sindelar became the first hero of Austrian Resistance.

Days after Sindelar's death another symbol of the Vienna-that-had-been fell—the *Neue Freie Presse* was shut down and, together with the *Neues Wiener Journal*, incorporated into the *Neues Wiener Tagblatt* (*NWT*). The *NFP* was the only German-language paper read by decision makers in the Balkans. An outraged Walter Rafelsberger, Bürckel's economic adviser, called the closing "a major setback for our Southeast policy." Nobody read the *VB* in the region, he said, and the *NWT* "is a classified ad paper of only local significance."

Bürckel and press chief Otto Dietrich tried to save the paper but it was too late. Nazi media czar Max Amman—he was president of the Reich press chamber and ran Franz Eher Nachf, the NSDAP's publishing house—had recently acquired the *NWT* and wanted to stabilize its shaky finances by shutting down the competition, whose financial position was even shakier. The *NFP* alone needed a subsidy of RM 60,000 a month in order to survive, and, Amman said, the putative benefits weren't worth the money.

In November he wrote Hitler a memo explaining the media situation in Vienna and how he planned to improve it. The city had four tabloid newspapers that reached across the lower social spectrum and had a combined circulation of 600,000, large enough to make all of them economically viable. The *NWT*'s three editions sold 65,000 copies a day. The two papers he wanted to fold had a combined circulation of 30,000 (roughly about 15,000 each) and the *NFP* had only 1,600 subscribers in southeastern Europe. With editorial talent from the other two papers Amman could turn the *NWT* into the quality paper of choice, better able to deliver the Reich's message abroad than the *NFP* and the *Journal* with their historic ties to the empire and the Schuschnigg regime.[14]

On January 30 newspapers published a short, laconic item: The Führer had granted Odilo Globocnik's request to retire as Gauleiter of Vienna and had appointed Bürckel in his place. Bürckel would remain as Reich commissioner for reunification and Gauleiter of the Saarpfalz. The announcement was the culmination of a five-month-long struggle. Globocnik had proved every bit as much of a disaster as Christian Opdenhoff (the party official who monitored Austrian affairs) had feared when he opposed his nomination in May. Impetuous, disorganized, loaded with energy, and full of the ruthless cruelty that characterized so many Austrian Nazis, Globocnik had plunged into his job with almost wild fury.

He named incompetent cronies to party jobs and engaged in what Luza called "freewheeling financial policies," meaning he paid no heed to NS rules and regulations and bucked the party treasury, a largely independent office directly responsible to the Führer.[15] In September 1938, a party report said he could not account for 1.5 million schillings

(RM1,000,000) taken from the Fatherland Front, and that he also ran two other secret accounts into which he sluiced a total of RM 700,000, monies raised via forced donations. He even tried to sell papier-mâché emblems for the Nuremberg party congress that year at the same price as those made of bronze, an effort the treasurer managed to block.

Globocnik was not out to enrich himself but used the money to further party goals, as Bürckel had told him to do. But when Bürckel himself ran into problems with the treasury, Globocnik was a convenient fall guy with no political base in Vienna and the kind of rough manners that outraged the city's "illegals." In short, Globocnik was too young and too raw, too insensitive to nuance, too arrogant to bother with the cumbersome business of building coalitions. By late August possible successors were being traded on the political rumor market.

Bürckel favored Hubert Klausner, the last leader of the illegal Austrian Nazi party, because Klausner was more likely to do his bidding and he was less abrasive. Hitler, however, said no. "Vienna needs an outstanding orator," Bürckel quoted Hitler as telling him, "but given all of Klausner's good qualities he is not that."[16] Since he could not agree on another successor, Globocnik got a second chance by default. He botched that, too, continuing his loose-cannon rampage and spending money. In December Bürckel put shackles on Globocnik's spending, and Seyss-Inquart also turned against him.

By Christmas he was pretty much finished politically in Vienna; he published his good-bye in the New Year's edition of the *VB*, praising Bürckel for integrating the Ostmark but claiming credit for what the party had achieved. He spent another month in Vienna cleaning up his financial affairs, then left to join Himmler's staff. Eventually he moved to Lublin where he would become one of the most brutal and ruthless mass murderers in the Nazi hierarchy.

With all the contenders for the Vienna job gone, Bürckel pushed to add the city to his job portfolio and thus remain a major Nazi player. His mandate as Reich commissioner was due to expire in April, leaving him with only the Saarpfalz at a time when Seyss-Inquart was slated to join the cabinet in Berlin. Add Vienna, however, and he would control two key corners of the Reich. Hitler named him to the job on February 1, 1939.

Bürckel made his first speech as Gauleiter on February 4, the day the Nazis kicked off Fasching or carnival. They had determined to make the Vienna celebrations the biggest ever, modeling them on the Rhineland's, even down to using German carnival dress to smother Vienna's old identity.[17] Festivities would have both an economic and a political focus. An advertising blitz was to attract visitors from the Altreich. Globocnik came up with the slogan—"Vienna dances"—while vice-mayor Blaschke promised that this Fasching would turn Vienna into "a single laughing, joyful, singing, and dancing city." Sunday, February 19, would be the highlight: the festive procession of Prince Carnival, a first for Vienna, which had heretofore looked on Fasching as an indoor amusement.

The political dimension came in a carnival newspaper KdF published. This was "the first year in which Vienna would celebrate its own carnival, the first genuine people's festivity. For what the old Vienna celebrated as carnival had become, under the protection of bayonets, the death dance of the ruling system." And what would make this year special was the absence of the "chosen people"—stock exchange swindlers and other economic criminals.

The *NWT* sounded what for many Viennese must have been a discordant note. It said that since the Anschluss the Viennese danced with more precision and discipline. Gone were *Schlamperei* and imagination on the dance floor—thanks to German dancing masters Goebbels had imported, presumably to teach the Viennese how to goose step in three-quarter time.

German discipline was most evident, however, in Prince Carnival's parade. Nothing was left to chance. Organizers sent cards to every house-owner in the city with instructions on how to put out more flags. The SA distributed more than 10,000 escutcheons made of stiff cardboard and decorated with pictures of a bibulous Rathausmann (the statue on top of city hall).

The result was worth the expense, the newspapers said, as hundreds of thousands lined the streets to cheer the Prussian Prince and his fire-cracking train of revelers. But the Nazi extravaganza left no traces. Fasching would not be celebrated until after the war and then the Viennese wanted no part of Rhenish pleasures.

Throughout the first few months of 1939, the debate on what to do about Vienna continued across a Nazi hierarchy increasingly aware that the title "Hamburg of the Southeast" did not resonate among the city's population. Perhaps proclaiming Vienna as "the city of fashion" would do better.

After all the Führer himself had wanted to make Vienna "the city of German fashion," and so a new home was found for "The House of Fashion," a trade organization, in the Palais Lobkowitz, a splendor of baroque architecture with space for fashion shows and room for a small café.

Mayor Neubacher formally opened the new facility on February 22, 1939, while the new director pointed to the importance of fashion exports for Ostmark's economy.[18] These exports had totaled RM 45 million in 1937, and the mayor predicted that they would grow substantially in 1939. A fashion academy was opened in March to offer training in all the fashion arts and provide the underpinning for industry growth. But Vienna did not—and would not—have a clear path to fashion preeminence. Berlin had no intention of stepping aside.

Weeks later the "fashion house" showed off a Berlin collection. "Berlin Elegance came to the Danube" the *VB* crowed. "All the clothes shown had a joyful, youthful élan with the expression of measured grace so characteristic for Berlin. . . . When the show was over it was clear that Berlin fashion had conquered Vienna." Not exactly an auspicious start for a new center of the rag trade.

From the outset Vienna would claim a prominent place in the Reich's cultural scene, something the regime was willing to concede, but made more difficult to achieve through an ongoing campaign of demonizing whatever Schuschnigg had done. The city's musical glory had crumbled and would have to recover lost ground now that the "new wind blowing through the Reich had begun to waken Vienna from its sleeping beauty slumber," as one newspaper put it.[19] The city's cultural affairs chief, vicemayor Hanns Blaschke, bemoaned the decay of the city's art treasures under the "system" but said the rot had been halted and would soon be reversed. Given party support, Vienna still had the energy for artistic rebirth. The tone newspapers used in writing about cultural affairs, therefore, was vaguely defensive and uncertain.[20]

Goebbels' promise to make Vienna a center of film production did not give culture much of a lift. He made it clear that the city would rank behind Berlin and Munich and focus on low-brow entertainment—musicals and other froth to take the audience's minds off their troubles. A Strauss family biography was one of the first vehicles scheduled to roll for Wien Film. (Hitler had simply ignored the Strausses Jewish taint, as he had had Franz Lehar's, and made them all honorary Aryans.)[21]

A month after Bürckel succeeded Globocnik he announced all-out war against those who crossed the price guidelines he had tried to impose ever since the Anschluss. In a major speech given an eight-column banner headline in the *VB*, he demanded that merchants slash prices. He blamed the Jews, or rather, since Jews were gone from businesses, Jewish habits that had taken root with the Aryans who succeeded them. The Jew may have walked out the door, Bürckel said, but the Aryan who came in after him was just as much of a Jew even if he could trace his Aryan ancestors back to the Crusades.

Like Jews these "white Hebrews" never stopped talking, and like Jews they stole the people's money. "We will have to liberate Vienna from these 'me too' Aryan merchants who don't deserve that name of honor and who obviously suffer from Jewish foot-and-mouth disease. The merchant possessed by Jewish greed steals money out of the pockets of workers, and takes the bread out of the mouths of his children. And his stores must be closed."[22]

Bürckel followed up the speech with a price-cutting blitz. All the city's media headlined the campaign, printing names of new industries and stores that had promised to charge less. On March 5 the *VB* announced "radical price reductions for textiles and shoes" beginning on March 10. The price of shirts was to drop by half and ladies' stockings by 52 percent. A loden cloth jacket, which cost stores RM 11.30 to buy and which some were selling for RM 22, would henceforth cost no more than RM 15.83. Two days later Bürckel decreed that all stores would have to show old and new prices on goods displayed in store windows. A week after his speech he told a press briefing that "We appealed to the honest German merchant and today we can already see signs of success." He cited shoes, textiles, furniture, household goods, and hotel-room rates, which were down 25 percent, a move sure to boost tourist revenues.

But like all efforts to control prices by government fiat, this one had unpleasant side effects, specifically periodic shortages. The *VB* admitted as much but tongue-lashed those housewives who complained. "Temporary bottlenecks in food supplies, such as those we experienced this winter, lead housewives to yell and bicker. Sure, they don't always have it easy. But should we really allow such absurdities to spoil the great and dignified days in which we created a new Europe? Surely not."[23]

Few Viennese were persuaded, as an anonymous letter Bürckel received in April demonstrated. The writer cited chapter and verse on the reality and myth of price cuts. Lower prices for sugar, milk, and bread amounted to a per capita saving of 1.8 pfennigs in a city with a 1.8 million population, and for a family of four a monthly saving of RM 2.25. "This is the more than modest result of endless laws, decrees, regulations, threats, punishments, human misery, personal restrictions, endless speeches, and brave newspaper stories. . . . Doesn't anybody in authority realize what impact speeches and preaching, bragging and bragging and bragging, coercion and compulsion have on people?" [24]

The letter was more eloquent than most, but it was only one of many, and the sentiments expressed in them began to erode still further the once-popular Gauleiter's already shaky base. Nor did new crackdowns on price-gougers help much. Despite sometimes draconian fines—RM 300,000 each imposed on a clothing firm and a wholesale pork butcher, for example—merchants continued to evade and exceed the guidelines. And no matter how hard the Gauleiter cracked down, it was not enough to stop merchants from squeezing out extra profits. This was not exactly resistance to Nazi rule, but it was an unmistakable sign that the party was losing ground in Vienna and that it did not know how to handle an increasingly disgruntled population.

As the first anniversary of the Anschluss approached, lavish preparations were made to celebrate the event, beginning with a torchlight parade on the Heldenplatz on the evening of March 11 and culminating with a giant military parade on March 15—to be reviewed by the Führer himself. As usual the choreography was near perfect. At 7:30 P.M. squads of SA lit torches, and searchlights built a cathedral of light across the walls of the Neue Hofburg where huge swastika flags hung between the pillars. At exactly eight o'clock the music struck up, and the insignia and flags of the party began moving out of the darkness into the pools of light around the statues of Prince Eugene and the Archduke Charles. A series of boiler-plate speeches followed; by ten o'clock the last torch had left the square.

Everyone now looked forward to the great parade on March 15 when the Führer himself would re-ignite the NS flame as the armed forces marched past his reviewing stand. However, on that day both Hitler and his troops were otherwise engaged.

In fact, Hitler had never planned to come to Vienna then. It had all been a ruse. In the middle of February he had decided to end Czech independence, what was left of it, cut loose Slovakia as a German satellite, and give another part of it to Hungary, while keeping Bohemia and Moravia under German control. Staccato style, Viennese headlines began to hit readers on Anschluss day with much the same content as during the Sudeten crisis: Czechs were suppressing Slovak autonomy; ethnic Germans were being beaten and tortured. The Reich, therefore, would have to act. Desperate Czech efforts to halt invasion failed, and when the Czechs came to Berlin to negotiate, Hitler threatened to carpet-bomb Prague. The weakened government caved in. On the evening of March 15 Hitler stood on the Hradcin, the old castle-palace overlooking Prague, and proclaimed Bohemia and Moravia as German protectorates.

It all happened so fast that the Viennese did not have time to worry about war as they had in the fall. Western reaction, too, had been slow and what condemnation there was the papers glossed over.

Three days later than scheduled, on March 18, Hitler arrived in Vienna, not for an Anschluss parade but to spend the night. He had been on the move for forty-eight hours and was clearly fatigued when his motorcade turned into the Ring, heading for the Hotel Imperial. Hitler walked past the honor company drawn up on Schwarzenbergplatz and appeared briefly on the balcony of his hotel suite.[25] The next morning at ten he was gone. Few noticed that he had used the city as a stopover, a place to sleep after an exhausting trip, and nothing more. Clearly, Vienna would have little place in the flow of great events in the Third Reich.

Just how little became apparent during the festivities honoring Hitler's fiftieth birthday on April 20. The pomp and circumstance were displayed in Berlin while Vienna's celebrations were those of a backwater, starting with the same front page in the Vienna edition of the *VB* as everywhere else in the Reich. The next day's headlines said in effect—we too had a nice time. Units of the Wehrmacht, the SS, and the air force had marched around the Ring and gathered on Adolf Hitler Platz outside city hall.

The *VB*'s prose ran to deep purple: "And now they approach in a broad front. The head of the marching column is still at the university. We see a block of gray that moves closer and closer. The beat of the marchers grows louder and louder. The broad front moves ever closer. And now we know: no power on earth can stop this front. It is something unique, unsurpassable. It is the German soldier!"[26]

Two days after his birthday Hitler issued the Ostmark laws that would govern the legal status of the seven Reichsgauen (administrative regions) of the former Austria.[27] They had been more than eight months in the making. Bürckel and his top aide Karl Barth had drafted a first version in July 1938, but the proposal would have given Vorarlberg to Bavaria and too much power to the Gauleiters who, as Reichsstatthalters would become de facto Reich ministers responsible only to Hitler himself. Bureaucratic warfare ensued. Interior minister Wilhelm Frick fought fiercely to retain ministerial authority and opposed ceding Vorarlberg. He prevailed, and in August Hitler returned the bill for redrafting. Never much interested in administrative reform, the Führer put Bürckel's proposal on ice while he handled the Sudeten crisis. In the ensuing months the debate over how much power to give the Gauleiter continued, with the tide of opinion running slowly in Bürckel's favor. A consensus emerged that the Ostmark Gauleiters be given some power to make decisions involving activities of Reich ministries. The question was how much. Bürckel pushed for across the board governmental authority at his January meeting with Hitler, but the Führer was not yet willing to go that far. He was a cautious decision maker on administrative matters.

Finally, on April 13 at a meeting in his aerie in Berchtesgaden attended by Bürckel, Frick, Seyss-Inquart, and Hans Lammers, the Reich minister who ran the chancellor's office, Hitler finally agreed to the text of the new law. It was promulgated a week later.

The law divided Austria into seven Reichsgaue with the Gauleiter of each one becoming Reichsstatthalter at the same time, thus combining leadership of the party and of Gau government—local and national—in one hand. Each Gau would have a "Regierungspräsident," or RP, an old Prussian title that literally meant "president of the government," who would be in charge of all Reich affairs and institutions except for rails, post, finance, and justice (for example, the RP controlled local labor, forest, and agricultural insurance offices). He would be an official of the Reich paid by Berlin. The Gauhauptmann (district captain) would handle local administration and draw his paycheck from Gau coffers. Matters were a little different in Vienna because it was both a state *and* a city, in other words, a Reichsgau and an independent community. Bürckel named Barth as his RP in Vienna to deal with Reich ministries and kept Neubacher as mayor to handle city matters, although with vastly reduced powers. The law was to be fully implemented by September 30, 1939, with the Landeshauptmann or governor still in charge of Gau—Salzburg, Carinthia, the Tyrol—administration until the switchover was completed.

Bürckel took over Seyss-Inquart's function as Reichstatthalter of the Ostmark and was charged with liquidating the Austrian provincial government by the due date. Seyss-Inquart joined the Reich cabinet as a minister without portfolio—and without much to do until the fall, when he was sent to Poland, except stir up mischief.

The law streamlined government procedures, cut through red tape, and made lines of authority much clearer. The Gauleiter had direct access to Hitler without reporting to anybody else. It also strengthened regional autonomy and over time the Gauleiter-Reichstatthalters became, as Luza pointed out, "territorial princes." In the case of Vienna this would lead to unexpected friction, especially under Schirach who tended to go his own way, and to sharper rivalry with Berlin—often to Goebbels's and Hitler's extreme displeasure.

On May 3, 1939 Bürckel announced a new administrative structure for the city.[28] He scrapped the vice-mayor's office—there had been three of them—and named them and four others as "Beigeordnete" or deputies to run various city departments and agencies like housing, transportation, culture, sports, youth, and health. Most were veterans. Blaschke added transportation to culture. Rafelsberger would be in charge of markets, food supplies, and city-owned enterprises as well as Göring's four-year plan for Vienna. He would also continue as the Gau's economic advisor, a job that included Aryanization of Jewish-owned businesses. Forty-five "Ratsherrn" or councilors were to act as advisors. They were an odd lot and reflected Bürckel's commitment to German socialism and the working class. They included an insurance agent, a locksmith, a mechanic, a metal worker, a mining engineer, a writer of popular fiction, a streetcar conductor, a professor, and the director of the Burgtheater, as well as the mandatory number of SS and SA officers.

Nazi ideology was not neglected. On May 6 the touring exhibit of "degenerate art" finally reached Vienna. The show featured 650 paintings and sculpture—including 17 pictures by Paul Klee—culled from 16,000 modern art works the Nazis had confiscated from their owners. The Nazis had had six years to drum their concept of degenerate visual arts as a Jewish-Bolshevik conspiracy into the mind of the Altreich but only a year to do the same thing in Vienna, so the propaganda barrage was particularly fierce.

"The gruesome art of cultural Bolsheviks. The mentally ill were the better painters. In a witches' cauldron of indescribable aberration," ran the headlines in *Das Kleine Volksblatt*. Degenerate art, the paper went on, was a "planned, devilish attack against the essence and the future of all art. Nothing that we hold holy was not dragged into the mud by these Bolshevik and Jewish artists. You feel as if you are in a mad house."[29]

Some 65,000 visitors had come in the first three weeks, 11,000 on Pentecost Sunday alone, and at times the exhibit had to be closed because of overcrowding. Still, it is hard to say just how much real influence it had. One anecdotal piece of evidence suggests that it did not have much: Rudolf Hausner, after the war one of Vienna's most famous painters, would visit the show with like-minded friends. "We would sit there," he recalled, "enraptured by what we saw and joyously sharing our impressions—until someone else walked by. Then we would fire off all the Nazi invective about degeneracy until the danger had passed and we could lean back and say to ourselves 'how lovely, how beautiful, how masterful.'"[30] They were not alone.

Goebbels arrived in Vienna in early June to open the Reich Theater Week, which would again be held in the city, a decision that led art "observers" into paroxysms of delight. They saw the city's selection for a second year in a row as a sign of revitalization and rebirth, confirmation that Vienna was a cultural center to rival Berlin. Goebbels clearly did not. In his state-of-the-German-theater speech, delivered once again from a flower-decked lectern in the Opera, he treated Vienna as just another city. His focus, instead, was on the history of German theater and its direct connection to Greek tragedy. He painted an arc from the thespian carts of the Middle Ages to Lessing's Hamburg dramaturgy—the theoretical foundation of modern drama. He said that Germans care about theater the way no other peoples do, and they do so with passion. "For theater without passion—and even frenzy—is not theater but light entertainment." As was his wont, the speech was intelligent, cohesive, and well researched.[31]

The Viennese brought passion to the theater, all right, but not the kind that led to "heated intellectual discussion," as Goebbels had demanded. At a performance of Schiller's *Maria Stuart* featuring Maria Eis, an established Burgtheater star, and Käthe Dorsch, a Berlin import, the audience began to chant "*Eis, Eis, Eis,*" when Dorsch appeared. They felt the import had been given a bigger buildup than the local favorite, and made no secret of their feelings.[32]

Hitler himself arrived in Vienna unannounced on Saturday, June 10, to take part in Richard Strauss's seventy-fifth birthday celebration. In white tie and tails, his standard theater attire, he attended the first performance of a new Strauss opera, *Friedenstage*. When it was over, his motorcade roared off to a hotel in the hills for a sit-down dinner for sixty prominent actors and singers.

On Sunday Hitler looked at art in the Hofburg and had tea and cake at a nearby café, distributing cake to all the children present. At night he went to the Burgtheater to attend *Einen Jux Will Er Sich Machen* (*He Wants to Have a Good Time*), a play by Johann Nestroy, a prolific nineteenth-century playwright who dissected the foibles of Viennese society with acid wit. (At the time Thornton Wilder was tinkering with a first English adaptation, *The Merchant of Yonkers*, which in turn became *Hello Dolly*). In photographs awe, mixed with an almost strange joy, played around Hitler's face as he looked up from his box at the white and silver glory he had first seen as a teenager.[33] The ovation that greeted him may have touched him more deeply than did any of the others. It was the only time in the seven years he was master of Vienna that Hitler attended the Burgtheater, yet as Goebbels noted in his diary the house had been a fundamental influence in shaping his view of the performing arts, and he told his propaganda minister as much as they were driving home afterwards.[34] The next morning the Führer was gone. He was not someone to linger in this town.

At the end of January 1939 Josef Löwenherz submitted one of his regular reports to Adolf Eichmann. The number of Jews able to leave the Reich in the past month had shrunk to less than 500 compared to several thousand the previous month, largely, Löwenherz wrote, because foreign consulates were closed over the Christmas and New Year's holidays. The largest number, 134, had gone to China and another 100 or so to Great Britain. Latin American countries had taken 62, the United States 31, and Palestine 27. But the number of Jews anxious to emigrate continued to grow, he wrote, noting the large number of people who crowded the IKG offices every day asking for passport forms. A shortage of foreign exchange accounted for the fact that far fewer people actually emigrated than had applied to leave. "The IKG simply is not in a position to meet the demands for landing fees and cash requirements so that a number of people are in danger of losing permission to enter foreign countries that had been obtained with great difficulty." Still, in January alone 2,600 Jews had been attended to. Children's transports were being organized. More than 230 children had been sent out in January, most of them to Great Britain, and the IKG had the names of several thousand others who needed to go.[35]

Jewish poverty was reaching desperate levels. The IKG had increased the number of soup kitchens from fourteen to sixteen and was feeding almost 21,000 people daily, a number Löwenherz expected to rise to 30,000. IKG was spending more than RM 150,000 a month in cash subsidies to the indigent and would soon have to spend more than RM 200,000. His budget for such payments was only RM 175,000. The IKG old-age home was far beyond capacity with a waiting list of 2,100. Löwenherz continued to offer retraining courses to teach Jews trades they could use abroad. Two Western aid organizations, The American Joint Distribution Committee and the British Council for German Jewry, had provided IKG with almost $700,000 and Löwenherz expected another $50,000 soon, but as of January 25, 1939, he faced a deficit of $66,623.54.

In his March report Löwenherz noted that since the IKG had resumed its activities in May 1938, it had helped a total of 20,646 people emigrate and that month had handled applications from 4,659 persons. It was now feeding 32,000 people a day and had spent almost RM 275,000 in cash payments to cover rent, food, education, and welfare for poor Jews. Since January he had won approval for extra old-age home space and expected to add 150 new beds. The Jewish hospital on the Währinger Gürtel could barely keep up with the load of indigent Jewish patients. In February and March British and American charitable groups had added more than $200,000 in foreign exchange to IKG coffers for a total of $967,000, thus helping to cut the deficit to $29,000.

At the time the IKG was not alone in helping Jews escape. A month after the Anschluss a Dutch philanthropist named Frank van Gheel-Gildemeester had set up a group to help poor Jews and non-Aryans escape, and he introduced several innovations Eichmann would copy. Wealthy Jews who contributed 10 percent of their fortune to the Gildemeester fund could use its facilities to emigrate, while their money would also help indigent Jews to leave. Before it shut down in 1940 and its activities integrated into the IKG, Gildemeester helped some 30,000 non-Aryans to emigrate.[36]

As 1939 headed into summer and Jews waited for necessary documents or plotted their illegal escapes, Jewish life, however precarious, took on some form of stability and cohesion, even a wrenching kind of normality. A few examples:

The so-called Palestine office, which helped train Jews in new jobs and then emigrate to Palestine, got Ernest Schindler into a Zionist school where he learned Hebrew, German, math, and Jewish history in the morning and was trained as a gardener and electrician in the afternoon, skills that came in handy when his efforts to emigrate failed and he was pushed into forced labor.[37]

Hans Kann was a "confessional" Jew, a term used for members of the Hebrew faith, no matter what their ancestry. Kann's mother was an Aryan and his father a Jew, so technically he was only a "half-Jew." Since he had been raised in the Jewish religion that didn't seem to count, and neither did the fact that he had converted to Catholicism in 1938. The Nuremberg laws declared all conversions after September 15, 1935, invalid as far as determination of race was concerned. Kann was sent to a *Hauptschule* or intermediate school because gymnasiums, which offered the more classical education, were closed to him. "The funny thing is that the school was very good because the teachers were Jews who had taught at gymnasiums so that our educational level was very high. We took analytic geometry, stuff you usually only got in a gymnasium."[38]

Michael Kehlmann stayed at the Döblinger Gymnasium until he was almost sixteen and was permitted to lead a reasonable social life with Aryan friends. "I could go to their houses and they could come to mine, although in theory Aryan children were prohibited from playing with half-Jews. When I got older I could have nothing to do with Aryan girls. Even kissing one would be *Rassenschande* (literally, racial shame)."[39]

Erich Lessing, a future famous Magnum photographer, found a sign of humanity in a Viennese policeman.

One night he ran into half a dozen Hitler Youth—the Aryan heroes never risked confronting without crushing superiority—who surrounded him and began to needle the "Jew boy." A man came by, he recalled, and said that this "Jew boy has been bothering you and they said yes he had so the man said well we'll take him to the police station and report him. So we get there and the man said well look this Jew boy bothered the

HaJot [HJ]. So the policeman said, 'aha, the HaJot boys bothered this gentleman.' So the man said, 'no, I told you, he bothered them.' And the cop said, 'yeah, I understand, the HaJot boys bothered that very well dressed gentleman.' The man said 'no, it's the other way around.' Then the policeman said 'okay then we'll keep him here and the rest of you can leave.' Then the cop looked at me and said, 'are you nuts? You're going home and you're never again going out dressed in that fancy over-coat in the evening. Now get out of here.'"[40]

Tamara Rainer was fifteen when the Nazis came. A half-Jew, she was ejected from fashion school and forced to work in a tailor shop "with a lot of other Jewish girls. At first we were treated pretty well. Later they tightened the screws, like we couldn't take the streetcar to work but had to walk. We were too young to worry much. We were optimists."[41]

Optimism, however, was a luxury. Throughout 1939 the net tight-ened. Jews had to give up their driver's licenses. "It would be intolerable for the folkish community to have our German streets remain a play-ground for Jews," the *VB* commented. Jews had to add Sara or Israel to their first names by April 1. In June Jews were barred from the Prater, the city's largest stretch of open land in the second district and close to where the city's Jewish quarter had been. Jews would, however, be al-lowed to use their own park "on the left bank of the Danube canal"—an uncultivated and weedy stretch of land.

With Jews banned from swimming pools, hygiene became a problem since they also could no longer take their weekly showers at public bath-ing establishments. After cumbersome negotiations a limited number of private pools agreed to let Jews use their showers. But what about the summer? The city agreed to buy and renovate a dilapidated private pool near the western rail tracks just outside of town. It was opened on May 13, 1939, and days later Aryans threw broken glass into the water and damaged or stole the shower heads. A bather was injured by a thrown rock. At the end of July Jewish bathers retaliated. When a troop train passed the pool, Jewish women showed their bottoms while men circled their foreheads with their forefingers in unmistakable signs of disrespect. The train engineer demanded that the pool be closed. City hall tried to blunt the attack by promising to let benches decay and grass die from neglect, but that wasn't enough to satisfy the steamed Aryans. On Sep-tember 17, not three weeks after the outbreak of war, the Jewish pool was closed, not just for the season but for good.[42]

Perhaps the most triumphant story about Jews the *VB* ran in the first half of 1939 came on May 14: "To date 100,000 Jews of the Hebrew faith have emigrated from the Ostmark. Welcome progress in Jewish cleansing: They're leaving!" In the first ten months of its activities, the Central Office for Jewish Emigration (Adolf Eichmann's operation) had been instrumental in the exodus of 99,672 religious Jews. Before the Anschluss 175,000 religious Jews had lived in "totally Jew-infested" Vienna and at least another 120,000 "Nuremberg" Jews—agnostics, atheists, or Christians who could not muster the requisite number of Aryan grandparents—but their exact number could not be determined until the next census.

After the sacking of the episcopal palace, violence against the Catholic church was sporadic but could be savage and dangerous. On November 20 an SS man in a careening car fired twice into the lighted window of a church rectory, barely missing the priest inside. Four days later the parish house in another suburb was demolished, and the rectory windows were smashed. On November 26 the gate of a church was splintered, a crucifix broken, and the altar damaged. A Gestapo report, dated November 29, summed up the incidents and said the archdiocese had the number of the speeding car and planned to lodge a protest, blaming Bürckel's October speech for the violence.[43]

Far more dangerous, however, were Nazi attacks on church education, money, and membership.[44] Catholic schools were privatized in July 1938, leaving them without official certification. In October school prayer was abolished and religious instruction made voluntary where it had been mandatory. The party vetted priests who offered such instruction to make sure their teachings did not contradict the dogma of National Socialism.

Pressure on Catholics to leave the church also mounted and was amazingly successful, given the fact that such departure required a formal, legal renunciation. In 1938 more than 78,000 left the archdiocese of Vienna alone, the bulk, 72,000, in the fourth quarter of the year. By 1942 more than 213,000 had formally left the church. One trigger for the exodus was money. On April 28, 1939, the Nazis ended the long tradition of state support for all churches.

Henceforth the church would have to raise money by demanding mandatory contributions from the faithful. Members who refused to pay up could be taken to court—but they could also leave the church, and, after a three months waiting period, no longer pay the "contribution." (the government carefully avoided the word "tax" used in the Altreich, a semantic ruse that robbed the Austrian church of its official character.)[45]

The new law, the *VB* said, assured the church of financial independence.[46] That of course was not the Nazi's goal, but ironically the law did just that: those who stayed were willing to pay without coercion. In 1940 alone, church revenues grew by 67 percent, from RM 3 million to RM 5 million, enough for Innitzer to assign RM 300,000 to other Austrian dioceses. The Nazis avoided open confrontation, however, fearful of turning priests and bishops into martyrs and thus kindling centers of opposition. Innitzer was just as unwilling to enter a fight he knew he would lose, so he took the church into an enclave where parish priests and parish houses became centers for those who still cared about their faith.

Not that the cardinal was immune to attack. In July 1939 he walked out of a provincial church near Vienna to find some 30 HJ boys waiting for him. They quickly surrounded him, yelled insults, accused him of complicity in the execution of Dollfuss's murderers, and shouted, "There is blood on your hands." Then they threw rocks and rotten eggs. Pius XII wrote him a letter of condolence.[47]

Ever since the Hamburg of the Southeast idea had been launched, thoughtful Nazis had wondered how to give the concept some practical meaning, which could actually boost German industrial exports to the region and assure the Reich of its granary and raw materials—including Romania's oil fields. The idea had been discussed for a year without acquiring substance or momentum.

But incorporation of Bohemia and Moravia as protectorates, Slovakia's status as Nazi satellite, and Hungary's decision in the spring of 1939 to join the anti-Comintern pact put a geographic dagger in place, pointing southeast. Clearly, more than rhetoric would be needed to make Vienna a gateway. The nuts and bolts of how to do it would come from Guido Schmidt, Austria's last foreign minister, who now held a key industrial job in Berlin. He laid out problems and opportunities in a memo about "opening a Southeast trading post" in Vienna.[48]

He warned of turf battles among various Reich institutions like the Reichsbank, and the foreign and economics ministries that could be avoided by drawing them all into the gateway project. The business structure of the Ostmark would have to be modified. An umbrella organization could spur creation of export cooperatives and remove bureaucratic and other obstacles. It would have to develop specific information on what goods would do best where, use the semiannual Vienna trade fair as a Southeast showcase, and encourage large German companies to open export offices in Vienna where buyers from the region could deal directly with the source of product. He also suggested building an economic intelligence service to carry out in-depth studies on each country's potential to buy German goods, support private initiatives, and launch advertising campaigns for Reich products.

It took another six months before anything concrete was done; but on February 8, 1940, the Südosteuropagesellschaft (Society for Southeast Europe, known as SOEG) was established under the protection of economics minister Walter Funk, with Bürckel as president and Rafelsberger, an SOEG vice-president, as driving force.[49] To a large extent Schmidt's advice was followed, especially in the information sector. No company interested in the seven countries his memo covered—Yugoslavia, Romania, Hungary, Slovakia, Bulgaria, Greece, and Turkey—could complain about lack of detailed intelligence. Austrian archives still bulge with stenciled weekly reports on events in the Balkans.

Schmidt's proposal made a larger point, however—give Vienna a policy-making role that could help evolve into capital of a Danube federation. Bürckel supported the trade aspect of the proposal—at least he did not kill it—but had little use for the broader context. Baldur von Schirach, however, did. His advent as Gauleiter of Vienna now was just a little more than a year away.

On June 3, 1939, Christian Opdenhoff fired the first shot that helped prepare the change-over, even as Bürckel seemed more solidly in control. He wrote a devastating report to the Brown House party headquarters in Munich on the political conditions of the Vienna Gau.[50] Bürckel had wasted almost all the goodwill capital that had greeted his arrival. Total reliance on his cronies from the Pfalz had aroused popular opposition. The Vienna consensus was simple: "Bürckel and his Pfälzer don't know us and can't adapt to our ways." In the morning, he continued, "Bürckel breakfasts with his Pfälzer, during the day he works only with them, at lunch he sits with them, and in the evening he goes to the Stadtkrug (a posh restaurant that had been a Nazi hangout for years) with them. At night he is back in his house with his Pfälzer." Most of them were incompetent. Key jobs were shuffled all the time so that most jobholders were fearful of doing anything lest they lose their jobs.

Bürckel himself was competent enough and it would make sense to give him a strong administrative aide—if he let go of his Pfälzer. But since he wasn't going to do that the party should look for a replacement. As he had a year earlier, Opdenhoff pushed for Albert Frauenfeld, even though he conceded that Frauenfeld was not ideal. For one thing he had been mentioned for the job too much and thus lost credibility, for another he wasn't sure if Frauenfeld was an artist or an actor. "An artist would fit in Vienna; I'd be afraid of an actor. One thing seems sure: Frauenfeld's strength lies in his high spirits, his ebullience, his energy, and his knowledge of local conditions. He probably lacks a consistent work ethic and will need an organizer to do the work."

Nothing came of the Frauenfeld trial balloon, but Opdenhoff's insight into the Viennese character was shrewd: the city needed an artist more than an actor, though an artist with acting abilities would be ideal, and Baldur von Schirach was both in just the right proportions—he was the poet laureate of the Reich, producing a poem for any occasion, and as Reich youth leader he knew how to perform on the political stage, two reasons why Hitler would pick him to lead Vienna.

Bürckel, meanwhile, fought his last battles with Seyss-Inquart, who predictably lost. Before leaving office in Vienna, Seyss made a grab for the city's cultural institutions, a grab Bürckel correctly saw as a first step in setting up an Ostmark cultural ministry, and which he thwarted, arguing that the Ostmark laws gave him control. He followed up by firing Mühlmann, allegedly for failure to curb an anti-Prussian cabaret. For Seyss that was the last straw; on June 23 he fired off an angry letter protesting Mühlmann's dismissal and cataloging Bürckel's many failures including his psychologically flawed treatment of the Viennese.[51]

Bürckel waited until August 8, and then he sent his rival a devastating, eleven-page barrage designed to knock him out of the Vienna ring for good.[52] His basic argument stated that Seyss wanted to conserve Austria while Bürckel followed the Führer's orders to liquidate it. He cited chapter and verse: Seyss had close ties to the church; Schuschnigg had trusted him; he had sent Dollfuss a telegram congratulating him for his escape from an earlier assassination attempt; even in office he had prepared secret plans for an Ostmark ministry or at least one for culture; he had no real ties to the party; he did not really believe in Greater

Germany. Bürckel's sarcastic prose may have lacked stylistic elegance or legal precision but when he was through so was Seyss-Inquart: "You may be a clever man but there is one thing you cannot do: replace National Socialism with cleverness." As Mühlmann had put it "The doctor [Seyss-Inquart] can undertake very little in these things because Bürckel always comes on like a raging bull to oppose them."[53]

Even before the final showdown Bürckel had moved into the cultural arena Seyss-Inquart had coveted. He announced plans for a Gau cultural week in mid-October that would feature the Philharmonic performing Beethoven's Ninth Symphony. He began negotiations to bind Wilhelm Furtwängler more closely to Vienna and to bring the director of the Hamburg opera, Heinrich Strohm, to Vienna as opera chief.

Resistance to Nazi rule had always been spotty and was expressed more in *Raunzen*, that peculiar Viennese whining so characteristic of the city, than in direct action, and the people as a whole didn't start complaining much until the fall of 1938. There was scattered action before that, most of it coming from the political extremes—the underground Communists, revolutionary socialists, and young Catholic supporters of the corporate state whose elders had been arrested. From the beginning the Communists were the most active. They distributed leaflets with slogans like "Hitler means war" and "Austria for the Austrians." And of course they were the first Gestapo target.

Young Catholic intellectuals like Otto Molden and his friends drifted into Resistance from Catholic youth groups that were also an early target. But because they were young, they were not tied to the corporate state and were largely without ideological bias. "We had lost our homeland, our country, and we wanted it back," Molden's younger brother Fritz explained.[54]

In the summer of 1938 the Moldens and some of their friends printed 4,000 anti-Nazi leaflets in an Innsbruck parish house, scattered them across the city, and dispersed before the Gestapo could track them down.[55] In Vienna members of another group smeared a white *Krukenkreuz* (crooked cross, the symbol of the Fatherland Front) on Schwarzenbergplatz together with the slogan "Long Live Austria" and they changed the street signs of the Höhenstrasse that leads through the Vienna Woods to "Dollfuss Strasse."[56]

But only during and after the Sudeten crisis did resistance go beyond young students distributing mimeographed leaflets. In an optical plant in Favoriten unknown workers wrote on a grindstone, "we thank our Führer for the new taxes."[57] A brief strike erupted in a Floridsdorf factory over dismissal of an employee. Members of a Communist cell in a bricks work destroyed machinery. Others lit outside fires on nights when the Nazis decreed blackout exercises. Johann Macho was seized for "derogatory comments" about his Wehrmacht draft notice. Wilhelm Skok was arrested for saying he wouldn't work under this violent regime, but only under the Social Democrats. Wilhelm Martien had shouted in a restaurant "long live Stalin. I'm a socialist and will remain a socialist." Josef Wanra and Rudolf Schiener had worn red carnations in their buttonholes in a "provocative manner." On New Year's Eve Ignaz Markisch had sung a socialist youth hymn and announced "I'm a Red and I'll stay a Red." He too was arrested.[58]

Things got serious enough in September for the local Gestapo to cable Heydrich in Berlin that Communists and revolutionary socialists were building organizations and a leadership cadre, raising money, and successfully producing illegal materials. And the growing number of industrial "accidents" revealed a clearly political design. The Gestapo tracked the Resistance closely but did not strike until early December, 1938, arresting fifty suspects. A second wave of arrests took place in August 1939 when more than a hundred suspects were seized. Sentences were still fairly mild. One group of revolutionary socialists got eighteen to thirty months in jail for distributing money to fuel resistance.

On the Catholic Right there was less organization and more improvisation. The Left had operated underground for four years. They knew the ropes, the risks, and how to snap back from defeat and betrayal. They had contacts in Moscow and in the West. The Catholics did not. They had been in power, and overnight their leadership was gone. The Moldens and their friends had guts and took risks, but they lacked experience and organization. The leadership would have to come from somewhere else—the church and the professions, from the intellectual upper middle class, untainted by Judaism and to some extent protected by their pan-German bias.

The most charismatic among them was Karl Roman Scholz, an Augustinian monk at the Klosterneuburg monastery. He had briefly been interested in the Nazis but then turned savagely against them. In 1937 he lived in England and made contact with British authorities as an information provider. He returned just before the Anschluss and in the fall founded a Resistance group of like-minded young men. Mostly they talked about a free Austria after Hitler was overthrown, and by the time war broke out Scholz had attracted 400 members to his "Austrian Freedom Movement" (ÖFB—Österreichische Freiheits Bewegung).

Dr. Karl Lederer, a liberal Catholic, had founded a Resistance group also by the name of the Austrian Freedom Movement. He wanted to make contact with the West, like Scholz, but unlike him, Lederer thought of sabotage. Dr. Jakob Kastelic, a Catholic lawyer, founded a third Resistance group. He thought more in terms of a central European federation, a thought reflected in the name he gave his group, "The Greater Austrian Freedom Movement."

The three groups had developed independently of each other and made contact only in the summer and fall of 1939 when war was close or had already broken out. All three were convinced that war was inevitable and that Hitler would be defeated. Austria, and perhaps some more modern version of the empire that might include Bavaria, would rise from the ashes.[59]

Not much happened in Vienna in the summer of 1939. The weather was hot, and the headlines spoke only of Poland. Domestic news came out of Berlin, as it had for fifteen months, underlining Vienna's diminished role—a city to which things happened but that did not make them happen. Vienna hadn't been in the news since Kristallnacht, and then only for the excesses Austrian Nazis committed. Locally, the media reported that Seyss-Inquart had celebrated his forty-seventh birthday and had received a congratulatory cable from the Führer. A watchmakers' convention opened in the Nordwestbahnhalle in late July, and on the 25th the Nazis celebrated the failed 1934 putsch against Dollfuss. On July 29 Wehrmacht bands marched around the Ring in the afternoon to—literally—beat the drum for their stadium concert that night. Not much new news at all.

The last week of August saw an international student sports festival roam across the city. Germany took forty-two medals. The night before it closed, a wine festival was held in Grinzing. The old village was festooned in flags and colored paper lamps. Vintners marched through the streets. Pretty girls brought out drinks of honor for the participants, and everybody danced into the deepening twilight.[60]

Now headlines from Poland broke the mid-summer torpor, and they grew ever more ominous, even if tone and content had become numbingly familiar. Poles mistreated Germans. Poland threatened the Reich. Poland had plans to conquer East Prussia. Poles mistreated the people of Danzig. Poles demand that Germany be razed like Carthage.

At home preparations for war were stepped up. Rationing, which had gradually been put into place, moved ahead swiftly. Shoe and clothing stores were closed temporarily until a new distribution system, complete with rationing cards, was ready. Air defenses were mobilized, and air raid protection measures implemented.

The German-Soviet nonaggression pact hit the papers like a bomb. "Everybody now thought war was impossible and that the conflict with Poland and the western powers had been won. The occupation of Danzig and the liquidation of Poland would be child's play. The danger of a world war was over," Josef Schöner, a young Austrian diplomat the Nazis had dismissed from the foreign service, noted in his diary.

But Schöner, who had moved from diplomacy into the family restaurant business and thus had wide contacts across society, also noted more pessimistic voices, especially when the British government reacted to the news by reaffirming its Polish commitments. One of his colleagues saw a Soviet plot. The agreement would free the Reich to attack Poland, the West would declare war, and Communism would be the victor.

Nor did the initial euphoria about the pact last. Schöner wrote, "Suddenly the fear of war is back, stronger than ever, stronger even than at the high point of the September crisis (before Munich). War is expected to break out any day. The general mood is serious and depressed, but there is no sign of panic. On Sunday the Viennese went to the wine gardens or the swimming pools as they always do. Their gaiety, however, was restrained. Business is pretty much at a standstill, especially since so many stores are closed for inventory. Today's distribution of ration cards was accepted apathetically."

On August 28 Schöner again reported: "We are in a situation without an exit. No demonstrations, not for or against the war, only a fatalistic silence and waiting. Not even new jokes. . . . The weather continues hot and humid, and weighs heavily on my nerves."[61]

CHAPTER 7

Decline and Fall

From Bürckel to Schirach:
September 2, 1939–August 8, 1940

Since 5:40 A.M. fire is being returned." The war was on. On
September 2 *Das Kleine Volksblatt* summed up events of the past twenty-
four hours in a series of succinct front-page headlines that tabloids do
so well:

"The Führer before the German Reichstag."

"I only want to be the first soldier of the Reich."

"German troops in Polish territory on all fronts."

"The Luftwaffe in control of Polish skies."

"No German will listen to foreign radio broadcasts."

"On the march with our soldiers."

"It came after all," Schöner wrote. "The convulsive optimism of the
Viennese that produced a kind of peace psychosis, has proved an empty
illusion. Hitler's speech [announcing the beginning of war] brought the
expected explanation. I heard it at the Carlton [a family-owned café];
the place was jammed with 'listening guests.' All with very serious expressions on their faces. No applause. A small group of people on St.
Stephen's Square. Those close to the loudspeakers lifted their arms when

149

the Deutschland hymn began, those who stood further away did not. People are careful not to express any opinions. Punishments for 'defeatism,' such as listening to foreign radio broadcasts, are draconic. Nightly blackouts don't help. What didn't my father tell me about the enthusiasm with which we went to war in August 1914."[1]

On September 2 Göring named Bürckel as Reich defense commissioner for "Military District XVII"—Vienna, Upper, and Lower Danube. The appointment added to Bürckel's already considerable powers, an augmentation he did not need. More empathy with the feelings of the people he governed was required; empathy, however, was a concept Bürckel did not understand, nor would have had much use for even if he did.

Now, one shock followed another: the sudden blackout of all doors and windows, the introduction of rationing and other economic restrictions, a 50-percent tax increase, a freeze on pay hikes, no changes in working conditions for new hires, new curbs on the use of gasoline—pleasure driving was forbidden and cars used for business got far less fuel than they needed—no *Schlagobers* (whipped cream) or foreign newspapers in the cafés, restaurant menus stripped down to essentials—Schöner's family business couldn't get meat for days. The *VB* urged housewives to buy tomatoes and can them. The 1939 crops were huge and must be used, not wasted. The newspaper itself announced smaller editions to save paper until supplies stabilized. Deputy Gauleiter Karl Scharitzer told 900 merchants that they were the best propagandists to explain the ins and outs of economic warfare. Rafelsberger said that a "totally just" distribution of goods and services was essential and merchants could help by making sure it was. Another official assured Vienna that there was enough grain on hand on September 8, not counting the current harvest, to feed the German people for a year.[2]

"Not a trace of enthusiasm," Schöner noted on September 5, "although the masses have been convinced by really quite brilliant propaganda that England forced the war on us." A week later he wrote that the mood had improved—thanks to Germany's lightning military victories. "The conquest of Krakow and Warsaw within eight days of war has made a big impression. Some are talking about an early end to the war because the English and the French won't dare tackle the west wall [the Siegfried line] and after the conquest of Poland they'll quiet down." Schöner disagreed. He looked for a long war because "the Western powers were out to destroy National Socialism." Few bothered obeying the ban on listening to foreign radios. Even party members were tuning in to German-language broadcasts from Radio Strasbourg.

Relaxation of blackout regulations a week into the war helped turn the popular mood around. While homes, offices, and places of public amusement were still required to obey them, streetlights had been turned back on. A change in how meat was distributed may also have helped. Housewives who had time to hit butcher shops in the morning got the choicest cuts, while working women who shopped after office hours often found nothing left. As the *VB* admitted, the system that had been introduced in the spring—each store selling meat and meat products drew up lists of customers—had not worked out. Housewives had simply registered in two or three stores and gotten meat wherever they were first in line. The NS women's organization was charged with drawing up new, tamper-proof lists.

Indeed, during the first few months of war Vienna's women became prime targets of propaganda. On September 9 the *VB* said that "Viennese women, whom we recently called soldiers in skirts, honor that title. They're coming up with new recipes, adapting their menus to daily market conditions, and have adjusted surprisingly quickly to purchase permits for clothing. Viennese women buy what they really need and they are getting it."

Mandatory conscription was—and is—a commonplace in Europe, and the Germans wasted no time putting young Viennese and other Austrian men into uniform. Before the war was out some 600,000 of them had served in the Wehrmacht. This drain on manpower worsened an already tight labor market with defense industries sucking in more and more workers. Not surprisingly, more and more women were recruited to take over traditionally male jobs—streetcar conductors, cinema projectionists, even entering the male bastion of the coffee house where women trained as "daughters of the hall"—since the term "waitress" was too demeaning for so august a job.

Basic Nazi attitudes toward women, however, did not change. They remained anchored in the "three Ks"—Kinder, Kirche, Küche (children, church, and kitchen)—as the *VB* noted in a feature about schools in the Altreich that trained brides for their roles as wives and mothers.[3]

The huge Gothic windows of St. Stephen's were removed to a safe place, and a wooden scaffold was built to protect the cathedral's entrance. In reporting on these safety measures, the *VB* poked fun at British charges that the Wehrmacht had damaged Poland's Catholic icon, the black Madonna of Czestochowa. "How we German 'barbarians' protect church properties is shown by how we are protecting the church of St. Stephen." [4]

The way German "barbarians" treated Viennese history where Poles were concerned was something else. King Jan Sobieski is generally credited with lifting the Turkish siege of Vienna in 1683. Myth, the *VB* said contemptuously.[5] Poles had invented that fairy tale "in their pathological vanity. This card-deck king never stood on our side but was always in the way." In its "true" account the *VB* mixed fact and fiction, a staple of Goebbels's media fare. But whether the story helped lift Vienna's mood may justly be doubted.

Nor was a heavy-handed *VB* effort at humor about ration cards likely to help: "This man came into a restaurant and ordered a succulent beef goulash. But he hadn't read his *VB* very closely. First he learned that today was Monday and Monday was a meatless day. But the waiter offered him a nice vegetable Schnitzel instead. When he asked for a roll the waiter demanded ration stamps for bread. He didn't have it so he didn't get his roll. But plum dumplings made with potato flour was a nice dessert and could be had without stamps. Besides every restaurant had to offer one dish a day ration-free."

The annual fall trade fair opened on October 16. Officials boasted about holding a fair in war time and about the strong representation from neutral nations in the Southeast and Italy. Economics Minister Walter Funk proclaimed that "Vienna had a mission to fulfill" and pitched its importance as trading hub and, eventually, Europe's largest inland port. The *VB* published a special fair edition thick with data and statistics including growing German car sales in the Southeast, the surge in electronics exports, and the show's importance as window for the newest Viennese fashions; in short another rote repetition of the city's new role in the Third Reich. It was beginning to sound shopworn, even to committed Viennese Nazis.

Perhaps that was one reason why Bürckel's opening speech was uncompromisingly ideological and paid little heed to the fair. "In economic matters we National Socialists direct our appeal to blood and heart. For us the people come first." Down the line he expressed his rigid support for his version of "German socialism," a creed no longer much in favor in the Reich, but that had served him well in Vienna.[6]

Perhaps it had served him too well and he knew it, for no matter how secure his position seemed to be, he never stopped fighting his enemies, perceived or real. With Seyss-Inquart gone he again focused on Mayor Neubacher (whom he had been trying to remove for a year).[7] It was tough going. Neubacher had powerful friends, including Göring. But under Bürckel's steady fire—Neubacher didn't get along with other party members, he wasn't a true illegal Nazi (even though Schuschnigg had jailed him), he was too arrogant, he should leave Vienna—so the mayor began to lose ground. Austrian Nazis had long resented his intelligence, wit, and sharp tongue. Early in 1940 he gave up, taking a temporary leave to become chief German economic negotiator in Bucharest. Neubacher formally remained mayor until December 1940, but his role in Vienna had been played out.

But the more Bürckel won, the more disruptive he became, waging petty feuds with subordinates and targeting other Nazi officials for dismissal or removal. As a result, both Berlin and party headquarters in Munich began to look at Vienna with growing concern, concern the Fitzhum affair heightened.[8]

Josef Fitzhum, the deputy police commissioner and an SS Oberführer, was high on Bürckel's hit list. He backed the failed nomination of Albert Frauenfeld for Gauleiter of Vienna and accused Bürckel of treating old Austrian Nazis badly. Bürckel went for the jugular: Fitzhum had taken bribes to steer choice businesses marked for Aryanization to his cronies. He was involved in the shady dealings of an SS sergeant named Alfred Swoboda, and Bürckel had sworn testimony to back the charge. In fact, Bürckel had pressured the prosecutor into forcing the imprisoned Swoboda to make a false statement. But the atmosphere that summer was rife for SS complicity in such crimes. Himmler, a strict moralist in small matters, ordered Martin Tondok, an SS colonel who worked in party courts, to Vienna to investigate the affair.

Tondok spent several months sifting the evidence. Then he met Bürckel. He had barely begun laying out his case when Bürckel unloaded: Fitzhum had made recommendations in virtually every Aryanization case. Tondok, clearly a cool customer, said he had investigated eleven charges of Fitzhum involvement and found that Fitzhum had given only three recommendations—and they were "unbiased political judgments about the applicant as a National Socialist and an SS man." Bürckel then brought up the Swoboda case. Everything Swoboda had said was a lie,

Tondok replied, and he had admitted as much with an official of the Vienna court present. Bürckel refused to budge. He would call one of his district leaders as witness to Fitzhum's guilt. Tondok agreed to meet again, bringing his pertinent documents.

After he presented his evidence the next day Bürckel pulled back. But the duel was not over. When Tondok cited three officials, including Rafelsberger who agreed that Fitzhum's recommendations were routine, Bürckel blew his top. He tongue-lashed Rafelsberger on the phone, insisting that the economic advisor had always blamed Fitzhum. Rafelsberger denied it and Bürckel, now in a towering rage, slammed down the phone. When Bürckel calmed down he suggested transferring Fitzhum out of Vienna. Tondok demurred—not if the transfer implied he had found evidence against the Oberführer. It was a position Tondock maintained against Himmler, arguing that his investigation would be blamed, leaving more bad blood in the Vienna party. Six months later, however, Bürckel prevailed. Himmler agreed to a transfer, posting the loyal but politically insensitive Fitzhum to the Waffen SS in Danzig.[9]

Again Bürckel had won a political victory, but it had damaged his standing with his superiors. Even before Tondok's investigation, the Nazi brass at the Brown House (*das Braune Haus* was the NSDAP's headquarters) in Munich considered the party's situation in Vienna serious. In December 1939 Hitler discussed the problem with Hess and Borman but postponed a decision. He wanted somebody from the Reich in the job, preferably somebody with a flair for public relations and public presentation. Clearly he was already thinking about somebody very much like Baldur von Schirach.

The advent of war made the lives of Jews that much harder. On September 6 Neubacher decreed that "until further notice" Jews could shop only in retail stores between 2 and 4 P.M. Jews were also issued new identity cards and ration books—marked with a prominent J—that entitled them to less food than Aryans. The *VB* noted that Aryans now had plenty of time to shop without coming into contact with Jews. Some, however, enjoyed standing outside stores where Jews shopped to spit and curse at them. "It was like running a gauntlet," Gertrude Putschin, ten years old at the time, remembered.[10]

A total of 1,048 Jews who were Polish citizens, or who had once held Polish citizenship, were arrested on September 9 and September 11. The majority were over sixty or under eighteen. For three weeks they were "stored" in the city's soccer stadium in the Prater, turned into a camp for the occasion, and then deported to Buchenwald.[11] Very soon ashes and urns began to arrive at homes of family members; by February 1940 two-thirds of those arrested on those two days in September were dead.

All IKG members were ordered to visit community offices between September 10 and 20 to provide names and other personal data for a future emigration index file. On September 20 the SD ordered the confiscation of all Jewish-owned radios, and on the 25th word went out that Jews could not leave their homes at night. As the labor market tightened, more Jews were used for forced labor. Since the authorities specified that Jews were not to be used in their own professions, they performed heavy manual work in Autobahn construction and stone and gravel works. They were paid near starvation wages and had to fork over a 15-percent premium on top of regular taxes.[12]

The new rent law promulgated in May allowed the authorities to relocate the city's remaining Jews into the three districts where they had been most heavily represented—II, IX, and XX. It was the first clear and conscious effort to create a true ghetto, not quite as drastic as those measures taken in Poland to segregate millions of Jews, but harsh enough.[13]

In October resettlement efforts paused briefly because the Nazis had come up with another scheme—moving Jews into empty parts of conquered Poland. Heydrich had floated the plan at a meeting in Berlin on September 21, which Eichmann attended. Initially Jews were to be shipped from Vienna, Ostrava in the "protectorate" (Bohemia and Moravia), and Katowice in southern Poland to the area around Nisko close to the new border with the Soviet Union. Eichmann, who had moved to Prague in July to duplicate the Vienna emigration center, was to be in charge. He told Löwenherz to draw up a list of 1,200 healthy men, preferably construction workers, engineers and other skilled labor, as well as ten doctors. The IKG would have to come up with RM 5,000 to cover transportation costs. Trains would carry men, tools, and building materials.

But the undertaking ran into a major obstacle—lack of rolling stock. The Wehrmacht needed the railroads for a major troop redeployment. Trains finally left Ostrava and Vienna on October 18 and 20 respectively, with more than 1,800 men aboard; a third train took off from Vienna on October 26. When the first train from Vienna reached Nisko, SS and police beat the Jews and stole their watches. Skilled workers were marched to the camp site, the rest were driven to the border.

"Abruptly the men at the head of the column swung into a soaking wet meadow," one eyewitness reported. "The rain pelted down harder and harder. Suddenly the SS began to shoot wildly and yelled 'get moving. Forward. Anybody found within five kilometers in the next hour will be shot, so will anybody trying to get back to Nisko. Get over to your red brothers.'"[14] Their reception on the other side was frosty. Most were shipped to labor camps in Siberia, and soon the Russians told the Germans not to send them any more Jews.

Back in Vienna a now-suspicious Löwenherz met with Eichmann on October 28 but was reassured that the Jews were being well treated, that the Nuremberg laws would not apply in Poland, that Jews would have an opportunity to build new lives.[15] As lies go, this one too did not last. Several weeks later the truth had filtered back to Vienna. A resolute Löwenherz told the American Joint Distribution Committee, the IKG's major foreign financier, to stop sending hard currency to Vienna until the SS stopped shipping Jews to Poland. In late December 1939 Eichmann backed down and indeed no other transports were sent to Poland until February 1941.

Now Eichmann leaned on Löwenherz to speed up emigration.[16] Instead of the 2,500 a month leaving he wanted 4,000–5,000 to go. The goal was too ambitious. The IKG didn't have the money. Some 100,000 Jews had left by May 1939; with the war now in progress, the total rose only to 117,000 by the end of the year. At the same time the Nazis went back to ghetto building at home, pushing more and more Jews into all-Jewish buildings, even though fewer Jewish homes were left for Aryanization. In 1938 Aryans had grabbed 44,000 of the estimated 70,000 Jewish apartments, leaving less and less living space for the remainder.[17] Another 5,500 apartments changed hands from March to September 1939, and some 6,000 eviction cases were pending in October. Jews targeted for eviction rarely got more than a week or two to leave. The IKG would receive lists of apartments to be vacated within two weeks. When time was up the community office had to return the lists to the Gestapo, noting where the Jew had moved—and if he had moved. Jews on the list were told that if they failed to vacate, their furniture would be put out on the street, and they would be arrested and sent to a concentration camp.[18](17)

An underground chase through the passageways of the Neue Hofburg—not unsimilar to Harry Lime's flight through Vienna's sewers in *The Third Man*—hit the papers on November 6, 1939, and made for a pleasantly chilling "divertimento" from the uncertain gloom of the phony war. "Burglar Hunt in the Neue Hofburg," one headline said; another asked "What did the Man in the Mask want?—The suspicious light in the poison chamber of the Ethnographic Museum." (The poison chamber displayed poisons from different regions of the world.)

Late one Saturday afternoon museum guards had found the door to the stairway leading to the "poison chamber" open and the light switched on. They swarmed through the museum but found nothing suspicious. When the guards made their next sweep at 4 A.M. on Sunday morning they found a man near the same stairway. One of the guards called on him to stop and when he didn't, they fired a warning shot. The man, about six feet tall, wore a dark hunting coat and cap and a black half-mask. He fled toward the stairwell and as he ran, fired at his pursuers, grazing the jackboot of one of them. The guard shot back but missed, and the man disappeared. Police arrived but found no trace of the intruder. It was a typical *VB* story—no follow up, no additional details, just the remnants of a delicious pre-Nazi caper in the night; the rough draft for a Fritz Lang film. But *that* kind of talent was long since gone; Lang had fled Germany for the United States in 1933.

With the Polish campaign out of the way, Vienna, like the rest of the Reich, settled into the limbo world of the phony war. Dances were banned and the pre-Lenten carnival Fasching was cancelled. Use of taxis was restricted for essential business and to destinations not easily reachable via public transit. Cab drivers were told to quiz would-be passengers about purpose and destination. Shavers were urged to save soap by not washing out their brushes. Housewives were told how to clean clothes using less soap—or even no soap at all. Starting on October 16 any wash sent out to the laundry required soap stamps. Department stores began offering fashion consultation every Friday afternoon. The idea?—to show women how to recut their old clothes to make them more fashionable.

Pressure increased to give more money to charities, and the pressure had already been high. Brown shirts lined major thoroughfares on November 4 and 5 to solicit donations. They shook boxes at passersby while bands played military music at the Opera, on Mariahilferstrasse, and at the

Volksoper. Smaller groups marched through the streets playing loudly. The music was supposed to loosen the purses of passersby, and the money was to go to winter war aid.

There was a trickle of good news. The price of coke or coal for home heating went down slightly. Flour rations were increased. Special allocations of food and higher rations of meat, butter, and eggs were announced in early November. More rice and legumes were made available. Fish would be plentiful, especially the traditional carp for Christmas, provided consumers hoarded their ration stamps. Fish was not as simple to cut as meat and could only be sold in bulk quantities. Ocean fish went to North Germany, but carp and other river and lake fish would feed the Viennese.[19]

Higher education was geared to the war effort. The medical curriculum was changed to speed the training of doctors so that they could move more quickly through the theoretical subjects and get to work in hospitals, assist in private practices, and get out into the countryside. Other academic disciplines like engineering and the natural sciences—needed for the war effort—were encouraged with scholarships for talented children of peasants and workers.[20]

Cultural policy during Bürckel's reign was a stepchild to which he paid lip service, except when it became a matter of political power as it did in his struggle with Seyss-Inquart. Bürckel did not go to the Opera or the Burg for relaxation, nor was he awed by cultural institutions the way Hitler and Goebbels often were. Instead he saw these entertainments not only as vents through which the people could work off—and then forget —their political and economic frustrations, but also as instruments of power, to be used when they worked and to be fixed when they didn't. He clearly felt that the Opera, the city's crown jewel, needed help, and in the summer of 1939 settled on Heinrich Strohm, boss of the Hamburg opera and widely seen as a coming star, as the new Vienna chief. It took months to arrange the appointment, since Hitler reserved the right to approve the choice, but in December 1939, the *VB* announced that the new director would take over in April 1940. Strohm did not arrive until September 1940, however, and the delay would prove pivotal to the Opera's future. Goebbels's propaganda machine was sympathetic to the artists it liked. They were pampered and cosseted and kept in a kind of playpen with their activities controlled by layers and layers of bureaucracy that in their breadth and scope were truly mind-boggling.[21] The ministry of propaganda and public enlightenment, the ministry of the interior, and the chief cultural office of the NSDAP made up the top layer of control. Propaganda's section IV covered theater and supervised the activities of the Reich's propaganda office for theater. Goebbels retained personal control through his chairmanship of the Reich's chamber of culture, an umbrella organization to which chambers covering all the arts including theater had to report. The theater chamber, in turn, put tentacles down the bureaucratic ladder into local government at the Gau level. There the Gauleiter had input through the mayor's office and his cultural advisor. In short, levers of influence were everywhere and they were used often, most often with ideological intent.

Take the play *An Austrian Tragedy*, a drama about Field Marshall Ludwig August von Benedek, who lost the decisive battle of Königsgrätz to the Prussians but made a deathbed appeal to the emperor Franz Josef to make peace with his German enemy: "everything that is immortal in Austria's name is written on the pages of German history. Austria must come home.... [It] is German and will so remain." [22]

It would seem to be solid Nazi rhetoric, but the Austrian Nazis bitterly opposed staging the play at the Burgtheater. Burgtheater director Lothar Müthel, a German, put it on anyway, even if he did use a different title— *Benedek* instead of *An Austrian Tragedy*. But the local Nazis had a point. They feared any appearance of the House of Hapsburg on a stage.

A performance of the Austrian classic *König Ottokars Glück und Ende* (King Ottokar's Rise and Fall) led to sustained applause after speeches extolling Austria's special and unique virtues. The SD was worried enough to report the incident to Berlin, and to note that men and women of a "reactionary Austrian persuasion" were talking up the production among their friends.

Periodically the Nazis celebrated their cultural achievements in Vienna, now, as the VB headlined it on January 5, 1940, "A City Without Jews. Vienna—now more than ever a city of culture—Record audiences for cinemas, theaters and concerts." The number of visitors to cultural sites had seen an enormous increase in the first half of the 1939–40 winter season, such as this "dying fairy tale city" had not witnessed in many years, and thus giving the lie to a book written in the 1920s—Hugo Bettauer's *City Without Jews*.[23]

In the novel Jews are expelled from Austria and as a result the economy collapses, culture is in the toilet, and Vienna becomes a provincial village. Typical wishful Jewish thinking, the *VB* opined. Now Vienna was almost free of Jews, both as actors and consumers of culture, and culture was booming. Operas and concerts were sold out with lines stretching around the block. KdF had made good music available to workers at cheap prices. Movie audiences had doubled over the past year, and the biopic *Robert Koch* had drawn 100,000 during its six-week run. What the *VB* did not say was that the quality of cultural offerings had declined in order to reach a lower common denominator than that when Jews still made up a third of the audience, and it only hinted at the price factor—the heavy Goebbels subsidies that made cultural entertainment more affordable.

On March 3, 1940, Bürckel moved, belatedly, to establish his credentials as a leader in the cultural arena with a major administrative restructuring that put every institution—museums, theaters, orchestras, the Opera, the film industry, the art, acting, and music academies—under Gau control with Bürckel in overall charge of a new office of cultural affairs headed by a "Generalreferent" or general secretary.[24] In a speech that mixed pragmatic reforms with homage to Vienna's cultural past and glorious future under National Socialism, Bürckel promised that the new office would cut red tape, eliminate duplication, and force cultural institutions to cooperate and not compete, as museums did, in bidding for the same piece of art. The directors of theaters, museums, and the rest would effectively work for the general secretary as department heads. Actors, musicians, directors, and other artists would be recruited to bolster the teaching staffs at the various academies.

Bürckel had already persuaded Wilhelm Furtwängler to take the helm of the Vienna Philharmonic (a post he had held before and now would keep until the end of the war). He would beef up the faculty of the art academy, which had been sadly depleted (both Jews and Aryan "degenerates" having been removed days after the Anschluss) and had to be upgraded. It had, after all, played a certain role in the Führer's life, Bürckel said without mentioning what it was—the academy had twice refused to accept Hitler as a student. Blueprints for a major expansion of the Burgtheater had been readied at the Führer's personal request. More room would have to be found for the Albertina Museum of Graphic

Arts collection of drawings and for the treasures stored in the museum of natural history.

Bürckel's mandate as commissioner for the reunification of Austria with the German Reich finally expired on April 1, 1940, an occasion his top aide, Karl Barth, used for an expansive report on Bürckel's two-year stewardship.[25] Conditions had changed so much that a reunification commission was no longer needed, Barth wrote, indeed reunification had become so much a fact that the past had been extirpated from memory and consciousness, "as if it had never existed." Bürckel had destroyed the artificial construct that was Austria and removed its debris in every arena: in politics he provided firm leadership, in economics he gutted "the network of Jewish capitalism," and in government he dissolved the Ostmark as an administrative unit and thus allowed the individual Gaue to develop their own relationships with the Reich's central authority. Proclamation of the Ostmark laws had crowned that achievement and made Bürckel Gauleiter and Reichsstatthalter, uniting the chief offices of party and government in one set of hands.

But in fact Bürckel's anointment as Reichsstatthalter had been touch and go. Hitler had been slow to give Ostmark Gauleiters the additional title as the 1939 law stipulated. True, Bürckel had exercised the office without the title, but in the spring of 1940, despite all his brave efforts in spheres still new to him, such as culture, his power began to slip away. Hitler was in a quandary. Bürckel had been a loyal servant and had carried out the Führer's wishes with exemplary precision and with whatever ruthlessness was required. But Hitler also knew that something had to be done about Bürckel's divide-and-conquer rule of the party, and that it would be more difficult once he became Reichsstatthalter.

He went so far as to authorize a press release in March naming every Ostmark Gauleiter except Bürckel to the Statthalter post (Carinthia was also an exception since Hitler had not yet named anyone to succeed the late Hubert Klausner). The announcement was pulled at the last minute with the Führer finally deciding to giving Bürckel the post. The PR implications worried him—the Gauleiter would stand exposed and alone if he were singled out for exclusion, and that could complicate the assimilation process, which despite Barth's claims, had never been fully implemented.[26] The newspapers carried Hitler's decision on April 13, 1940, and they paid Bürckel tribute, much along the lines Barth had laid out for them—the Reichsgaue had developed in such a forceful manner that coordination from Vienna was no longer necessary. Days later Barth took his leave to return to the Saarpfalz. His replacement was Philipp Wilhelm Jung, another Pfälzer. While Neubacher was in Bucharest, Jung would take over his duties as mayor and was formally appointed RP in May.

War muted the city's celebrations, casting a somber shadow on New Year's Eve 1939. Bars, cafés, and restaurants closed early and began to fill up much sooner than usual as people fled from the now-darkened streets—blackouts had been reimposed in November—into the warm and well-lighted places of amusement. Cabarets, theaters, cinemas, and restaurants had long been booked solid—proof, the VB said, that the German people and with them the Viennese would not allow the warmongers to get them down. But down they clearly were, as the VB admitted that festivities were more somber than they had been in the past. At the stroke of midnight all public places fell dark for a moment and people kissed each other as tradition demanded. At 1 A.M. everybody closed up, and people met on the streets where moonlight brightened the darkness.

Anschluss festivities, too, were limited to speeches and pronouncements with much less of the pomp and circumstance of a year ago, nor was Hitler's birthday draped in the splendor of previous anniversaries. The first of May was honored in factories, department stores, and shops. Bürckel, still showing his red flag, had bought up all the seats in Vienna's theaters and distributed the tickets to workers for free. The fare was correspondingly lightweight—Lehar, Johann Strauss, and a string of shallow comedies.[27]

On April 19, 1940, the VB reported the death of eighty-seven-year-old Katharina Schratt two days earlier, who had died in her apartment at Kärntnerring 1. "Her close relationship to the Emperor Franz Josef was generally known," the VB commented dryly. And with her another part of the old Austria died. Schratt was an actress at the Burg as the nineteenth century wound down and the emperor's "good friend," a relationship the Empress Sissy encouraged. To this day the Viennese debate whether "the Schratt" had carnal knowledge of the emperor, but all are agreed she provided the lonely Franz Josef some warmth and companionship. The Nazis, clearly, had not thought it worthwhile to bother the old woman about her relationship to the long distant past.

In 1940 Ostmark's economy gave rise to some concern.[28] Liquidity was high, and the money supply was growing too quickly since funds were not flowing into savings. In part, Rafelsberger wrote in his regular report to Bürckel, the Viennese had misunderstood a speech that economics minister Funk had given in Salzburg stressing the primacy of savings for the war effort. Many saw his remarks as a precursor to forced savings and, as a result, the population spent discretionary income on hoarding goods and buying unrationed items like alcohol. Peasants bought typewriters, city-dwellers "bought anything that had permanent value." Far less money would rush into these "dark channels," Rafelsberger wrote, if people knew just how the war would be financed.

Construction was in the doldrums with only very few wartime projects underway in Vienna. Only large companies had the needed equipment, thus freezing out small and midsize firms. Some were working at only 10 to 20 percent of capacity. The metal-working industry suffered both from material shortages and a ban on use of certain metals. Ceramics, chemicals, paper, glass, and lumber businesses all complained about material and fuel shortages and the resultant cutbacks in output. Taxes were a problem, thanks to bureaucratic snafus by the Vienna city government. Some 20 percent of the tax forms business needed to calculate employee taxes for 1940 had been printed with major errors and needed to be replaced, costing employers time, energy, and effort. Bureaucrats had complained they couldn't meet the demand for forms and had to be browbeaten into producing them by the end of January, a good two months late.

Price-wage policies were not as stable in practice as Rafelsberger had claimed they were. He had barred both higher and lower prices on the grounds that the latter would increase popular buying power while the former would increase inflationary pressures. Inevitably shortages were leading to higher prices, a trend encouraged by party and government officials who thought prices played only a subordinate role in wartime economic life. As a result, the number of reported price violations had declined sharply, even in areas where such violations were on the increase and had in the past been more fully reported. The reporting decline was most notable in the bar and restaurant business although price violations there were clearly higher than elsewhere. At the Dorotheum, the city-owned auction house, antique furniture, sold under open market conditions, was fetching prices far higher than the auctioneers' estimates.

In an April 24, 1940, report the economic advisor noted that popular perception of steep price increases since the Anschluss had more merit than government indices of stable price development would suggest. For one thing, he argued, the indices were often flawed and could not express quality differences and indirect higher prices, and for another, once the index was broken down into its component parts substantial price differentials emerged. Prices in Vienna for food, electricity, heating, and various other consumer goods including textiles were from 5 to 16 percent higher than in Berlin. Moreover, higher prices were not offset by higher wages since pay scales had been curbed more rigorously. In a May 15 report Rafelsberger conceded that new producer prices for vegetables were higher than they had been, a factor of the war, which complicated foreign imports.[29] A sugar industry request to hike lump sugar prices had been denied, and the government foresaw a uniform reduction of beer prices across the Reich: after May 19, 1940, brewers could make only 6-percent beer.

The labor market provided a much brighter picture. January unemployment in Vienna had fallen to 36,000 with a third of the jobless unskilled day labor. By mid-May Vienna registered only 15,000 jobless of whom 2,000 were "fully functioning" and ready to work. Over two years— meaning from two months after the Anschluss—unemployment had dropped from 220,000 to the current low, 7 percent of the May 1938 total. Some 4,000 of the unemployed were Jews, and the non-Jewish 11,000 were the dregs of any large city.

In an earlier report, dated March 11, 1940, Rafelsberger had discussed the situation of Vienna's Jews. Emigration was much slower than Eichmann had hoped for in the fall. The IKG had managed the exit of only 586 Jews in February with the bulk, 450, going to the United States. Still, it was about the same as January—608—and Rafelsberger hoped that the March total would pass 1,500 now that the American Joint Distribution Committee had pledged an extra $100,000 in hard currency on top of the regular monthly stipend it sent the IKG. American relatives had also sent almost $30,000 to help cover boat tickets and other travel expenses for emigrating Jews.

Rafelsberger observed that Jews were still getting away with much more than they deserved or that the laws allowed. Jews had been seen buying in stores at all hours of the day, not just in the times set aside for them.

Store personnel sometimes gave Jews preferential treatment, explaining that, after all, Jews were people too. Rafelsberger's examples of this preferential treatment included a dairy in the twelfth district, a coal wholesaler in Liesing, and the Heller candy store on Kärntnerstrasse where a Jewess was able to buy a kilogram of biscuits whereas other customers could purchase them only in 100-gram increments. In general, he continued, regulations covering sales to Jews were honored more in the breach, and Jews had been buying unrationed items in great quantities. Finally, he noted that Vienna still had a large number of Jewish families with cleaning ladies.

Rafelsberger's sober assessment of Vienna through the spring of 1940 provided a realistic background for the growing discontent of the population that was reflected in an SD report issued six months later: "The economic concerns in Vienna are the same as they have always been. The depressing lack of fruit, the small quantity of favorite vegetables, price hikes in so many areas, and the general increase in the cost of living are the factors contributing to the generally depressed mood in the city. These are the circumstances that make so many 'Volksgenossen' [literally "people's comrades," a term used to refer to anybody who was not a party member] look with such concern at the coming second winter of war, especially with wood and coal so tight."[30]

More overt opposition to the Nazi regime had picked up with the beginning of the war. The three Catholic groups had made contact and begun discussing the possibility of common action. The Communists were the best organized, as they had been from the beginning, but they were also the most exposed since the Gestapo paid them the most attention. The church continued under pressure and confined itself largely to pastoral duties, but Innitzer did support one Jesuit's efforts to help non-Aryan Catholics, meaning people who had Jewish grandparents but who had converted.[31] These non-Aryan Catholics were in no man's land. The IKG did not help them. Their religion did not protect them from the Nuremberg laws, and even many Catholics thought Jewish conversions were more pragmatic than spiritual. Georg Bichlmair had worked with converts before the Anschluss, and in May he asked Innitzer to act as patron and financier for an organization that would help them cope with the new realities. It was risky business since the operation was at best semilegal. The so-called "Action Bichlmair" worked with the Quakers and the Gildemeester-Aktion people in helping non-Aryan Catholics to survive and to leave the Reich. (Some say that the Gildemeester-Aktion used monies from the Jews to finance non-Aryans.) Money was scarce—RM 3,000 a month was all Innitzer could scrape up for starters. The war cut into emigration and forced Bichlmair to take larger risks—even placing so-called U-boats—Jews who hid out with Aryans and who managed to disappear below the surface of daily life— in private houses. The Gestapo had struck on November 9, 1938—on Kristallnacht, arrested the Jesuit, and exiled him to Upper Silesia. The staff was left to work alone until June 1940, when Innitzer found another Jesuit, Ludger Born, to run the "Archbishop's Relief Agency for non-Aryan Catholics." Born was shrewd and cautious, and over time won near legal status, meeting regularly with Gestapo officials. Innitzer begged and borrowed the needed money, now RM 7,000 a month, from the Vatican and private sources. It helped as many as fifty non-Aryan Catholics a day escape until emigration was halted. Later, packages were sent to those in concentration camps.

The Communists, though small in number—they were never a factor in Austrian politics on their own—remained busy, with the KPÖ, or Communist Party of Austria, stung into a new activism by the German-Soviet pact. More print propaganda was needed to explain the Moscow line about the war—a fight between capitalist-imperialist blocks and one for which Paris and London were more responsible than Berlin. Communist publications, however, also carried other news from abroad, which was in short supply given the ban on foreign radio broadcasts. The Gestapo, fearful that the Communists had built up a second leadership network, stepped up surveillance and struck in December 1939, arresting 119 suspects. One leader managed to evade capture until March 1940, but once again the Nazis had succeeded in crippling Communist activities, cutting propaganda efforts to a sputter. The Communists, however, were a tough bunch who knew how to bounce back. By the time Bürckel left Vienna, the KPÖ had a third generation of leadership in place.[32]

When war broke out the three Catholic groups had spent a year adding recruits and trying to figure out agendas and missions.[33] Roman Scholz was on a second trip to England in August to expand the sources he had developed two years ago, and with war drawing closer he hurried home. He began to realize that as important as conversation, debate, and other intellectual endeavors were, they were not enough. Over two months he wrote seven reports to his British contacts in English, covering political and religious conditions in Austria. He sent emissaries to Czechoslovakia to develop ties with the Czech Resistance and to Budapest for talks at the French legation. Both undertakings seemed promising. The French even gave Scholz's movement a code name that members could use when talking to French diplomats. His group was becoming tightly organized into small individual cells with only three members and in groups of one hundred. As more and more of his membership was called up for military duty, he developed stamp-size identity cards that could be shown to the Allies and would allow the Austrians to join up and fight Hitler.

Most importantly, Scholz had made contact with the other two freedom groups, Dr. Karl Lederer's "Austrian Freedom Movement" and Dr. Jakob Kastelic's "Greater Austrian Freedom Movement." Lederer had moved beyond talk. He published fliers titled "What you won't read in the *VB*," which contained up-to-the-minute information on what was really going on in Austria and that found a wide readership. Kastelic tended to dream about a postwar Danube Federation including Bavaria, and perhaps the Habsburgs back on the throne.

Conversations among the three moved ahead slowly with all of them probing and talking, not ready to engage into hands-on action Communist style. When they were finally willing to do something concrete it was too late—they were betrayed to the Gestapo. The Judas of this story was in many ways a typical figure for the time and the place.

Otto Hartmann was a minor actor at the Burg who had joined various military formations of the Fatherland Front. On March 13, 1938, he donned an SA uniform and was part of an honor guard outside the Brown House Am Hof, claiming to have been an illegal Nazi who had denounced his Fatherland Front fellows to the Gestapo. Fred Hennings, the Burg's star Nazi, yelled that his behavior was "common betrayal," but Hartman just shrugged his shoulders and said, "Yeah, that's what it is." Hennings, Bettac, and Volters then went to Gestapo headquarters on Morzinplatz demanding to know more about their colleague's activities. But the Gestapo man was not forthcoming, saying that if they had given Hartmann the lead in one of Schiller's plays "he wouldn't have come up with such ideas (such as betraying his erstwhile friends)." Efforts to dismiss

Hartmann from the Burg failed. Hennings was cited to a brown-shirt colonel and chided for daring to call so committed a National Socialist "politically unreliable."[34] Clearly, Hartmann had friends in high places. He also had no morals.

He told Fritz Lehmann, a Burgtheater colleague, that he had joined the Nazis only in order to act against them. Lehmann, a member of Scholz's group, therefore took Hartmann to meet the cleric, and by the end of 1939 Hartmann was ensconced in the Austrian Freedom Movement as one of its most belligerent and important members.

He demanded action: he wanted to destroy telephone cells, pour acid in mail boxes, blow up the gas works, Gestapo headquarters, and a munitions depot. His truculence impressed the ascetic Augustinian Scholz, theologian and poet. But still he took his time melding the three Resistance groups into one large organization well-connected enough to have some impact. In March 1940 the three groups agreed to coordinate activities more closely but to remain separate for the time being. In July just before they were to take the final step, the Gestapo struck. Scholz was arrested on July 22, 1940, and within a few weeks 240 members of the Resistance groups, including Lederer and Kastelic, were also jailed. Their Calvary lasted for three-and-a-half years. A people's court finally sentenced the leaders to death on February 23, 1944; on May 10 some twenty Austrian patriots were beheaded, the guillotine slicing off a head every four minutes. "For Christ and Austria," Scholz said as he mounted the scaffold. Otto Hartmann was paid RM 30,000. He continued to work under cover for the Gestapo for the rest of the war, mostly in actions against Communists. The Burg was incensed enough for director Lothar Müthel to yell "that swine Hartmann isn't coming into my theater" and making the ban stick despite Nazi pressure. (Hartmann was tried for high treason in 1947, sentenced to life imprisonment, and pardoned twelve years later, allegedly for "ill health.")[35]

Resistance also took other forms, especially among the Catholic young who stuck together in parish houses and private homes. They were unorganized, loose, and loped together through life like packs of young dogs, and as such they had survived the Nazi crackdown on the church and its activities that followed the rosary demonstration at St. Stephen's in October 1938. Two years later a concert by the Don Cossack chorus at the Konzerthaus provided the venue for another such demonstration. Russian songs were a staple of Catholic campfires and since they were not forbidden could be sung freely. When Fritz Molden, Felix Fuchs, and some of their friends heard about the concert, they decided to go and found the place jammed with teenagers like themselves, mostly fifteen to seventeen years old. The young crowd began to sing with the Cossacks and demand more of their favorites; their frenetic applause drew six encores. Meanwhile, a Hitler Youth had slipped out to call the Gestapo to report an anti-Nazi riot taking place. And when the leather coats—the unmistakable Gestapo garb—arrived, some of the Catholic youth were singing the banned songs of their movement. The "Green Henrys," as the Vienna Police's prison vans were called, waited outside to take hundreds of youths to the "Liesl," the police prison on Rossauer-lände. The youngsters kept singing in the vans to the amusement of the Viennese cops, who said no one had sung in them since illegal Hitler Youth had in 1937. The police were still tolerant when the hundreds of prisoners arrived. Fuchs was jammed into an eight-man cell with seventeen others. But when they continued to sing police threatened to close the window "and then you guys can choke to death." One by one Fuchs's cell mates were taken to Gestapo headquarters on Morzin Platz. Fuchs was the last one out, and when he sat across from the Gestapo agent he faced a three-inch-thick dossier that included his songbooks, photos of Catholic processions in which he had taken part, letters, books, and other materials confiscated from his home. "He only wanted to know one thing: did we have lists of members. Well thank God we didn't. We weren't organized. We were just friends who hung out and didn't like the Nazis."[36] A month after his arrest Fuchs was let go; Molden had gotten out earlier. The imprisoned were not beaten or mistreated, not yet, but it was suggested that seventeen-year-old Felix Fuchs volunteer early for Wehrmacht service. The incident had elements of a lark but it hardened the bonds of resistance among the young.

As the Nazis swept across Norway, the Low Countries, and France, and it seemed as if England too must fall, Hitler began to ponder domestic concerns. Something had to be done about Vienna. At the end of June 1940 he ordered Hitler Youth leader Baldur von Schirach, then a lieutenant in the Wehrmacht, to his headquarters in the Black Forest. Schirach had volunteered for the army, figuring that at thirty-three he was too old to continue as HJ boss. Hitler met him with open arms. "Now that you've had your wish, [to join the army] I need you for something else.

You're going to Vienna as Reichsstatthalter. The situation in Vienna is completely out of hand. Gauleiter Bürckel did not understand how to win the Viennese for the Reich. I can't afford to have a mutinous large city at the southeast corner of the Reich. Somebody with psychological tact must go to Vienna and I think you're the right man for the job. In Vienna you need sensitivity and tact for questions of cultural policy, and that's why I thought of you." He would be in complete charge, Hitler added, and nobody, not even Goebbels "will be allowed to contradict you."[37] And Hitler kept Schirach as Reichsleiter in charge of youth affairs—including supervision of the Hitler Youth—with an office in the chancellery in Berlin.

Schirach's appointment was announced on August 2, 1940, and a week later he had exchanged his gray uniform for a gray flannel suit and jumped into a black two-seater Mercedes racing car. He and a friend, he told his wife, would drive to Vienna with a stop at the monastery in Melk to look at the library. "I'll call you from the Cobenzel on Friday night," he said and roared off—as befits a young man in a hurry.[38]

CHAPTER 8

Vienna's Second Chance

Baldur von Schirach:
August 10, 1940–June 24, 1943

Baldur von Schirach's inauguration as Gauleiter and Reichs-statthalter of Vienna took place on Saturday evening August 10 in the usual venue for such events—the Konzerthaus—and with the usual pomp and circumstance of flags, eagles, military music, and the serried ranks of the formations—SS, SA, the Wehrmacht, and, in Schirach's honor, columns of Hitler Youth flanking the entrance. The Vienna Philharmonic struck up Beethoven's *Coriolanus Overture*, but the music was quickly drowned in applause for Rudolf Hess, the Führer's deputy, who brought the Führer's greetings and his expressions of confidence in both men.[1]

In his farewell remarks Bürckel, the tough, gruff street fighter with, for once, a jacket over his brown shirt, dripped treacly sentiment: Vienna had become his second home. Nobody who had ever felt the spell of this city could ever come free of it. Whenever the white lilacs bloom in Sievering he would return to his second home (a remark that led to bitter Viennese jokes about uprooting all the white lilacs), and he was overjoyed that Vienna had made him an honorary citizen "so that I may belong to you in all the futures to come."

Schirach's speech, in contrast, was proof that Hitler knew what he was doing when he sent him to Vienna. His language reflected sentiment without sentimentality, expressed genuine pleasure at his new assignment without undue flattery of his listeners, and exhibited a shrewd assessment of what they wanted to hear. "I don't want to make a pro-grammatic speech. I don't hold much for them. I won't make you any promises. I want to work for you. Here I see my new life's work." But he also told the assembled party leaders that he expected them to obey his orders, do their duty, and refrain from intrigue and personal attack (al-though he phrased that thought more diplomatically).

With Bürckel gone, Schirach wasted no time putting his mark on his new fiefdom. In the first few weeks and months of his rule he was every-where. One speech followed another as he made personal appearances at every institution of the city—from backstage at the Opera to the work halls of factories.[2] He spoke to blind war veterans, promising to inte-grate them into the political process. He told 785 retired streetcar con-ductors how much he appreciated the tireless efforts of faithful city workers like themselves. He received a delegation of Spanish journalists, lectured them on their new responsibilities in the new Europe, and asked them to bring his greetings to Spanish youth. He reminded local party leaders that the NSDAP was one big family, gave guidelines to leaders of the BDM (the Bund deutscher Mädchen was the female equivalent of the Hitler Youth) in his function as Reichsleiter for German Youth—"every young woman carries within her the dignity of the Reich,"—and told a meeting of private enterprise managers that he was "a worker in the reconstruction of Vienna." He attended every major first night at the Burg and the Opera and the Philharmonic when star conductors like Wilhelm Furtwängler or Hans Knappertsbusch stood on the podium. No dignitary, foreign or domestic, passed through the city without Schirach's dragging him—or her—to a cultural event. Thus he took Emmi Göring to *Maria Stuart* at the Burg and weeks later the Reichs-marshall himself to the *Rosenkavalier* at the Opera.

On August 15 Schirach moved his personal office from the old Aus-trian parliament, which he now dubbed the "Gauhaus," to the Ballhausplatz, seat of Austrian power since Metternich's day, and he had the prince's own desk dug out of a museum and put in the spacious hall where the Con-gress of Vienna had met. The gesture had a clear meaning—Schirach would be a link to a glorious past, not its destroyer as Bürckel had been, and would lead that past into an equally glorious future.[3]

The day before he moved he had penned a three-page memo to Rafelsberger about Vienna's role in the Reich's Southeast Europe policy. Schirach wanted to know just how Vienna could play a major part in development of the Reich's trade with the Balkans, specifically whether the transport infrastructure needed expansion, what capital and warehousing was available, and how many companies had the needed regional know-how. Clearly, Schirach was anxious to play a foreign policy card from his new springboard on the Danube.[4]

Days later he won a chance to shine in the spotlight of Axis geopolitical activity. On August 28 Hitler met the Italian foreign minister, Count Galeazzo Ciano, in his mountain lair to discuss growing Hungarian-Romanian territorial differences over Transylvania that threatened to erupt into armed conflict, and thus interfere with regular Romanian oil deliveries to the Reich's refineries. Italy and Germany would have to referee the dispute and settle it—within forty-eight hours, the Führer decreed. Vienna was selected as site of the conference and Schirach given two days to make all the arrangements; in other words, prepare the show-business framework—fleets of limousines, flowers, red carpets, the formations and marching bands— for a settlement the Axis would dictate, largely the return of territory to Hungary the Allies had awarded to Romania in 1919. Schirach was good at pomp and circumstance and stole one of Ribbentrop's protocol officers to help, a move that infuriated the thin-skinned diplomat and worsened the already shaky relationship between them.[5]

Not that Schirach had much policy input in what was at best a staged event, but it allowed him to play host and to appear to the Viennese as a man of much more substance than Bürckel had been, an appearance the *VB* went out of its way to promote: The meeting was another demonstration of the important role Vienna had to play in the Third Reich. Editorials talked grandly about the Axis' design for peace and mutually beneficial trade in Southeast Europe and about the equality of all the partners to the discussions. In truth, there was not much equality. The Romanians were ordered to give up large parts of Transylvania and to remove their troops from the region within fourteen days. Headlines spoke of "permanent security and peace in Southeast Europe."[6]

Schirach got another chance to trumpet his Balkan policies during preparations for the opening of the Vienna international trade fair in the fall of 1940.[7] The preparations had been thorough and reflected the greater sophistication of Schirach's PR apparatus, based, as it was, on his nationwide Hitler Youth network. Five Italian cabinet ministers had been invited to attend, as well as the trade, economic, and finance ministers from a dozen countries including Hungary, Yugoslavia, and Bulgaria. Goebbels had agreed to broadcast opening ceremonies. Newsreel cameras were set up to record the event. Top Nazi dignitaries including economics minister Walther Funk, postal minister Wilhelm Ohnesorge, and labor front leader Robert Ley would attend and speak. Funk's speechwriter in Berlin had been massaged to prepare a draft praising Vienna's role in Southeast policy making, and the minister's chief of staff agreed that SOEG (the Southeast Europe society) was a "soap bubble" without much content, thus providing Schirach with another outlet for his policy-making intent.[8] Accordingly, Funk's speech praised Vienna's new role in the Southeast but without pushing the Hamburg analogy or limiting the city to that of a trading post. Instead, Funk paid more attention to Vienna's historic role as hub for all East–West exchanges—intellectual, cultural, political, and economic, and not just trade—and how the NS state was leading the city to new heights in all of them. And he brought in one other element to which the German victories of recent months had given new relevance—the idea of a new Europe under Axis hegemony.

It was a point Schirach picked up on quickly. Vienna was more, much more, than just an East–West trading post but was the depository of the entire southeast tradition of "the first Reich" (that of Charlemagne and the Holy Roman Empire of the German nation) and it is "certain that the still young Southeast Tradition of the Third Reich will be bound closely to the name and strength of this city." The trade fair itself bore witness to Vienna's new position that went far beyond the Southeast and put it among the front ranks of global cities—a claim no Nazi had yet made and that had to soothe the hearts of many Viennese who bitterly resented the gradual decline of their once proud and vibrant city.[9]

Clearly Schirach had bolder things in mind than trade—providing substance to the "soap bubble" of SOEG, for example, by moving various industrial and economic groupings that handled Balkan affairs from Berlin and other centers to Vienna. When labor minister Franz Seldte's plans for opening a new international labor office in Germany became public, Schirach pushed hard for placing the new institution in Vienna. When a foreign office job opened up in his Gau, Schirach fired off a letter to Ribbentrop suggesting that it be given to Schirach's aide Günther Kaufmann. In addition, he proposed that Ribbentrop agree to have an umbrella organization for all southeast activities located in Vienna.

He was tireless in making contacts with any foreigner who visited or was stationed in Vienna. He attended a reception for the departing Bulgarian consul, received a delegation of Japanese doctors, opened a Japanese railroad exhibit, greeted foreign students who had completed a summer course of study, received a group of Romanian youth leaders, greeted a delegation of seventeen Norwegian architects, and gave receptions for the Hungarian minister of culture at the Ballhausplatz and for members of the Hungarian-German society at the Hotel Bristol. And he was often on the road. A week after the Vienna fair he was in Bratislava to visit the Slovak trade show. He traveled to Flanders for a speech and to Amsterdam to lend support to a Vienna cultural week, was often in Berlin on youth matters, and flew to Bucharest as the Reich's representative at a state funeral.

His foreign policy ambitions got another boost when Hungary opted to join the three-power Axis pact (concluded in Berlin on September 27, 1940), and Hitler decided to hold the signing ceremonies at the Belvedere Palace in Vienna on November 20.[10] It was an occasion to trumpet once more the Nazi concept of the "new Europe," a concept for which Schirach was an articulate proponent, with Vienna as a significant centerpiece. The *Neues Wiener Tagblatt* put his thoughts well in an editorial that credited the NS and the fascist revolutions with setting in motion "the great European revolutionary process," which was leading to an "intercontinental new order." Vienna had seen a significant number of the changes, beginning with the Vienna arbitration agreement in September 1938. "Authoritarian diplomacy" would convert the triumph of "free and peaceful peoples" into stable policy. Never, the *NWT* added somewhat incoherently, has war been so directly a function of peace as this war against England.[11]

Of course, foreign policy was for Schirach, as it is for most statesmen, the most attractive aspect of power, but it was not one that fell naturally into his lap. He strove hard to carve a role for himself and correspondingly paid less attention to the mundane chores of his office—holding the wage-price line, the battle against the black market in meat and other rationed items, the perennial housing crisis, general economic conditions, and perhaps the toughest nut of all—the 60,000 Jews who had remained in Vienna.

The black market and wage-price guideline violations continued unabated in 1940 even though German victories had opened huge food reserves. Meat was a sought-after black market item, and meat whole-salers caught with illegal veal, beef, and pork, which they sold outside the regulated distribution channels, were heavily punished—one who sold 7,000 kilograms (15,432 pounds) got seven years in jail and RM 5,000 in fines.[12] And hardly a day went by when the media did not cover trials of merchants who sold food and textiles into the black market. Wage-price and black market issues would bedevil Schirach's nearly five-year rule in Vienna, as it had Bürckel's tenure. He tried to tackle these issues in a speech he made in December in which he promised "a hard hand" for all those who engaged in black market and other illegal activities. At the same time he acknowledged that he had not been able to master wage-price problems. He blamed the usual suspects—much lower productivity than in the Altreich, antiquated machinery, not enough years since the Anschluss to tackle economic issues.[13]

Holding the wage-price line was not a promise Schirach could keep, anymore than the perennial Nazi pledge to do something about housing. He and labor minister Seldte visited some of the barracks and shanty-towns on the far side of the Danube, but all they could do was preach patience and promise that things would soon be different. Seldte ran housing but could do little to help. City housing czar Leopold Tavs blamed the socialists—in the 1920s they had built only 65,000 apartments when 240,000 were needed. But he had no solutions beyond juggling available housing and limiting landlord rights to turn down would-be tenants.[14] Deputy Gauleiter Scharitzer suggested—one more time—kicking out all the Jews. On September 24, 1940, he sent out a circular demanding the immediate resettlement of Jews to free up more apartments. Not many Jewish flats were left, however, and Jews had to live somewhere, even if four and five people were jammed into one room with only rudimentary cooking and sanitation facilities.

Expulsion of the remaining Jews from Vienna had been one of the major mandates Hitler had given Schirach. Little had been done in the ten months since Eichmann had shelved his efforts to resettle Jews in Poland, but Schirach was determined to give the Polish option another try. On October 2, 1940, he proposed it during a Berlin luncheon with Hitler, Bormann, Hans Frank, the governor general of German-occupied Poland, and Erich Koch, the Gauleiter of East Prussia.[15] Koch also wanted to unload his Jews. Frank protested vehemently. He couldn't take any

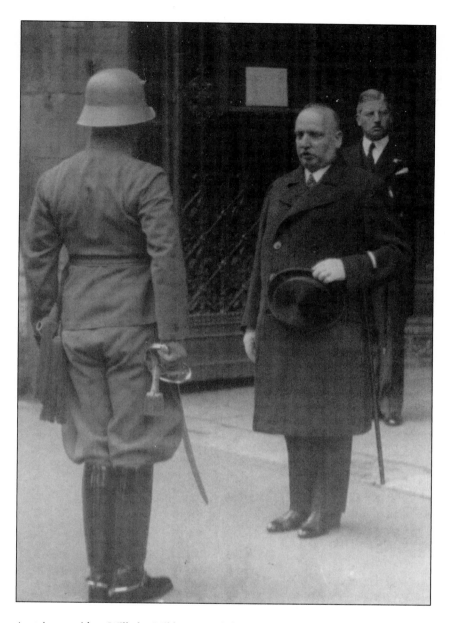

Austrian president Wilhelm Miklas around the time of the Anschluss. Chancellor
Kurt von Schuschnigg stands behind him. An Austrian officer stands at attention.
Verein für Geschichte der Arbeiterbewegung (VGA). 1626068.

Seyss-Inquart and his cabinet on the balcony of the Ballhausplatz chancellery at 12:30 A.M. on March 12, 1938. *Bildarchiv der österreichischen Nationalbibliothek. 1560807.*

Facing page, top

Chancellor Kurt von Schuschnigg arrives at the Innsbruck railroad station on March 9, 1938, prior to making his speech announcing a plebiscite on March 13, on the question of Austrian independence. *Documentationsarchiv des österreichischen Widerstandes.*

Facing page, bottom

Seyss Inquart's two-day cabinet. The chancellor is fifth from the left. Glaise-Horstenau, the vice-chancellor, is third from right. *Verein für Geschichte der Arbeiterbewegung (VGA). 1625227.*

Right

Chancellor Engelbert Dollfuss. The Nazis murdered him on July 25, 1934. *Documentationsarchiv des österreichischen Widerstandes.*

Below

The masses gathered on the Heldenplatz on March 15, 1938, for Hitler's Anschluss speech. The picture is taken from the Hofburg balcony where Hitler spoke. Equestrian statue is of Prince Eugene of Savoy, an 18th century Austrian general. *Österreichische Gesellschaft für Zeitgeschichte, Wien-Bildarchiv. 1072857.*

A young Jew is forced to write "Jew" on the wall of his father's store right after the Anschluss. *Österreichische Gesellschaft für Zeitgeschichte, Wien-Bildarchiv. 1073447.*

An oversize Hitler billboard is mounted on a Luegerplatz building. The banner proclaims "One Reich, one people, one leader." The tower of St. Stephen's cathedral is in the background. *Bildarchiv der Österreichischen Nationalbibliothek. 1558419.*

Facing page, top

Ja (yes). Propaganda for the plebiscite erected around a tobacco kiosk outside the Scottish Church on the Freyung in downtown Vienna. *Bildarchiv der Österreichischen Nationalbibliothek. 1558379.*

Facing page, bottom

Plebiscite propaganda decorates a house built by the noted modernist architect Adolf Loos. The banner says "common blood belongs in a common Reich." *Österreichischen Gesellschaft für Zeitgeschichte, Wien-Bildarchiv. 346654.*

Hitler's motorcade drives up to City Hall on April 9, 1938. The Burgtheater, the Austrian state theater, stands in the background. *Verein für Geschichte der Arbeiterbewegung (VGA). 1438294.*

Hitler on the steps of Vienna's City Hall on April 9, 1938. The man in the raincoat in the middle is Gauleiter Josef Bürckel. Propaganda Minister Dr. Paul Joseph Goebbels stands next to him. *Österreichische Gesellschaft für Zeitgeschichte, Wien-Bildarchiv. 357518.*

Cardinal Theodor Innitzer, archbishop of Vienna, leaves his polling place after having voted *Ja* without going into a closed voting booth. *Bildarchiv der österreichischen Nationalbibliothek. 1552622.*

Facing page, top

Seyss Inquart votes in the April 10, 1938, plebiscite. *Österreichische Gesellschaft für Zeitgeschichte, Wien-Bildarchiv. 356629.*

Facing page, bottom

The paper ballot used in the plebiscite. Note how large the *Ja* is compared to the small *Nein*. *Verein für Geschichte der Arbeiterbewegung (VGA). 1270961.*

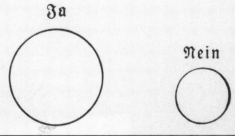

Volksabstimmung am 10. April 1938

Stimmzettel

Stimmst Du, deutscher Soldat, der am 13. März 1938 vollzogenen
Wiedervereinigung Österreichs mit dem Deutschen Reich zu?

Ja

Nein

Odilo Globocnik, first Nazi Gauleiter of Vienna, during a speech in the spring of 1938. *Dokumentationsarchiv des österreichischen Widerstandes.*

Poster outside the Nordwestbahnhalle for the anti-Semitic exhibit "Der ewige Jude": the eternal Jew. *Documentationsarchiv des österreichischen Widerstandes.*

Vienna police take an oath to the Führer. Gauleiter Bürckel in the middle in his rain coat. Himmler is on the left. Scene is the Heldenplatz. *Österreichische Gesellschaft für Zeitgeschichte, Wien-Bildarchiv. 348712.*

"Scrubbing party" on Kirstallnacht in Vienna. Jews wash the pavement as Hitler Youth stand by. *Verein für Geschichte der Arbeiterbewegung (VGA). 1271655.*

Hitler at the Vienna state opera for the premiere of Richard Strauss's opera "Ein Friedenstag" (a day of peace) during the 1939 theater festival week. Hitler, in white tie and tails, sits between Bürckel in a brown shirt uniform and Goebbels. *Österreichische Gesellschaft für Zeitgeschichte, Wien-Bildarchiv. 347956.*

Hitler in the old imperial box at the Burgtheater in 1939, the only time he visited the house during his Vienna reign. He is flanked by Bürckel and Goebbels. *Österreichische Gesellschaft für Zeitgeschichte, Wien-Bildarchiv. 347949.*

Left

Baldur von Schirach in his Reich Youth Leader uniform. *Österreichische Gesellschaft für Zeitgeschichte, Wien-Bildarchiv. 1254547.*

Below

Baldur von Schirach at a training session for Hitler Youth ready to go into the Volkssturm to die in the hopeless defense of Vienna. *Österreichische Gesellschaft für Zeitgeschichte, Wien-Bildarchiv. 1271627.*

General music director Hans Knappertsbusch conducts the Vienna Philharmonic at a concert for workers in a factory in 1944. The concert is being filmed. *Österreichische Gesellschaft für Zeitgeschichte, Wien-Bildarchiv. 358043.*

The Prater, Vienna's largest amusement park, after allied bombing in the winter of 1945. The giant Ferris wheel (later famous from the film *The Third Man*) is the only thing left standing. *Bildarchiv der Österreichischen Nationalbibliothek. 1553555.*

The opera in flames. Allied bombs triggered the fire storm on March 12, 1945. *Verein für Geschichte der Arbeiterbewegung (VGA). 1276217.*

more Jews, he already had too many in Poland. For the time being Hitler agreed but supported the game of musical chairs in Vienna itself that would leave more Jews with fewer houses. Two months later, however, Schirach was told that the 60,000 Viennese Jews would indeed be transported to Poland beginning early in 1941 and to start making the necessary preparations—in secret so that the Jews would not hear about them.[16] Schirach was a self-professed anti-Semite, and his speeches often resonated with flourishes of insidious rhetoric about the Jewish virus gnawing away at European culture, but he lacked the anti-Semitic passion of a Hitler, a Goebbels, or a Himmler so that he tended to dawdle over this problem as he did over so many others that did not really interest him.

Culture did, and here he fulfilled all of Hitler's expectations and more, for this was his true milieu. He turned down Hitler's suggestion that he live in the Hofburg or at least in the Palais Schwarzenberg[17] and instead opted for a capacious villa on the Hohe Warte, complete with a Rothschild park, which stretched halfway down the hill to the Danube Canal. From the living room windows the Schirachs could look across the Danube. It had fewer Greek pillars than Bürckel's house in Grinzing—though it had a few—and more graceful lines. Even the five red chimneys were fitted into the architectural design. A dining room that seated only twelve played to Schirach's penchant for making policy at intimate receptions. It was the kind of background that fitted into Schirach's unusual Nazi success story.

Baldur von Schirach was born in Berlin in 1907, the son of a cavalry officer.[18] A year later the family moved to Weimar where Schirach's father was to manage the Grand Duke of Saxony-Weimar's court theater. He grew up speaking only English until he was five. In 1855 Schirach's great grandfather had emigrated with his family to America. "My grandfather, Friedrich Karl von Schirach, fought in the American Civil War as a major in the Northern army and lost a leg in the battle of Bull Run," Schirach would write in his memoirs. "When President Lincoln was murdered my grandfather, with a leg made of cork, stood among the guard of honor." The leg did not prevent Friedrich Karl from dancing at postwar balls. At one of them he met and fell in love with Elisabeth Bailey Norris, a scion of one of the oldest and richest families in Philadelphia. In 1871 Friedrich Karl, now an American citizen, returned to Germany with his young wife and settled first in Kiel and then in Lübeck, Thomas

Mann's city, where his son, Baldur's father, went to school with the future Nobel Prize laureate.[19] Karl Bailey Norris von Schirach was an American citizen until he entered the Prussian army. Nevertheless, when he returned to the United States on a visit to his relatives he fell in love with a member of the Norris clan, Emma Middleton Lynah Tillou, and brought her back to Germany. She loved Berlin.

She liked Weimar a lot less but adjusted to the stiff court ceremonial that accompanied her husband's post in the Athens of Germany, Goethe's own town. Young Baldur Schirach was sent to a posh boarding school—American money sustained the family through the inflationary period—where, he would write, "a three-quarters American became a nationalist German," a development hastened by the suicide of his elder brother Karl in 1919 whose farewell note said that he did not wish to survive Germany's defeat. In 1925 young Baldur met Adolf Hitler during a performance of the *Walküre* at the Weimar court theater. The next day Hitler came to tea with flowers for Schirach's mother and knowledgeable conversation about Wagner and German literature. A year later Baldur was an arts student in Munich and a member of the SA. When the NSDAP held its second Reich party congress in Weimar, young Baldur was an organizer and messenger close to Hitler and already aware of his peccadilloes. A talented speaker and a mediocre poet but one who could make his verses sound significant to the unlettered, Baldur von Schirach became a student leader in Munich and in a matter of years had literally stamped a nationwide Hitler Youth organization out of the ground. Hitler named him Reich youth leader in 1931 and the following year sent him to the Reichstag and made him Reichsleiter for youth education. He was in play early as a possible successor to Hitler himself.

He truly believed in Hitler, as the title of his memoirs, *Ich Glaubte an Hitler* (*I Believed in Hitler*), suggests. He had a chance to break out of the Führer's spell and did not take it. In 1928 his mother took him to New York where a great-uncle suggested the young man chuck Europe and go into American banking. Schirach never gave it a serious thought.

By the time he came to Vienna his reputation was slightly soiled. His initial successes with the Hitler Youth were beyond question, but his organizational talents were not. He was a good idea man and presenter but not much on follow-through. He was good at Nazi politics and Hitler's fondness for him—he had married the daughter of the Führer's court photographer, Heinrich Hoffmann—made up for his other short-comings. Still, he had wanted to add the education portfolio to his Reichsleiter's job and thus be in charge of every aspect of German youth—from cradle to manhood—and this he did not get. He wanted the embassy in Washington but not under Ribbentrop, whom he disliked and whose job he coveted. Still, he saw Vienna as a great opportunity to display and unfold his talents as a man of culture and a patron of the arts. He would not show up at the opera in a business suit, as Bürckel allegedly had done, nor doff his jacket in the Hotel Imperial's dining room and eat in his suspenders. True or not, for Hitler such things mattered a great deal, even if Eva Braun's Vienna friends were the source of such gossip.[20] Schirach also knew that he needed good people to run cultural policy—and that they could not be Viennese. Their reputation for throat-cutting and backstabbing in the arts was too well established and too well known. How he stumbled on a man by the name of Walter Thomas is murky, but more than anyone else Thomas gave Schirach the cultural panache the Gauleiter sought.

Thomas was a bookish youth from the Ruhr with mildly left-wing leanings who eschewed a university education for a job in a bookstore and a bohemian life style.[21] He adored Thomas Mann, and read everything from Dostoevsky to André Gide, wrote book reviews, essays, and short stories, and much of his output had an anti-Nazi slant. But he must have had some charm and a lack of clear political outlook—he was, after all only twenty-four years old when Hitler seized power—for the Nazis forgave him, let him keep his job at a local newspaper, and, when he was no longer viable, allowed him to slip into a reasonably cushy post as a dramaturge at the theater in Bochum, an industrial town in the Ruhr with a good reputation for drama. He clearly had talent. At one point in the 1930s he was seriously considered for a cultural job in Berlin but was turned down because of his politics. Although he had joined the party in the late thirties (a fact he was anxious to hide after the war) he was taken aback when, on a rainy late summer day in 1940, he received a telegram to come to Vienna for a job interview. Mystified, he wondered if they would offer him management of a provincial theater like Klagenfurt. His interviewer at the Ballhausplatz smiled. Not at all. The job they had in mind had nothing to do with managing a theater—he would become the cultural czar of Vienna in charge of all its institutions—museums, orchestras, theaters, the opera, exhibitions, concerts, writers, publishers, actors, and singers, as a kind of secretary general for the arts. (Bürckel had established the post but never done much with it). Schirach wanted Vienna's cultural establishment to rival Berlin's, and, if possible, even to exceed it. "You came to our attention through your work," the interviewer said. "You have what we need: youth, imagination and energy."[22]

Thomas demurred. He lacked two things: he wasn't Viennese and was not an exponent of the party. Again the man smiled. No Viennese was wanted but a neutral expert from the Altreich who understood the business of culture and had no ties to any Viennese faction. No, the job was not political. They knew about the incident in Berlin, but there the *party* had the last word. In Vienna, that honor belonged to Schirach. But why was Thomas so worried about politics? Surely he was not opposed to the party? The pause seemed endless while Thomas raced through his options. One wrong word, he knew, and he was headed into a death battalion where he would surely die for Führer and Fatherland, if not end up immediately in a concentration camp. "I believe that culture and politics are two separate and distinct arenas," he said. "We can talk about that later," the interviewer replied and scheduled an appointment with Schirach for the next morning at ten.

The Reichsleiter wore the uniform of his political office, neither brown shirt nor black but redolent of a Ruritanian general, which Thomas felt did not suit him or his face—"the face of a spoiled unmilitary son of a wealthy and cultivated home." Schirach leaned back in his chair, rolling a Brazilian cigar between index and middle finger, and launched into a monologue about his plans for Vienna. It was routine stuff—even for Thomas: building a new harbor and other construction projects designed to regenerate the city and ready it for full-blown expansion once the war was over, in about a year or so. Then he swung into Vienna's role in the Balkans, and here he did plow up new ground. "Vienna is no longer attractive for many of the Puszta (the Hungarian Plains) magnates. The Christian Democrats removed many of the attractions the city had. I plan to open several elegant brothels and bring nightlife up to speed. I'd rather have Vienna as a den of iniquity than a prayer hall for Austrian reactionaries." Finally he got down to business. "I understand you have several reservations. They don't exist for me. I don't want a party functionary in this job who measures everything with Rosenberg's yardstick, and I don't want a representative of the Hitler Youth, but a professional. There is one caveat: no differences with the party because in that case I would be powerless. Well, you've had a day to think it over. How about it?" To which Thomas replied in a veiled voice: "I hope to fulfill everything you expect of me."[23] For a young man in his early thirties it was a job beyond his wildest dreams, hopes, and expectations, and despite his reservations Thomas knew it. Like Faust he was willing to sell his soul to the devil, and, like Faust, he was sure he could keep it nevertheless.

Thomas started his new job on September 4, feeling his way through fuzzy instructions to improve the city's overall cultural performance and early warnings to watch out for the local knife wielders. Like so many Germans he fell in love with Vienna at once, but unlike most he kept a critical eye on performance. The opera, he knew, was in trouble with its quality sometimes under the level of mediocre provincial houses. Actors at the various theaters, private and public, could be wonderful, but the required stage discipline was often wanting. He was also charged with making the arts a more civil place in which backstabbing was kept to a minimum. That, perhaps, was his hardest task, given the city's long tradition of cultural intrigues.

Clearly, the Opera would be Thomas's first concern and he, like everybody else in Vienna's cultural establishment, knew that Heinrich Strohm, Bürckel's choice for Opera director, would be a disaster. A shy, gentle man, Strohm had built his reputation on a modestly avant-garde approach to opera and his career—to some extent at least—on the fact that he had gone to boarding school with Goebbels, who supported him because he thought a shy and gentle man was just what Vienna needed.

Strohm was installed on September 18 with Schirach extolling Germany's role as a great cultural, as well as political and military, power. Strohm, Schirach said, would make the opera—where the Führer had first experienced the glories of German music and whose spirit still filled a house that would "remain forever Adolf Hitler's"—the first stage of the Reich.[24] Strohm dutifully promised to give new life to its splendid tradition. The poor man did not know what he was in for. In the arts, Vienna takes no prisoners.

In late October Goebbels came to town. The Führer's decision to give Schirach control of cultural policies including the opera and the theaters had not made Goebbels happy, and he had not accepted the decision as final, one reason he would come often to Vienna, make speeches, and play every cultural card he held. On October 27 he delivered a tirade against England, but began his remarks with a warning against "yesterday's men"[25] eager to foment conflict between Vienna and Berlin, a clear signal that Viennese resentment against the Prussian city was an ongoing problem that rhetoric alone could not solve but that would have to be addressed on an ongoing basis.

The warning was triggered by an *NWT* piece titled "Vienna—refuge of the German soul." When Goebbels read it in late September he was so furious he fired the author, Dr. Aurel Wolfram, on the spot. (This being Vienna, however, Schirach and Blaschke found the offending author a spot in the theater section of the city's cultural office.) Goebbels's fury was understandable, for Wolfram's essay was a paean to Vienna's glories and a condescending putdown of the Reich's capital as a "city machine" with the exercise of economic and political power its only function, and culture an insignificant adjunct. Berlin was the center of an incredible dynamic. "It burns itself out every day in its own flames. It is a constant upheaval. It has a lot in common with Americanism. It marches across the past without sentiment and reshapes the cityscape with new North–South and East–West axes as the situation demands." Not so, of course, Vienna. Move a stone in that edifice and its whole soul collapses. For Vienna, would anybody think of it, a North–South axis would be a dagger stabbed through its heart. Hands off, therefore, for all ambitious city planners, builders, and other speculators. Vienna must be preserved from the spirit of untrammeled progress because only then could Vienna be "the capital of the inner Reich, the refuge of the German soul."[26]

Given two densely printed pages of such insidious rhetoric, it is a wonder Wolfram escaped Dachau. But Goebbels also knew that Wolfram was right about Vienna and that the time had come to throw the Viennese some red meat. The next day he announced that after the war the annual Reich Theater week—which had been suspended after 1939—would be held permanently in Vienna. The *VB* sang hosannas of praise for Goebbels's generous action in bestowing on Vienna so great a mark of distinction—and on himself the mark of a city benefactor.

The carefully calibrated announcement came within another context—the installation of Günther Kaufmann as head of the Reich Propaganda Office in Vienna, a move that bought Goebbels a stake in the ambitious young man who so far had owed his career exclusively to Schirach, and through him in the city's cultural policy.[27] Kaufmann said all the right things about Vienna's new role in the Reich as center of culture, fashion, and commerce, and made it clear he was ready to serve two masters.

On November 18, 1940, some 52,000 fans jammed into Vienna's soccer stadium in the Prater for a game between Vienna's Admira and the German champion Schalke 04. The stadium crowd was unruly and ready for trouble. And trouble, political trouble, there was aplenty, despite a massive display of uniformed and plainclothes police and the presence of an impressive array of Nazi brass led by Schirach and his wife. Let a German player commit a foul, or worse, get away with it, and the fans' anger exploded into anti-German, even anti-Nazi, expletives. As the *NWT* noted, the crowd ignored Austrian infractions, or worse, cheered them. It didn't help that Schalke played a tough, even brutal, brand of football. And when the referee disallowed Admira's go-ahead goal after the teams were tied 1 to 1, the crowd exploded with soccer war style fury. Fans grew totally out of hand when an Admira forward headed the ball into the net, and the referee called that goal back too and the game ended in a tie. Whatever the truth of the matter, the *NWT* wrote, crowd reaction was out of all proportions. "The tumult would not end even after the game was over." And the paper suggested that partisan fans had endangered Vienna's reputation as a mecca of soccer.

That the authorities were deeply concerned by what they had obviously seen as an anti-Nazi soccer riot became apparent in a *NWT* story on November 20. It warned that Vienna's stadium threatened to win a reputation as a "hot iron"—meaning a site where crowds roughed up visiting teams. Rivalry between Altreich and Ostmark teams was healthy, "but unfortunately it was used by some to express their most base instincts. People who see themselves as class-conscious gangs are winning the upper hand and are damaging the reputation of Viennese fans and indeed of the city itself." If the hooligans couldn't be tamed it would be better to close down the sport.

That it took the Nazis three days to bid up their soccer rhetoric was a reflection of indecision, both of action and analysis. Just how serious was the riot? The Gestapo cabled uncertain reports back and forth from Berlin, suggesting that they would need 10,000 police to pick out ringleaders of so large a mob. What's more, even with the sizable contingent of police on hand that day, nobody was around when so-called hooligans smashed the windows of Schirach's limousine and slashed its tires. Soccer would remain a Gestapo problem for the rest of the war; especially when, seven months later, the Viennese got revenge of a different sort. Before 90,000 fans in Berlin's stadium Rapid cannonaded Schalke 04 into submission. Down three–nil after halftime, the Viennese pounded three goals into the German net in fifteen minutes, put in the winner in the 72nd minute and scored the winning goal to become German champion for 1940–41. Viennese media played up their victory, but not on the front page. The same day German tanks had rolled into Russia.[28]

Goebbels came to Vienna again on December 7, 1940. He clearly had a good time. He took a drive into the Vienna Woods, visited an exhibit of tapestries and the city's clock museum. At night he saw a new production of *Romeo and Juliet* at the Burg and listened to Müthel whine about Viennese critics.

"I promise to sort them out on his behalf. He is very happy about this," Goebbels wrote in his diary. He was also impressed enough to reserve twenty Burgtheater repertory performances for workers in various city enterprises and for soldiers on leave in Vienna—tickets would not cost them a pfennig.

Goebbels also took care of another cultural problem—the excesses of the political cabaret Wiener Werkel, which had been poking fun at the Nazis since early 1939. Goebbels's diary reads: "Put the manager in his place. This establishment flatters itself that it can get away with sly subversion and typically Viennese griping. I draw the gentleman's attention to the dangers of his activities in no uncertain terms. He will be more careful from now on."[29]

In typical Viennese fashion, the cabaret obeyed Goebbels and did not obey him. To understand the contradiction a little history is needed. Wiener Werkel was founded by an enterprising actor and illegal NSDAP member named Adolf Müllner-Reitzer. He thought the Third Reich could do with cabaret and persuaded the Gau propaganda office to issue a license. He recruited a solidly anti-Nazi crew, knowing that the humorless Nazis couldn't poke fun at themselves, and opened for business on January 20, 1939. The cross-talk included items such as this:

Husband: "You'll see, we won't have strawberries next spring." Wife: "Why won't we have strawberries?" Husband: First of all 'cause they're red, and second be-

184

cause the Prussians will probably make rayon out of them." Wife: "What have you always got against the Prussians?" Husband: "Nothing. But for you, of course, every Prussian is a Lohengrin."

The second show was more daring, masking the Anschluss as the Japanese occupation of China, a skit that included the line: "Don't worry, we'll demoralize them quick enough." The incensed Gestapo ordered the show closed. Müllher-Reitzner appealed to Bürckel, got a postponement, invited Bürckel to attend the second performance, plied him with drinks beforehand, and had the actors gloss over the more insulting lines. The mildly plastered Bürckel told the Gestapo to lay off. Word got out quickly—and the Wiener Werkel was sold out for months.[30]

But a program that featured skits titled "Ulysses' Journey through Greater Greece" and the "Janus Head" were another matter, a bitter satire on the red tape that kept Ulysses on the road for ten years studded with verbal digs at Nazi manners and morals. An incensed Goebbels had both skits taken out of the show. Nevertheless, the theater survived until Goebbels closed all the theaters in 1944; it was, in the end, the only political cabaret in Greater Germany.

At 5 A.M. on December 10, 1940, Hitler allegedly picked up the phone to call Schirach at his villa on the Hohe Warte. "I need a present for the French," Henriette Schirach quotes Hitler as telling her husband. "You have a coffin in the Capuchin Tombs of the King of Rome, Napoleon's son. I want him sent to Paris."[31]

As church bells tolled noon on December 14, 1940, the artfully forged iron gates of the Capuchin Tombs, where all the Habsburgs are buried, swung open and a bronze sarcophagus weighing nearly two thousand pounds was brought out by the brawny men of the Vienna mortuary office and placed on a "gala carriage" drawn by four horses. Only a few people were on the street at the time and they rushed up, as the Viennese always do, to watch the spectacle. Many raised their hands in the Hitler salute. The horses trotted past the opera to the West station. It was one of the coldest days of the year, and onlookers were sparse with only a very few aware of who was passing by. High-ranking Wehrmacht officers boarded the special railroad car as a guard of honor. They arrived in Paris around midnight. The catafalque was carried through the dark and silent streets to the Invalides where the German soldiers surrendered the coffin to French gendarmes. On Sunday the archbishop of

Paris celebrated the mass for the dead. The Duke of Albufera represented Napoleon II's family; Admiral François Darlan the Vichy government. A German honor company stood on the square outside to salute the coming and going of the French officials. Then the Parisians crowded into the Invalides and did so until late that evening. December 15, 1940, a hundred years to the day since Napoleon I had been brought home to Paris from St. Helena. At last "*L'Aiglon est revenu pres de l'Aigle.*" (The Eaglet has come back to the Eagle.)[32]

Whether "the Führer's generous gesture," as Viennese newspapers hailed it, helped improve relations may be doubted. Perhaps one snag, inevitable when half-educated men are charged with symbolic action, dampened French enthusiasm. Both Hitler and Schirach had forgotten, or more likely, never knew, that they had left a vital icon behind—like all Habsburgs (and the *Aiglon* was, after all, the son of the Archduchess Marie Louise), his heart had been encased in silver and left in the tomb. None of the Austrian bureaucrats charged with the transfer had bothered telling their Nazi masters.[33]

During the first fifteen months of the war daily life in Vienna had not changed much, once the first shocks of blackout, rationing, the ban on foreign broadcasts, and other restrictions had been absorbed. The Viennese griped a little more than usual, but the unbroken string of Nazi victories made burdens easier to bear. Life was drabber. By the fall of 1940 only 800 cabs were on the road compared with 1,600 in the spring, but the *NWT* insisted that the number was enough. A memorial service was held at the Konzerthaus for those who had died in combat. *Parsifal* was performed on All Souls' Day, as tradition demanded. German women were honored with a special exhibit depicting "the German woman in the course of history" and reminding women that motherhood was their primary function. Victorious troops home from the Western front marched around the Ring. Pensions of city employees were improved— Bürckel's parting gift to his bureaucracy. Dr. Julius Wagner von Jaurreg, the doctor who won a Nobel Prize in 1927 for the malaria treatment of progressive syphilitic paralysis, died on September 28 at the age of eighty-three. The media paid tribute to his scientific achievement, while at his funeral Dr. Tavs praised him as a man of "Germanic convictions."

The 125th anniversary of the founding of Vienna's Technichsche Hochschule—the university of engineering and science, the oldest such institution in Europe—was celebrated as a "day of honor" for German research and science. All sixty chancellors of Greater Germany's universities shuffled into the Musikverein dressed in medieval robes with the insignia of office around their necks, while the Vienna Philharmonic played Franz Schmidt's *Royal Fanfares*. [34]

In October the party launched its annual month-long propaganda wave with daily meetings held across the city. "This is not a promotion campaign but a drive for public enlightenment," the *NWT* wrote. "The general public is to be instructed about what is happening and should draw its own logical conclusions." To that end, the paper said, the party was putting its best orators on the podium under the motto "the party at war."[35] Accounts of a large turnout are probably accurate and a function of both continuing strong Nazi sympathies and strict party discipline down to the local level; in other words, party leaders acted as enforcers.

A year-end session of the city council noted that city taxes would not be raised in 1941. The Prince of Liechtenstein had given the city some property in Mödling for construction of a Hitler Youth home. A hospital had been purchased in Gersthof. Construction of the first basin of the planned Danube harbor would continue. Rafelsberger, whose many jobs included running city-owned enterprises, reported on growing use of gas and electricity and the resultant increase in revenues.

Philipp Jung, whom Bürckel had brought in as RP to run the Reich side of Gau administration—local affairs were handled by the mayor while the RP dealt with Reich ministries—headed the session. He still had the title but not the office. Schirach had named a close aide, Dr. Hans Delbrügge, as RP in early September, leaving Jung to manage city affairs, while mayor Neubacher was on special assignment in Romania. Neubacher had hoped for a comeback but Bürckel had told Schirach he was not to be trusted. Vice-mayor Thomas Kozich would recall what happened when the two men met:

> After waiting for fifteen minutes Neubacher was allowed to enter Schirach's office. The Reichsleiter sat behind Metternich's desk at the far end of the capacious room, apparently reading a file, and took no notice of his visitor. Neubacher walked across the stone floor. When he reached the desk Schirach did not get up nor ask his visitor to sit down. So Neubacher was forced to report that he had come to discuss city matters. Schirach looked up and said coldly, "Herr Dr. Neubacher I do not plan to discuss any projects of the city of Vienna with you since I do not plan to work with you."[36]

The embarrassing interview was over. In a matter of months Neubacher managed a transfer to the German Foreign Service. (He spent the rest of the war in the Balkans with the personal rank of minister.)

As the New Year dawned Schirach had his political, economic, and cultural team in place. He backed up Kaufmann with local Nazis—Eduard Frauenfeld, brother of the illegal Gauleiter Alfred Frauenfeld, was named to head the propaganda department in Kaufmann's office; Hermann Stuppäck, a lyric poet and illegal Nazi who had lined up candidates for Vienna's top cultural jobs right after the Anschluss, took over the culture department. Here he could keep an eye on the already troublesome Thomas. Schirach had addressed all his constituencies, including the workers to whom he tried to sell Bürckel's German socialism but with little success and less conviction. Schirach looked like an aristocrat, and although he was a better speaker than Bürckel, his worker audiences did not believe him. Finally, he had thrown his considerable energies into boosting city culture. The Opera headed the "to do" list. Strohm had proved to be the disaster everybody expected.

In October Strohm took the Philharmonic and the Opera on tour in Holland, which was a great success, and when he returned little of the shy and gentle man he allegedly had been was left.[37] Strohm had become a vest-pocket Napoleon. He told one and all that Vienna had a lousy opera and that bringing it up to speed would be a mammoth undertaking. He tore the tapestries off the walls of the director's office, a room where Gustav Mahler had once ruled, and built a new exit directly onto Kärntnerstrasse. He made no allies, let alone friends.[38] He did not understand Vienna and made no efforts to try. He was quickly bewildered—and it showed. His first "innovation" was a changed opera program that left operagoers, who didn't much care about what was printed in it, bewildered and more convinced than ever that he was just another body Bürckel had brought in from the Altreich—not a conductor, not even a musician, but a representative of Berlin's cultural centralism.

Thomas would note that Strohm couldn't have done much to stop his critics. The Third Reich's musical pope, conductor Wilhelm Furtwängler, didn't like him, and nearly eight weeks after Strohm's appointment Schirach told Thomas the same thing: "I don't like that man. He has bad luck. I need people who are successful. I need a brilliant opera for political reasons and I can't afford scandals. The man has to go."[39] Things at the Opera became steadily worse. Nobody was in charge. Strohm's deputy was in a hospital and Strohm lacked guts to knock heads together. Conductors Knappertsbusch and Furtwängler were at odds. Oscar Fritz Schuh, brought from Hamburg to stage operas, declared his artistic independence. Shortly before Christmas, Schirach gave Strohm a dressing down for his artistic inadequacy. Whereupon Strohm had a nervous breakdown and was shipped off to a clinic to recover. He returned in January and things got worse, as Kaufmann wrote to Goebbels on February 5 seeking permission for a change in management.[40] Days earlier Schirach had once again sent Strohm to a clinic. Strohm knew he was finished and had told Thomas so before his first breakdown. An outsider was needed to run things, so Schirach himself would take over the Opera and Thomas would manage it for him.

At first, Thomas was more shocked than pleased.[41] He was plagued with self-doubt and with fear of failure. He came from the stage. He knew how theaters worked from the inside out. He understood actors, playwrights and directors but he was a musical amateur who could barely read a score, but Schirach had picked him for a reason: when the chips were down Thomas delivered (even if his name is still rarely mentioned in the cultural history of the times). He made decisions and he stuck by them. He told orchestra, singers, and stagehands what to do, and he did so without braggadocio or hysterics. He saved the season. Performances improved. He spent the millions Goebbels had funneled into the Opera with caution and some wisdom. He bought, borrowed, and begged singers from other houses. When he wanted something he flattered those whose egos needed massaging. He made the improvements Schirach needed and from which Schirach could catapult to other achievements.

The Gauleiter had already sketched out two major projects for 1941—a week honoring the 150th birthday of the Austrian poet and playwright Franz Grillparzer in January, and the "Mozart Week of the German Reich" in December to commemorate the 150th anniversary of that "great *German* composer's" death.

The first event of the New Year, however, belonged to Goebbels, the down payment of his promise to send workers and soldiers to the Burg for free to see *Romeo and Juliet*. On January 3, Günther Kaufmann—a true servant of two masters—mounted the Burg's stage. He had the kind of classical education that both Schirach and Goebbels valued in their top aides, and his speech showed it. He talked much about the role of the arts in the building of the Reich, of how artists had always marched ahead of politicians. None of 1940s victories was more important than Vienna's rise from the cultural ashes. And then he stretched his hand out for the brass ring of drama—Shakespeare. "That the poet of this evening is an Englishman who, next to Grillparzer, had given most dramatic life to the impact of love on human existence does not concern us. He is a loner among his own people, without much following among the playwrights of his nation. Like Goethe he belongs to the world, only with this difference—he found his eternal home with us where the creative genius of a German spirit was discovered early and always loved. Nor do we wage this war against Shakespeare but against Churchill."[42]

Grillparzer should have been a risky choice for the Nazis. True, he wrote classic drama in the tradition of Goethe and Schiller, but the fate of the Habsburg dynasty loomed large in his plays, and his love song to Austria in *King Ottokar's Rise and Fall* always brought Viennese audiences to their feet and the SD to the teletype. This was Schirach's meat and drink. He would treat the poet like any political hero: trumpets and wreaths at his tomb on the morning of January 14; the festive opening of a Grillparzer exhibit at city hall at noon with Schirach presiding; the awarding of special Grillparzer prizes and finally, that evening, Schirach's festive reception at the Hofburg.

His opening speech the next day, moreover, showed just how clever the Reichsleiter could be in the integration of Austrian genius into the greater German Reich. "We Germans," he said, "have the tendency to praise our great sons only after their death." The honors heaped on Grillparzer for his eightieth birthday "came too late and did more to disturb his solitude than confirm his victory. The cliché that genius runs ahead of his times has been proved on his 150th birthday, for only today has his mission been fulfilled. A poet of Greater Germany is being honored within the greater German framework and in a manner that does justice to his being and his personality." Germans, he continued, were marked by the polarity between logical thought and artistic creation, by the contrast between Kant and Beethoven, Prussia and Austria.[43]

From the day he arrived in Vienna one of Schirach's goals was to make the city the fashion capital of the Reich. Certainly, it had the history to back the claim. Under the empire Vienna had been a magnet for the fashion-conscious in Eastern Europe and beyond. If the city could not rival Paris's haute couture, Vienna did turn out more glamorous gowns than Berlin, Prague, or even Budapest. In the first republic fashion was one of the "taste" industries—pastries, the decorative arts, furniture, cutlery, porcelain, and handicraft—that led Austrian exports.

Hitler himself had expressed some interest in giving Vienna the fashion mandate, and since the Führer took a personal interest in all the arts and reserved for himself policy-making decisions—such as who would be director of the Vienna State Opera—such support could be decisive. But Hitler also had a tendency to change his mind and to lose interest in domestic affairs. Moreover, his attitude toward Vienna was ambivalent since he both admired and detested the place, and was wary of any claims the city might make that would challenge Berlin's role as center of the Reich. His support, therefore, could not always be counted upon.

On August 20, 1940, Günther Kaufmann sent Schirach a memo outlining the problems that stood in the way of giving Vienna fashion supremacy. "The tendency to put the emphasis on Berlin in matters of fashion is very strong," Kaufmann wrote. A new fashion magazine, he noted as one example, that was to be published in Vienna had been assigned to a Berlin publisher.

Both Goebbels and Dr. Robert Ley, the Reichsleiter in charge of DAF (the German Labor Front) were interested in winning control of the fashion industry, Kaufmann went on to say, and Schirach should exploit their differences to Vienna's advantage.[44] It was sage advice but difficult to follow because the lines of conflict between Goebbels and Ley were never that sharply drawn. Whatever decisions were made about a German fashion capital never seemed to be final and were always subject to revision.

Nevertheless, Vienna pushed ahead resolutely. On August 26, 1940, Schirach's office received a proposal for establishment of a fashion studio within the house of fashion that would train fashion specialists. An eight-page brochure with a print run of 5,000 had been prepared to publicize the new venture. Organizers also asked the Gauleiter's propaganda office to prod newspapers into giving the studio ample coverage.

On September 2, Rafelsberger opened a fashion show at the Palais Lobkowitz in conjunction with the fall 1940 international trade fair. The show, the *VB* said, demonstrated that Viennese fashion was now free of all Parisian influence. In early November the *VB* grew more expansive. Plans had been developed among the city's fifty leading fashion salons—coordinated by the House of Fashion—that would assure "Vienna of the first rank among the fashion centers of the newly awakened Europe." Even Parisian women's clothing stores had signs in their windows touting "Vienna fashion." Viennese clothes still dominated the Balkans, the *VB* continued, and were making headway in the Nordic countries. The *NWT* concurred: Viennese fashion didn't need Paris anymore.[45]

The stories reflected political developments. On November 9, Kaufmann informed the ministry of propaganda in Berlin that Schirach had met with Ley, who in the meantime had been put in charge of fashion, at least nominally (Kaufmann knew perfectly well that Goebbels would never give up his right to meddle in anything he chose to). The two men, he continued, had agreed on locating "all creative fashion work and all training facilities" in Vienna. The DAF would put up the funds needed to make Vienna the center of the new European fashion, and that therefore the fashion emphasis would shift from Berlin to Vienna.

That would seem to have been that, but it was not. On January 25, 1941, Kaufmann asked Goebbels to give Vienna financial and propaganda support as the Reich's new fashion capital. Such backing was needed to avoid a brewing battle among German cities vying to become fashion centers. Unless a definite center emerged, no effective propaganda campaign for German fashion could be launched abroad or at home. Vienna was best suited for the fashion role, Kaufmann argued, and should Dr. Ley, as expected, locate production of high fashion in Vienna to buttress the creative end already in the city, fashion propaganda would have to emanate from Vienna. Kaufmann estimated the cost of such a campaign at RM 800,000.[46]

Kaufmann never got the money or Goebbels' help, while Ley had to be persuaded over and over to make good on his November 1940 pledge to award Vienna the fashion palm. In a memo Kaufmann wrote to Schirach the same day, January 25, he stressed the need for obtaining Ley's "hundred percent commitment to put high fashion in Vienna," which he had not yet given. So Schirach tried again. On February 19, Ley was in Vienna to discuss the fashion situation at the Ballhausplatz. Schirach lined up all the heavy guns on his staff to persuade Ley once and for all that German fashion belonged in Vienna. Again he got only half-hearted agreement. The Ley aide in charge of fashion clearly wanted authority over it to remain in Berlin and gave ground only grudgingly. Goebbels held back because he did not want Ley to accumulate political capital from his role as fashion czar, and to do so at Goebbels's expense—

one reason why the propaganda chief tacitly supported Berlin, Munich, and Frankfurt's claims for a share of the fashion pie.

Schirach's fashion ambitions ran into opposition in Vienna as well. Rafelsberger did not want to give up city control over the industry, as he would have to if the DAF were to assume the financial and administrative burden. The economic advisor was content with keeping Vienna as one among several fashion players. Kaufmann was not. He persuaded Schirach to opt for the fashion capital prize, and in May it looked as if the Viennese were close to wrapping up a deal with the DAF. But, as spring turned into summer, new obstacles arose. Efforts to bring Frankfurt's fashion chief, a native Viennese, back home failed. Frankfurt's mayor wouldn't let her go. Even worse, Ley's point man wanted to bring the woman to Berlin behind Kaufmann's back.

Kaufmann tried to wrap up the situation in an early summer memo in which he concluded that the situation was too much in flux for Vienna to win any clear-cut victory soon. Goebbels had shifted ground—he now openly supported fashion decentralization. Schirach, Kaufmann suggested, should meet with Goebbels in Berlin and change his mind. Schirach tried but failed. Ley, Kaufmann said, would not make a final decision about Vienna until after he had seen how successful a planned fashion show in the spring of 1942 would be. The whole process, Kaufmann added, was shot through with bureaucratic intrigue so that Schirach could not afford to drop his guard or take Berlin's promises at face value.

He was right. The question of fashion supremacy was never fully resolved, even though Fred Adlmüller, the city's postwar fashion czar who had made his reputation designing for the wives of high-ranking occupation officials, claimed that Vienna had indeed been the Third Reich's fashion capital.[47] Suffice it to say that Schirach used fashion to boost the city's image—and by extension his own—throughout his tenure. Journalists from seventeen nations, for example, came to Vienna in November 1941 for the third fashion week that brought a preview of designs for 1942. It was a time when the swastika still flew high.

The war was going well, and Vienna had occasionally played a ceremonial part in its politics. It did so again in early March 1941 when Bulgaria agreed to join the Axis, and the negotiations to do so were again held in the Belvedere Palace with the Führer himself in attendance.[48]

193

His arrival was already ritual. Thousands lined the route from the West station to the Imperial Hotel; the crowd at the hotel forced the Führer to step outside to acknowledge their "love and devotion." The next day German troops marched into Bulgaria, and two days later Göring was in Vienna to confer with Romania's strongman General Antonescu about deepening economic and commercial ties. All were reasons enough for editorialists to crow about Vienna's continuing role as center of policy developments in the Southeast.

Vienna was being noticed. The Reich seemed willing to give the city new importance. Goebbels had earmarked more than RM 20 million to help poor families cope. "The ink was not yet dry under the Belvedere agreements," Kaufmann wrote, "when that act of statesmanship documenting the important role of this city in the Southeast of Europe was followed by a socialist measure that demonstrated the Reich's love and care for this great city."[49] On March 13 Goebbels came to Vienna and, together with Schirach, held a mass meeting on the Heldenplatz to celebrate the third anniversary of the Anschluss; this celebration became a much bigger deal than it had been the year before, a clear effort to win back the still disaffected Viennese.

So both Schirach and Goebbels began their speeches on the Heldenplatz with praise of Vienna's essential Germanness. "This is Adolf Hitler's most loyal city," Schirach said, while Goebbels opened with "Men and women of the German city of Vienna." He conceded that the Reich had not solved the wage-price problem, but pointed to the RM 20 million of bridging assistance as proof that the Reich "cared." He called loss of Vienna's political position "the dowry placed on the table of German unity." In return the Reich had given Vienna the important role of bridgehead to the Southeast and cultural center of the first rank.[50]

German efforts to make the Balkans their backyard with "keep out" signs directed at Russia and Great Britain seemed close to success, especially when the Yugoslav regent committed his country to the Axis on March 24, after another (this time secret) meeting in Vienna. Two days later, however, rebellious generals staged a coup in Belgrade, ousted the regent, and installed eighteen-year-old King Peter II as the ruler. Enraged, Hitler postponed his planned invasion of Russia and prepared a quick strike into the Balkans. The drums he sounded were the same as in all his other aggressions—mistreatment of local Germans. From the start of the Balkan campaign Vienna was something of a staging and planning area: Hitler hit Belgrade from the air on April 6, took the city a week later, and on April 27 the swastika flew over the Acropolis. A month later the Germans had conquered Crete; all events the Viennese press chronicled with glee and malice, and as if the city had played a major part in them.[51]

Real life was different and much of it was reflected more accurately in the city's courts and in Gestapo reports than in the triumphalism of the media. Black market activities were clearly increasing and so were the punishments meted out. Butchers and restaurant owners were early targets for charges of illegal slaughter of cattle and swine. One butcher was accused of selling 2,000 kilograms (some 4,400 pounds) of pork to restaurants without asking his customers for ration stamps, but also without charging them higher prices. A Vienna court ruled that he was not a war profiteer, and he was sentenced only for violating local ordinances. A Reich court overturned the verdict and in the process ruled that illegal slaughterers were indeed war criminals. By July the Reich court ruling began to bite. Heinrich Götzelmann, at the age of forty-five, was sentenced to death. As a city official he had sold meat ration stamps for 21,000 kilograms (46,300 pounds)of meat and profited to the tune of more than RM 20,000. "No mercy for price gougers" one headline proclaimed over a story that Elisabeth Spendl's vegetable stand was closed for good and she was banned from ever running one again for persistently charging higher than legal prices, while wine merchant Josef Messinger was fined RM 5,000 for price gouging. When he appealed the court upped the fine another RM 600. A man who ran a sausage stand in the Prater sold 600 frankfurters without stamps. The court was merciful: he got only three months. A delicatessen merchant got three years for selling spoiled fig paste to the Wehrmacht at inflated prices.

Common crime remained part of daily life and spiced up newspaper fare, even that of the staid *VB*. True, crime was not that different from crime in any other big city, but the Nazis prided themselves for having changed the crime scene. They had little mercy for robbers and killers. The death penalty was common, a fact in which newspapers like the *VB* took great pride. It separated their "law and order" state from lax Jewish justice under Schuschnigg when criminals literally got away with murder. National Socialism was different. It paid little heed to mental problems, for example, although occasionally a criminal's social circumstances influenced sentencing. But Nazi crime reporting showed that even so closed and rigidly controlled a society as Nazi Germany could not do any better suppressing crime than the lax democracies, no matter how harsh its criminal justice system, nor was that system consistent with a marked haphazardness in its sentencing.

Take the case of Nikolaus Fronys, age twenty-three. He was sentenced to death for matricide. The young man had been in and out of mental institutions and one psychiatrist said he couldn't distinguish between right and wrong. But a court appointed psychiatrist disagreed and said Fronys knew what he was doing when he choked his mother, stuck his fist down her throat and stabbed her fifteen times with a kitchen knife. The death sentence was carried out promptly. But the courts could also be fair, even to those who were denounced for treasonous behavior. Albert Hoffmann, a tailor, went to the police in the ninth district and accused the owner of a café near the Franz Josef station of listening to foreign broadcasts. The Gestapo investigated and found that the owner was innocent. Hoffmann said he was drunk and didn't know what he was doing. That defense, the court ruled, was not good enough and gave him eight months for slander.[52]

Sexual relations were often criminalized and punished more harshly than in other societies. In August the *VB* ran a story headlined "Women who besmirch Germany's honor. Prison for intimate relations with prisoners of war." Emma Zeller and Elisabeth Rohrer had husbands at the front but nevertheless had engaged in sexual intercourse with prisoners of war "in total disregard of their womanly honor and despite the ban against social contact with POWs." Both women had probably led loose lives, but since neither had previous convictions, the court was lenient: Zeller got two years, Rohrer only a year. Morality in the Third Reich was writ large.[53]

The Gestapo reported a large number of other violations to the courts that covered an often-bewildering waterfront. Marie Muhri, a fifty-five-year-old owner of an apartment house and a cleaning establishment, had failed to put containers for scrap metal collections outside the house, and she had refused to put out more flags on Hitler's birthday. Three workers were arrested at a theater for spreading sneezing powder among the audience during a performance. A dentist was arrested for telling a German sergeant that one reason for dental problems among soldiers was poor nutrition. A bricklayer was seized because he called an SA man "a shit" and said that the current regime was "against the workers." The state railroad administration denounced a worker to the Gestapo because he had refused to attend a course in pistol shooting. Told he was violating the rules of war the man said, "I shit on the rules of war. My family comes first." When the owner of a milk store learned that his son had died in Russia, one of his customers pointed to Hitler's picture on the wall and yelled, "Tear him down, the dog." The Gestapo was informed but could not find out the woman's name. Adolf Treml, an actor and writer, was arrested because he remained seated in a café reading his paper while national songs were sung. The Gestapo said he would be jailed for eight days.[54]

As Schirach's cultural program unfolded during 1941 it became clear that he was taking bold risks to expand the frontiers of artistic freedom. While the Grillparzer week was conventional, and a speech in February contrasting the glories of German culture with the penury of England's contribution—over the centuries England had not produced a single noteworthy musical composition—fitted the Nazi line, the production of a new opera, *Johanna Balk*, by Rudolf Wagner-Regeny did not. It was part of a contemporary music week held in April 1941 that also featured works by Carl Orff and Werner Egk. The three young composers were the limits of modern music allowed in the Third Reich, even though Wagner-Regeny had worked with Bertold Brecht and his music was said to have overtones of Kurt Weil. Still, two of his operas were produced in the 1930s and had won him success and fame, despite historical themes that might have been interpreted as anti-Nazi. So could that of *Johanna Balk*—a tale of Magyar suppression of Siebenbürgers (Transylvanians) centuries ago—and the unease of Berlin's cultural bosses grew as opening night in Vienna neared. They disliked both text and music and banned the opera forty-eight hours before the curtain was to rise, ostensibly for foreign policy reasons: the Hungarians might be offended. The real reason, of course, was the opera's context—suppression of another people. Hitler had already banned Schiller's *Wilhelm Tell* for telling a similar tale.

Now Walter Thomas was quick on his feet. He summoned a meeting of author, composer, and stage director, and fired off a cable to Berlin: "Foreign policy dangers impossible stop On own initiative changed all names of places and people, and time of action so no relationship to history possible stop Since this only reason performance of new version set for tomorrow."[55] The cable bought them a precious few hours since no new version was ready, but when the curtain rose the text had been changed and the singers goose-stepped through it. But with or without the changes this was not a work Viennese audiences (properly cleansed of Jews who might have liked it) could tolerate. It ran counter to everything the Viennese cared for, what Furtwängler once called their love of "full-bosomed" music that allowed them to wallow in chromatic waves. It was ascetic, antiromantic, bereft of tonal carnality. A fugue played between the second and third act was "a motor-driven piece of music," Thomas would write, "whose dissonances lacked any harmonic transitions." [56] The Philharmonic was furious. The musicians clearly suffered under the staccatos and shrill rhythms, and the public stomped and whistled—a sign of high displeasure. Goebbels had the performance recorded and sent the disks to Hitler to prove that the Viennese played "atonal humbug in the style of the *Three-Penny Opera*." The work was banned in the Altreich and the Vienna Opera was urged not to repeat the performance for "reasons of public safety." (It was, however, several times with similar results—booing audiences.)

Schirach seized the occasion of the scandal to unveil his "Vienna cultural program" in a Burgtheater speech that defended the opera and laid out his approach to the arts.[57] True, *Johanna Balk* had engendered controversy. Some liked it, others registered violent protest. So what, said Schirach. "Why shouldn't we have discussions? If audiences argue about whether an opera is good or bad, are they a danger to the state or the city, or to art itself? I don't think so. Such discussions are useful and fertilize our cultural life. We don't want a cultural cemetery."

He then proceeded to discuss in exhaustive detail the plans he had for every cultural institution and event—the Mozart Week, a European musical festival early in 1942 to celebrate the 100th anniversary of the Vienna Philharmonic, new funds for the Volkstheater whose financial problems threatened bankruptcy, expansion of the city opera—the old Volksoper—so it could rival the state opera, new plans for the architecture of the Burgtheater, contracts with major conductors like Furtwängler, Clemens Krauss, Knappertsbusch, and Karl Böhm. He announced that Lothar Müthel would become "Generalintendant"(a kind of general manager) for both Burg and Opera in the next season and that Thomas would conduct Opera affairs until then. (In fact, Ernst August Schneider was called in from Cologne to handle day-to-day management from the fall of 1941 on). Schirach promised new architectural projects that would enhance, not damage, the city's core heritage, new centers of learning for the arts and the applied arts, for music, dance, and acting. Universities would focus on problems of the Southeast. Museum collections would be renewed and enriched, and art exhibition space expanded. More a catalogue than a cohesive program, the speech would be Schirach's reference point for cultural matters in the months to come.

Müthel was formally anointed as boss of the state theaters on April 21. The Führer himself issued the decree—another sign of how deeply Hitler involved himself in the cultural affairs of the city—and Goebbels sent a congratulatory cable.[58] A new exhibit opened at the Kunsthalle on May 12; many works displayed were those of young artists who painted them while on leave from the front, a sure sign, one critic wrote, of the creative impulses that service in the Wehrmacht engendered. In July the city observed the 100th anniversary of the birth of architect Otto Wagner, a towering figure in fin-de-siècle Vienna and the changing cityscape it brought forth. Modern architecture, clearly, was more acceptable to the Nazis than painting or music.

At the end of September 1941, Schirach broke more new ground with a speech at the opening in Düsseldorf of an exhibit of modern Viennese art that challenged the dogma of "the truth of reality," meaning that art should be a true depiction of nature, as Hitler and Goebbels demanded.[59] Apply it, Schirach said, and all art from antiquity to romanticism would lose all meaning, and color photography would advance "to the greatest artistic achievement of our age." But paintings that look like color photographs are as degenerate as portraits with two eyes on one side of the face. "Art does not serve reality," he said, "but truth. The apple of a Dutch genre painter is as unreal as that of Courbet or Vincent van Gogh. But all these apples are true. . . . God save us from a new materialism in art that says we need only reproduce reality in order to achieve truth . . . (and) . . . that demands the real because it cannot bear the true. Nature is real and true at the same time. Art and nature have truth in common but their reality is different."

Vienna's media did not comment on the speech and did not give the text much space. This was incendiary stuff and they knew it. Schirach knew it too since he took the quote—"the truth of reality"—from a Nazi magazine rather than attributing the thought to Hitler himself, an attack he dared not risk. But the speech was noted in Berlin where Goebbels continued to store ammunition for the cultural conquest of Vienna. His initial opinion that he could mentor Schirach had given way to a growing wariness; Vienna was too independent, too set on going its own way, and the doctor did not like it. Days after the attack on Russia he had made a grab for control of Burg and Opera, announcing that henceforth both theaters would depend on him for their financing. Schirach struck back quickly: under those conditions he could not fulfill the Führer's mandate. Hitler agreed and Goebbels had to pull back.[60] But it was a tactical retreat. Goebbels bided his time.

Schirach, meanwhile, achieved an opera coup. Gustav Gründgens, then—and in the years after the war—Germany's greatest actor-director, came to Vienna to direct the 150th anniversary production of Mozart's *Magic Flute* on October 2. Gründgens cut out the slapstick and coarse humor that so often marred productions of the Mozart opera. Instead, he presented, as the *VB* put it, "a fairy tale opera that reminded one of the world of a thousand and one nights."

Two weeks later Thomas reported to the cultural press about how much of Schirach's April program had already been implemented: the Volkstheater had been saved from financial ruin.[61] The Josefstadt would add serious new Nazi plays to its repertory; the Volksoper had a new director who would push up the performance level and train young singers for the Staatsoper. Several theaters that had closed after the Anschluss because of dwindling demand would be reopened to meet the rush of new theatergoers; art exhibits would be reorganized and a new schedule of art shows developed for the 1941–42 season.

The cultural highlight of the year was the Mozart Week that ran from November 28 to December 5, 1941, even though it encountered an icy reception in Berlin. As a Reich festival it needed approval from the propaganda ministry. So Thomas traveled to Berlin and submitted plans for eighteen concerts and seven opera performances. That was all well and good, he was told, the ministry approved honoring Mozart, but why only in Vienna? Goebbels himself would have to approve this one. Goebbels did but insisted that Berlin have oversight responsibilities, fearing that the musical extravaganza might have Austrian, Viennese, or even worse "separatist" overtones. It did, of course. The demand for tickets—64,000 people had applied, far outstripping the available theater space—showed that.[62] Schirach decided to add a Vienna Mozart Week with sixty concerts and other events, which, since it was a local matter, did not need Goebbels's approval.

It was not an easy event to organize. The radio wanted an advanced text of Schirach's opening speech, which was to be broadcast nation-wide. Sorry, Thomas said, the Gauleiter doesn't even give out his topic. Playing the national hymns before the "Jupiter" symphony also led to a tussle before the Nazis won out. Lists of foreign guests contradicted each other. Not enough food stamps were handed out so that special supple-ments had to be found. Nothing earth shaking, of course, but good ex-amples of how the vaunted German efficiency could become bollixed in Viennese *Schlamperei* (a truly untranslatable term whose dictionary defi-nition of "sloveniless" does not reflect its true meaning, which is more a state of mind and a relaxed attitude to the vagaries of life.)[63]

The festival itself would prove as much an exercise in Nazi propa-ganda as a celebration of Mozart and his music, although just about everything he ever wrote, including half-finished works dug up by avid German musicologists, was performed—and with the kind of panache conductors like Karl Böhm could draw from musicians and singers.

Schirach used his opening speech to launch an attack on the cultural impoverishment of Great Britain and the United States: "What a poor world it would be were it dependent on English or American music. Their cultural sterility is proverbial. They may try to hide their feelings of inferiority by claiming to fight for human culture, but we know what's behind that claim. Bolshevism and the driving force of the British Em-pire have one thing in common: the infertility of their spirit. But we are a creative nation."[64]

Goebbels came for the last two days of the festival, attending first the Gründgens-staged *Magic Flute*. One of his flunkies called the elegant production—all white and gray instead of the radiant colors used so of-ten—a scandal: "This is supposed to be a festival production. Herr Minis-ter, it is a travesty." Goebbels, Thomas wrote, agreed. It was a travesty.

The next afternoon Goebbels delivered his homage to genius, speak-ing to a half-empty house, an insult Schirach had engineered by failing to mobilize the troops, something the Nazis were good at. Yet it was a sensitive speech, far better than Schirach's, full of empathy and insight— Goebbels knew that Mozart's was indeed the voice of God, that here was a universal genius Germany may have claimed as its own but who be-longed to mankind, and that after Mozart no one need search for the nature of genius. "Here it lies clean and immaculate with all its mystic secrets clear for all to see. . . . If art has the task of lifting up the hearts of a tortured mankind and to move them into a better world, if in a life full of hardship and contradiction it can show us the ideal of joyful perfection or at least to let us sense it, how great is the artistry of this genius! One would have to invent a new language to do it justice in words."[65]

That evening Furtwängler led the Vienna Philharmonic through Mozart's *Requiem*. The performance was to be recorded and aired later that night. Halfway through the concert Goebbels scribbled three words on the back of his program and handed it to an aide. He had forbidden the broadcast, a move fueled by his resentment over how he had been treated that afternoon at the Opera when so small a crowd had listened to his speech, a resentment that suddenly bubbled over and led to the ban. Later at a reception in the salon behind the state box Goebbels let loose. The whole world would laugh at him for letting Catholic Vienna conduct religious propaganda under cover of a Mozart festival and then putting it on the air. "All we'd need is a congratulatory telegram from the Holy Father to his contrite son returned to the bosom of the church. That's just like me." He was furious. He left abruptly after telling Thomas to report to his suite at the Hotel Bristol at once. When he arrived Goebbels delivered a savage tongue-lashing. "You're the guilty one, you alone. You support Vienna separatism. Your policies are hostile to the Reich. You've been seduced by the liberalistic reactionaries in Vienna. This Mozart Week is a scandal that has nothing to do with us. It had only one aim—to give Vienna a monopoly on the arts. But you won't succeed. Berlin is and will remain the capital. I have it in my power to make Vienna a cultural village. You go ahead without my permission to invite Frenchmen, Belgians, Romania, Hungary, and God knows who else in order to swindle Viennese illusionism." Then he told Thomas to get out.[66] In reality, Thomas lasted another year and a half. Schirach was loath to let him go because he was gutsy, knew his business, and had the kind of provocative ideas the Reichsleiter felt he needed, even if Thomas was sometimes politically naïve and behaved foolishly, for example by helping Jews in trouble.

The trouble of Viennese Jews was growing exponentially. A week after the Gestapo had told Löwenherz on January 23, 1941, that they knew of no plans to deport Jews to Poland, he was informed that the first transport with about a thousand Jews on it would leave on February 15. The second, he would write in his report, was to depart on February 19, and then once a week every Wednesday. Some 10,000 Jews were to be re-settled by May. Instructions were specific. Each Jew could take two suit-cases weighing no more than 50 kilograms (a little more than 100 pounds), two warm blankets, and two pairs of shoes. The IKG should see to it that Jews with more shoes should give one pair to emigrants who didn't have a spare. The central office would select Jews for resettle-ment and they would be moved on a family basis. Those selected were to report to "transit camps" in the second district. They were to lock their apartments on leaving. The Gestapo would then seal them. Once in the detention center they were to surrender ration cards and apartment keys. They could take as much cash as they had, but the Gestapo would change the marks into Polish zloty. Finally, the Jews had to provide a list of all assets—provided they still had any—which would be sold to cover their transportation costs. The IKG was to feed the deportees in the detention center until they were shipped out. Jews who did not report freely would be rounded up and severely punished. In February and March some 5,000 Viennese Jews were sent to Poland. Then, on March 16, the SD ordered a halt for the same reason as in 1939: a shortage of rolling stock. Hitler was planning to invade Russia, and the Wehrmacht could not spare the transport.[67]

Behind Löwenherz's bureaucratic and dry account lay thousands of individual tragedies.

A ninety-year-old woman had always said she would never go to Po-land. When the SS came she asked to go to the bathroom and then lie down. She never got up. She had taken poison. Edith Holzer had worked as a nurse in a Jewish old-age home when the SS came and cleaned it out. "They took everyone," she remembered. "One man was simply lifted out of his wheelchair and tossed into a waiting truck. Some people struggled and tried to defend themselves, but the SS just picked them up and pushed them into the vehicle."[68]

Mano Fischer, fourteen, lived with his mother in a converted pigsty—the Nazis had kicked the family out of their flat in the Karl Marx Hof—when the SS came looking for him. They weren't interested in his mother because she was an Aryan, but she went with him anyway. The Nazis took the boy's bike and stuffed it, along with mother and son, into one of the waiting trucks. They spent several days in a school used as a transit camp.

One night Fisher and his mother went out to the toilet. They noted that the door to the courtyard was open and that Fischer's bike stood there, waiting and tempting. The door to the street was also open. "Lets go," his mother said, and they pushed the bike onto the street and walked home. It was three in the morning. Fischer survived thanks to an accommodating bureaucrat in the local labor office who gave him a work permit that paved the way for a job at a weaving mill. But without an official identity card he was in constant danger of being discovered.[69]

Deportations were not resumed until the fall with both the IKG and the Nazis using this down time to prepare for the future. The central office tightened control over Jewish life. Jews, for example, could no longer move to a different house or apartment without permission. Beginning September 1941 all Jews had to wear the yellow star stitched on their clothing. The *VB* was specific: the star was to be worn, clearly visible, on the left side of the chest. Its introduction was an "absolute necessity to enhance and complete the Nuremberg racial laws." The IKG made the stars and sold them for eight pfennigs a piece. Jews were forbidden to use public transport. Some exceptions were made though: Jews could buy a ticket after showing photo ID but were not permitted to board during rush hour.

Over the summer the final solution began to be put into practice, well before the Wannsee conference of January 1942 where it was formalized and documented. The Nazis began experimenting with gas trucks that killed passengers.

Early in September Löwenherz asked Eichmann in Berlin if rumors of new deportations were true. Eichmann denied them, by then a clear signal that indeed they were true. On September 30 Löwenherz met with Alois Brunner, an SS officer who now ran Eichmann's central office for Jewish emigration in Vienna. Alois would become known as Brunner I to distinguish him from his namesake Anton (they were not related), who would succeed Alois at the central office to become Brunner II; both SS men were among the most brutal Nazis. Alois Brunner told Löwenherz that Jews from across the Reich, including Vienna, would be sent to Lodz in Poland and that his office was to put together lists of deportees. The IKG would have to notify the victims and cover their costs. This time, however, they would be allowed to take only RM100. Again Löwenherz fought a bureaucratic battle to keep special categories of Jews in Vienna, notably those who worked for him, orphans, the sick, and the lame, as he had done in February, and again with mixed success. He saved some and had to sacrifice others. The day Löwenherz met Brunner happened to be Yom Kippur, and when he stood in the synagogue on Seittenstettengasse that evening to take part in reading the Torah, the tears ran down his face and the congregation knew that the worst had happened.

In five transports over a period of less than three weeks beginning on October 15, more than 5,000 Viennese Jews were sent to Lodz. In all 20,000 Jews were shipped to that Polish city between October and November. Less than a year later only 2,500 or so were still alive. The others had been murdered as part of "Aktion Reinhard," former Vienna Gauleiter Odilo Globocnik's efficient killing machine in that region. In December 1941 about 40,000 Nuremberg Jews remained in Vienna, a problem Eichmann addressed in February 1942 when he had half a dozen Jewish leaders, including Löwenherz, come to Berlin. His message was brief: all Jews were to be removed from Reich territory. Impossible, Löwenherz said. Massive emigration from the city—a last 6,000 had departed in 1941 before the doors to emigration closed in November—had left only the old and the sick who could not be transported and those Jews protected through marriage to an Aryan. Eichmann shrugged but said he would see what he could do. His answer was Theresienstadt, a small Czech town the Nazis had turned into a model ghetto and shown off to the Swiss Red Cross as a shining example of Nazi mercy. The old, the sick, the privileged—mostly highly decorated veterans of World War I—would be "stored" there with the first transport leaving on June 20, 1942. That fall almost 15,000, including what prominent Jews were left, notably Dr. Viktor Frankl who won postwar fame for his "third" Viennese school of psychotherapy, and his family, and members of the IKG staff had arrived in Theresienstadt. In the end even the model facade had peeled off the camp, most of whose inhabitants were shipped to Auschwitz.

The techniques of mass deportation did not change much in 1942. The central office issued lists of Jews for deportation but no longer relied on voluntary compliance. Instead, it used a combination of Jewish police, meaning Jews who had been forced or had volunteered for enforcer roles, and SS supervisors. Some of the JUPOs, as the Jewish police was known, were rougher than others. But their goal was the same: help Jews pack their belongings, list their assets, turn over apartment keys, and get them into the trucks that would take them to the transit camps.

Jews were shipped to the East in batches of 1,000. If the lists did not bring in enough Jews in time for train departures, SS trucks grabbed them off the streets until the quota was met. Brutality was fierce, with both Brunners the most feared by their victims. Alois Brunner squeezed the last pfennig from Jews loaded onto trains and put on white gloves when he beat Jews, so as not to pollute himself. Anton Brunner indulged in equally horrific beatings. He tore earrings from women and broke gold teeth out of old men's mouths. He beat one Orthodox Jew into a bloody pulp because the man had taken off his hat but not his yarmulke.

The Wehrmacht's failure to conquer Moscow in December 1941 and the Russian counteroffensive that month led to a change in strategy. In the summer of 1941, when it looked as if the Russian campaign would be over on schedule, plans had called for Jews to be transported into the Ukraine and other eastern territories whose wide-open spaces could accommodate the millions the Germans wanted to get rid of. But now the strategy of leaving Jews to the elements and the open spaces had become too risky; they could fall into Russian hands who would accept them more eagerly now that Germany was the enemy, not a friend, as had been the case at Nisko. This was yet another reason to formalize the final solution. Governor General Hans Frank still had too many Jews in Poland. If he couldn't ship them east, they would have to be killed on site. Gas trucks multiplied, as did concentration camps and eventually the more efficient gas ovens.

By that time the mass exodus of Vienna's Jews was over. Only 22,000 were left in the spring of 1942, and in October the mass transports of the remaining Jews, with most of them headed for Theresienstadt, were completed. By the end of the year only about 8,000 racial Jews—those who did not conform to the Nuremberg laws—remained, with some 6,000 protected through Aryan marriages. In November the IKG was dissolved and a Council of Elders set up to handle Jewish affairs, with Dr. Löwenherz still in charge.

To read about the suffering of individual Jews becomes repetitive and to some extent deadening, but take one man out of the many and it can still be heartbreaking. Armin Tyroler, a non-Aryan (meaning he had converted to Christianity but had Jewish grandparents) married to a Jew, was sixty-eight years old in the winter of 1941. He had been a member of the Vienna Philharmonic for forty-two years when he retired in 1937 with a pension and the honorary title of "professor." In December

1941 he wrote to the director of the Philharmonic, reminding him that on his retirement the director had said to come see him whenever he was in need and that "our doors are always open to you." He had not done so because he had always managed by himself. But what he now faced was beyond his powers. "My situation is so terrible and so well known to you that I need not discuss it further." In language redolent of the lost monarchy and another century Tyroler pleaded with the director to use his influence "to preserve me from forced evacuation." He had spent his life giving pleasure to others through music and had done so to the satisfaction of his superiors. "That gives me the courage to beseech you not to leave me in my nameless misery. Honored Herr Direktor! Time is short and the danger I face is very great. Take pity on me and don't deny me your help." [70] The director replied that he would forward the plea to Walter Thomas who had successfully intervened in similar cases. Thomas did intervene but could only delay the inevitable. He got him an extra nine months in Vienna, even if the musician had to move from his home in the ninth district to a "Jewish" apartment in the second district. Then on August 27, 1942, two months after the first transport left for Theresienstadt, Tyroler and his wife were on a train to that hamlet in Bohemia. He survived for a little more than two years but on October 28, 1944, now seventy-one years old, he was shipped to Auschwitz where he was gassed. [71]

Walter Thomas had won a reputation for trying to save Jews. Vienna's arts community had been heavily involved with that lost Vienna in which Jews played such leading roles. Theo Lingen and Hans Moser, two comic actors with considerable appeal even outside the Third Reich, were both married to Jews and in constant need of protection. Even otherwise solid Nazi supporters turned to him. Thus the actress Paula Wessely, who had lent her name to incessant Nazi propaganda, called Thomas: her secretary was married to a Jew and faced deportation, could he help? Thomas himself professed to be daunted by the task, but his name occurs in enough archival material to make his own claim of attempting to help plausible.

He led an active social life within the arts community, and was accessible to the noncomformists, and even to Jews, who felt safe in his presence. He attended parties in the homes of actors, directors, artists, and singers where conversation often broke the bounds of orthodoxy. One such occasion made his reputation. It had grown late and those present had drunk too much alcohol. They devised a game—everybody should say what he or she wished as they left the party. Ursula Schuh, an artist married to Oscar Fritz Schuh, the Opera's innovative director of Mozart works, drained her glass and called out "I wish Hitler were on the gallows." The group froze. Thomas was a party member—a fact he hid in his book *Until the Curtain Falls*—and one of Schirach's closest collaborators. But after a few seconds Thomas turned to his wife and said, "I think it's time we all went home." Milan Dubrovic wrote in his book *Embezzled History* that "now we all knew that we could trust Thomas fully and could come to him with pleas to help persecuted friends."[72] And Thomas came through, sometimes using Schirach's stationery without his permission to save homes or find new ones for the threatened and persecuted.

But he was not at ease in his skin, and his occasional despair is documented by a visit he paid to Alois Brunner at the central office in an effort to help Jewish artists who had made sizable contributions to the city's culture. Brunner was polite but sarcastic. "Please sit down. What brings you here? We don't usually wander along the high road of humanity as artists do with whom you usually have dealings. Our business is a lot more realistic." When Thomas explained why he had come Brunner said, "I know that you are very much engaged for these people. You signed several applications that ended up here, so we think that you are a friend of the Jews. But we can't make any exceptions. A Jew is a Jew, and the deserving Jews are the worst. I don't have to make any decisions. I follow orders, and my orders say that at a certain point in time no Jew may remain in Vienna. There is no recourse. Even if the Reichsstatthalter supports a petition, it won't help. I don't answer to any local authority, not even Schirach." He had the last word, Brunner continued, and Thomas could save mail and time by coming directly to him, but that it wouldn't do him any good. "This is a dangerous business. Lay off. It doesn't matter if your artists separate from their wives tomorrow or in six months, one day they will, no matter how hard you try. Take my advice. You can't stop anything and only put yourself in a bad light trying."[73]

Thomas kept trying anyway, on behalf of the Jews and the cultural projects in which he was engaged. True, Brunner may have been in a position to decide about life and death for Jews. but his reach was not ubiquitous; for example, it did not extend to living space. In March 1942 Brunner tried to assign a Jewish apartment to a Nazi official, but Thomas intervened and his intervention had Schirach's official stamp on it. Brunner had to admit his "orders" did not extend that far. Still, it meant one more black mark on Thomas's Gestapo record.

The fight with Goebbels during Mozart Week did not dent Thomas's cultural aspirations or the backing they received from Schirach who, in 1942, still enjoyed unstinting support from the Führer. Hitler was pleased both with Schirach's cultural activism and his cheerleading for massive Jewish deportations—Schirach did not take an active part in them but made sure that those who did got all the official help they needed, including ideological speeches denouncing world Jewry. Indeed, in a speech in April 1942 he claimed credit for making Vienna *judenrein* (clean of Jews). He noted that the Jewish question had not been much discussed in recent years, but "we have deported them by the train load and in doing so have eased both provisioning this city and the housing situation."

In March Vienna celebrated the one hundredth anniversary of the Vienna Philharmonic. Schirach opened the festivities on March 28, ending his speech with an almost passionate defense of art under fire: Goya's paintings were a revolution hated by his contemporaries; Van Gogh was so "far ahead of his time that we haven't caught up with him yet"; Mozart and Bruckner had broken new ground and run into critical spears, but criticism couldn't measure a Werner Egk with the yardsticks of other composers. He thanked the Philharmonic for helping him bring contemporary music to the Viennese public, because "all music, including music of the present, must have a home in Vienna." Indeed, he added, "Here in Vienna all art is at home."[74]

And for the next year or so it seemed that it was. Festivals of new music and homage to dramatists like Friedrich Hebbel were to be followed with the crowning event in November—a spectacular celebration of playwright Gerhard Hauptmann's eightieth birthday. The prospect did not make Berlin happy. Hauptmann may have won the Nobel Prize, but for ideologues like Alfred Rosenberg he was not enough of a Nazi, and for Goebbels too much a pacifist. Still no one interfered.

Schirach went all out. He traveled to Germany to escort the playwright to Vienna personally and put him and his wife up at the downtown Palais Pallavicini. He gave receptions and dinners, invited the usual coterie of honored guests to watch a flurry of Hauptmann plays strut across Vienna stages. Hitler and Goebbels sent grudging telegrams. Thomas opened the festivities at a matinee where he expressed Vienna's joy at hosting the play-wright. Raul Aslan, the Burg's unchallenged star, recited a special poem Josef Weinheber had written for the occasion. The Burg put together an exhibit of Hauptmann memorabilia. At the end of the Hauptmann week on November 22, the eighty-year-old was glad to leave. He had a weakness for wine; the late hours and the rich food did the rest.[75]

Clearly, money for such extravaganzas was no problem. Thomas had RM 11 million a year to spend on the theaters alone, and more millions for museums, exhibits, and other cultural institutions. With such sums buildings could be refurbished, new exhibition space opened, and new acquisitions made. He bought two Rembrandts, rushing to Berlin once he heard of their availability, conned an Austrian in the ministry of fi-nance into advancing the money, and arranged for purchase of several Italian, German, and Dutch masterpieces. The Austrian Gallery in the Belvedere got two Corots, a Monet, a Toulouse-Lautrec, and a Maillol. He told the director of the Museum of Applied Arts that he could go ahead and buy the priceless oriental rugs from the famed Clam-Gallas collection that the Austrian government had tried to acquire beginning in 1922 but could not afford.

But even as the collections expanded, provisions were made for hid-ing them in old monasteries and the cellars of small castles in the coun-tryside to protect them, not only from the ravages of war but also from freebooters who stole art for various Nazi patrons—most notably from Kajetan Mühlmann, Seyss-Inquart's arts-chief-become-chief-art-thief for Hermann Göring. Thomas succeeded. Not even Göring could walk off with a Vienna picture or statue, try as he might.

Thomas also made sure that new acquisitions and other art were open to the public. In 1941 the art museum showed off its new treasures, re-configured the Egyptian and antiquity collections, and launched a spe-cial exhibit of heraldic costumes from the Habsburgs' treasure trove. A year later a second exhibit of new acquisitions followed. But Thomas also shoved in more daring and controversial work that would give Vienna a reputation in 1942 as the culturally freest city of the Third Reich, a magnet for artists and writers.

He put together special shows from the Albertina's holdings, one "Drawings from the Turn of the Century," for example, included Gustav Klimt—just acceptable—and Egon Schiele—mostly degenerate—and

Käthe Kollwitz, whose work the Nazi press ignored. Most daring, perhaps, he opened a show of drawings by the Belgian James Ensor, a painter and printmaker whose work ranged from postimpressionism to symbolism and expressionism, styles not exactly in favor. And he tried to have the German expressionist Emil Nolde relocate to Vienna to live, an effort that failed. Once Schirach learned that Hitler hated Nolde he withdrew his support, but not before Thomas had arranged a private showing of Nolde's latest watercolors. The artist himself came to Vienna and attended the show. Then Nolde returned to his inner exile in the North, leaving indelible impressions of art that was and would be again.

Thomas was more successful with Richard Strauss in a coup that strengthened Vienna's position as cultural center—he arranged for the composer's move from his villa in Bavaria to his small palais in Janquingasse in Vienna. Strauss was no longer perceived as the musical god he had been in the 1930s. His son had married a Jew; his grandsons were half-Jews. He made remarks the Nazis found offensive. But he was still Germany's greatest living composer, and Goebbels was willing to make exceptions for him. But for Strauss they were not enough. His daughter-in-law had been insulted, his grandsons barred from secondary school. Strauss would come to Vienna provided Schirach met his demands—they were not easy for a Nazi to fulfill.[76]

Schirach did indeed meet the demands, and went beyond: he could not assure food rations equivalent to those of a Gauleiter but he would see to it that the Strauss family had plenty to eat; he authorized Thomas to talk to Strauss as if guarantees had been offered. The composer bought into this gossamer agreement, and by 1942 he and his entourage were settled in the Janquingasse.

Allied propaganda saw the move as another Strauss commitment to Nazi cultural policy, while top Goebbels officials viewed it as more support for Vienna's separatist intentions. Still, on December 16, 1942, Beethoven's birthday, the composer received the Vienna city council's first Beethoven prize.

In October 1942 Thomas demonstrated his ability to synthesize and provoke by opening a new exhibit titled "Art and Culture of a Century." It was a comprehensive show designed to give visual form to the theatrical, scientific, musical, literary, and artistic development of the city—without, of course, any reference to the Jewish contribution. He had run into some opposition when he unfolded his plans but then found united support.

211

Even the city government's cultural boss, Hanns Blaschke, who had feuded with Thomas from the day he arrived—"You want to run my Burg-theater, my Opera," he had told him in deep Viennese dialect, "What do you know about it? You're a Prussian and politically you're a nothing"—thought the show was a good idea and said so at the opening.[77] The show, Thomas would write, had not pleased Berlin because "it became a demonstration of Vienna's cultural conscience and a commitment to its own tradition."

Berlin was already uneasy enough about Thomas's free-wheeling ways and had blocked appointment of well-known scholars to chairs at Vienna's institutes of higher learning. Many remained vacant or were occupied by nonentities. As one Goebbels official told Thomas, his ministry wanted to prevent "an accumulation of too much quality" in Vienna that could challenge Berlin's hegemony. But challenge it had—and did.

Although Hitler still held Schirach in high personal regard, he was queasy about Schirach's expansive cultural policies and shared his feelings with Goebbels who stoked his doubts. Goebbels noted in his diary that the Führer was "determined to break Vienna's cultural hegemony. He doesn't want the Reich to have two capitals that compete with one another. Vienna is just another city with a million people like Hamburg, nothing more. Schirach is on the wrong path. The Führer hates Vienna's atmosphere. He spent so many unpleasant years in this city that his aversion to Vienna is easy to understand."[78] A month later he wrote that Schirach was not up to the job in Vienna, interfered too much with his ministry's activities, and was "about to repeat all the mistakes we have made since 1933."[79]

Schirach was not unaware that he was under fire and that Thomas drew most of it, but he still gave him wide latitude. Once they even had a long conversation about Thomas Mann in which Schirach conceded his brilliance as a writer but rejected his work for "reasons of state." Such discussions gave Thomas the courage to exercise his convictions, even though he wondered every time he opened a letter from the Reichsstatt-halter's office whether he was being dismissed.

Finally, Schirach had been pushed too far. In mid-1942 he summoned Thomas to the Ballhausplatz. Schirach went over the reasons he had hired him in the first place, essentially because he did not want one of Goebbels's minions in the job. Thomas had enjoyed some success, the arts community was behind him, but Schirach had serious concerns. Thomas had enemies and he, Schirach, had a hard time holding them at bay. True, he could fire Thomas, but that would be an admission that he had made a mistake. Goebbels would triumph and claim that Schirach had bent to his will. "I can't afford that. I will have to look for other ways."

Thomas soon felt his master's ire. His name was stricken from the major invitation lists. Hermann Stuppäck moved from the propaganda office to a job as Thomas's deputy who had access to his mail, phone calls, and other records. On the surface little had changed, but Thomas felt like a dead man on leave. Nonetheless, he arranged the Hauptmann week and was going full throttle in other areas as his program for the 1942–43 season attests.[80] It was packed with concerts and recitals from Furtwängler and Böhm to the Schneiderhahn Quartet and pianist Walter Gieseking, featured more than a dozen new plays and as many new productions of standard opera fare, had a Verdi festival on the calendar for April, a flock of new art exhibits, and a clutch of scientific lectures. It would also feature an exhibition of "Young Art in the German Reich" that would finish Thomas's career and damage Schirach's political viability.

Schirach was already in trouble, despite Hitler's continued support. He had taken too many chances in pushing a liberal cultural agenda, and he had made too many enemies. Himmler had expressed contempt for his literary ambitions, Bormann had taken umbrage at Schirach's arrogance, and Ribbentrop's thin skin had been rubbed raw by real and imagined slights—Schirach had failed to show up at the railroad station to bid him good-bye, for example. Goebbels hovered nearby, waiting to pounce, as his diary entries document.

What weakened Schirach the most was his inability to persuade the public at large to fully integrate with the Reich and to support its policies, especially after Hitler attacked Russia and the city's mood turned sour. As manpower needs increased more, and more men were drafted, it became harder to win deferments for essential work. Shortages persisted and general annoyance rose. No overt or widespread opposition to the Nazi regime existed as yet, but griping at the *Piefkes*—the disdainful term the Viennese used in referring to Altreich Germans and especially the Prussians—had become endemic.

The *VB* tried a feeble riposte in October 1941 with a "sarcastic" Leo Schödl column titled "The End of Piefkitis" in which the author described a woman from the Altreich who sprays insults about Vienna and the Viennese in every venue from the trade fair to St. Stephen's Square. In fact, Schödel wrote, the woman didn't exist but was invented by those "who bore the mark of Cain—defamation and sedition—in their hearts and on their chests. May God and the Gestapo have no mercy on them for they know damn well what they do. They want to bring the fungus of Piefkitis among the people and maintain and deepen divisions that are slowly receding."[81] But the divisions, in fact, were growing.

Concern over Ostmark separatism, that is, maintenance of a Viennese and an Ostmark—not necessarily an Austrian—identity within the structure of the Reich, informed much of Schirach's and the Nazi party's politics even before the Balkan campaign and the Russian invasion. At the end of October 1941 Schirach told Hitler that construction of new housing was urgent, despite the war, in order to quell Viennese complaints. Hitler refused Schirach's request to expand city housing. He instructed Bormann to tell Schirach to suppress such dissent, brutally if need be. His job in Vienna was not to build more housing but to clean up the situation, deporting the Jews, then the Czechs and other minorities so that the population would be cut back to 1.4 million thus solving the housing crisis.[82]

But Viennese discontent was also fueled among some by fear of American intervention in the war. In his book Thomas described Colin Ross's visit to the Schirach villa months before Pearl Harbor as one example. Ross was a German globetrotter who turned out travel books by the yard that sold millions in Germany and in translation. He was a self-styled U.S. expert—and Schirach had never lost interest in his maternal home. Ross was blunt. "If war with America comes, everything will be lost," he said and asked Schirach to arrange a meeting with Hitler so he could tell him that the United States was a thousand times more technologically advanced than Germany and could build an air armada in a year "that will destroy everything."[83] Ross never saw Hitler, nor did the headlines after Pearl Harbor reflect his insights. "War monger Roosevelt has reached his goal," one said, while others pledged "battle with all means at our disposal till final victory."

By then the brief fever of being the center of attention—or perceiving itself as such—of the Balkan campaign had faded. Hitler was consumed by the war in the East, and Ribbentrop had never let the diplomacy of the Southeast slip out of his hands. Nevertheless, Schirach kept a hand in what he still saw as his coming empire—a Nazi version of the Habsburg realm.

Much of it was dreams—like the "state dinners" he gave using the dynasty's gold, silver, porcelain, and crystal—but some of it was indeed real.

The SOEG, for example, did take on more substance than that of a soap bubble. By 1941 it had a solid economic reporting structure in place across the Balkans. The stream of information that flowed into Vienna was distributed widely and widely relied upon. "Businessmen benefited from what was in essence often industrial or agricultural espionage," Dietrich Orlow wrote in *The Nazis in the Balkans*,[84] and the German government used the data in negotiations with Balkan countries. But Schirach had kept SOEG out of Ribbentrop's hands by making economics minister Walther Funk the group's patron while he kept the presidency. For Vienna it meant more prestige and buffed the city's image as international center.

In mid-June 1941 Schirach put SOEG on display at the Konzerthaus with all the usual hoopla including, this time, the Vienna Symphony, in a meeting that the *VB* said had far more than local importance. Funk was the star with a "programmatic" speech about German foreign trade in war time. He claimed that trade volume in 1940 had reached peacetime levels through reorientation to the Southeast and was working to create a large-scale European economy. For Schirach the speech was an opportunity to beat Vienna's Southeast drum. No city in the Reich would understand Funk better, the *VB* quoted him as saying, no city was better suited to contribute to the work of cooperating with the nations of the Southeast and the Near East.[85]

At home in 1942 Schirach did his domestic political duty. He pitched the workers in February, urging them to work harder but promising that every hour worked contributed to the Reich's socialist achievements.[86] For the fourth anniversary of the Anschluss, Schirach shared a platform with Goebbels on the Heldenplatz where the party gathered 100,000 people. Their message: work and sacrifice; victory at any price. "When the Reich calls upon us," Schirach said, "we know only one watchword: everything for Greater Germany, everything for Adolf Hitler." Goebbels made fun of Churchill for claiming the gap between Berlin and Vienna would never be bridged. It had been, and for a long time, he said, although in truth he knew better.[87] Even committed Nazis like Blaschke remained hostile to the Prussians, and Schirach had not succeeded in firing up mass enthusiasm for the party's programs. The Viennese were not opposed to Nazism per se, but the shock value had worn off. Massive crowds were no longer easy to mobilize. Fewer than 70,000 turned out to celebrate the Führer's fifty-third birthday.

Schirach's major focus that year was not domestic concerns but a mixture of his favorite interests—youth, foreign affairs, and culture. He would hold a European youth festival in Vienna in September.[88] It was both a catastrophe and a success, and as such typical for the man. Schirach thought big. He would invite representatives from all of Hitler's vassal states. The event would be another congress of Vienna—parades, receptions, festive signing of documents, acts of brotherhood, gala performances at the Burg and the Opera. Months before the event he shifted staff from his Reich youth movement in Berlin to Vienna. Everybody worked around the clock—posters had to be approved, parade routes laid out, the decoration of streets and houses decided upon, and foreign dignitaries invited—heads of governments, ministers, ambassadors. He saw himself as accomplishing what Ribbentrop's foreign office could not—impressing the enemy with the unity and determination of the new Europe under Nazi hegemony.

But he had not counted on the one group he needed to impress the most—the Nazi hierarchy, which dismissed the whole thing as "Baldur's children's festival." Ribbentrop annulled all the invitations. Italian foreign minister Ciano sent his regrets after having accepted. So did everybody else, including ambassadors from the Balkan states. Goebbels gleefully barred press coverage in the Altreich. No radio, no newsreel cameras.

But Berlin could not stop the event from taking place. Schirach had taken hundreds of gas-guzzling limousines out of mothballs and sent them whizzing through the streets even though the dignitaries they were supposed to transport had not come. Instead, low-ranking officials and members of the Hitler Youth and of other youth organizations had the time of their lives tooting around the Ring or driving up the Höhenstrasse. For the youth had come—Italians, Spaniards, Walloons, Flemish, French, Norwegians, Finns, Bulgarian, Romanians, Slovaks, and Hungarians—all piled into the stadiums and receptions; they ate off gold dishes and stormed the cold buffet. Some even turned the Hofburg into a forbidden dance floor and made such a ruckus that Schirach fled home before midnight.

But not everything was fun and games. Schirach gave several political speeches in which he attacked FDR and the Jews with vicious and cold-hearted hatred. In one he accused Roosevelt of aiming to become world president, said Eleanor was less noted for her beauty than for her "unscrupulous" business dealings, and called FDR a "physical wreck" who could stand up only with braces, but even worse was a "moral wreck" with the blood of youth on his hands because he had made a speech calling on world youth to reject fascist values.[89]

His opening speech on September 14 was even more savage. He accused Jews of propagating "untamed sexual lust" among youth and heaping contempt on decency. "Every Jew active in Europe is a danger for European culture. To those who accuse me of having sent tens of thousands of Jews out of this city, which was once the metropolis of European Jewry, I would have to reply that I see in this a contribution to European culture." And he called the European Youth Organization, which was formed as part of the Congress, "a weapon in the battles of this war."[90]

The speech was so savage that when Schirach asked Thomas about the reaction of Vienna's cultural community, the latter could only shrug. The night before some of his actor friends had been outraged. "I knew it," Schirach said. "Oh, these artists. If you say something whose background they don't understand they curse you. What must a politician say even if he feels quite differently." As he spoke he looked at a small sculpture next to a copy of Rodin's *Le Penseur* on his desk.[91]

The local media escaped Goebbels's edict and gave the Youth Congress blanket coverage. Schirach would be honorary president of the new organization, and his successor at the Hitler Youth, Artur Axman, would run it. Spaniards and others would manage working committees, including one for young women. And all the papers picked up on Vienna's choice as festival site. As the *Südost Echo* noted, "Vienna is and remains the clearing house for creative achievements in all areas of art and culture and is therefore the servant of European solidarity."[92]

The man in Vienna's streets was less impressed. The German summer offensive in Russia had reached Stalingrad and not punched much beyond it. The makings of the tragedy to come were not yet clear, but the Panzers had begun to sputter—which led to local jokes: "Do you know why our tanks aren't rolling past the Volga? They had to give up all that gasoline for Baldur's kid festival."[93] That may have been a joke in Vienna but not in Berlin or in the Führer's headquarters on the Eastern front. Martin Bormann complained that German soldiers were dying at

Stalingrad while Vienna celebrated. Goebbels replied sarcastically, "Soldiers fight but the Congress dances in Vienna." Hitler's brow reportedly knitted in anger. It was the first time he was seriously annoyed with his protégé. It would not be the last, but for the time being Schirach's fervor in resettling Jews and his fury over SD chief Reinhard Heydrich's murder by Czech patriots on May 27, 1942—he wanted to expel all Czechs from Vienna as soon as all the Jews were gone—kept him afloat. And at the turn of 1943 Hitler called his Vienna Gauleiter from the Wolf's Lair, his headquarters on the Eastern front, to wish him happiness, success, and good health.

Schirach finally fell out of Hitler's favor two months into 1943 over yet another art exhibit Thomas had organized. It opened at the Künstlerhaus on February 7, 1943, a day late and without official ceremony. Thomas had solicited and gathered 587 works from 175 artists across the Reich that lay outside the art of color photography and therefore violated the strict canons of reproductive painting. But if the pictures were not abstract or revolutionary in the sense of Ernst Barlach or Nolde himself, they were different—personal expressions of how artists saw the world. Schirach had approved the show and given it ample display in the Hitler Youth magazine *Wille und Macht* (Will and Power). The *VB* gave the show a full page on February 9 and printed two pictures. The critic said the pictures showed "the inner reality" behind the painting.

It was perhaps not the best of times to take such risks. The last German soldier had surrendered in Stalingrad on February 3. The specter of defeat in war loomed over the Reich and certainly over Vienna. And worst of all, Hitler was not amused. He summoned Schirach to Berchtesgaden. The scene was explosive. They stood in the great hall of the Berghof with the panoramic window that looked out on the mountain scenery as if it were a painting—the ultimate combination of truth and reality. Bormann gave Hitler an open copy of the magazine. "A green dog," the Führer hissed. "And you have a quarter of a million copies printed which mobilizes all the cultural Bolsheviks and reactionaries against me. This isn't youth education but sabotage."[94] A Nazi art expert had walked through the show, declared some of the pictures degenerate, and urged Goebbels to close it. Now the Führer himself gave orders to shut it down—unobtrusively. On March 7 the *NWT* reported the ex-

218

hibit would close the next day to save personnel costs and to ease congestion on the Reichsbahn because so many people had come from all over the Reich to see the show.

Back in Vienna Schirach called Thomas to his office in the Gauhaus, the old parliament, not to the Ballhausplatz. Thomas went over his cultural schedule, but when he came to the Verdi festival Schirach interrupted. "Another festival. German cities are collapsing in ruins but Vienna pretends there are reasons to celebrate. When is this festival supposed to take place?" When Thomas told him April, Schirach made a note of the date and said. "Let's assume it's possible but if it is, it will be the last one. I can't afford special Vienna politics. They're provocative and create more enemies for me. I had to listen to some very unpleasant things. The Führer spoke of cultural opposition, about Vienna's liberalism in the arts. And Goebbels helped out. I know nothing will happen to me. But I have to make some changes. I went too far out front and let things happen that should not have happened. Your name was mentioned often up there in the mountains. And not only by Goebbels. You were designated as the root of all evil."[95]

He would send Thomas to the Eastern front to show that a liberal artistic weakling was able to fight for his nation and his Führer. He gave him a compass in case he got lost and a small pistol "in case there is no other way out." He also allowed him to manage the Verdi festival before he put on a uniform. So on April 4 Thomas stood in the Emperor's Hall in the state opera before a clutch of dignitaries, including Schirach and the Italian ambassador, to deliver his last hurrah—the Verdi cycle was an homage to Italian genius. Verdi's operas did not only have cultural but political value, which justified holding these performances in the fourth year of the war when the total commitment of the nation had been made to preserve European culture. His remarks, the *NWT* noted, "were warmly received."

Not, of course, by Goebbels. He was triumphant. The Führer had closed the exhibition, he wrote in his diary in March, and had turned sharply against Schirach. "He has decided to place cultural policy in Vienna under my direction." And later he wrote "Schirach feels pretty small right now. He sent Thomas to the soldiers. I believe that in the foreseeable future we won't have any problems with art policy in Vienna."[96] He was right. Before he was drafted Thomas spent several weeks in the city as an observer of the cultural scene—long enough to see the rapid changes Goebbels had decreed. Everybody and anybody who was not racially or politically pure was bounced out of his cultural job. Stuppäck took over Thomas's position—it took another eight months before he got the title—and demonstrated just how *real* Nazis handled culture. He did not dismantle what Thomas had built, but he kept everything strictly within political guidelines. Cultural coverage in the *VB*, for example, began to look back much more than it did to the present or the future. Long essays on such topics as "Germans and Knighthood in the Niebelungen Epic" or short stories by tested warhorses like Bruno Brehm began to replace racier coverage of cultural events.

In short, Vienna's role as magnet of artistic freedom within the Reich had been played out, even if the level of the performing arts remained high. In 1943 Karl Böhm finally came to Vienna to take over the Opera. He had been in Dresden and was long in play for the post in Vienna but reportedly Hitler did not want him there—he thought him a poor conductor, a judgment based on a snap visit to the Dresden opera where a journeyman performance was underway, which Böhm did not even conduct. By 1943 Hitler had forgotten his opposition and Goebbels put his own man—for Böhm was that despite his postwar fame—in place. Böhm arrived in January 1943—weeks before Thomas's disgrace—and said at his inauguration on January 14 how much he was looking forward to working together with "general secretary Thomas." So much for prescience in cultural politics.

Böhm also pledged, as Strohm had done, to give the Opera new glory. He was, however, more specific. He would push Mozart and Wagner and prepare a new repertory of Richard Strauss's operas to present as a birthday gift for the composer's eightieth birthday in June 1944. Thomas ran through the recent history of the Opera and paid particular tribute to Furtwängler, Krauss, and Knappertsbusch for helping restore the house after the Anschluss. He was generous to Strohm—incapacitated by illness and forced to give up his post—and to Ernst August Schneider, who had run the Opera after Thomas stepped down. Schneider would continue to manage the house.[97]

Now, Schirach's own position deteriorated far more rapidly than he had ever expected, even after his tongue-lashing from Hitler. He worried about the conduct of the war and began to doubt victory. He became convinced that only a negotiated peace could save the Third Reich even though FDR and Churchill had demanded unconditional surrender when they met at Casablanca on January 11, 1943.[98] The Allied landing in North Africa had been a success. The Russians were preparing to annihilate the German Sixth Army at Stalingrad; American and British generals were planning to invade Sicily and Italy, whose government began to wobble. Schirach looked for an opportunity to discuss war policy with Hitler himself, but arranging such a meeting would be difficult. In February Goebbels had proclaimed "total war" in a Berlin speech—he and other top Nazis felt that Schirach had not fallen into line. On April 24 Goebbels noted in his diary "Schirach has no idea of what total war means and tries constantly to torpedo it." The Führer told munitions minister Albert Speer that Schirach had become a prisoner of Vienna reactionaries. "He lacks political sensitivity and he's not a real Nazi," Goebbels wrote. "He spends too much time with artists and that does him no good. In any case, the Führer no longer has any great plans for him," a judgment in which Speer concurred. Schirach had been taken off the list of possible successors.

So Schirach opted for a letter, which he had his brother-in-law—like his father a photographer and assigned to HQ on the Eastern front— give Hitler directly, thus circumventing Bormann who controlled the mail flow.[99] In it Schirach argued that Germany could no longer impose a peace on Russia or the United States and that Hitler should negotiate either with Stalin or FDR. Schirach favored Roosevelt and offered himself and Colin Ross as negotiators. Hitler did not bother answering.

Meanwhile, Schirach adjusted to the new realities as best he could. In his speeches he bragged about past successes of his stewardship ranging from improved medical care for workers to the party's stepped up propaganda campaign to keep the Viennese loyal and enthused. He pushed efforts to bring more women into the work force and tried to soothe women's fears of working in factories. For many, especially in the middle class, the workplace seemed strange and somehow dangerous.[100] A week after Stalingrad fell Schirach issued a decree closing bars and night clubs in the inner city, largely to free up more labor but also as symbol for somber times that had no room for frivolous celebrations (and which, incidentally, killed his plans for a thriving night life). Luxury shops were shut down including jewelry, flower, book, candy, and toy stores. Children would be able to buy chocolate in other food outlets. Most fashion houses were shuttered except those whose output was sold abroad.

Implementation of those decrees, however, was not as complete as the Nazis might have wished. Rafelsberger was in charge of the closings but he too had to settle for what he could get, lest he rattle the business community too much. Thus coffeehouses were exempt since, as Schirach noted, most of them had become restaurants. Besides, in war time coffeehouses had little to do with coffee—a reference to the dreadful brew of malt and chicory these establishments were forced to serve. And an order to ban beauty parlors from giving clients hair perms had to be relaxed (to some extent because Eva Braun, alarmed by her Viennese friends, urged Hitler to ease the order.)[101] The *VB* explained that perms would again be permitted, but appealed to readers to use them sparingly, but hair coloring was reserved for women with gray hair.

Schirach swung onto the propaganda circuit to sell the new realities to the party's rank and file—and to the people at large beyond them. Throughout February 1943 he delivered speeches in every *Kreis*—there were ten such political districts in the city—exhorting political leaders to make people work harder. He used every venue, from coffeehouses in the Prater to the spacious reception areas of city hall, to get his message across. On March 7 he delivered a radio speech full of pathos about Stalingrad: "The sorrow has stabbed our people through the heart. Now the people must arise. A battle has been lost, but the war will be won." He urged women to enter factories. Vienna, he noted, had more working women than any other Gau.

On March 13, 1943, Schirach delivered the obligatory Anschluss oration to celebrate the fifth anniversary of the return of the Alpine and Danube Gaue to the Reich, nomenclature that showed how thoroughly even the term *Ostmark* had been cleansed from the Nazi vocabulary. The day reminds us, Schirach said, "that we cannot think or work for anything but ultimate victory." A week later the Viennese were forced to celebrate a memorial day for those who had died in battle but who, in dying, had been victorious. For the most part the pomp and circumstance was standard fare, but the presence of old soldiers in imperial uniforms, the singing of Luther's hymn "A Mighty Fortress is our God," and the use in speeches and other public pronouncements of the phrase "for us Stalingrad is holy," added a different dimension, a first sense that the giddy euphoria of early victories had faded for good.[102]

Hitler's birthday a month later continued the new somber note in Schirach's post-Stalingrad rhetoric. The pleading tone was unmistakable: Hitler was the nation's only hope for victory. He alone carried the burden of the nation. "The Führer leads. We follow and serve him and know this: no people on earth has such a man. God sent him to us and may he keep him in the year to come as forceful, healthy, and energetic as he stands before us today."[103]

In private Schirach was a lot less sure. He was still desperate to talk to Hitler, to push his peace proposals, to find allies among the hierarchy. But if there was a peace camp in the party—a doubtful proposition at best—it had little clout. Göring came to Vienna on May 7, 1943, ostensibly to talk about the Vienna Gau's military problems. But when Schirach asked him about Hitler, the Field Marshall shrugged. The Führer barely tolerated Göring at military briefings, and nobody paid any attention to his opinions.[104]

Late that spring—somewhere between Easter and June—Eva Braun called to invite the Schirachs to spend a few days at the Berghof. Henriette Schirach had just returned from Amsterdam. One night from her hotel window she had seen SS men herd together Jewish women for deportation to the East. She wanted to tell the Führer. Schirach claimed he told his wife not to bother, that they couldn't do anything about it anyway, but she insisted.

The first night after dinner when Hitler's guests, including Bormann, Goebbels, Eva Braun, and Speer, were sitting around the fireplace in the great hall, Schirach proposed an idea that Günther Kaufmann, now gone from Vienna to become a full-time war correspondent, had suggested: instead of suppressing the Ukrainians enlist them in the Nazi cause. Hitler's face darkened. "Don't talk about things that don't concern you," Schirach quoted him as saying. "Those Slavs are in no position to govern themselves."[105] The subject was dropped. But according to Goebbels's diary it triggered one of Hitler's famous outbursts of temper—the hate he had felt for Vienna all his life, his fury at Schirach and his policies. Hitler pledged to make Berlin the most beautiful city in the world. He would not tolerate efforts to rebuild Vienna to rival Berlin. He knew the magic attraction Vienna had for visitors, but when he was through Berlin would trump it. Vienna had the right to make cultural policies in grand style and the Reich would support them, but he would not permit a dualism between the two cities about who led the Reich. Berlin must be the chosen capital, Vienna pushed back into the role of a provincial city.[106]

Whether Henriette brought up her Dutch experiences that night or the next is unclear. She had always been able to say things to Hitler that others could not. He had known her since childhood and treated her as family. But now Hitler erupted. "You're sentimental. What do you care about Jewesses in Holland?"[107] She had heard him scream before, but never at her. The Schirachs left before dawn to drive back to Vienna. He knew, in Goebbels words, that he was a dead man politically. Periodically Hitler would talk about relieving him or pushing him into the diplomatic corps, but he never did. And Schirach retained more clout than he would admit at Nuremberg. He was invited back to the mountain redoubt and even arranged a meeting between Hitler and the Norwegian Nobel Prize-winner Knut Hamsun.[108] But he was no longer the young prince with the freedom to do as he pleased. He had enjoyed a great ride. Thomas's description of a day in the life of "the young gentleman" is proof of that. At 9:03 P.M. his valet knocked gently on his bedroom door. It had been a late night. He had left the Hofburg at 2:34 A.M. after consuming rich food, champagne, cognac, and heavy cigars. It took a while before Schirach could growl, "come in." The valet pushed the curtains aside, went into the bathroom to open hot and cold water taps, measured the water temperature with a thermometer, gathered the shaving kit, put out bottles of mouthwash and other toiletries, and placed thick towels on the heating rack. Then he told the young gentleman that his bath was ready. While Schirach conducted his ablutions, the valet laid out his uniform, shirt, and under garments. He tied Schirach's tie and held out the uniform jacket with thick silk lining so that the young gentleman could slip in easily. Downstairs an equally hungover adjutant was waiting. While Schirach drank coffee and ate toast with smoked meat on it, the adjutant read off the day's schedule with not a minute free until 10:30 P.M. when he was to board the salon car of a train taking him to a cultural festival. As he left the house the valet handed him cap and gloves, and he stepped into the waiting Mercedes. A smaller car for security was parked behind the limo. On the drive to the Ballhausplatz police stopped traffic to assure free passage. He walked across a huge wine-red carpet to Metternich's desk—there had been none when Neubacher had walked across the stone floor back in August 1940—and sat down in the red upholstered chair another flunky had pulled back to tackle the day's mail. Forty minutes later he was ready to receive his first visitors held over from the previous day—the general in command of the Vienna military district, and his RP. The general wanted more troops, suggesting the closing of nonessential factories and drafting the workers. Schirach agreed but balked at releasing artists for military service. He needed opera and Burg for propaganda reasons. The RP was told to keep it short, the Gauleiter was behind schedule. When Schirach finally left for a city hall luncheon, two visitors were still waiting upstairs. So were the luncheon guests. He had been due at noon. It was now 12:45 and the soup was cold. But the meal was rich—salmon and eggs as appetizers, the soup, roasted fish, Schnitzel, a cream cake, three kinds of wine. Schirach made a short speech and left before the ice cream was served. His next stop was a factory for one of his German socialism speeches only the managers applauded while workers sat on their hands in the back rows. Then back to the villa where the valet helped him out of his uniform and laid out fresh clothes, including an elegant gray flannel suit, while Schirach took a quick shower. Then it was downstairs to a tea reception for a famous actor making one of Goebbels's kitsch movies on the Rosenhügel. About twenty artists, actors, writers, and musicians were invited for sandwiches, rich pastries, tea, and afterward peaches in champagne. When they left at last he was still running late: Verdi's *Othello* at the opera with an Italian general as guest. The curtain rose—sixteen minutes late—when he finally took his seat in the old imperial box. Another reception in the salon two steps behind the box during the intermission with a table groaning under the weight of venison, fowl, pates, cheeses, fruit, and petit fours. An exhausted Schirach nodded off during the performance only to wake for the final applause. His special railroad car waited at the station. A small supper in the dining section, more excellent brandy to go with a recitation of the next day's program, then comfortably to bed. In his speech the next day Schirach would demand sacrifice and abstinence, a willingness to die for Führer and Fatherland, the greatness of a hero's death.

CHAPTER 9

Prelude to Disaster

Schirach Loses Control:
May 8, 1943–June 11, 1944

For the common people of Vienna a life of luxury and variety such as Schirach led was beyond imagining. In the years before the city fell within the perimeter of war and was subject to the same bombardment as the Altreich, life was, for the most part, drab and boring. There was little diversion for adolescents beyond Hitler Youth meetings, family outings, hiking or biking in the country, movies, and soccer. For the culturally adventurous there was standing room at Opera and Burg. And for young women from upper-middle-class families—bright, good-looking, in their twenties—there was a modicum of luxury at home and in the sputtering nightlife Schirach had tried to ignite before he had to put out the fire.

"There were only two things you could do as a kid," Kurt Neubauer, who would work for United Press and run an American newsletter operation, remembered, "go to soccer matches and to the movies.

> I was at the Stadium when Admira played Schalke 04 and yelled my head off at the Piefkes. Soccer gave you a chance to protest. I was at the last international match, Germany vs. Switzerland, in 1942 I think. Little Switzerland beat the Germans 3 to 2 and when they played the Deutschland hymn nobody sang it. The newspapers were furious. They said losing didn't matter, but of course it did, and the way people behaved when they played the German national anthem was unacceptable, and of course it was.
> I saw *Jüd Süss* [a notorious propaganda film made to foment hatred of the Jews] three times. I wasn't an anti-Semite, I really wasn't—I was the only one in

226

my building to say hello to a Jewish lady who lived there—but I was fifteen years old and there is one scene where this woman takes off her blouse and you can see her naked breasts. We couldn't see that any place else. The last American picture I saw before Hitler declared war was a gangster movie with Anthony Quinn. You couldn't get tickets. It was always sold out.[1]

Most films were, and the dumber they were the better the public liked them. Goebbels may have believed he was offering quality entertainment, but the bulk of the movies Wien Film and Tobis ground out in the Rosenhügel Studio were shallow romances, costume pieces, musicals, and comedies with Hans Moser and Theo Lingen. Both were accomplished actors but both also played to formula, a Teutonic version of Abbot and Costello, only nowhere near as funny. One thing these kitsch films had in common was lack of explicit Nazi ideology. *Wiener Blut* (*Vienna Blood*, the title of a Strauss waltz) had the fourth highest gross among the thirty most successful wartime films, and *Operette*, another piece of musical froth, ranked twelfth.[2]

Not that Goebbels shortchanged propaganda. *Linen from Ireland* was as savagely anti-Semitic as *Jud Süss*, and *Homecoming* a shameless piece of propaganda that justified Hitler's attack on Poland by depicting Polish savagery against ethnic Germans. The movie ranked fifteenth, largely because Paula Wessely, a truly extraordinary actress, but one with pronounced Nazi sympathies (despite her appeal to Thomas to save her secretary), gave a stunning performance.

Some newspapers avoided Goebbels's ban on criticism by printing reviews from Italian newspapers. Thus the *Corriere della Sera* said of a German gangster movie that the Germans should leave such films to the Americans because "they're better at it and have more gangsters." It was a clear signal that the film stank, but, Neubauer recalled, that didn't hold down movie attendance. "You went to every film to which you could get tickets. It didn't matter how bad it was. You went to get some variety in your life." Attendance numbers backed him up—they grew sharply all through the war.

Attendance at meetings of the various youth groups—the HJ, Hitler Youth, for boys from fourteen to eighteen, the *Jungvolk*, also known as *Pimpfe*, for boys ten to fourteen, the *Jungmädchen*, girls ten to fourteen, and the BDM, *Bund deutscher Mädchen*,—was mandatory, but a surprising number of youngsters in Vienna managed not to go at all or attend only sporadically, especially as the war dragged on.

In September 1943 the *NWT* noted that police could now force truant boys to go to HJ meetings—an embarrassing admission of poor attendance since the HJ was proud of the "voluntary" nature of service, despite a law mandating membership. Precise numbers, of course, are impossible to obtain but there is plenty of anecdotal evidence.

Karl Lichtenecker, a future Austrian diplomat, spent the obligatory four years among the Pimpfe but avoided the HJ altogether because a noted psychiatrist wrote an expert opinion that the fourteen-year-old's nerves were too weak for the rigors of the HJ.[3]

Adolf Holl slid out of the HJ after a lightninglike career as a Pimpf. The future apostate priest was ten when he joined in 1940 and advanced quickly to squad leader. "I had thirty boys under me and we would meet once a week, tie knots, sing songs, and march through the countryside." But Holl was responsible for kids' attendance, which had fallen badly by 1942–43, so that sometimes only three boys came. That meant calling at home and reminding everybody to show up. One night when he was about thirteen, several older boys accosted him as he came out of a building. They were sixteen or seventeen and had long hair—a sure sign of the dreaded *Schlurfs* (literally "shufflers"), teenage rowdies who listened to swing and were in and out of trouble. "They beat me up because I was out rounding up kids for meetings. That got me thinking and I transferred to another group where I wasn't so visible." In 1944 when he transitioned into the HJ, he picked the Motor HJ, basically a motorcycle gang. "All they wanted to do was ride their bikes."[4]

Traudl Lessing, who would work for *Time* in Eastern Europe and marry photographer Erich Lessing, rose equally quickly in the Jungmädchen group to run a squad of ten girls who were equally hard to round up. She tramped from house to house and found one girl who would never come. "She was sick one week or had to study the next and still was not okay the third, so I gave up. I thought, she doesn't want to come and that's that. Now if my father had been a party district leader and I let it drop the girl wasn't coming, results could have been serious—especially since she lived in a communal building, meaning that her family probably had socialist ties." When it was time to join the BDM, Lessing put it off for a year and then claimed she had to study for her *Matura*, the certificate needed for higher education. "I just didn't want to go to the BDM. I thought it boring. Nothing happened to me. Nobody came to make me go."[5]

Inge Zembsch's experiences—she would teach German and gymnastics in a Gymnasium—were similar. She joined the Jungmädchen, and "because I was smart was picked for a leadership role." Like the others that meant running around getting girls to attend meetings. In her case that also meant missing piano lessons, which incensed her mother enough to go to the Jungmädchen. "She told them that if this doesn't change she wouldn't let me come anymore. It didn't and I didn't [but] I wrote good essays and I jumped farther and ran faster than the others and that made up for it. You had wide latitude so long as you were identified with the Nazi regime. So you didn't have to march and run around and do everything they wanted you to do. But if you spoke out against the Nazis you were in trouble and we knew that."[6]

Unlike others, Kurt Neubauer was disillusioned early. The HJ would have big rallies in the Prater on Sunday for 2,000 to 3,000 boys. Everybody brought a lunch. His mother packed Schnitzel. But at the lunch break the HJ leaders demanded that each boy turn in his food for equal distribution. Kurt ended up with a piece of bread and lard. From week to week the number of Schnitzels the boys brought decreased as incensed mothers asked why they should pack Schnitzel when meat is expensive. In the end though, all the boys had to eat was bread with lard or jam on it. But Neubauer found ducking meetings in his neighborhood difficult. "If you didn't show up two or three times they'd send somebody to your parents. So my mother would say 'you idiot, go. I don't want any trouble.'"

Anton Zembsch, a future high official in the Austrian ministry of Trade (and Inge's husband), and Holl, the future priest, brought a second perspective to their HJ experience—religion. Like many young Viennese, Holl had been pushed to the church by his mother. She was an active anti-Nazi and one of the few who had voted no in the plebiscite. When her son had come home bragging about the thousand-year Reich she remarked dryly that only "God is eternal," and, Holl said, "She must have thought that a little counterpoison wouldn't hurt. So she sent me to religion class in the local church. They looked at me a little funny because they knew I was an enthusiastic Pimpf. But some of the things I heard in church must have touched me." The turning point came when he was evacuated to the country in 1944 and became an altar boy, something the HJ didn't like. Holl went anyway, sometimes in HJ uniform. "It was okay to be religious."

Zembsch, too, had been an altar boy and regarded the Carmelite church in his neighborhood as a second home. His mother was religious and her example had great influence. But it never bothered him that Arthur Radinger and I, both half-Jews and his best friends, were suddenly gone. "I knew Jews weren't wanted in the Third Reich and we understood that." He became a Pimpf and then transitioned into the HJ. "It was really simple. The HJ aroused the basic instincts of every boy. You hike through the countryside with a compass. You sit around the campfire and sleep in tents. These are things that interest children today and satisfy their romantic yearnings."

He became deeply enmeshed in the ideology of the Third Reich. His father died a year after the Anschluss, and Hitler became a "kind of super father." He felt drawn into the maelstrom of the movement, a victim of a mass psychosis he could not oppose because he had not been equipped by family or church to do so. Still, his mother and a local priest, Father Thiresius, prevented him from "doing evil."

One day when a company of Pimpfs marched past the church, Zembsch saw the priest on the steps and yelled out "Hi, Father Thiresius" and no one much cared. "You could be a Nazi *and* a Christian. That was possible. The others looked at you funny but as long as you followed the Nazi ideology it was all right. It would spoil your career, though, if you wanted to be a Nazi bigwig."

He did not, but when he found out that the priest listened to the BBC he was disturbed. "I didn't like a Catholic priest listening to the BBC when he knew it was forbidden. He let me know he was listening, too. Perhaps he thought he could recruit me to resist but he soon realized that I disapproved. You didn't do that. It wasn't moral."

Social life was sparse. "We didn't have any," Neubauer said. "When I didn't go to the movies or to soccer games I sat home and read. I wasn't invited out." Girls were a problem. He went to a boys' school and didn't know very many girls. Sometimes he walked one home but found no opportunity for necking. "You couldn't do it in the park during the day, and your parents didn't let you out at night. No nice girl let you near her. Growing up I had only one wish: to sleep with a girl just once before I died."

"Until I was eighteen I had no social life," Traudl Lessing said, "even though I did go to dancing school when I was fifteen." Like all well-brought-up Viennese children—and those who hoped to be—she attended Lieutenant Colonel Willy Elmayer's dancing establishment (still today the ne plus ultra of budding social life for young Viennese, decades after the colonel's death). By the time she got there, however, most of the boys two or three years older had been drafted and she was left with the pimpled and the snot-nosed. Elmayer did not only teach dancing but the social graces—boys and girls walked arm in arm in a circle around the room to practice conversation. "So I tried desperately to talk to the young man next to me but he poked me in the ribs and said 'look, Miss, please be quiet I want to hear what my buddy back there is saying.' I didn't go back very often after that."

Elfie Neustädtle spent most of the war years in the Vienna Opera ballet school, and later danced in the corps de ballet. The Opera meant social cachet and in her late teens handsome HJ leaders and Wehrmacht ensigns on leave buzzed around her. Luftwaffe pilots were considered the most glamorous. They grew their hair longer than the Prussian crew-cut norm and wore white silk scarves. But wartime flirtations were brief. The soldiers returned to the front. There would be letters and packages and sometimes death notices.[7]

Maria Czedik was a student in her twenties. She kept a meticulous diary that showed that for some, life under the Nazis was not all that drab, but that even a wartime *dolce vita* often had a bitter aftertaste. In one of her 1942 entries she wrote: "On Friday met Achim and Gretl in the "Mounierstube" [a food and drink bar on Kärntnerstrasse that survived into the 1950s] and we started with *Sekt* [the German version of Champagne] and then we went to eat at the Stadkrug, and afterwards to the Bachusstube [another bar] where Mamlas and Jane showed up. It was very nice. Achim is 1. a Piefke, 2. a political leader, and 3. a God believer [a form of secular religion favored by leading Nazis], but nevertheless very nice. He has a lot of charm. Yesterday they all came to my house. Finally a short good-bye and a glowing kiss and three beautiful days are over before you knew it." In the summer she wrote "I don't know what I want, except to eat, eat, and eat again. This always being dissatisfied comes from never having quite enough to eat and from not being in love. But where are you going to find enough to eat and a man to fall in love with?"

Nor was she happy with the regime. "I hate this war and this system. . . . The other day I dreamt that I wanted to kill Hitler, too bad that I can't do it, that dammed beast. There isn't anything bad enough you can say to do him justice."

And on February 3, 1943, "Stalingrad fell today. Official mourning from today until Saturday. We are retreating everywhere and somehow it is terribly tragic having to watch the inexorable collapse and downfall of one's own people. Perhaps Europe will recover enough in ten years so you can build a secure life but till then our best years are running away. We had such an impoverished youth. We never knew real peace and never had a chance to develop spiritually and intellectually. We don't have anything— no real religion, no solid faith in any idea. We're not like normal young people who want to storm ahead but like old folks who want peace and quiet. Will we ever know real happiness?"[8]

Outside accounts of life in Vienna in 1943 are sparse, but on November 14 the *Neue Zürcher Zeitung* published one by a Swiss businessman who had spent time in the city. The food, he wrote, was the worst in the Reich, the vaunted Viennese cuisine had descended into indifference. Restaurants were jammed and dirty, service almost nonexistent, yet nobody seemed to care. There was enough to eat for everyone but the joy had gone out of it. A weak "unity" beer was served—in contrast to Munich where several varieties, some quite good, were available. A glass of wine was hard to get and required a "relationship" with the waiter or the owner.

Fruit and fresh vegetables were in short supply. Over four months an individual received two kilos (a little more than four pounds) of fresh fruit. More vegetables were on hand but not on a consistent basis. Small wonder Viennese women scoured the countryside to buy food at higher prices—paid in cash or tobacco. The black market boomed—a fact confirmed by the increasingly harsh sentences courts handed down to black marketers. But with some Viennese willing to pay RM 200 for a kilo of coffee, RM 100 for 100 grams of tea, RM 80 for butter, and RM 40 for white flour, authorities were hard put to stamp it out.

Luxury and other stores were shuttered and shops still open had little to sell. Some had signs in the window saying they would be closed for the duration, while others labeled products shown as "only for decoration." Everybody seemed to have plenty of money but little to spend it on. Theaters and operas were jammed and regularly sold out tickets within minutes of opening the box office. People lined up at the Opera two hours before the curtain rose hoping for standing room.

The mood in Vienna deteriorated as the war news worsened. Fear of bolshevism was deep-rooted, with some Viennese saying "we can afford to lose the war against England but never against Russia." In the fall there was more talk of new secret weapons that might turn the tide. Finally, the *NZZ* noted a much heavier political hand—controls of trains had become much more severe, and the number of red posters announcing execution of traitors and other "undesirables" had multiplied.[9]

Most of the able-bodied—and even not so able-bodied—Jews left in Vienna had long been pushed into forced labor, alongside the growing number of foreign workers. Most of the Jews who remained had some Aryan blood, which gave them a measure of protection.

As an indeterminate Jewish mixture—nobody ever quite figured out how Jewish his family was thanks to his father's ability to mix up documents—Michael Kehlmann had managed to stay at the Döblinger Gymnasium until he was sixteen. But when his "pure" Aryan contemporaries were being hauled into flack duty, Kehlmann was kicked out of school. His father found him a laborer's job in a factory.[10]

For Hans Kann things had been tougher. When he left school in 1941 his mother was in jail, sentenced to two years for listening to Radio Moscow and the BBC. By 1942 Hans and his father worked side by side at a bottle-and-can dump. They worked twelve-hour days—"I hated it. Manual labor stupefies your mind. We worked alongside Jewish lawyers, judges, and mathematicians. The workers were the worst. They hated us not because we were Jews but because so many Jews were intellectuals. We worked alongside French, Serbian, and Italian POWs. Hours were long and working conditions were horrible. We carried three sacks weighing twenty-five kilos[about fifty-five pounds] each when loading ships and had to carry them across pontoon bridges."[11]

Alexander Altschul was twenty-four when the Nazis came. He had hoped to emigrate to England but never got a visa. Instead he was pushed into forced labor, assigned to garbage disposal where he had to separate out metal, glass, textiles, paper, and bones. Most of the Aryans who worked with him were social outcasts—*Schlurfs* and prostitutes who turned tricks at night and worked in garbage during the day. "They were okay," Altschul remembered, "they weren't hostile." Like Kann he met Jewish doctors, lawyers, journalists, and engineers, and became friendly with some of them. He wore the Jewish star, but attached it with pins so he could take it off when in town to attend the Opera or the Burg. "I still had a good suit."

One night he came home around two in the morning, saw three tell-tale gray trucks outside his house and knew his hour had struck. He fled and went underground, dependent on the "kindness of strangers" for his sustenance and eventual escape to Switzerland.[12]

Paul Grosz and his family had failed to emigrate, but Paul had taken locksmith and electrician courses at the IKG. In 1940, barely fifteen years old, he was pushed into forced labor in a factory that made uniforms. "I can't really remember the time frame," he said. "Everything melted together into a gray picture. It was a time in which my life was in constant danger, even if I didn't feel that way every day. Hunger and fear had become routine. You couldn't trust anybody because you lived in such a hostile environment."[13]

Franzi Löw, twenty-two years old when the Nazis came, had a degree in social work and a job with IKG. When the city of Vienna relinquished guardianship over 200 illegitimate Jewish children in late 1938, Löw was appointed their guardian and placed them into three IKG orphanages. In addition, she was guardian for some twenty retarded youngsters left behind by emigrating parents. In the early 1940s she received a call that her retarded charges would be transported to the insane asylum at Steinhof.

Desperate, Löw went to the Rothschild hospital where the noted psychoanalyst Viktor Frankl, who himself would be deported months later, was head of psychiatry. He agreed to take and hide five of the youngsters, but she had to take the rest to Steinhof. She pleaded with the insane asylum's director not to send them away—to no avail. The group was sent to Hartheim, a castle in Upper Danube that the Nazis used for euthanasia. As guardian she received their death certificates. The cause of death: heart failure.

In 1942–43 Löw had one case of *Sophie's Choice*, this one with a happy ending. A young woman became pregnant in jail. At first doctors thought she had a tumor but then realized the truth. The Gestapo checked, discovered the prospective father, and killed him. Days after the child was born in the Jewish hospital, the Gestapo told Löw to give the young mother this choice: take the child and go to Theresienstadt, or leave the baby behind and face deportation to Ravensbrück. The mother never hesitated. "Please, Frau Löw, take Denny, I'm going to Ravensbrück." She survived and was reunited with her son.

Another half-Jewish orphan came under Löw's care when his foster mother was deported in 1941. Two years later, when he was a locksmith's apprentice, Franzi Löw was ordered to bring him to a transition camp. They arrived around eleven at night and met with Brunner II (Anton). She told him her charge was a half-Jew. "Bring proof that he was baptized before 1935 and I'll let him go," Brunner told her. Löw had good contacts at the archdiocese and went at once to Pater Ludger Born, who had run the cardinal's mission for non-Aryan Christians. Would he issue a baptismal certificate showing the boy had been baptized before the cutoff date? The clock pushed toward midnight. Born fell to his knees in front of a crucifix and prayed for what seemed like a long time. Then he rose, signed and stamped the certificate, and wished Löw well. Shortly after midnight she was back at the camp. Brunner looked at the certificate and said, "Okay, the boy can go." When they were out of hearing range he asked, "But Aunt Franzi, how come I have a baptismal certificate, I'm a Jew?" She would tell him later, she said, and hurried him home.

The next day when she arrived at the IKG at 6 A.M. Löwenherz was furious. She managed to calm him down but he still said, "What will we do when the Gestapo finds out?" But they never did. The child remained in the home until liberation and was reunited with his foster mother. Few such stories had a happy end. In early 1942 Löw had seventy children in the home. A year later the number was down to thirty, and they had been hard to save. For those with a documented Aryan father she had to dig up the so-called *Ariernachweis*—a paper trail that proved the father had four Aryan grandparents. For the others she picked names out of baptismal records and got copies of their certificates from local churches and used them to uncover other needed documentation. In 1966 the city of Vienna finally got around to giving her a medal.[14]

On January 1, 1943, Löwenherz was put in charge of the council of elders, which had replaced the IKG on November 1, 1942; he was also given responsibility for all other organizations that had cared for non-Aryan Christians and agnostics. At the time only 7,989 Jews were left in Vienna. In December 1943 their numbers had shrunk to 6,259, which broke down this way: 1,080 professed to another religion; 85 had foreign citizenship; 3,702 lived in a "privileged" marriage with an Aryan, which gave them a measure of protection; 1,392 in an "unprivileged" one—like Hans Kann. The staff of the council totaled 254 at the beginning of 1943, compared to 1,088 a year earlier. Most of Vienna's remaining Jews, at least those who could still walk, had been pulled into forced labor.

The council still had a lot to do. It updated files on Jews still in Vienna and gathered what information it could on Jews who had emigrated. The Gestapo regularly collected the updates. The IKG handled the mail and parcel flow to Theresienstadt, paid burial costs, and disposed the assets of the dead. During the course of the year about another thousand Jews were deported. In May the weekly *Jewish Information Bulletin* was changed into a biweekly, and on December 31, 1943, Goebbels closed it.[15]

Throughout the spring and summer of 1943 Schirach's position deteriorated, and his political clout waned. Efforts to replace him were sporadic. In November and December Hitler considered half a dozen candidates but could not settle on any one. Dr. Hugo Jury, the Gauleiter of Lower Danube, was approached, but Hitler was wary about giving him control of two Gaue because that might foment separatist tendencies, and Jury did not want to give up Lower Danube. He also warned Bormann not to appoint another German because he would grate on raw Viennese nerves, which by this time had become not so much anti-Nazi as anti-German.

But since no other Austrian Nazi seemed to have the stature and clout needed for the job, Schirach stayed, though he was never far out of the line of fire. He had made too many enemies including Martin Bormann, a man close to Hitler and one on whom the Führer depended. Borman, like many other top Nazis, took umbrage at Schirach's aristocratic manners and his tendency to condescend to those he thought his social inferiors. Both Bormann and Goebbels accused Schirach of not taking "total war" seriously.[16] He had, for example, not done enough that summer to prepare Vienna for the coming air war. Hitler sent him to Westphalia to study how things were done in those Gaue under steady allied bombardment. Schirach took the lessons to heart and began planning for an underground air command post and an elaborate warning network. He also turned the catacombs deep under Vienna's many churches into air raid shelters for 150,000.

It wasn't enough. Ribbentrop testified in Nuremberg that he had witnessed a conversation between Himmler and Hitler in mid-1943 in which the SS chief had suggested putting Schirach on trial before a people's court for his defeatist pronouncements—the Reichsleiter had doubts about a German victory going back to the invasion of Russia.[17] The idea got nowhere. But it was indicative of Schirach's eroding support; so were rumors in Vienna in July 1943 that Schirach and his family had fled to Switzerland, or, alternatively, that the Schirachs had been apprehended and shot on the spot. The rumors were prevalent enough for the SD to cable them to Berlin.[18]

Growing isolation from the party and the party's uniformed formations complicated Schirach's political problems. He had never joined the SS and quarreled with the SA because they tried to absorb senior HJ cadres. Moreover, by the summer of 1943 power rested with the party and the SS, especially after Himmler became minister of the interior in August. Like Bormann, he despised Schirach, and, when the ploy to have him executed failed, Himmler began to meddle more seriously in Viennese affairs. But he too failed to "get" Schirach.[19]

He was not easy to dispose of. No ranking embassy was available. Nor could he simply disappear from the political scene. He was too well known and still had the loyalty of the Hitler Youth. Nor did Schirach act like a political corpse. He was too shrewd and too aware of what modern public relations could do not to maintain a vibrant facade. After returning from the Berghof he was everywhere—in defense plants, in Slovakia to inspect camps for children, at a military hospital talking to the wounded, in the fields to visit with farmers, and at the Palais Schwarzenberg to hector his political leaders. And he repeated his German socialism speech in factory after factory, no matter how meager the response.

He won some PR mileage by Hitler's decision to rename the Fortyfourth Infantry Division, in which many Austrians had fought and died at Stalingrad, as the grenadier division of the *Hoch und Deutschmeister*—in the days of the empire Vienna's home regiment (literally "the high and German masters"). The name change was a conspicuous honor. "The Führer," one headline read, "honors Vienna and its sons."[20]

Forced to give up his avant-garde cultural ambitions, Schirach settled for "culture in total war," meaning culture without frills: fewer new theater and opera productions, less opulent stage designs and fewer costumes, soldiers, the wounded, and defense workers as "honored guests." In the fall of 1943, Stuppäck, still only deputy secretary general for culture, tried to implement the new look by dusting off Thomas's plans for the 1943–44 season and presenting them as his own. It was solid stuff but lacked the daring of Schirach's more liberal years. Classics and Nazi historical pageants at the Burg, Richard Strauss all the time at the Opera in preparation for his eightieth birthday, and the Philharmonic under Furtwängler.

Viennese music wasn't limited to the classics. The city's pop tradition had become a staple of radio programs beamed to the front where soldiers craved dance music. The problem, the *NWT* hinted, was the lust for swing and jazz of which the Nazis disapproved because in both rhythm dominated melody, while Vienna pop featured the sing-along style the soldiers allegedly preferred. In fact they did not, and the most popular piece bands were allowed to play was "The Tiger Rag."[21]

A bevy of new art exhibits was also planned. One of them warned the Viennese against buying expensive kitsch disguised as "art." Ceramic angels, tile plates, and useless boxes were fetching astronomical sums and breaking price ceilings. It didn't work: the rush from currency into collectibles was too strong, not only in Vienna but across the Reich.

Perhaps that rush was one reason why two Viennese critics tried to rehabilitate the expressionist painter Egon Schiele. Both the *NWT* and the *VB* ran stories in October 1943 to commemorate the twenty-fifth anniversary of his death and to separate out his folkish from his degenerate side—this at a time when Schiele was still considered degenerate in the Reich.

Salvage operations were on in the theater too, with Shakespeare the target of rescue efforts in case Goebbels decided to turn against the bard of Avon—always a possibility given the propaganda minister's intellectual fickleness; in the 1940s he had banned Schiller's *Wilhelm Tell* because he now found the play's antidictatorial message uncomfortable. In the thirties Tell had been much admired within the Nazi hierarchy. Lothar Müthel, therefore, decided to stage the *Merchant of Venice* as a wildly anti-Semitic play. Werner Krauss, the greatest thespian of his day, played Shylock in a red wig and decked out to resemble a caricature from Julius Streicher's infamous newspaper *Der Stürmer*.[22] In Müthel's version Shylock's daughter is adopted and thus untainted by Jewish blood. Heinz Kindermann, professor of drama, followed with the claim that German theater, on the back of the nineteenth-century Tieck-Schlegel translation, had made Shakespeare popular across Europe, so much so that even the English had come to Vienna to see how *Hamlet* should be played. Like many Germans and Austrians to this day, Kindermann believed that the translation was better than the original.

In 1943 Vienna was a rapidly changing city. The murdered and exiled Jews had been replaced by new minorities—forced labor imported from all over Europe to keep Vienna's defense plants humming. With the city still out of reach of Allied planes, the Germans had moved key industries to the Vienna region—nearby Wiener Neustadt was a center of aircraft production, and the city itself had chemical plants, oil refineries, and munitions factories, many of them newly built. Several hundred thousand laborers had been imported to work in them. Some lived in camps and barracks, others were allowed to find private quarters. They had some freedom, and their presence had become part of the daily cityscape.

The Nazis boasted about how well foreign workers were cared for. Even sports events were arranged for them—soccer matches and boxing bouts with attendance limited to foreign workers. Pay was good, the Nazis claimed. In March 1944 Serbs had sent home 5 million dinars. Workers had been brought in legally. Berlin had signed contracts with twenty-one governments (a lie but in line with the persistent fiction that the Reich was a law-abiding state.) Foreign workers were housed in special, well-equipped camps that paid attention to their national identity. Germans were in overall charge to assure law and order and provide medical care.[23]

The truth, of course, was something else. Workers were not brought in under contract but often seized on the streets and shipped to the Reich where they were exploited, poorly housed and fed, often driven to work past exhaustion. Many of them died. Polish workers—by 1944 there were 100,000 of them in Austria—were treated with special savagery. They had to wear a large *P* cut out of a lilac-yellow piece of cloth. What little contractual coverage existed for other foreign workers did not extend to Poles. They worked a minimum of twelve hours a day. Pay was arbitrary. Taxes and other duties and contributions were deducted from meager wages and included payment for lodging in bedbug-infested barracks. Food rations plummeted from a meager 1,800 calories a day in 1942 to 1,000 a year later. Polish children were barred from religious instruction. Sex with a German meant death. Hangings were frequent, and other Poles were rounded up to watch them.[24] Some, obviously, had greater freedom than others. French, Italian, Belgian, Serb, and Greek workers got a better deal than Poles and Russians; some perhaps because they took bigger risks. In 1942, five French jazz musicians who played at the Club Ventadour in Paris were seized in a particularly vicious Gestapo raid and ended up as forced laborers in Vienna. They managed to stay in touch, perhaps because in some respects the city was looser than other

Nazi strongholds, and to reactivate their quintet, which played at various labor camps. Over time they made contact with Austrian musicians and began to play professionally. Quintet leader Arthur Motta ended up playing drums for the German "Radio Europe" dance band. But the French musicians were also in touch with a musical underground—Viennese teenagers who played jazz and swing. Eventually, the French group ended up playing more or less regularly—and more or less with Nazi tolerance—in a cellar on Riemergasse in the inner city, even after Schirach closed all the night clubs.[25]

Milo Dor was twenty when he came to Vienna from Belgrade in the late summer of 1943. Imprisoned for Communist activities he was freed provided he "volunteered" to work in the Reich. Dor's father, a prosperous Belgrade doctor with good contacts in Vienna, arranged a job for him in a defense plant. Since Dor spoke German, French, and Serbo-Croatian he was put in an office to distribute materials and instructions to other foreign workers. He had a room in the eighth district and led a near normal life. "I wasn't paid enough to live on," the now eighty-year-old Austrian novelist and polemicist remembered, "but my father sent me money. Still, it was like a vacation in hell. The Gestapo had me on their list and they would check regularly to make sure I was doing a good job."[26]

If Balkan intellectuals were part of the cityscape, so were Ukrainian peasant women who congregated in the Prater on Sunday afternoon. A reporter for a tabloid caught up with two of them, "sturdy, blue-eyed peasant girls with round faces and great teeth." They came from a small village, wore kerchiefs on their heads, and boots and skirts of clearly poor soviet quality. They had never been to a large city and found Vienna quite wonderful. "You don't have winters here," one of them said, while the other remarked "you only see capitalists. Everybody is so well dressed." One of them looked enviously at the reporter's dress and sighed "I would die for a such a dress."[27]

On a Sunday in 1944, Italian workers thronged the Apollo cinema for a matinee of Italian music arranged by local Italian fascists who made snappy speeches about ultimate victory before the theater rocked with melodies from *Butterfly*, *Trovatore*, *Aida*, and other Italian favorites.

The Nazi press began to pay more attention to Vienna's new multilingual face. Italian workers sang "O Sole Mio" on the way to work, the *NWT* wrote in 1944, while Russians sang of the vast steppes while toting vats of garbage. The owner of a paint shop asked a friend for an Italian dictionary. He knew a little Italian and employed Serbs, Greeks, and French who all understood a little bit too, making communications easier. The new multilingualism was a good thing, the paper said, because it showed that Vienna was once again the middleman of Europe.[28]

That may have been a bit much. Tolerance of foreigners was becoming a problem. Where should the Nazis draw the line between acceptance and distance? Germans, the *VB* said, should be tolerant, polite, and friendly, but observe limits, meaning not too familiar and God forbid not intimate. These are foreigners with whom the Reich had been at war. Many were raised under bolshevism and some were still Communist agents. So mum was the word on politics and the military. And should any German engage in barter with foreigners he should be denounced and punished.[29]

By midsummer of 1943 the possibility of air raids on the Vienna region became more likely, and the warnings in the media more urgent: Don't overload cellars, keep only essentials—clothes, towels, heavy blankets. Know the way out so well you can navigate in the dark. Stop believing the fiction that Vienna would not be bombed.

The Americans stopped it for them. They attacked on August 13, flying in from bases in Tunisia to bomb military targets in Wiener Neustadt, an industrial hub thirty miles south of Vienna. The official communiqué was brief, noting that the bombs had not done much damage although some civilians had been killed. In fact, the Americans dropped 187 tons of high explosives on a Messerschmidt fighter plant, cutting August output to 187 from 270 planes in July. The raid came as a total surprise, thus accounting for high civilian casualties—185 dead, 20 missing, and more than 800 wounded. With only one fighter squadron based in Austria the Germans could do little to ward off the attack.[30]

The *VB* noted—almost with smug satisfaction—that Vienna was no longer an island of the blessed, immune from "the criminal terror lust of our opponents." Indeed, the raid had its good side: it woke up sleepy burghers and reminded them that in total war the whole Reich had become a "total battle field."[31]

Evacuation plans for mothers, children, and the elderly were revealed in mid-November. They included instructions on leaving homes ready for attack—curtains taken down, rugs rolled up, furniture moved away from the wall. They also contained promises that other people would not be billeted in the empty flats.

The first families left Vienna in February 1944, and their departure went off without a hitch. Hitler Youth and BDM were at the station to help mothers and children with their luggage. Deputy Gauleiter Scharitzer showed up to wish the evacuees well. Everyone, the *VB* assured readers, left with happy smiles on their faces.[32]

The smiles did not last. Rumors spread quickly that those who left Vienna would lose their apartments to other bombing victims. The *VB* repeatedly condemned such "rumors" as evil lies and printed "authoritative" statements from Nazi brass that apartments were safe. But no matter how hard the Nazis tried, the Viennese did not believe them.

Throughout the spring and summer of 1944, Allied air raids on the Vienna region were sporadic and therefore all the more shocking. After each one the party organized memorial services that became increasingly elaborate as bombs began to fall on Vienna itself. The rhetoric was harsh, sarcastic, exhortative, and sometimes close to hysteria. "Homes and a cemetery as 'military' targets," one headline read. On April 12, 1944, a hundred people were killed in a raid on the outskirts.[33] A week later Schirach came to deliver the funeral oration in front of a black iron cross flanked by two pylons draped in black and crowned by two offertory vessels from which somber flames licked skyward. Wehrmacht and party flags on either side flew at half-mast.

"We are gathered here to honor the dead struck down last Wednesday by cowardly murderers' hands," Schirach began. Murdered by "organized American crime" they had died for "peace and freedom" and so long as "we are ready to sacrifice blood and treasure rather than our ideals and our honor the German folkish community will emerge victorious," the *VB* reported on April 19, 1943.

On September 12, 1943, the *NWT* recalled the 250th anniversary of the lifting of the Turkish siege of Vienna in 1683, and commemorated Vienna's role in standing guard for Western civilization. It may have been an effort to link the city to the coming German triumph. But that fall it was just as likely to remind the Viennese of their own identity, and rekindle the idea of an independent Austria after the war. It had already taken hold among Catholics and Socialists active in prewar politics who had largely accepted Anschluss. Now they began to wonder.

242

One trigger were those Germans who had begun to think about toppling Hitler and forming a government that could negotiate peace with the Allies, but would keep many of Hitler's conquests, notably Austria, the Sudetenland, and Memel. To that end the nascent underground sent emissaries to Austria as early as October 1942 to seek support for Anschluss beyond Hitler. Jakob Kaiser, the chairman of the Christian trade unions in the Weimar republic, made the first contact. He visited Lois Weinberger, a former Catholic union official and a friend, to hint about the scope of anti-Hitler activity in the Altreich. It had reached across parties and the other divisions that had marred Weimar. The Austrians should do the same. Days later Kaiser brought Dr. Carl Gördeler, the former mayor of Leipzig, to a meeting at Weinberger's apartment attended by Dr. Felix Hurdes, a Catholic lawyer. (Both Weinberger and Hurdes would play pivotal roles in the early history of the second republic—Weinberger as vice-mayor of Vienna and Hurdes as minister of education.) Gördeler had thought long and hard about his peace plan, and his initial drafts were the genesis for the July 20 plot.[34] Weinberger and Hurdes, however, would have none of it. They told Gördeler they would support him but that Austria was not part of the package. They wanted a free and independent Austria.

In May 1943 Karl Leuschner, a German Social Democrat, came to Vienna to win the support for continued Anschluss from Dr. Adolf Schärf, a Socialist lawyer who in 1938 had Aryanized a Jewish law practice. With former socialist mayor Karl Seitz isolated and under surveillance, and Austria's first post–World War I chancellor, Karl Renner, living in the country, Schärf was the leading pre-1934 Socialist politician still in Vienna.

Leuschner told Schärf that the Hitler regime would be overthrown that fall with the help of the military, that Gördeler would be chancellor, and he, Leuschner, vice-chancellor, that Schuschnigg would join the cabinet and that all of them wanted to keep Austria inside the Reich.

It should have been an easy sell. Schärf had adjusted smoothly to the Anschluss, to being German. "Ever since I had learned to know and love the treasures of the German mind I had always dreamt that my spiritual home was not Austria but Weimar. But during our conversation I had an epiphany. I interrupted my visitor and said, 'the Anschluss is dead. The love for the German Reich has been driven out of the Austrians. I know and treasure some of the Germans who have come to Vienna, but

I see the day when they will be driven out of Austria as the Jews once were.' When I said these words I had the feeling as if somebody else, not I, were speaking, as if it were somebody else's voice."[35]

Leuschner also went to see Weinberger and Hurdes and was told the same thing. But he had paved the way for closer contact between Schärf and Hurdes, who began to talk more frequently and found they could bury past differences. Seitz and Renner slowly came around to accepting the truth of Schärf's outburst. And after the Allies issued the Moscow declaration in November 1943, stamping Austria as Hitler's first victim and supporting re-creation of the nation within its prewar borders, the Austrian Socialist leaders came to accept the concept of independence and statehood. They had not been active members of the Resistance, but they began to build careful ties to the few who were still active.

Toward the end of 1943, Austrian resistance to the Nazis had increased, but this time it was neither Communist-inspired nor fueled by idealistic young Catholic intellectuals. Communists had done most of the heavy lifting in the early resistance movements and had risen phoenixlike every time the Gestapo struck.[36] But an infusion of Socialists unwilling to take orders from Moscow and the steady bleeding of their own leadership had sapped their resiliency, and by the end of 1943 the party had been badly crippled.

Hartmann's treachery had done in the best and the brightest among young Catholics. Those not arrested and eventually executed were drafted and fought first in the West and then in Russia. Many of them, like young Fritz Molden, were put in death battalions and marked for battlefield slaughter. And even if they survived they were too far from the scene to have any impact, at least not till the last six months or so of the war.

Instead, older, more experienced men, many released from concentration camps—presumably to make room for Jews—took up the cudgel. They had been in the forge of politics before Hitler and knew that enthusiasm and taking unnecessary risks were not enough, that thought, analysis, commitment, and pragmatism were needed. And that pragmatism mandated bridging the ideological divide that had separated Catholics and Socialists. Resistance groups were still small, few had as many as a hundred members, but unlike earlier efforts contacts among them increased so that by 1944, a network was in place that reached from one end of the country to the other. Acts of sabotage rose with rail and road communications between key towns disrupted, such as the line from Vienna to Wiener Neustadt.

The Gestapo, of course, was well aware of the new activism, and more and more Austrians were dragged into Peoples Courts where sentences grew increasingly draconian. Communist activity, for example, carried the death penalty, which generally was more widely applied as the war news worsened. No exact figures exist on how many non-Jewish Austrians were executed—estimates range from 7,000 to 35,000. In Vienna decapitation at the Landesgericht (the Vienna district court) took seven seconds.[37]

Crime seemed to become more garish and more daring during the course of 1943; certainly it was so perceived by many people, as the *VB* attested in a scolding piece on November 28. Ten days before, two policemen had been shot and killed when they approached two youths unloading pigs from a truck. Five days later police found and killed the gunman who had a long record in the illegal slaughter trade. A cut-and-dried case, the *VB* said, but unfortunately the murders had aroused concern in much of southern Vienna, concern that was without foundation. Rumormongers had worked overtime—stories about murdered passersby, corpses of nude women found in roadside ditches, and sewer gates deliberately left open near cinemas so that moviegoers would trip and break their legs, were rampant. Crime was no worse than it had been at other times in so large a city as Vienna, the *VB* said. The only difference? Under Schuschnigg slimy Jewish lawyers got off murderers or held them to short sentences while today "not only murderers but all violent criminals are put to death."

Still, crimes against old women were not all rumors. Josef Cermak, age twenty-four, was sentenced to death as a "dangerous habitual criminal"— he had already served four jail terms for theft—because he broke into a Viennese villa, tied up an eighty-two-year-old woman, and locked her in a room. Police nabbed him days later while he was trying to rob a hotel clerk. Friedrich Tuttnauer, a twenty-three-year-old half-Jew, was beheaded for a series of crimes that began in January 1943 when he grabbed a suitcase in a Viennese hotel full of food and silk underwear, which he sold. He followed up with four thefts of chicken and rabbit coops.

One of the juicier shootouts took place in mid-May 1944. For weeks police had tracked a gang believed responsible for a series of store and auto thefts. On May 16 cops broke into an apartment in the second district only to meet a hail of bullets as gang members shot their way out of the trap, seriously injuring one of the policemen. The next day Vienna's finest tracked them down to another apartment and arrested four men with guns. A fifth, gang leader Paul Lakolis, who was more heavily armed than the others, escaped and led police through a chase of nearby streets, firing as he ran. He climbed over the wall of one house, ran through the garden of a second into a third building, where he hid in the cellar. As police came he opened a murderous fire, killing one cop and wounding five others. The gun battle last seven hours before Lakolis gave up, although, police said, he still had a thousand rounds of ammunition left.[38]

In December 1943 Himmler finally exercised his new muscle in Vienna. He forced Schirach to appoint Hanns Blaschke, a vice-mayor and SS Oberführer as mayor. In a way, it was a belated triumph of the "old fighters" in Austria who had been ignored for so long. Blaschke, a patent lawyer, had joined the NSDAP in 1931. He was tall, slim with a thatch of silver hair combed off the face, a Roman nose, narrow eyes, and full lips. He was something of a ladies' man, using his Viennese Schmäh—a mixture of charm and blarney—to good effect. He sang Viennese songs in a light baritone and accompanied himself on the piano with just the right touch of the lachrymose his constituents loved. In many ways he was typical of his breed—a loyal son of Vienna and a devoted follower of the Führer.[39]

He gave his administration a more Viennese cast than even Neubacher had managed. He changed the city council, adding more workers and white-collar employees. He tried if not to democratize the city machinery then to make it more populist, to cast a wider net than the other mayors had done. In February he delivered a series of speeches that led the NWT to talk about "a new wind blowing through city hall." Blaschke said he wanted to move city government closer to the people, to cut red tape and reduce paper work. He would open city council meetings to the media, and have problems discussed openly and frankly. He had no use for "bicycle riders"—who bow going up and kick coming down—or for the perennial yes-men. Everybody in government should be free to say what he thinks and to suggest improvements.

Blaschke's more outgoing personality put a sheen on city hall it had lacked. He was out and about, visiting everybody from farmers to the wounded. Wherever he went he preached a new gospel of openness—more personality, less authority. He exuded a genuine optimism that reflected the golden glow of the first few months after the Anschluss.[40] Vienna could recover the glory of those days, perhaps even exceed them, now that the rightful heirs were in power. Hitler used his birthday to announce Blaschke's promotion to SS Brigardeführer, giving him a general's rank.

Homage to Richard Strauss started early. For more than a month a dozen Strauss operas graced Viennese stages. The eighty-year-old attended most of the performances and rose to acknowledge audience cheers. On June 11, 1944, his actual birthday, cultural Vienna went all out.[41] In the morning Schirach gave the maestro a jewel-encrusted baton. The academy of fine arts awarded him a commemorative medal. The city opera presented *Adriane auf Naxos*. And at the Musikverein the Vienna Philharmonic gathered at noon for a musical tribute. Böhm conducted the waltzes from the *Rosenkavalier* and then Strauss himself swung his birthday baton for *Till Eulenspiegel*. Everybody who was anybody in Vienna attended. Schirach and Blaschke of course. Goebbels, who disliked Strauss for both his political views and his racial ties, sent a telegram; so did the Führer, and both wished Schirach had not made such a fuss.

With the Allies already ashore in Normandy and in possession of Rome, it was too late for substantive reforms, nor could music soothe Vienna's jitters. The war was going badly. The mood of the city kept darkening and not because the population had suddenly turned against the regime. The Viennese liked the Nazis just fine—better when they were winning, of course, but well enough. The darkness was fueled by fear, by the memories of 1918, by the near certainty that they would be on the losing end of another war. And no amount of bread and circuses could alleviate that foreboding.

CHAPTER 10

The Last Year

Destruction from the Sky:
July 1, 1944– March 1, 1945

On July 16, 1944, planes of the Fifteenth U.S. Air Force based in Foggia in southern Italy attacked airplane engine production sites, warehouses, and supply bases in and around Vienna, killing 119 civilians.[1] Flack was heavy as airman Robert Hyde jumped from his burning flying fortress. Observers on the ground saw his parachute billow open above a forest near Weidenbach in the Vienna Woods. A five-man civil patrol set out at once to search for him. Hyde landed in the deep woods, stripped off his parachute, and plunged into the trees. After several hours he came to a clearing with a farmhouse on it. Anna Stangl, the owner, wasn't home, so Hyde sat down on a bench outside and waited.

When Stangl returned he asked her for something to drink. She gave him a glass of milk and a piece of bread. He ate and drank sitting on a box that sat astride the road leading to the house so he could see the patrol—they wore swastika armbands—march up. He moved quickly into the main room of the house. The leader of the patrol, a local dentist, followed him, leaving the rest standing guard outside. He pulled a gun, told the American to raise his hands, put his gun away, and began to frisk him. When he had gone down to the hips, Hyde pulled an 11-mm pistol from his flack jacket, but before he could aim his weapon the patrol leader grabbed his wrists and pulled them down. One of the men standing watch outside with his rifle at the ready saw the struggle and fired a warning shot. The bullet grazed the back of Hyde's hand, which cramped in pain and loosened a shot from his pistol. This bullet, the Nazi who would write the report said, struck the rifleman in the clavicle just under the neck and tore the main artery, killing him instantly.[2] The other men rushed in, quickly overpowered Hyde, pulled his arms behind his back, handcuffed him, and took him to the gendarme post in nearby Mödling.

The next day Hyde testified before a military tribunal that he had been told that Germans took no prisoners and that the civil patrol would lynch any American flyer they captured. Therefore he was determined to sell his life as dearly as he could. A German military court subsequently sentenced him to five years for manslaughter.

Hyde was not the only allied flyer caught on the ground. A week before Hyde was shot down, a RAF pilot jumped from his crippled plane and landed in the Danube swamps. That time the civil patrols had a harder time—they couldn't find him. But the next day Philip Lahner, a retired railroad worker, was loading hay in the swamps when he heard a noise in the bushes. Thinking it was a deer, he paid no attention. But when a man in a brown vest stepped into the clearing Lehner began to think he might be the British flyer. Armed with a pitchfork he pointed his "weapon" at the enemy and called out "hands up." Dutifully the pilot did as he was told and Lahner turned him over to the authorities.[3]

In the summer of 1944 such incidents were, if not common, not totally outrageous. Allied air raids on Vienna had become part of the city's overall reality but not yet an everyday occurrence—in July and August the Americans attacked targets in and around Vienna some ten times. Still, damage was often heavy, and German propagandists made the most of it in describing the horror of destruction and the impact bombs had on individuals.

> A little girl sits on a windowsill at street level. Her right hand is bandaged. "It doesn't hurt anymore," the child says. From the debris of a house that is nothing more than a rubble heap survivors, mostly women, search for the remnants of their possessions. Their homes have been destroyed but no one despairs. A young woman shrugs. "I'm not afraid anymore," she says, "you get used to danger."[4]

Vienna was integrated into the July 20 plot early on with Captain Carl Szokoll as point man.[5] A professional soldier commissioned in Schuschnigg's army and transferred to the Wehrmacht after 1938, he was an ardent anti-Nazi and an early recruit for the plotters in Berlin. Badly wounded in France, he had held desk jobs ever since. In 1943 he ran section "1b/org" at the deputy general command of military district seventeen, which was responsible for organizing, equipping, and dispatching troops to the front, a cockpit position from which he could move troops, assign soldiers, and maintain an overview of military events in the district. He was given a draft of "Operation Walküre" in August 1943, weeks after Colonel Claus Schenk von Stauffenberg completed work on the doomed plan to seize power.

It was simple and compelling. Some 10 million foreigners worked in the Reich and were they to revolt, it could cripple the defense industry. The threat could be met with small, mobile battle groups able to occupy key installations at a moment's notice. Hitler, unaware that once in place these groups could topple the government under the mantle of protecting it, loved the idea and gave it full support.

Szokoll scheduled a first test for Walküre on August 12 in Stockerau outside Vienna.[6] When he and Colonel Heinrich Kodré, the district's chief of staff, arrived at 2 A.M. to launch Walküre the response was so awful that the colonel ordered Szokoll to repeat the tests over and over until Walküre units had developed into a powerful striking force. Szokoll seeded his staff with reliable foes of the regime and had them practice alerts until they had the operation down pat. In February 1944 Szokoll met Stauffenberg in Berlin to discuss final details. He returned home confident that the charismatic colonel's enthusiasm would carry the plotters to victory. He foresaw an end to the war that summer.

At 5 P.M. on July 20, Kodré, who was not in on the plot, handed Szokoll a telex from Berlin. Hitler was dead, it reported. A party clique had tried to seize power, and the government had declared martial law. It was time for Walküre.[7] Szokoll put armed guards on all the entrances to the building—the old Austrian war ministry on the Ring—and began barking orders over the phone to all the Walküre units. Across the city soldiers grabbed their guns and began to move out, with no idea that they were part of an anti-Nazi plot. Within an hour all the units were on the streets, and they quickly occupied post and telegraph offices, railroad terminals, and other strategic objectives.

Next all the Nazi brass—party, SS, SD, and SA—were told to come to the old ministry. As they arrived they were disarmed and then taken to Kodre's office where he showed them the telex. Eduard Frauenfeld, the

Gau's propaganda chief, was the only one to smell a rat. "I know the Führer is alive," he said, "I just know it."[8]

At this point the coup in Vienna seemed to have been a total success. Szokoll was on the phone giving orders to dissolve the SS. In one room dissident officers played Jewish songs on the phonograph and drank champagne toasts—but they had celebrated too soon. Minutes later word came from Berlin that Hitler was indeed alive and that the putsch had failed. The detained Nazis were freed, and the Gestapo ordered filing cabinets combed for names. Szokoll survived. He was seen as the man who only followed orders, and two weeks later he was promoted to major and left to fight the Nazis another day.

The official version made no mention of Walküre's local success. The media gave fervent thanks for the Führer's salvation. A thanksgiving meeting was held on July 21 on Schwarzenbergplatz with 350,000 in attendance. Workers were trooped in from factories hoisting signs: "Death to the Traitors" and "With Adolf Hitler to Victory."

The Gestapo arrested 600 "traitors" right away and thousands later. Weinberger and Hurdes were seized, so was Leopold Figl, a future chancellor, who was sent to a concentration camp for the second time. The Gestapo was thorough. It ransacked its files for names, and everybody who had ever been under surveillance was seized, not right away but over the course of the next several months.

Among them was Milo Dor, arrested on September 5 because his name was on a list of those under surveillance. The Gestapo beat him on the soles of his feet until the skin popped and blood spurted to the ground. "They wanted me to confess that I was here to organize a cell. But I couldn't help them. I didn't know."[9]

On August 24, 1944, Goebbels issued a series of new directives designed to free up several hundred thousand people for essential war work. In effect, he closed down the Reich's cultural establishment. Theaters, operas, and concert halls were shuttered, so were circuses except those needed to maintain "stocks of valuable animals." Newspapers were combined—in Vienna the four tabloids were folded into the *Kleine Wiener Kriegszeitung* (*KKZ*—the *Little War Paper*)—or shut down, while those that continued publishing, like the Vienna edition of the *VB* and the *NWT*, were held to four pages and six-times-weekly publishing schedules. Higher education was limited to those disciplines essential to the war effort, chiefly medicine, engineering, and related subjects. Schools that taught the arts were closed, so were art exhibits. The workweek was extended to a minimum of sixty hours with one late afternoon a week free for essential shopping, provided that minimum worktime requirements were met. The decrees were to go into effect September 1.[10]

They hurt, especially in a city as devoted to theater as Vienna, something the *VB* acknowledged, noting that audiences had bid a nostalgic and melancholy good-bye to the art that had meant so much to them. Understandable, the *VB* said, but no reason for sentimentality and regret given the bitter reality of war. Besides, film and radio would meet the cultural needs of the battlefront and the home front.

Well, not quite, as mayor Blaschke explained in mid-September. He promised to expand party cultural activities in the morning and the evening so that musicians could play for workers. Lending libraries would stay open longer. The city would also broaden cultural activities in the home, especially house music. In general, Blaschke added, families should be drawn more closely into cultural activities. It was small beer and Blaschke knew it.

Early in October Goebbels tightened the screws. Army doctors stationed in the Reich were to treat civilians and ease the burden on the few doctors still left at home. All congresses and public meetings were banned. Civil decorations would no longer be awarded. Administration would be simplified and red tape cut. In Vienna plans were announced to turn the city opera into a large movie house. The Vienna Symphony, the city orchestra, was disbanded.

Still, Blaschke and Schirach made sure that the city was not a total cultural desert. The Vienna Philharmonic gave periodic concerts at the Opera, the Musikverein, and at lunch-hour "musicales" in outlying factories.[11] Audiences usually comprised defense workers and the wounded, although ordinary citizens snagged the occasional ticket. The Vienna Boys Choir took the stage before Christmas. But as the months passed the cultural fare grew thinner—popular lectures on Italy with pictures or more sober discussions such as those held to commemorate Friedrich Nietzsche's one hundredth birthday—perhaps a function of the almost daily aerial pounding the city was taking.

The air war over Vienna began in earnest on September 10, when American planes attacked oil facilities but also dropped bombs for the first time on the inner city. Damage was heavy and some priceless architecture was destroyed. The Palais Harrach on the Freyung, a Baroque jewel, took a direct hit and the *NWT* doubted if it could ever be repaired (it would be). The Heiligenkreuzerhof, a Gothic-Renaissance structure in the oldest part of town, was heavily damaged. The Ballhausplatz took a direct hit. The Pasqualatti house, where Beethoven had once lived, "stares with dead eyes into the sky." Alfons von Regius, a retired judge, noted more soberly in his diary that in his third-district neighborhood "mountains of broken glass lie heaped on the streets in small splinters."[12]

Schöner watched from the roof of his office as a gray-green wall of smoke pulled across the sixth district so that the corner houses on nearby Mariahilferstrasse were hidden.[13] When he left his office at 1 P.M. no streetcars ran. He walked downtown, confirmed the damage done to the chancellery, thanked God that the Hofburg had not been hit, only to note that a Baroque archangel had been ripped from the entrance to St. Michael's on Michaelerplatz. Outside the Café Central, where Trotsky had once played chess, Wehrmacht soldiers were busily nailing wooden planks across shattered windows. The old Hungarian embassy on Bankgasse had been hit; so had the Starhemberg Palais. One bomb had struck behind the Burgtheater, hitting the cellar where several people were still buried. Another had carved a crater out of the Ringstrasse in front of the Café Landtmann, while a third had slammed a hole in City Hall Park. Masses of people walked on the Ring in late afternoon. For the most part they were more curious than frightened. But a group of singing forced laborers was roundly cursed.[14]

For the media the destruction wrought on September 10 was fodder for exhortation and propaganda. Thus the *Kleine Wiener Kriegszeitung* (*KKZ*), wrote that the "air murderers" had killed with the "same, mechanical ice-cold cruelty as they had over Germany." But if they had hoped to split the population they were sadly mistaken. The only result? A "glowing, deep-seated, silent hatred that thinks only about one thing: revenge and retribution."[15] The language in other media was similar.

On a more practical level, the September 10 raid pushed authorities into confiscating even more apartments, and to demand that those who had an extra room or two take in those who had lost their homes. No appeals to generosity were made; this had the force of law and included rooms with "normal" occupation, meaning one or two persons.

Apartment owners had the absolute duty to make any confiscated room available to others. Those who refused would be prosecuted.

The Fifteenth U.S. Air Force pounded the city again on October 11. The targets were oil refineries, but population centers were also hit. Schöner noted that is was a short but violent attack that lasted a bare hour. "Flack fired wildly and for the first time while I was in the cellar I heard the thunder of falling bombs."[16] Afterward he saw columns of smoke rise above his neighborhood and black clouds in the east that visibly darkened the sun. An alarm on the 12th proved false. The following day industrial targets across the Danube were bombed. "You begin to accept the alarms with resignation," Schöner wrote. "When I leave the house in the morning I wonder if I will return to an intact flat."

The Americans launched another "terror attack" against Vienna on October 17, and once again the media responded with language designed to whip up the popular will to resist. "In a matter of moments cold, unfeeling murderers brought great harm to the peaceful residents of our city," the Little War Paper wrote.

Schöner called it a black day and said it was the worst raid since September 10. He saw little smoke or fire. Apparently the Allies had dropped high explosives. Afterward most streetcar lines were down and major thoroughfares were black with people walking home from work. Few trams ran the next day. Gas was turned off. The Schöner family restaurants had nothing to sell—no coffee, beer, or mineral water.[17] For the rest of the month alarms were frequent but raids few—and then more pinpricks than real bloodletting.

That changed on November 5 when the Fifteenth Air Force sent 500 B-17s and B-24s against Vienna. The planes dropped 1,100 tons of bombs on oil refinery targets but some explosives went awry and did heavy damage to the core city.[18] For the first time, Schöner said, the Americans used firebombs massively, and fires burned everywhere. Streets smelled of phosphorous. Fire trucks roared up and down main traffic arteries. After the all clear sounded people streamed through the streets. No water, no gas, no public transit. "Thank God we still had power," he noted. At lunch the "Austrians" in his office said they could not understand such heavy attacks on the inner city "when we are supposed to be liberated." Schöner's dry comment: "They forget six years of war and the 99 percent Ja votes in 1938."[19]

Later that afternoon he went downtown to the cathedral. The faithful, including many soldiers, crowded around the altar where a priest was conducting afternoon services. Houses burned on virtually every street he passed and people stood outside, picking through the possessions they had saved. From his wife's house he saw a red night sky over the second district where the northwest train station was burning.

Hella Kinn, who worked for a German chemical firm, walked down the street that morning when she heard the cuckoo warning come from shattered windows—the "death clock" as she called it.[20] (The signal on the radio alerting the population that enemy planes were approaching the city was dubbed "the cuckoo" for the two-tone sound it made.) When she reached her room she heard the sirens, grabbed the bag she had kept packed, and headed for the cellar. Flack began almost immediately; so did the whistling sound of bombs. Explosions grew closer and closer. Then a blast shook the cellar. Crying people rushed to the exits in fear of being buried alive. But the bomb had struck two houses farther on.

Half a dozen raids followed over the next two weeks with oil refineries in and around Vienna the major targets. Results were impressive. Production was down to 31 percent of what it had been in the spring.[21] The inner districts were not hit much, though cuckoo warnings had become a constant.

Hella Kinn had managed to obtain a rare ticket for the Philharmonic on November 22. She rushed home after work to dress up—a gray silk dress she has worn for three years, stockings and shoes that date back to the "Schuschnigg years"—and just made it to the all-Mozart concert. "Since the beginning of the war Mozart is my passion. He alone can lift me above this present to give me peace and harmony. Beethoven, the so beloved, and I hate to say this, is often depressing, especially the Fifth Symphony with its victory apotheosis. And the Ninth—'All men are brothers,' who can bear that today?" In the middle of Mozart's violin concerto the air raid sirens howled. The orchestra stopped playing. The audience ran pell-mell to the exits. The cloakroom was chaos with people struggling to reach the exits. The air raid shelter underneath the Musikverein was a joke—a few small rooms totally inadequate for so large an audience. The air stank. People grew sick. But it was a false alarm and after an hour the all clear sounded. The concert resumed, but the mood of joy was over. Not even Mozart could change that.

Two months of air war had transformed city life. Disruption became the norm. People geared their activities to the availability of gas, water, and power. Erratic streetcar schedules and the districts they served—they literally changed every day—led to terrible overcrowding. People hung on the open platforms of the old trams like bunched grapes. Schöner noted that as many public transit accidents occurred in a week as had once taken place in six months. Barber shops and beauty parlors cut services drastically. Women would be permitted only one permanent every six months, and this time there was no Eva Braun to protest. The piles of rubble grew, and clean up crews could barely keep pace. Phone service was frequently disrupted. Family members often worried for days about relatives they were unable to reach.

Air raid shelters had become a way of life. The Americans usually attacked between 11 A.M. and 2 P.M. so many headed for shelters rather than to the office. On December 3, near 10 A.M., Hella Kinn saw mobs of people loaded with suitcases and bundles rushing for the catacombs. The underground network ran two stories beneath the streets, across much of the inner city and from church to church, and afforded the best protection. Punctually at eleven, Kinn noted in her diary, the sirens howled. She had stopped going to the cellar in her house, which was just below street level and vulnerable. A woman who sat next to her in the catacombs complained bitterly about the alarm because she had planned to see a movie. When the all clear sounded after three hours, she said, "They did that for me, so I could go to the movies."

Raids in mid-December had left 25,000 people homeless in the tenth district alone, a fact, she wrote, "you only hear on the grapevine," and not from official reports or from the newspapers—they only reported on the help given bombing victims. Starting on December 15 the cuckoo sounded in Vienna every day, including Christmas and New Year's Eve, even if some were false alarms. On a work-free Saturday Kinn rose at seven, dragged coal from the cellar, and rushed to finish her errands before the cuckoo called punctually at 10:30 A.M. This time it was a false alarm, but on the 19th Allied bombs knocked out the rail link west, making train trips difficult and dangerous. American bombers had begun to pass low above moving trains and open up with machine guns.

"Fear," she wrote, "is the emotion that dominates all others. We are afraid when we get up in the morning and when we go to bed at night.

Fear when we leave the house, fear when thinking about people close to us. Fear in every hour and minute of our existence."

On New Year's Eve Margaret Bajez, who worked as a copy editor in a publishing house, reflected on the year just past. "What a year," she wrote in her diary. "The Russians are battling for Budapest. We know that Vienna is next, and the question on everybody's mind is will Vienna be defended? Will God show mercy to our city, or will it be completely destroyed in the madness of our times?"[22]

The New Year brought no respite. As the Allies drove closer to the Reich, bombers flew shorter distances and encountered less resistance. On January 15, 1945, some 400 American planes attacked Vienna in the heaviest raid to date. Results were mixed. Some rail hubs were destroyed, but residential and business districts were hit hardest.[23] Hella Kinn had been to another Philharmonic concert the night before: Hans Pfitzner's *From the German Soul*. The work had not appealed but the musicianship of orchestra and singers had. It was past 11 A.M. as she wrote and no advent of enemy planes had been reported. "Eleven thirty. The cuckoo calls." What followed, she wrote the next day, "was among the most horrible we have experienced so far. Waves of death passed over us without respite so you couldn't hear the antiaircraft guns." The all clear sounded three hours later. She planned to visit a friend, a long walk away with no streetcars running.

She managed to cross a huge crater only to find herself in a desert—destroyed houses all around, the road blocked with rubbish and delayed-action bombs, and fire wherever she turned. "I couldn't get through anywhere. People tried to push through the snow and mud. Soldiers with stretchers ran to and fro. A woman stormed out of a half-ruined house yelling 'isn't anybody coming? He's bleeding to death.'" Kinn finally gave up and walked back home through a black sky brightened by fires "that raged like torches of death."

Bad weather bought the battered city some relief, with only one major raid through the rest of the month. But in February the Americans hit the city hard, flying a series of raids with 400 and 500 bombers, and doing heavy damage to oil and transportation targets as well as to residential areas.[24] On February 19 a bomb hit Schönbrunn—allegedly the Germans had sited a high military office in the Habsburg summer palace—and destroyed the zoo, one of the oldest in Europe. None of the beasts of prey escaped, the *NWT* reported, but an elephant and rhinoceros were shot and killed; their cadavers still lay on the broken roofs of their cages.[25] Some 1,200 exotic birds were killed or had escaped. The newspaper issued an urgent appeal to the population to bring any rare species they found back to the zoo.

The anatomical institute was destroyed in another February raid. Heinz Fidelsberger was taking his anatomy exam in the cellar that day. Stumped by one question he repeated it, playing for time, and suddenly found himself slammed against one wall with the lights out. "We simply hadn't heard the sound of the explosion." Seconds later the assistant yelled "Fire, fire, fire." The force of the blast had burst many thousands of glass vials in which body parts floated in alcohol, and now thousands of liters of burning liquid ran down the stairs; soon the whole building was engulfed in flames. They got out onto the street where the professor stood dazed and shocked. All his scientific work, twenty years of labor, were locked in the safe of his study. Fidelsberger took his keys and ran back inside. He grabbed the papers from the safe as the whole ceiling collapsed behind him, and then the floor underneath. He managed to reach the main stone staircase and jump past puddles of burning liquid and out of the collapsing building. When he returned late that afternoon to help with the cleanup, the professor remembered the interrupted exam and said "I'll pass you, is that all right?" It was.[26]

On February 21 Ernst Andreas, a twenty-two-year-old private first class assigned as a clerk to a pioneer battalion office in the Hofburg, sat in the palace cellar forty feet below street level during a massive raid that damaged the university, ripped the roof off city hall, and tore open streets all the way to Schwarzenbergplatz. A B-17 crashed behind the Burgtheater. The pilot, Raimund Klutz (Imagine, a German name! Andreas noted in his diary), bailed out and landed squat in the middle of a virtually empty Heldenplatz. A lone fireguard, a wizened old man, crept up behind the American, who was trying to untangle his parachute, and slammed Klutz over the head with his German helmet. Then he dragged the six-foot-six dazed American into the shelter. "No wonder the man was crying. Clearly he thought he would be killed. And indeed there were many ready to do just that but our soldiers protected him. He was searched for weapons and then two sergeants took him to a nearby room. Imprisoned officers are always guarded by non-coms with pistols."[27]

On February 26 Maria Czedik wrote that most mornings at eleven the city resembled an ant hill. "Masses of humanity push and shove each other to get into the public cellars. The Wiedner Hauptstrasse (a main thoroughfare in the fourth district) is a mass migration flowing out of the tenth district. We finally have water in our house. You can only buy bread in the morning and there is none later in the day anywhere in town. Anker and Hammer (Vienna's two major bakeries) were hit in a raid. Everything freezes and everybody wants a decent meal. My nails split and break. I'm supposed to have a tooth pulled."

Even before American bombs became part of Vienna's daily fare, the population had turned apathetic and desolate. Indeed the mood was so bad that SD chief Kaltenbrunner felt something had to be done at once. He had spent time in Vienna in September and on the 14th fired off a letter to Bormann demanding change. The Viennese, he wrote, did not know where to turn, and no strong personality was able to provide political direction. Plans to build a Southeast defense wall from Slovakia past the Neusiedler Lake to the Semmering region were not taken seriously, and were more likely to cause panic than to reassure an already nervous population. The city's defeatist mood made people willing to believe all the bad news from the Southeast including "lying propaganda," to display "certain Austria tendencies," and of course to swallow all kinds of Communist propaganda. The only solution, Kaltenbrunner wrote, was replacing Schirach with a Gauleiter who could bring momentum, organizational talent, personal toughness, and political self-confidence to the job. He nominated Alfred Frauenfeld—the perennial candidate.[28]

Himmler, too, backed Frauenfeld as new Gauleiter. But Bormann was not so sure. On September 17, 1944, he sent a trusted aide, Helmut Friedrichs, to Vienna to take another reading. He met with Lower Danube's ailing Dr. Jury, who was too sick to do more than work a couple of hours a day from home, and with Deputy Gauleiter Scharitzer. Both thought that Schirach was doing a bad job as Gauleiter, but both warned the party not to replace him, at least not now, and not with Frauenfeld. Jury said Frauenfeld should have been made mayor of Vienna instead of Blaschke but, despite his popularity and organizational talent, he should not replace Schirach. Scharitzer was blunter: Frauenfeld was a bluffer. He lived in a large, pretentious villa in posh Hietzing and had been roundly criticized for it. His extravagant life style would quickly make him vulnerable to even greater attack. Schirach may have lived equally if not more extravagantly, but somehow the Viennese believed he deserved to. "They call him the baron," Scharitzer said, "who lives in another world but that's something people don't mind." Moreover, Frauenfeld's advent would revive the "old cliques," meaning the Austrian Nazis who, with Blaschke's anointment, felt a new wind at their back.

While Jury was only mildly critical of Blaschke, Scharitzer called his appointment a major blunder. As mayor he was a washout—he had no administrative skills and all his focus was on culture. He was unlikely to withstand the pressures of a worsening political or military situation. His suggestion of drawing nonparty members into governance was absurd—any move toward democratization had to be, in the Nazi world view—and therefore he could not be taken seriously politically.

Schirach's own failings should have been well known in Munich, but Friedrichs treated them as fresh news: He was focused on the arts, on youth affairs, and Southeast policy. He was playful and not interested in matters of substance. His personal staff so guarded his privacy that he had little contact with district leaders and other party officials. And he had little influence on—or interest in—the activities of his RP Delbrügge or Mayor Blaschke.

Both agreed that Schirach was a decent man, personally courageous—he had gone to Slovakia to evacuate a children's camp threatened by partisan activities—well thought of in Vienna, and with absolute authority over the people who worked for him. But both rated his human relations skills and leadership qualities as negligible. Jury described Schirach's method of governance as being "*in* society" but not *among* people. "He rules but he does not lead. He shuttles back and forth between the Hohe Warte and the Ballhausplatz and receives artists and the like but doesn't visit factories very often to hold speeches," an unfair criticism since newspaper reports put him there regularly. For Scharitzer, Schirach "lives in another world where he pursues his hobbies. He thinks about foreign policy and wants to put that in order. But he doesn't see the real problems that, as Gauleiter, he needs to solve. At a recent political meeting he talked about the servant problem and said that if he lost his maids he'd have to shine his own shoes and fetch food stamps."

Friedrichs conclusions were obvious. A change of Gauleiters in Vienna was out of the question. Schirach was better than Frauenfeld. Scharitzer needed better and stronger men in key posts and had to persuade Schirach to take a larger hand in the nitty-gritty of party work. In short Schirach had once again escaped the ax.[29]

260

Now the party cracked down harder than it had before July 20. Peoples Courts became more active and handed down brutal sentences. The *VB*'s descriptions of their activities in Vienna in the fall of 1944 are horrific in their cynicism and callousness. Anyone who doesn't toe the Nazi line— for whatever reason—will face the harshest punishment, it said. "We don't need informers or an inquisition. Whoever is openly against us must be wiped out! The judgment of the people's court is harsh but just." The paper then took readers inside the court:

"The gas-bag before the court is as ugly as an ape and his past puts him outside society. He was once married to an Orthodox Jew according to Hebrew rites. His testimony is as twisted as his whole being." The court adjourned proceedings pending further evidence.

An accountant is accused of spreading destructive rumors and quoting from the Talmud—it is better to be a coward for five minutes than to be dead a life long. "The spineless Talmudist makes a nervous impression. The witnesses are sure, calm and collected. There can be only one judgment—death."

A chemist is charged with spreading rumors. "You can see and feel that this man does not belong to us," the *VB* noted. "He is unmanly and unprincipled." He escapes death, however, and is given a heavy prison sentence instead. A fore-man, on the other hand, is clearly the victim of slander. He is solid and upright, his accusers are nervous and inconsistent. "The indictment bursts like a soap bubble. The man is acquitted." A female doctor and a fortune teller are sen-tenced to death. Invective is heaped on both—they are ugly inside and out.

"We will not tolerate cowards and criminals who attempt to stab our soldiers in the back as they did in 1918," the president [judge] of the court told the *VB*. "We will relentlessly punish every attempt at treason, defeatism or subversion of our soldiers. But we do not want to hold show trials on the Bolshevik model. We don't have torture cells like the GPU [the Soviet Secret Police] does. Our only task is to find the truth." A hard sell when that "truth" was manifest in the red death notices that had begun to sprout across the city.[30]

On October 18, 1944, Hitler announced formation of the Volkssturm (people's guard)—an amalgam of the dregs left in the manpower pool of everyone from ages sixteen to sixty. Two days later Schirach called for a mass demonstration and harangued the crowd with the usual clichés: "we are tougher than fate," "every hour our fortifications grow deeper," "Vienna stands under the sign of Prince Eugene, under the sign of the arts of war. This Gau will become bulwark and symbol of battle."[31]

Schöner was skeptical. "As far as I can observe the public reaction is feeble and resigned, as is every response to desperate propaganda mea-sures, even though the Goebbels machine is attempting to exceed all its own past achievements. Slogans painted on all walls and shop windows for several weeks now—'battle until victory' and 'victory at any price'— are finding no resonance."[32] This didn't mean that Goebbels was giving up. Days later a newspaper editor told Schöner about new directives to drum "Volkssturm and nothing but Volkssturm" into the ears of readers. Everything must serve to make people even more fanatic.

On September 28, 1944, Josef Bürckel died, allegedly from a two-day bout of pneumonia, but rumors that he had committed suicide persisted. The Führer ordered the pomp and circumstance of a state funeral. Rosenberg held the funeral oration. Schirach traveled to Saarbrücken to represent the Gau that Bürckel had once headed. The Vienna media paid the funeral respectful attention, but very few people seemed to care. For "Bierleiter Gauckel" ("beer leader clown"!) good riddance was more in line with the popular mood.[33] In Hungary, regent Miklós Horthy resigned and the fascists of the Arrow Cross consolidated governmental powers. They had moved, the *NWT* said, to block "traitors" from following Bulgaria and Romania in seeking an armistice with Russia. The new men around Prime Minister Ferenc Szalasy would assure marshalling all resources to continue the war. Schöner, who had good contacts in the Balkans, wrote that the Jews who had escaped mass deportation and murder in the provinces by fleeing to Budapest were now being systematically liquidated. The situation, he added, was reminiscent of Vienna in March 1938, augmented by six years of war and "the Asiatic residue in the Hungarian temperament."

Despite local party criticism and Schirach's lack of interest, Blaschke continued his campaign to bring city government closer to the people. In a city council session on September 6, Blaschke welcomed thirteen new councilmen. They included a farmer, an accountant, a metal worker, and a locksmith as well as the rector (president) of the University of Vienna, and a colonel in the NSKK, the Nazi motor corps. He did not want to lead by giving orders, Blaschke said, but to gather competent advisors who could help him govern. He planned to hold council meetings every month to develop new ideas and monitor the success of old ones.[34]

But in October his focus was already on the new version of total war: he would cut the bureaucracy 30 percent by shutting down the tourist office, limiting library and archival work, and closing all exhibits.[35] At subsequent sessions the councilmen discussed the growing rat problem and the increasing difficulties of burying the dead. Rats thrived on rubbish and rubble, and had already caused the loss of 66,000 kilograms (about 146,000 pounds) of grain. Geography would determine the cemeteries where families could bury their dead. Transporting corpses across the city used too much gas. One councilman pushed cremation but the response in Catholic Vienna was tepid.[36]

In mid-November disruptions in city life—lack of gas, water, power, and public transit—had grown great enough for Blaschke to explain to the public that overaged infrastructure took longer to repair. Gas pipes, for example, had been buried too deeply for easy access. At the November council meeting Blaschke denied a feud with Schirach that had become the talk of the town; so much so that the papers *had* to pick it up to deny it. Bad blood between the two, of course, had long been a matter of record.[37]

The last Christmas of the war was gray, cold, and desolate, with little holiday spirit. The newspaper claque tried to infuse some joy but without much success, for what could shoppers do with headlines like the *KKZ*'s "Even the smallest things can make us happy?" The KdF opened a show featuring homemade presents: carved wooden toys, paper dolls, braided belts, and handbags of twisted straw. It's not what is given but how—with love and devotion, as tokens of affection, the newspaper decreed.

The *VB* conceded there was little to buy. Mothers looking for toy trains, dolls, and other traditional items would not find any. They were not being manufactured because the skilled workers who made them were turning out guns and bombs. The paper did note that a run on chamber pots in one store was so great that management limited sales to one per customer—prompting many to telephone family members to come on down and buy. Not that they all needed to use them at night, but the pots were good barter items, which could be traded for food in the country. For those who lacked time and imagination for homemade presents there was always money. Banknotes could be wrapped in festive paper—provided there was any—and placed under the tree.

There was plenty of money around but very few trees. Hella Kinn got her Christmas bonus on December 1, which, she wrote, despite enormous taxes, still amounted to a nice sum. "I would have been glad for the money in other times, but now it leaves me indifferent. There is nothing to buy." As for Christmas trees, they were a treasure. Schöner noted that the rare pedestrian walking down Mariahilferstrasse with a tiny tree tucked under his arm was the object of envy. At one corner a small mob had gathered—a man was selling branches from a fir tree.

Maria Czedik was upbeat. "Despite all the horror around us some kind of Christmas spirit has arisen. Everybody ate as if his life depended on it. Everybody must have thought it would be for the last time." (Black market food was still available.) She even had a good time on New Year's Eve, largely because good-looking boys were around. Gas was turned on for the evening. Bars, restaurants, and other places of amusement could stay open as long as they wished—on Himmler's personal orders—and streetcars ran two-and-a-half hours longer.

The Ardennes offensive in the West helped bolster the mood in Vienna, mostly among committed Nazis and those Viennese who had been running after the rabbit since Schuschnigg's time. Once the tide turned, so did they. And clearly the number of committed Nazis began to shrink in earnest in the New Year. Kinn recorded a visit to a friend who had long ago given up hope of final victory. But her husband, home from the front, clearly had not. "The mentality of committed Nazis is strange," she wrote, "and I am not clear if they really believe what they are saying or if they only pretend to." When she told him about her fears that the Russians might come to Vienna, he laughed out loud. Few others did. Fear of the Russians was rising across the city and with it growing exasperation with the Nazi regime, which clearly was no longer in a position to defend the people or their interests. But lack of support no longer mattered to the Nazis who simply tightened the screws.

Thus the rise in the number of executions was far larger than the number of posters suggested. "They're only whispered about," Kinn noted, "but unfortunately they are fact." A friend had been at the central cemetery to visit the grave of her parents. She was late. Twilight had fallen when she saw a truck drive up. Suddenly uneasy, she hid in a bush. She noted a freshly dug grave nearby where the truck stopped. She saw the men unload blood-soaked bags, which they emptied into the grave. Severed heads fell out.

On January 9, 1945, a fellow worker told Kinn this joke, surely symptomatic for the moment: An inspector came to a Nazi boarding school and called one of the boys to the stage. Who is your father? he asked.

Adolf Hitler, the boy replied. Who is your mother? Greater Germany. Where do you come from? Berlin. What do you want to become? A soldier. You're a good boy. Next. The lad was from Hamburg. He acknowledged his paternity and said he wanted to be a sailor. The third boy was from Vienna and he too answered the paternity question correctly. But when asked what he wanted to become he replied "an orphan."

Three weeks later Kinn made fun of new restrictions on use of natural gas—it would be curbed two days a week. "That's a joke since most of the city doesn't have any gas anyway. At times we don't have any power. Sometimes the lights go out without warning—a particular joy sitting in a dentist's chair." On January 28 she snagged a ticket to the Philharmonic under Furtwängler—Cesar Franck's Symphony in D Minor and Brahms's Second. "I listen to music with devotion and ardor as never before because each time I think perhaps this is the last time."

As the military situation worsened, Nazi rhetoric became harsher. Schirach's New Year's message paid tribute to the Viennese for withstanding many months of aerial pounding. The turn of the year, he said, would be a turn of the fates, "So we march into the New Year unafraid and confident of victory."[38] A week later Schirach dutifully echoed the Führer's call for "popular sacrifice," meaning that every German should scour his attic and contribute what he found to the common good—textiles, clothes, shoes, anything soldiers and especially the children and old men called into the Volkssturm could wear into battle.

In the first two months of 1945 Schirach's popularity dropped precipitously. A new shrillness had entered his rhetoric, and the Viennese were no longer willing to forgive him his extravagant lifestyle. His lack of compassion began to irritate. Word about the elaborate bunker and command post he had built in the Vienna Woods had begun to spread. He had imported workers from the Ruhr who dug down twenty-five meters (eighty-two feet), brought in cement—a water truck had to come up three times a day to speed the work—and built an expansive bunker, which, an engineer who had worked on the project noted after the war, could have withstood an atomic bomb. No expense was spared—wood-paneled walls, a massive conference table, leather chairs, a lavish kitchen, and state-of-the-art telecommunications centers. Once the cuckoo sang, Schirach's limousine—and those of other party leaders—could be seen rushing from the Hohe Warte or the Ballhausplatz to the safety of the bunker. As he passed onlookers roundly cursed him. The Viennese saw his excesses as personal insults.[39]

Ralf Roland Ringler, an ex-Hitler Youth leader returned from the front and charged with training teenagers in the arts of war, was ordered to the bunker in February together with other HJ leaders. The group sat down to a meal of chicken and rice served by three waiters in white tie and tails. Conversation came around to alleged worker riots in the tenth district (Hella Kinn had also alluded to them in her diary). Schirach's face darkened. The corners of his mouth pulled down. "If the mob in Vienna dares rise I will use all means at my disposal to gun them down." Gone were the German socialism speeches he had used for so long with so little effect. What remained was the spoiled child of German aristocracy and American money. "The Reichsleiter hovers above things and anybody who tries to hinder his hovering is eliminated," Ringler noted.[40]

The indigenous Austrian Resistance had survived the aftershock of the July 20 uprising reasonably well. Few Austrian civilians were involved, and Major Szokoll had kept his anti-Nazi team intact. True, Hurdes, Weinberger, former mayor Seitz, and others who had been in touch with Gördeler had been arrested, but the loose resistance structure that had taken shape in the wake of Stalingrad was only slightly damaged. Hans Sidonius von Becker, propaganda chief for the Fatherland Front, had begun pulling the disparate strands of resistance together. After he was released from Mauthausen in 1941 he set up a central coordinating committee that gave the groups and grouplets a sharper, more professional focus than they had in the past when the Gestapo succeeded in regularly smashing Resistance cells. But Stalingrad had brought deep change to resistance psychology and sparked more spontaneous opposition, often around a strong local personality, and while these groups remained autonomous they had far greater contact with each other. By early summer 1944 something close to a Resistance block had taken shape—close enough in any event for a code name to gather them together: O5. O stood for Österreich (Austria) and the five for the letter *e*, the fifth in the alphabet, making the meaning clear—*Oe*, as in the phonetic spelling *Oesterreich*, still a forbidden word in post-Anschluss Austria. Days later the slogan was smeared on streets, houses, and public buildings in three Vienna districts, and soon O5 was plastered all over the city including St. Stephen's cathedral. A week later the Gestapo had established a special section to handle O5 matters.[41]

Unlike the idealists of 1940 who cared about ideas and political structures, the O5 groups took direct action. Thus in June 1944 the Resistance knocked out a transformer in Vienna and streetcar traffic was disrupted for days. Another group disabled ninety phone cells. Key rail lines were disrupted—not for long but often enough for the disruptions to sting, especially one that linked Vienna to the Zistersdorf oil wells to the East, and the line to Wiener Neustadt in the South. Resistance cells set up courier services to Tito's partisans and to American forces in Caserta in Italy, making initial contacts with American intelligence. Months later the OSS would supply radio transmitters and other equipment. An Austrian officer set up a shop to manufacture false papers and other identity documents. A new sense of professionalism entered the ranks as operations become both slicker and more confident. Anti-Nazi doctors increased the hospital stays of dissidents and made sure they did not have to return to the front. A growing number of deserters found shelter and protection in safe houses. The Austrian Freedom Movement, founded in April 1944, began publishing a news sheet in May that was distributed across working-class districts and which urged workers to fight for "peace, freedom, and Austria."

In early December of 1944 O5 decided to form a seven-member steering committee to better coordinate the now disparate but far more widespread resistance activities and to give political direction to what had been till then a purely military organization.[42] Becker headed the group, which ranged across politics from Catholic-liberal to Communist, but did not have a Socialist member. It was called POEN for *Provisorisches Österreichisches Nationalkommittee* or Provisional Austrian National Committee. Members included Dr. Ernst Molden, the deputy editor of the *Neue Freie Presse* before 1938, and Major Alfons von Stillfried, a man with wide contacts among anti-Nazi officers in the Wehrmacht that ran from what was left of Admiral Canaris's *Abwehr* counterintelligence service to such key figures as Szokoll and Major Karl Biedermann, the chief of Vienna's military police. Even more important, Stillfried had contacts in Croatia, Hungary, and Italy. Becker and other POEN leaders realized early that they needed to build a solid relationship with various Allied centers before Germany's defeat in order to make credible Austria's claim for independence under the Moscow declaration. A passage in that document had demanded that Austrians do something to speed their own liberation. This would prove a problem since most Viennese—and other Austrians—did not give the Resistance the kind of public support the Maquis had in France. The Viennese may have become disillusioned with the failures and defeats of the Nazi regime but in general did not share— at least not then and some never did—the Resistance's hopes, aims, and dreams. The Russians scared them far more. Schöner found no signs anywhere of a general uprising. Gradually contacts with the allies increased— in Italy, in Switzerland, where young Fritz Molden, barely twenty years old, sat in Allen Dulles's Bern office to lecture the spy master with an arrogance peculiarly his own, about what was really going on in Austria, and into France and even England.[43] The young couriers impressed their Allied contacts enough to provide some support. OSS officers, usually Austrians who had fled the Nazis and become Americans, were parachuted into the country, bringing communications equipment, know-how, and trust. They would be the basis for Austrian military action in late March and April.

O5 and POEN were careful, mindful that the Gestapo could strike anytime. The key lay in barring O5 penetration by Nazi agents. Becker understood the danger, one reason why his organization remained so loose and why members kept to circumscribed activities. He also had his own contacts within the SD and the Gestapo. But he was never able to obtain a list of so-called V-Men (*Vertrauensmänner*)—Nazi infiltrators into his organization, and in January and February 1945 the Gestapo shut down one group after the other. Becker himself was arrested in February when the SS moved onto the student organization and he happened to be at their headquarters. One of the students opened fire, killing two Gestapo men. "They burned holes into his flesh with candles," Becker would write, but he survived.

So did O5. Budapest finally fell in mid-February, and the Russians already were beyond Lake Balaton and would soon march along the north side of the Danube. With the end of the war clearly only a matter of months, if not weeks, away, the Resistance was able to scramble and reassemble its forces in March and April. Most important the Nazis had not struck at the Stillfried-Biedermann-Szokoll triangle within the armed forces. They would prove one key to the coming battle for Vienna.

CHAPTER 11

The Battle for Vienna

Death and Transfiguration:
March 1–April 29, 1945

When the all clear sounded on March 12, 1945, at 2:30 P.M., Hella Kinn stepped out of her half-destroyed office building into another city. Bombs had sheared off a corner of the art museum and the statue in front had lost its head. Trees lay smashed and broken. When she looked down the other side of the Ring she screamed. The Opera was on fire. "For a moment I lost it. I don't want to see it, I shouted, and hid my face in my hands. Nevertheless, I ran in the direction of the flames, as if drawn by magic. As I ran I heard myself say over and over 'the Opera is on fire.' I didn't get very far. At Goethe's statue the Ring was closed. I tried to get into the inner city by climbing up the ramp to the Albertina but rubble blocked my way." Wherever she looked buildings were on fire—the Phillipshof across from the Albertina and the Heinrichshof across from the Opera, and of course the Opera itself. "The fire swelled and grew and expanded until it engulfed heaven and earth." She closed her eyes again and remembered the first time her parents had brought her to Vienna from their home in Transylvania to see and hear *The Flying Dutchman*. Then and there she had determined that she would live in this magic city for the rest of her life. *Fidelio, Don Giovanni, Meistersinger*. The memories crowded her mind, "but when I thought of them it seemed to me as if they too were shrouded in flames. Had I ever thought I would stand here and see this destruction? Then the great hall collapsed with a terrible thunder. A true believer who sees the temple of his god burn cannot have felt any different than I did at that moment."

She was not alone in feeling that loss of the Opera was the deepest wound war had inflicted on the city. Schöner called it "the blackest day for our beloved city and for me and our family." The cuckoo sang at 12:15 but nobody paid much attention. Vienna had not been subject to a major air attack since February 21, and indeed the two hours or so he had spent in a cellar had not been very different from other air raids. But when he called his father after the all clear he learned that the Opera and the Heinrichshof—where the family owned a café—were on fire, and that another of their restaurants, the Casa Piccolo, had been badly damaged.

He rushed downtown—on foot since no streetcars were running. The cupola of the art museum was only a skeleton, and he thought it a miracle that the heavy facades had remained standing. The Heinrichshof café was beyond salvage. The Casa Piccola had been shattered, but the kitchen and the pantry had been left intact. When he first passed the Opera it was still standing with black smoke billowing through the roof. Later, as darkness fell, he saw fire lunging out from the stage and up onto the first floor where fire fighters were silhouetted against the flames. It all appeared "so unreal and operatic."

For Ernst Andreas, destruction of the Opera was the worst blow of a day that saw cultural landmarks fall like ninepins—Opera, art museum, the imperial stables, the Spanish riding school, the Academy of Fine Arts, the stock exchange on the Ring. A bomb had torn the balcony off the Hofburg where Hitler had harangued the multitudes in 1938. The Burgtheater and Volkstheater had been damaged, though not badly.

Nor was injury limited to the city's icons. Adele Hufnagel, a dental assistant in a city clinic, recorded the Opera's fall in her diary, but worried more about the ruined streets and houses in Ottakring and Hernals, working-class districts beyond the Gürtel. "They carpet-bombed our neighborhoods. Jörgerstrasse is destroyed from the Gürtel to the public bath. Today is the anniversary of the Anschluss and that's why they attacked us so hard."[1] A matter-of-fact resignation marked the recorded comments of most citizens. Stephanie Bamer, a young lawyer, noted that the opera had burned, that the vestry of St. Stephen's had been destroyed. "Many dead. The inner city is on fire."[2] Alfons von Regius wrote that the destruction was "such a great pity."

The media lamented with greater force, even with some empathy for what loss of the Opera meant to the city. True, the *Little War Paper* headlined its story with "against brutal destruction, icy hatred" and ranted against "the messengers of Mr. Roosevelt," whose barbarism was no different from the murder and destruction of bolshevism and which every true Viennese would meet with "murderous hatred." The *NWT* was closer to the pulse of popular sentiment in describing the Opera as the city's most populist institution, not limited by class or wealth but accessible to all who loved music. But neither the tempered sorrow of the *NWT* nor the shrill rhetoric of the *KKZ* could shape the emotions of the Viennese. The Russians were too close in Hungary: the vaunted German counteroffensive had stalled. Naked fear had flamed across the city, a fear the destruction of the Opera only intensified. In his diary Schöner caught Vienna's downward-spiraling mood very well.

On March 1 the Schöner restaurants still had no running water. To keep going they pumped water from the nearby imperial stables and pushed tubs and pots on carts and dollies to their kitchens. Toilets that did not flush silted up and stank terribly. But the family businesses soldiered on, whereas many of their competitors—the Café Mozart of *Third Man* fame, for one—did not. One result: the restaurants and cafes were swamped. "People fight for a free chair, wait patiently, and court the favor of nervous and overburdened waiters." At home Schöner arranged to reuse flushed water a second time. Baths were out of the question. "I never knew you could wash with so little water."

On March 2 he still had little hope or faith in any Austrian resistance. "The fear of the Gestapo, SD, and SS is too great. People are less actively opposed to the regime than they are tired and resigned. The situation reminds me of Austria in early 1938—everybody sees the end coming but keeps muddling through."[3] Walking by a grocery store, he saw this sign in a window: "Bread sold out. No cheese. No vegetables." Garbage piled up everywhere. The streets were filthy. "Thank God people are getting used to it." The family restaurants managed to get their refuse collected by giving the garbage men a glass of wine. "Money is no use as a tip. Cigarettes are the best currency." Burying the dead had become a serious issue. Most corpses were dumped into mass graves in the central cemetery with crosses marking the spot so relatives could rebury their loved ones after the war. Coffins had become almost impossible to get. Most of the dead were buried in paper bags or not at all. One of Schöner's friends had to live with a corpse for days because no one came to remove it. The diarist noted that three to four weeks could pass between death and burial.

The radical cut in bread rations drove up the prices for bread and ration stamps on the black market. Schöner recorded that people were paying up to RM 50 or twenty cigarettes for a kilo whereas a week previous, bread had cost ten cigarettes. Lard was now RM 200 a kilo, sugar RM 150. Political discussion had grown franker with the postwar period the focus of many conversations. Opposition to the Nazis is no sure alibi, Schöner told friends, a point someone active in the underground left-wing movement had made to him: "The fact that the Nazis sent somebody to Dachau is no excuse in our eyes for his past sins. We haven't forgotten February 1934."[4]

A report from military district XVII, issued on March 6, 1945, supported Schöner's gloomy assessment: "The mood here is very depressed. Everybody is tired of the war. Outright destructive tendencies are noticeable. Only a very few still believe in victory."[5] More and more people were listening to "enemy broadcasts." Propaganda claims of new wonder weapons in the offing that would surpass the V-1 and V-2 were openly ridiculed. And, worst of all, agitation for the so-called Free Austria Movement was winning strong resonance among the artistic community and what was left of high society. On March 10 the local SD sent Kaltenbrunner a corroborating report. Workers had adopted an especially hostile attitude toward the party after heavy air raids and were no longer afraid to speak their minds. Even the Führer was no longer off limits. The SD report quoted one worker as saying, "Isn't there anybody who can get rid of him?" As for Schirach, the Viennese had only contempt. "Where is he? You never see or hear him during a raid. We can die here and the good man sits comfortably in his secure bunker."[6]

But in early March the Viennese were encouraged by an unusual sight: division after division of fresh young soldiers in pressed uniforms and new weapons rode through the city on shiny new Panzers headed toward the Hungarian front.[7] Hitler had decided on another gamble. He moved SS Obergruppenführer and Colonel General Sepp Dietrich's Sixth Panzer Army from central Germany to the East. The general was ordered to smash the Russians in the Lake Balaton region and then punch holes in their lines to recapture Budapest, stabilize the whole front, and keep Vienna safe. The Germans attacked during the first two weeks of

March, but success was sparse. Still, Schöner thought that after a week, the front had stabilized and that the Russians were not planning a major offensive in that region. He was wrong.

On March 16 Marshall Tolbuchin's Third Ukrainian Front and Marshall Malinovsky's Second Ukrainian Front attacked on a line from Lake Balaton to the Danube, thrusting south toward Croatia. The battle was fierce and Russian losses were enormous. But after three days Soviet troops tore two holes into German-Hungarian lines, threatening the whole German army group south with collapse. Defying Hitler's hysterical commands to hold the front at all costs, German generals, including Sepp Dietrich, began to retreat to save what they could. In the ensuing fighting the Sixth Panzers lost most of its tanks and the Sixth Army, which fought alongside, most of its artillery. The Germans were forced to evacuate the southern banks of the Danube and mass armor on the other side of the river, which helped the Panzers slow Malinovsky's drive on Bratislava. But on March 25 the Russians stood outside Gyoer, the last major Hungarian town between Marshall Tolbuchin and the Austrian frontier. Vienna was now a little more than an hour away by train.[8]

The seriousness of the situation, however, seemed to have escaped the Nazi bureaucracy in the once and future capital. Schöner had been ordered to the HQ of Military District XVII to discuss soldier replacement and labor questions. He was appalled at the naïve lack of concern he found among the brass. They simply ignored failing morale, lack of discipline, and the unwillingness of the rank and file to obey orders. All the Nazis could talk about was the application of "necessary" force.[9]

The seeming normality of life among the ruins had an almost surreal sheen. Ralf Roland Ringler had tickets for a Wolfgang Schneiderhan concert. "Music and culture, those were things we believed were worth fighting for. I look at the faces around me and begin to doubt. Nothing could arouse these people. They'd never lift a finger to help themselves. They just want to preserve the values of culture, with or without battle."[10] Hella Kinn sat in an air raid shelter on March 16 and listened to people in an adjoining room laugh and shout as if they were sitting in a wine garden, while those in the shelter with her talked of suicide. A factory manager sent one of his messengers to his daughter's school with a bribe—he was to give the professor a kilo of lard, discreetly, so that she would pass his daughter to the next grade.

The lights went on at Anita Schöner's flat after a ten-day hiatus. Schöner and his wife had maintained separate apartments during the war, but now they celebrated with a dinner of sausage and potatoes and real coffee. After dinner they were sitting down to play a game of cards when the lights went out again. At city hall the councilors met for the last time on March 18 to discuss one disaster after another as if they were the most routine events. Thus Rafelsberger promised to have the elevated lines up and running by the end of the month. Erratic water supplies could be steadied by tapping into nineteenth century wells—as had already been done successfully in the tenth district.[11] The *Little War Paper* reported that a number of exotic birds had been returned to the Schönbrunn Zoo. They included parrots and several birds of prey that had flown from the zoo into open apartment windows miles away. Several eagles and vultures, however, were still flying around the palace grounds.

Air raids continued unabated. The day after the Opera fire, the Americans were astride the rail line between Vienna and Wiener Neustadt. Chemical factories on the edge of the city were hit on March 15 and oil refineries at both ends of Vienna—in Floridsdorf and Schwechat—on the 16th. The bulk of the March attacks had slammed transportation targets, specifically rail lines leading East—an effort to interdict supplies destined for the fizzling German offensive in Hungary—and once that objective was achieved, American bombardment of Vienna ceased. The last attack came on March 30, as the Russians were preparing to cross the old Austrian frontier.[12]

Advance units of the Forty-sixth Army, part of Marshall Malinovsky's Second Ukrainian Front, had reached the Austrian border near Güns on the 28th and crossed it on March 31. Tolbuchin's men poured in after them. Schirach's Southeast wall proved to be the myth Kaltenbrunner had thought it would be back in September: Russian tanks drove through it like hot knives through butter. One Russian flank smashed south from Güns toward the Semmering where troops of the German Sixth Army were posted; a second punched past the northern shore of Lake Neusiedler toward Vienna, an approach guarded by Sepp Dietrich's Sixth Panzers. Neither the German infantry nor the armor were effective fighting forces after the pummeling both of them had taken in Hungary.[13]

On March 30, Good Friday, Schirach declared martial law,[14] a step Schöner thought redundant. The government already had all the power it needed to order executions. All the order did was increase popular fear and uncertainty. The next day Schirach banned all private vehicles from leaving Vienna and ordered four battalions of motorized Volkssturm, mostly teenage boys, to the front. That triggered one of the few demonstrations of the war, and the only one by women. The mothers and sisters wanted more than to merely keep their boys home. They took to the streets to protest against fighting for Vienna at all. For weeks rumors had circulated that Vienna would be declared an "open city" as Rome had been, but the Nazi brass wouldn't hear of it. (Schirach had hoped he wouldn't have to fight; later he told Blaschke that he had little choice—Bormann had ordered the defense). But it was a shimmer of hope and when it was dashed, the city's mood worsened as a Nazi district report about the protest, dated April 2, attested. It acknowledged that the situation was getting worse every day, that the wildest rumors were spreading and were believed.[15]

With the Russians driving toward Vienna from the South, Schirach introduced Sepp Dietrich to the city's population via radio and the press. Nobody pretended anymore that the seriousness of the situation could be papered over.

"I'm not a man of big words or polished speech," Dietrich said, "besides, today deeds count for much, words for very little." He promised to do "everything humanly possible" to save Vienna. "More would be foolhardy. The battle will be hard, victory difficult."[16]

The next day the *Little War Paper* conceded that Russian troops had reached the outer limits of Greater Vienna. They had taken Wiener Neustadt, the key center of aircraft production, and were on the outskirts of Baden, a spa not twenty miles away.

The city's defensive perimeters were solid enough, but not as elaborate as the Soviets would later claim.[17] They were based on heavy antiaircraft guns turned into land artillery. The first belt ran from Mödling in the South to the Wilhelminenberg and Laaerberg mountains in the West. A second line was closer to the core city and ran north across the Danube to Grossjedlersdorf in the North and the Lobau in the South. Finally, the twenty-four five-inch guns mounted on the steel-and-concrete flak towers inside the Gürtel could form a third line. While the fire power was heavy, the guns' mobility was slight. They could be turned 360 degrees, but since they were mounted on concrete sockets they could not be moved from place to place. Still, the Germans had amassed a lot of guns—ninety heavy pieces and sixty light guns in Grossjedlersdorf alone, and their fire power sufficed to slow the Russian advance.

The German high command, however, was at sixes and sevens. On April 2 General der Infanterie (the equivalent to an American lieutenant general) Rudolf von Bünau was ordered to take over command of Vienna's defenses. He arrived on April 3 but found he had no clear mandate with Schirach and the commanding general of the Vienna area countermanding his orders. Bünau had ostensibly been put in charge of the defense but could not dispose of all the troops theoretically under his jurisdiction. After a quick survey of the situation, Bünau wrote in his diary that Vienna was indefensible—a conclusion Dietrich and others had also reached. But Bünau was bound by Berlin directives: should he fail to hold the line he would be put before a military court and his family held hostage. In the end he and his soldiers were put under Dietrich's command.

Nor was Dietrich's Panzer Army a fully functioning force. When he arrived in Vienna he told Schirach that they called it the Sixth Panzer Army because he had six Panzers left. He wasn't far from the truth. On April 5 he disposed of only twenty-eight battle-ready tanks.

Nevertheless, efforts to push more children into battle continued, largely on the orders of the art-loving Reichsleiter himself, the second act of barbarism he committed on top of sending 60,000 Jews to their death in 1940–42. Ringler, who had been told to put together a Hitler Jugend company, did more than most to protect and train his charges, but the bulk of the HJ shoehorned into the Volkssturm was used as cannon fodder.[18] He haunted the hospitals and clinics to assemble a truly motley crew to help him train the children under his charge—men with false legs, a missing foot or arm, or a head wound. But they all knew war and would help train his boys in everything from use of hand arms to bazookas. On Easter Sunday Ringler marched his troops, rifles on their shoulders, around the Ring to the Hofburg in a demonstration of armed might and the will to use it. They were to be sworn in. The ceremony was the same as it had been for seven years: serried ranks behind bundled banners, martial music, patriotic songs about death and glory, Schirach's speech about death, heroism, and transfiguration in the Führer's service. Days later Ringler decided to give his boys real—as opposed to

MARCH 1–APRIL 29, 1945

theoretical—bazooka training. A target was built besides Prince Eugene's horse on the Heldenplatz. The boys began firing. The noise was deafening. Two doctors rushed out of the Hofburg where a field hospital had been set up. The wounded were beside themselves—the noise had to stop. "I'll have you put before a court martial," one of the outraged doctors yelled. It was typical for the city's overwrought mood.

The Austrian resistance had not been idle. Major Carl Szokoll—who had survived the July 20 plot with a promotion—had conspired to make Vienna an open city and had even gone to Schirach's RP, Hans Delbrügge, to enlist his aid in persuading Berlin to surrender Vienna without battle. Instead, he was given a plan for Vienna's destruction, "Operation Gneisenau," named for a Prussian general. It was part of an order Hitler issued on March 19, 1945, which historians have labeled "Nero" and whose acronym was ARLZ. *L* was the key letter. It stood for *Lähmung* (paralysis). The order's gist: destroy every item of infrastructure in the Reich before it could fall into enemy hands. Hitler reserved the right to order implementation for individual cities. Szokoll was charged with drawing up the specifics for Vienna—gutting all railroad stations, blowing up bridges, mining the Danube, placing explosives in power plants, gas works, oil tanks, even the Anker bread factory.[19]

Szokoll thought long and hard. Perhaps he could use Stauffenberg's failed plans to save Vienna. First he had to change the operation's name. He picked "Radetzky," the most successful Austrian Field Marshal of the nineteenth century. His superior wanted to know why. Because, Szokoll replied, the Viennese would fight harder for their city under the mantle of a beloved general than under the name of a distant and unknown Prussian. It made sense, he was told. Szokoll was now in the same position he had been under Stauffenberg. He could put together Radetzky units with Austrian officers in command under orders to destroy the city but in reality ready to save it. He gathered a group of loyal commanders—at least he thought they were loyal—including Major Karl Biedermann, a key figure since he commanded the city's military police. Mindful that one reason for Walküre's failure had been lack of popular support, Szokoll made contact with O5 and POEN both to widen and coordinate operations. At Easter he felt he had enough Radetzky units in place to seize key installations as the Russians closed in, and thus avoid a prolonged battle for the city.

His next task was getting in touch with the Red Army and persuading the Russians to follow his plan: instead of striking from the South, the Soviets should push West and then North toward the Danube before looping East and attacking through the Vienna Woods. Szokoll would put Radetzky units into the region ready to open the back door. At the same time the Resistance would declare Vienna an open city and assist the Russians streaming in. In return the Russians would keep the aqueducts on the Semmering and the Schneeberg intact, assuring the city's threatened water supply; tell the Americans to stop bombing; and free all Austrians captured during the coming battle. Staff Sergeant Ferdinand Käs, Szokoll's top aide, volunteered to take the plan through the German lines. Szokoll assigned him his car and driver and drew up his orders: "Make contact with the Hungarian prime minister Ferenc Szalasy. Route through Burgenland, southern Lower Danube, Styria. All duty stations are to provide maximum support."

Käs drove off on Easter Sunday night, April 1, at 10 P.M. and reached the Semmering at dawn, April 2.[20] Battle lines were already drawn and the car was quickly under fire from both sides. Käs and his driver abandoned the vehicle, and at the bottom of a hill found two Red Army soldiers with machine pistols who took them prisoner. Some thirteen hours later they were taken to Hochwolkersdorf, a village that served as Soviet headquarters. Negotiations took till the afternoon of April 4 with agreement reached on all of Szokoll's major points—including the drive to the West and assurance of the city's water supply. The Russians also told Käs to report to the Resistance that Dr. Karl Renner, the first republic's first chancellor, was on his way to the Third Ukrainian Front's HQ. Stalin had personally selected him to head whatever provisional Austrian regime took shape after Vienna's fall.

When Käs returned, everything seemed in good order. Radetzky units were laced across the Vienna Woods. And on the evening of April 6 the Russians shot off the agreed-upon signals, red flares. The Resistance was to answer with green flares, which it did. Szokoll then left his office to confer with the Communist underground. He wanted to put together a unified committee representative of all Austrian politics. It would prove a fatal mistake. While Szokoll was away, one of Biedermann's lieutenants denounced the plot. Biedermann and two other plot leaders were arrested. Under torture they revealed the names of the others—including

Szokoll's. On April 8 Biedermann and his aides were hanged from a lamp-post in Floridsdorf. Szokoll had been warned before returning and fled.

Meanwhile, the Russians struck west and north. On April 6 the Ninth Russian Army was moving swiftly toward St. Pölten, while units of the Sixth Soviet Tank Army closed in on Tulln on the Danube and swung east toward Klosterneuburg, a town some ten kilometers northeast of Vienna. Armored columns also moved into the city from the West—from Hütteldorf and the surrounding parts of the Vienna Woods. But formations were more probing than strategic and battalions of Hitler Youth and police auxiliaries were actually able to stop the Russians and push them back, albeit briefly. Still, exploratory Soviet units probed as far as the West Station, and therefore the Gürtel defense line, before pulling back.

The battle for the city exploded the next day. Russian columns coming up from the South had reached the central cemetery—a vast expanse of land covering much of the tenth district—and had penetrated the urban sprawl of Favoriten itself against fierce German resistance. Units of the grenadier division "Der Führer" had reached Vienna that day and been immediately thrown into efforts to stop the enemy advance from the South. The Russians also crossed the Danube Canal where that river arm rejoins the Danube proper and were on the island that houses the Prater, the second and the twentieth districts, facing determined German opposition bolstered by other units of the newly arrived division.

The first signs of popular resistance to the Reich began to emerge. Workers offered to act as guides for the Red Army through the maze of city streets. The first white flags, usually sheets or towels, began to flutter from windows. Families offered shelter to German soldiers ready to desert, taking their uniforms and providing them with shoddy civilian clothes. In Floridsdorf housewives poured hot water onto soldiers of the Führer division on the move across the Danube. Marshall Tolbuchin had issued two proclamations urging the Austrians to resist and promising that the red army was in Vienna to liberate the city.[21] They clearly had some impact in restless working-class districts.

Schirach's office had issued the ARLZ alert Szokoll had prepared for gutting key infrastructure two days before. Mayor Blaschke moved to prevent the worst by declaring major installations out of bounds and banning their destruction. But he could not block Schirach's order to pull 3,700 fire fighters, virtually the entire city complement, and 600 fire trucks and other vehicles out of the city.[22] After April 7 only eighteen fire fighters remained with three damaged vehicles. The move assured more death and destruction than Russian ordinance ever could inflict.

Red Army cannon opened up on the morning of April 8 in an effort to knock out German artillery positions in the Prater and the Stadtpark near the Ring itself. The Germans shot back, and during the course of the day a host of new fires swept through the inner city and destroyed factory installations in the eleventh district. The flames burned unchecked. The cathedral was damaged for the first time. The Burgtheater, where the Nazis stored ammunition, blew up and burned so that only the facade was left standing.

Major Red Army forces had moved in from the West, and by nightfall the Russians had pushed through Ottakring and Hernals almost without a fight, operating on tips from working-class informers that the Germans were retreating. They reached the Gürtel from Nussdorf to the West Station, effectively Vienna's second line of defense, but they could not break through to Heiligenstädterstrasse south of Nussdorf, where German three-inch guns had destroyed several Soviet tanks. Instead, the Russians probed for other weak spots and found them. Although the plot had been betrayed, the Radetzky units were still in place—reason enough for Sepp Dietrich to order them back since he was not sure of their loyalty. As a result the Russians found it relatively easy to cross the Kahlenberg and descend into the wine-growing village of Grinzing. More importantly, the constant probing led to the collapse of a unified German command in the northeast of the city.

That move allowed the Russians to push across the Gürtel at Alserstrasse into the ninth district and move down to the general hospital. Their advance was stopped by the Panzer Grenadier regiment of the "Führer" division that happened to be moving across Alserstrasse to new positions just as the Red Army approached. The grenadiers halted the Soviet advance, which was then reversed—at least temporarily—by an odd crew of children, old men, students, the walking wounded, and other Nazi fanatics whom a retired Austrian Major General, Marian Wessely, had put together as "battle group Wessely."[23] They actually managed to push the Russians back to the Gürtel, thus winning time to evacuate the wounded from the hospital. But the respite was brief. The Führer division was being moved across the Danube, and it was clear that the Germans could not long hold the districts between Gürtel and Ring, and indeed the inner city itself. On the evening of April 9 the Germans retreated across the Danube Canal. At 4 A.M. on the tenth General Bünau left the old war ministry and crossed the last intact bridge over the canal, which was then blown up. At 4:30 German cannon opened fire on the abandoned inner city. The Russians moved in cautiously during the morning hours. They now controlled two-thirds of the city. The battle would last another three days.

Baldur von Schirach's activities after introducing Sepp Dietrich as Vienna's savior on April 2 are unclear. His wife and family had left the city weeks before. He moved erratically from his home on the Hohe Warte to his new office in the cellar of the Hofburg. As the city burned Schirach saw himself as hero in some Baroque opera, ready to die a hero's death— or to act as if he were. At the same time he continued his life as before.

On April 5 Ringler determined to move his HJ company out of Vienna. He would first ask Schirach's permission and if he didn't get it, he would arrest the Reichsleiter. In the growing chaos the idea was not totally implausible. He was admitted to Schirach's villa. The Reichsleiter was asleep but would be down shortly for breakfast. In his muddy uniform Ringler felt out of place. Finally Schirach appeared in his fancy uniform. He was polite, engaging, and friendly as he listened to Ringler explain why he wanted to move the boys out, but he did not respond. Instead, he spoke about the big picture, about the United States, about Japanese philosophy. He was truly out of it—floating above reality, and Ringler, acting on his own, moved his boys out of harm's way.[24]

Otto Skorzeny's impressions were similar when he visited Schirach at the Hofburg on April 6. The Austrian SS swashbuckler, who had snatched Mussolini off his mountaintop prison in the fall of 1943, was in Vienna to help break the plotters around Szokoll and Biedermann. "The floor was covered with magnificent carpets," Skorzeny wrote in his memoirs. "Portraits of eighteenth century generals and battle paintings hung on the walls. In the candlelit hall people ate, drank, and caroused." Skorzeny told Schirach he hadn't seen a single German soldier in town and invited him to a reconnaissance drive. Schirach declined. Instead he bent over a map and explained how Vienna would be saved. Two elite divisions were ready to move, one from the north the other from the west. The enemy would have to capitulate. That's what Prince Starhemberg had done in 1683. Skorzeny shrugged. Further discussion was useless. As he left, "Schirach looked at me and said: 'Skorzeny, my duty can be expressed in three words—victory or death.'" What he wanted to say, Skorzeny noted sarcastically, was victory or flight. Five hours later the Reichsleiter left the city and sought protection with the retreating German army.[25]

Vienna's newspapers published their last editions on April 7. The *VB*'s last headline: "In the sign of successful resistance—we look danger coolly in the eye." The city's desperate military situation was hardly mentioned, and neither was the Red Army's entry into Vienna. That was recorded in word-of-mouth lore, diary entries, and memories written down years after the fact.[26] These reports don't always agree with communiqués of the contending armies or with reconstructed historical records, but they have the virtue of freshness, immediacy, and personality.

On April 9 Hella Kinn was hiding in a cellar that had become home during the siege. Just as she was about to stretch out on a couch, someone called down "Ivan is here." Moments later a neighbor rushed in. "They're here. I shook hands with two of them. They said they wouldn't hurt us." Kinn ran upstairs. "Grete stood at the door and waved. 'We've survived,' she called out, and laughing and crying we fell into each other's arms. 'Thanks be to God,' I said. 'For us the war is over.' We walked down the street. A Russian soldier stood outside the house next door surrounded by laughing, gesticulating people. Russians stood on the corners. All the houses had white and red flags on them. On some you could see the circle where the swastika had been cut out.... And whatever may come now, we are free of this Führer and his creatures."

Maria Czedik somehow got wind of the Radetzky plot—indeed the information seems to have been carried on the wind—and wrote on April 5 that "Vienna is to be turned over to the Russians today at 9 A.M. God give that it is true. We've borne these Nazis for seven long years and now we shall finally be rid of them. Of course life will be terrible under the Russians but getting rid of this pest is worth hard times to come. My God, never having to hear *Heil Hitler* again, never again. No Gestapo, no war, no bombing. Dear, dear God, let it be true."

On April 8 she wrote that "of course the rumor was not true. Fighting continues and the artillery fires nonstop. Yesterday word had it the Russians were on the southern Gürtel and would have the city by nightfall. So everybody burned their swastika flags and prepared white sheets but it was all for nothing. They still haven't come." But the next morning she saw the first Russian tanks rumble past. "Everybody was out on the street and waved. In Vienna even war becomes an occasion for making mischief."

Margaret Ebenwaldner heard that the Russians were on Alserstrasse on the 8th. Women with white flags in their hands were jumping on the tanks and riding in with the soldiers. "They were not the wild-eyed Mongolians we had expected but definitely European types, well-fed, clean-clothed, and neatly shaven. Most of them were tall and well-built, and most of them could speak a little German."

Bertha Nickl never thought much of the Russians to begin with. "With their fur hats and slit eyes and the wild expressions on their faces they make us all afraid. Many people cry openly. So many years of battle and sacrifice and suffering and so many of our loved ones dead on the battlefield and the end is nothing but enormous suffering."

On April 8 Karl Sellner recorded heavy artillery fire in his ninth district neighborhood. In the afternoon Soviet armored reconnaissance pushed down to Lazarettgasse, three blocks north of the hospital. "We overturned the barricades the Nazis had put up," Karl Sellner wrote. "White flags flutter from some houses." They were too early. On the 9th the SS was back with house to house fighting raging until nightfall. When his mother stuck her head out the window to water the geraniums the Nazis opened fire. He had to grab her by the feet and pull her down. "Liberated! Dead Tired," Sellner wrote on April 10.

Margaret Bajez remembered that on the 7th mobs stormed railroad station depots and grabbed anything they could get, and the authorities did little to stop them. Men rolled wheels of cheese down the street. Stores were broken into and plundered. Garbage piled up but not the ordinary kind—"pictures of Hitler in every shape and size, and party and formation insignia."

"Mouth radio" spread reports of where bread, meat and coal could be obtained as depots were broken open. Bajez ran to a bakery and found an endless line but when her turn came she gathered a two-kilogram (about four pounds) loaf. Meat was available somewhere else. A coal depot soon had people loading up carts even if they would not need the fuel until winter. And nobody paid any attention to three dead soldiers in one corner.[27]

The Russians wasted valuable time securing the inner city. Their caution allowed the Germans to build a defensive line, albeit a tattered one, along the eastern bank of the canal from the island's "point" in Nussdorf, where it rejoined the Danube in the north, to the Augarten bridge in the second district above the Prater, where the Russians were already fighting. A fierce artillery duel began on April 10 when German guns laid waste all the buildings along the Franz Josefs Kai on the Vienna side of the canal and started fires in the inner city behind it. Russian guns were placed on St. Stephen's Square and in other open spaces. At midday on the 11th rumors spread that the SS planned a storm attack across the Augarten bridge. The Russians pulled their artillery out of the allegedly endangered area, while soldiers hid in houses. A white flag was hoisted from the cathedral spire, and for several hours the inner city was a no man's land. According to Manfred Rauchensteiner, (whose book is the most exhaustive on the 1945 fighting in Austria published to date) looters took over with horrific consequences. They plundered stores, took anything not tied down, and apparently set fires that soon engulfed the downtown from the Stephansplatz up the Kärntnerstrasse. With no fire fighters in the city the blaze quickly turned into a fire storm. The cathedral, Rauchensteiner claimed, had been damaged by German and Soviet artillery but was still standing and in relatively good shape. It could not, however, withstand the fire that burned for the next forty-eight hours. On April 13 the cathedral was a gutted shell. (Rauchensteiner's version contradicts earlier accounts that blamed Nazi gunners across the river for shooting off the church's roof—politically a far more acceptable story and one to which the Viennese stuck for decades. After all, it helped absolve them from Nazi crimes and that absolution would be the focus of so much post-war Austrian politics.)

On the night of April 11th the Red Army was across the Danube Canal at several points; on the 12th the Russians launched a general offensive that, during the course of the day, managed to push the Germans into a small triangle near the Florisdorf bridge in the north of the island. At the same time the Red Army captured the Reichsbrücke, the last intact bridge across the Danube itself. With sizable Red Army forces on the far side of the river, the battle for the city was effectively over. On the 13th SS and what was left of the Wehrmacht moved north.

Marshall Tolbuchin promptly reported the fall of Vienna to Stalin himself who ordered a 24-salvo salute fired by 324 guns, awarded 84 unit citations, and several thousand medals. General Birjukow, the corps commander in charge of the actual fighting, was named a hero of the Soviet Union.

Gradually the Viennese began to emerge from their cellars and return to what was left of their homes. The city was desolate. Fires burned unchecked. Buildings on both sides of the Danube Canal were in ruins, empty facades with gaping holes where windows had once been. Bridges were crumpled in the water. A photograph of the cathedral taken on April 14 showed that the fires had burned out leaving the church without a roof, the remaining walls blackened by the flames. Outside the burned-out Hotel Meissl & Schadn, once the home-away-from-home for Nazi brass, a graceful statue sat untouched on top of a well, surrounded by the shattered remains of the figures that had once accompanied her.

"Vienna was a dead city," Karl Mark, a social democrat who would run the nineteenth district that summer, noted. "People walked around but there was no running water, no gas, no power, no streetcars, no automobiles, no traffic, and nobody knew what would happen now." Indeed, the only thing the Viennese cared about during the next couple of weeks was avoiding Russian soldiers and foraging for food. They had already plundered in the final days of the Nazis, but now they made it big business—everybody did. "I saw a lady in a fur coat walk out of a store with a sack of flour on her shoulders. A well-known dentist in my district came out of a Meinl (the city's largest grocery and delicatessen chain) store with a crate of sugar."[28]

Fear of the Russian soldiers came in two waves—first, when the frontline troops marched in and the propaganda-sodden population expected rape and pillage; they were relieved to encounter only isolated incidents. Second, when the back-up troops arrived, rape and robbery did become common. Women from their teens to their eighties were ravished. The Russians grabbed any watch they could find, sometimes wearing six to eight of them on both arms. Even Nazi opponents like Schöner had to concede that on this point Nazi propaganda had been on target, although

Soviet officers explained the rapes away by saying their troops had been abstinent for so long. Russian behavior, though not nearly as bad as the embroidered Viennese accounts would later have it, quickly changed the public perception from "liberator" to "occupier." Nevertheless, nobody seemed to want the Nazis back. The committed had fled West with the Wehrmacht, while the others watched with concern when they saw Russian troops drive out of town.

Politics had begun to ferment as soon as the Russians neared the Austrian frontier, and it became clear even to the densest Viennese that the end of the war was only a matter of time, and not much time at that. O5 and POEN began to look beyond Resistance to the city and the country's political future. They set up headquarters at the Palais Auersperg behind parliament and close to city hall. Szokoll, who had fled to the Russians and returned with their blessing, showed up on the evening of the April 7 hoping to mount a last-minute rescue of Biedermann and the others.[29] He failed but his presence gave O5 a military anchor. Over the next few days the Auersperg became the hub of a new political consciousness, the only central authority in what was becoming an outlaw city.

Law and order was a distant dream. With no police on the streets, looting and crime continued. Men claimed authority based on nothing more than a red-white-red armband. The streets were unsafe during daylight, and after the 8 P.M. curfew they were unsafer still. Some 12,000 corpses lay on the streets. Many were buried in parks or private gardens, others left on the pavement. Phones and telegraphs didn't work. Time was out of kilter because the Russians operated on Moscow time, an hour behind Vienna. Districts the Russians occupied became Soviet fiefdoms with Red Army officers appointing locals—Communists or those who claimed they were—as district chiefs. But the Russians were not yet ready to move into the political scene. The Germans were across the Danube and had to be pursued. The war was far from over, so, at best, Red Army interference in local politics was haphazard.[30]

On April 12 the O5 took the first step toward asserting political control and with it some semblance of law and order. It summoned two leading socialists to the Auersperg. One was Dr. Adolf Schärf, the lawyer who had negotiated with Jakob Kaiser in 1943 and the leading Socialist in the city who had not been arrested. The other was Anton Weber, a former city councilor in charge of buildings. Dr. Raul Bumballa, who had taken over as head of POEN after Becker's arrest, told Weber that the committee of seven had decided he was to be provisional mayor with a Communist, Rudolf Prikryl, as his deputy.

Bumballa and POEN were politically naïve, with no experience in the rough and tumble of party politics. They thought the past could be buried with a new spirit of cooperation taking over. But Weber and Schärf, seasoned political infighters, were cautious about accepting the offer. Marshall Tolbuchin's declarations—now plastered across the city—had called for a return to the status quo before 1938, including prewar borders, which the Socialists read as meaning a return to the Schuschnigg regime, and they wanted no part of that. Instead, they favored a return to the 1920 constitution and a truly democratic government—a point they would win. Weber told Bumballa he would have to consult with the Socialist party before considering his offer. He and Schärf then called a meeting for the next day, Friday, April 13, in the Red Room of the badly damaged city hall.[31]

The meeting was attended by eight Social Democrats including Oskar Helmer, the future minister of the interior, and Theodor Körner, Schärf's chosen candidate for mayor. Known as the "Red General" Körner had been chief of staff of the Isonzo army in World War I and helped build the first Republican Army and the Socialist Schutzbund. He spoke fluent Russian, went without an overcoat in winter, had the bearing of an imperial general, and the custom of giving orders that were immediately obeyed. Clearly he could talk to the Russians one on one.

Schärf returned to the Auersperg with the new candidate and new demands—he wanted a 50-percent share of city council seats for the Socialists with the rest divided among Communists and members of the Resistance. O5 countered with a 40–40–20 proposal: 40 percent each for Socialists and Communists, 20 percent for themselves. Schärf demurred. He didn't care how the other two parties divided the rest, he wanted the 50 percent. He got them: O5 leaders like Bumballa were no match for his tactical skills and political ruthlessness the Nazi experience had only sharpened. O5 had not expected a return to pre-1933 party politics, indeed they had all been too young to take part in them. Soon Schärf was talking to the renascent Christian Social party, which named old-line politician Leopold Kunschak as their leader and nominated him for one of the vice-mayoral slots. The Communists, bolstered by the arrival of Moscow-trained exiles like party leader Johann Koplenig and Ernst Fischer, a cultural jack-of-all-trades, dropped Prikryl and, in their turn, named an old-line Communist for the second vice-mayor's post. By April 18, O5 was aced out. Tolbuchin agreed to Körner's appointment. The next day the Russians searched city hall for illegal arms; Körner and his team waited on a park bench before entering. Körner was now the only Austrian "in office."

Nor had the Russians been idle at the national level. Dr. Renner, the former Socialist chancellor, had indeed been brought to Russian headquarters and charged with organizing a provisional government. Orders to do so had come directly from Moscow, which relinquished little political control to the army. Even the marshals were told what to do. Clearly Moscow had hoped the seventy-four-year-old would be easy to manipulate. They were wrong. He had written letters to old colleagues, both from the Left and the Right, and, like Schärf, he wanted a return to pre-1933 governance. He arrived in Vienna on April 20 to begin negotiations with Left, Right, Center, and the Russians. It took a week to put a cabinet together. The Communists had never done much in free Austrian elections, but they had borne much of the burden of early resistance to the Nazis, and now they had the Red Army behind them. Consequently their demands were high—deputy chancellor, and the ministries of interior and education. The interior ministry would control the police and was thus the cockpit for seizing power—as would be the case in most of Eastern Europe. Renner, a product of the imperial bureaucracy that was the wellspring of Franz Kafka's world, devised a tortuous solution. Each cabinet member would have deputies from the other two parties—there were three in contention then, the Social Democrats, the Communists, and the old Christian Socials—to keep an eye on his activities. The result was a top-heavy government of more than thirty members. The Communists got interior and education posts, but Oskar Helmer, a tough street fighter from the Social Democrats who had refused Bürckel's demands that he talk workers into voting yes in 1938, was interior deputy and he would brook no Communist shenanigans.

On April 27 the new government met with Marshall Fjodor Tolbuchin, who recognized it in the name of the Red Army and the Soviet Union. The regime issued a declaration of Austrian independence that nullified the Anschluss and reinstated the 1920 constitution. Two days later the government met at city hall, where Körner greeted the members and conducted Renner and the others across city hall park to the old parliament building. An ebullient Renner swung his hat to thousands of cheering Viennese and proclaimed Austria's rebirth from the same rampart where the first Austrian republic had been proclaimed on November 12, 1918, not necessarily a great omen.

Renner's choice did not meet with universal approval. Many on the Left and the liberal Right could not forgive his call to vote yes for the Anschluss. Among his most vociferous opponents were Schöner and Viktor Matejka, a leader in adult education before the war who was sent to Dachau right after the Anschluss and released in 1944. Austrians in the concentration camps, he would remember, had sworn that Renner would never occupy an important place in postwar Austria.[32] During his imprisonment Matejka had moved from left-wing Catholic to right-wing Communist—he was someone the party was anxious to have. They put him in charge of the city's cultural affairs, a post he held for four years. On April 17 he attended a meeting of leading Communists and was told that Stalin himself had chosen Renner and that argument was futile. It would be as futile as Matejka's demands that Cardinal Innitzer be removed from his diocese. Clearly, the future would belong to the leaders of the past—albeit without the contribution the lost Vienna had made to the city.

Schöner, the ex-diplomat (and copious diarist) who helped reopen the foreign office on April 16, was appalled when Renner showed up on April 30 and delivered a speech in which he castigated the Austro-Fascists more than he did the Nazis. Workers had not forgotten February 1934, and no leading member of the Fatherland Front would play a role in the new Austria, Renner said, and neither would leading Nazis. However, small-fry Nazi party members would be treated with compassion, and those who professed loyalty to the new republic could remain in public service. Renner didn't expect the Nazis to change their worldview overnight but said they would in a year, just as the monarchists had in 1918 when he was chancellor for the first time. Schöner noted that of the fifty diplomats gathered at the Ballhausplatz, perhaps five had served in the German foreign office, the rest were convinced Austrian patriots. "Except for his antifascist tirade he spoke like an old pan-German. Now I understand his 1938 plea to vote yes, and for the first time. Apparently nobody can cut loose from the sins of his youth. . . ."[33]

Vienna lay in ruins. The physical setting Hitler had left his "pearl" was one of devastation. Bricks and stones could be repaired and restored, but the spiritual setting would be something else, and it would not be for the better. The men who launched the second republic had their roots in the first and in the empire, and they did not represent the best of either. Renner, Schärf, and their friends had formed the right-wing opposition to Otto Bauer, the Jewish intellectual who had created Austro-Marxism and built it into an ideological competitor of Marxism-Leninism. They wanted no part of the lost Vienna that had died on Kristallnacht. The Communists were out for power but could not attain it, because Stalin stuck to his agreement with the Western Allies to let Austria take a democratic course. The Christian Socials, gathered in the new People's Party, did not give a tinker's damn for the city. Although they exiled Schuschnigg, they hankered back to the days of the corporate state and were at best reluctant Democrats. The half-million members of the NSDAP spent four years in limbo but even while they were prosecuted—and some even executed—in an Allied-demanded denazification program, their potential votes weighed heavily in the electoral calculations of both major parties, and did so from the very beginning, as Renner made clear on April 30.

That calculation, too, was part of Hitler's bequest to those who would reshape the "pearl" now that he was gone—that . . . and a city without Jews.

CHAPTER 12

The New Shape of the Pearl

Vienna after Hitler: 1945–2004

When the Renner government buckled down to work in April 1945 it faced a city whose major landmarks were destroyed, whose infrastructure no longer functioned, whose people were impoverished and hungry, and whose future was very much in doubt. The Red Army brooded over the city like a malevolent vulture. The Western Allies were in the west of the country, and God knew when they would arrive in Vienna.

The photographs from that spring are stark. Rubble strewed the streets. Destroyed bridges hung in the water with precarious wooden planks leading across the canal. Women wandered down a sunny, burned-out Kärntnerstrasse, some already in summer dresses, looking vacantly into gutted store windows. People walked around St. Stephen's Square with the roofless cathedral behind them and paid no attention to the destruction.

Food was the most pressing problem. At least the Germans had kept distribution intact, so that while few had enough to eat and most complained about the deadly monotony of what there was, nobody starved. With the Russians in charge—intent on taking reparations and living off the land—distribution collapsed. Worm-eaten peas and old potatoes became the staple of city diets.

Ration cards were supposed to assure the population of 1,500 calories a day, but they seldom did. Over the next nine months that fell to a low of 800 calories, an amount that forced most residents to forage for food on the flourishing black markets, in the little gardens thousands kept in the outskirts, or in the countryside where they traded what hard goods they had for food, hoping they could get it back to Vienna without encountering marauding Russians. In August 1945 Schöner reported that he was living mostly off peas and bread; even potatoes were hard to get, with a kilo of old potatoes fetching RM 12.[1] Meat had been unavailable for a month. Sugar and fat could be bought only on the black market at steep prices—RM 1,500 for a kilo (two pounds) of lard, RM 1,000 for five kilos (eleven pounds) of sugar. (As a reference point for the RM inflation, in 1938, for example, one could get a champagne supper for two at the Sacher Hotel for RM 15; in 2002, 900 schillings would buy two beers and two pairs of long frankfurters.)

The Resslpark in front of the Karlskirche was the center for illegal transactions that summer, with literally everything for sale—from food and cigarettes to an airplane. Fritz Molden wrote that a friend had bought the plane, sold it to a Hungarian who dismantled it, brought the parts to Budapest, reassembled it, and made the plane the first craft of a national Hungarian airline. In return the seller received four cars, which he had rebuilt into three vehicles and then sold at great profit.[2] Russians were active participants in the "exchange," Schöner reported, swapping food for jewelry, watches, cameras, and gold coins, and on that market, at least, they did not cheat or rob.

The economy stuttered. In 1946 farmers produced 40 percent of the wheat they had in 1938, while meat and sausage output was 30 percent of the prewar total. Leather shoes were barely a quarter. The cost of living was 7 percent higher, and the wages of skilled workers 18 percent lower than in 1938. Laborers earned less than 70 percent of prewar pay. Not a single cigarette was distributed in the first month after the city's fall, sending black market tobacco prices through the roof.[3]

The smell of decaying garbage on streets became overwhelming; the city had no sanitation vehicles, and ex-party members charged with cleanup dumped the mess at collection points on main thoroughfares, but nothing was taken out of town. A late May heat wave worsened the stench. Streets near bomb craters were covered with layers of fine dust that led to eye and respiratory infections. A form of diarrhea, which required several days of fasting to cure, was rampant and often left victims too weak to work. Most stores were closed well into the summer. In late May, after seven weeks, Schöner was finally able to get a haircut.[4]

One sign of normalcy came on May 31 when the first Corpus Christi procession since the outbreak of war wound through the streets of the inner city. Cardinal Innitzer walked under a canopy, and the crowd noted how old and thin he looked. Leading People's Party politicians, with future chancellor Leopold Figl in front, walked behind the prelate, while former Austrian president Wilhelm Miklas—much older than he was seven years ago, with furrowed brow and wrinkled face, a too-thin neck sticking out of too-wide a shirt collar—brought up the rear of the dignitaries.

The Renner government did not have much reach that spring with its power limited to Vienna and surroundings, and even there it had little authority since the Russians had the last word on just about everything. As a result the Allies saw the regime as a Soviet tool and were not about to recognize its legitimacy. But lack of authority did not stop the government from developing policy, nor from bitter inter- and intraparty squabbling, much of it ideological.

On June 12, 1945, for example, Communist leader Ernst Fischer—he had been flown back from his Moscow exile in mid-April to guide the party's social policies—slashed back at a Renner speech, bemoaning the fate of the million Sudeten Germans that the Czechs, in righteous fury, had begun to expel. Renner wanted to use scarce foreign exchange to help them.

"I find it intolerable that we have not spent a penny on the families of those the Nazis executed and on the victims of concentration camps, but that we are ready to spend a million Czech crowns for Nazis in Czechoslovakia," Fischer shouted. Not so, tut-tutted Dr. Schärf. The Czechs were keeping the Nazi; only the "little guys" were being expelled and they were worth helping.

He did not comment on Fischer's other charge about failing to aid Nazi victims.[5] The government really wasn't interested in them, a point Renner had made in a cabinet session on May 10. He threatened to resign if unions, the Socialist party, and other groups whose funds the Austro-Fascists had confiscated in 1934 were not given priority in returning lost assets. It would be unconscionable, he said, "to compensate every little Jewish merchant or peddler" and not organizations that represented 47 percent of the people.[6]

Indeed, in treatment of Nazis and their victims the cabinet was at sixes and sevens. Most had no use for illegal Nazis or those who had achieved rank and position in the Third Reich. Some, like Renner and Fischer, held the Austrians responsible for having participated in Nazi crimes, arguing that Austria was part of the defeated Reich and would therefore have to expiate its guilt. Others, like Schöner, argued that Austria, as Hitler's first victim, should line up among the victors and claim innocence in anything Hitler had done. This was one reason, initially at least, why conservatives were more opposed to allowing large or small Nazis back into government than were the Socialists.

Renner and his supporters went out of their way to be nice to the "little guys," the Nazis who just went along for the ride, even if they had been party members. Instead, they unloaded their full fury against the Austro-Fascists who had tumbled Austria into Hitler's hands, no matter how many of them had spent the war in concentration camps and had played leading roles in the Austrian resistance—something the Socialist leadership had not done.

Bürckel and other high-ranking Nazis had treated the Socialist leadership well, part of the Gauleiter's efforts to win support of the working class. Renner, for one, lived off a comfortable pension in the country and was never bothered by the Gestapo or other party authorities. He would explain afterward that he was saving himself for his work as chancellor. He even went so far as to claim he had gone to the Russians on his own and told them that he was the only man able to take over a provisional government.

Once in power Renner had little use for the men of the Resistance. Schöner claimed they made him uncomfortable, that he felt they were not real Democrats because they held to no party allegiance, and that he saw democracy in terms of political parties. He regarded those who had emerged from concentration camps as "wild cards" and avoided using them in governmental affairs.

But such persons were seen with a different eye in the west of the country where the Allies—American, British, and French—had begun to establish their rule. In the Tyrol the O5 had seized control of Innsbruck while the Americans were still a day away. When U.S. Major Sheldon Elliott rolled into the city on the evening of May 3, he found houses decked out in red-white-red bunting, and, as he arrived at city hall, a huge American flag was unfurled. He was greeted by a tall, blond young man who introduced himself in flawless English as "I am the chief of the resistance movement." His name was Karl Gruber and he would become postwar Austria's first foreign minister. The Americans were impressed enough to make him governor of the Tyrol.[7]

For months Renner and his ministers wondered whether a second government would be established in the West, which the Allies would recognize and in which the men of the Resistance would play a major role. They need not have worried. The young men who had risked their lives and fought the Nazis wanted no part of postwar politics.

During the first international Alpbach seminar—an organization founded to bring scholars, artists, philosophers, economists, and politicians to the Alpine village to discuss European issues (it is still going strong after almost sixty years)—in August, young Molden, then an aide to Governor Gruber, discussed the problem of what the Resistance should do politically. One of his OSS colleagues, an Austrian in an American uniform, suggested that instead of paying court to the "decrepit" court councilors, they go to Vienna and seize power. Molden was on his way to Salzburg for a conference between Gruber's newly formed Austrian "state party" and the People's Party where he could act as a Resistance spokesman. In the end the young decided to avoid the political fray altogether and to stay away from politics.

"Our goal," Molden would write, "was only to drive out the National Socialists and the Third Reich and to free Austria. Domestic politics after liberation did not seem to me a matter for the Resistance movement."[8] Later he would admit that that had been a major mistake. In September Gruber had fused his regional grouping into the People's Party and gone to Vienna to become foreign minister, taking Molden along as his secretary.

By then the conservatives in both parties were solidly in power, the Allies had recognized the government, and the political switches had been thrown toward the past—not to the past of the lost Vienna but toward the provincial city Hitler had decreed after the Anschluss.

The end of the war had brought some intellectual ferment. A bevy of new literary and political magazines flooded the marketplace. New art shows opened with young painters tentatively stalking around the modern tradition, whose alleged "degeneracy" was still deeply embedded in the Viennese mind. Plays that had been forbidden showed up on some Viennese stages with the Josefstadt's production of Thornton Wilder's

The Skin of Our Teeth an early hit. It was a play with which the Viennese could identify. The German title: *Wir sind noch einmal davon gekommen*—We've gotten away with it one more time.

For the most part, however, the city's intellectuals looked to the past in order to catch up with the years that had left Vienna out of the Western mainstream and its own history banished. Kafka, Musil, Broch, and Karl Kraus had all been coins of the intellectual realm before the war but now, with those who had read them before the Anschluss gone and those who had remained decimated, they seemed new to the young, and because their books were hard to get, they became all the more desirable. The most influential of the new publications, *Der Plan*, published not only the forgotten Austrians but writers from the larger world beyond—T.S. Eliot, Huxley, Rimbaud, Walt Whitman, and Mayakowski. *Das Silberboot*, another literary magazine, featured fiction by Klaus Mann, an excerpt of correspondence between Proust and André Gide, and poetry by, among others, James Joyce. The monthly *Tagebuch* confronted the immediate past with a radio play about the Lidice massacre along with essays about Freud and the destruction of Belgrade in 1941.

Viktor Matejka, the Communist in charge of city culture, was the mainspring of intellectual renewal. He supported artists and writers, using his meager cultural budget to buy and exhibit art, and to help with publication of new texts. More than anyone else Matejka wanted to restore Vienna as the global cultural and intellectual center it had been between the wars, and he knew that meant bringing back as much of the talent that Hitler had exiled as was possible. Early on he demanded that the provisional government issue a blanket invitation to return for all those the Nazis had driven out. His efforts failed, however; one of the first signs that Vienna itself was not interested in once again becoming what it had been.

Three of his failures are instructive about the attitudes of city fathers toward their own history and to their future—or rather the lack of one.[9] The names involved are glittering: Franz Werfel, Oskar Kokoschka, and Arnold Schönberg, two Jews and one Aryan.

Werfel wanted to come home from his California exile right after the war. He had suffered two heart attacks, was depressed and despondent, and took little joy in his American successes that ranged from *The Song of Bernadette* to *Jakobowsky and the Colonel*. Matejka was delighted. Russians sat in Werfel's villa on the Hohe Warte, a stone's throw from

Schirach's residence, and the house had been damaged. Matejka wrote to Werfel that he had talked to the Russians, and cleaning crews were at work fixing the damage. Meanwhile he would find adequate housing. He didn't. Mayor Körner flat out refused to help. Returning POWs and victims of Allied bombs would have first choice. In August Franz Werfel was dead.

Matejka didn't have much better luck with Schönberg, seventy years old after the war and in poor health. True, Körner promised to help this time, relying on Matejka's judgment that Schönberg was a good man and a great composer. But he never did sign a letter promising decent living quarters. Matejka would learn that the mayor's staff had risen as one man to oppose the offer. The argument was the same they used in the Werfel case—it would set a precedence for other emigrants demanding homes, demands impossible to meet in the current housing crisis.

Undaunted, Matejka tried to enlist the help of other officials but to no avail. "If he's going to die soon anyway, why do we need to get him an apartment?" one colleague asked, while another said "Oh God, Matejka wants to smuggle in another Jewish composer nobody understands." And a third commented that "If he's got to be a Jewish musician why can't he compose music people like us can appreciate."[10] In 1949, two years before Schönberg died, Matejka did manage to obtain honorary citizenship— second class—for the composer, but it was a struggle.

Kokoschka had fled Vienna in 1934, first to Prague and then to London. Matejka was an old friend and after the war ended, tried at once to bring Kokoschka back. He even persuaded Körner to write an open letter in a magazine asking the painter to come home. Vienna had not paid him the tribute he deserved, Körner wrote, and was anxious to make it up to him. "We invite you to come to Vienna and to live your art here. Vienna needs to know that her greatest sons are inside its walls. We want to honor you on your arrival in Vienna."[11]

The painter arrived in Vienna in 1946 for a short visit and a show, but the honors promised by Körner were not forthcoming. Plans to give his brother a farm that Kokoschka could use as a center for the visual arts were dashed, and Matejka's efforts to make him an honorary citizen were foiled. The culture chief tried first when Kokoschka turned sixty but was told the painter was too young and the honor was reserved for politicians. The fact that Richard Strauss had been given that honor at the same age, sixty, was ignored by those in power at city hall.

Matejka tried again in 1951 when he was out of office but not without influence—or so he thought. His successor refused to award Kokoschka, now sixty-five, honorary citizenship first or second class. Instead he offered the third-highest decoration—the city ring. An indignant Kokoschka refused. He was not a third-rate artist. The new cultural czar boiled over. "This has never happened before," he fumed. "Kokoschka will never get anything from the city of Vienna."[12] And he never did.

Things were no easier in other areas of intellectual endeavor. Only one of the seven Nobel Prize-winners the Nazis had exiled returned, and he was given a minor chair at a provincial university. Karl Popper, the eminent British philosopher who would be knighted by Queen Elizabeth II, considered the idea of coming home. He spent time at the Alpbach seminar in the summers and in 1948 was offered an associate professorship at the University of Vienna. He turned it down.[13] It wasn't much of a title. Yet Popper flirted with Vienna for the rest of his life—one more sign of how strongly the city attracted those it had scorned. Friedrich Hayek, who would win a Nobel Prize in economics in 1974, was never offered a chair in Vienna; when he returned to Europe from Chicago in 1962 he taught at the University of Freiburg in West Germany and later in Salzburg. Belatedly, in the 1970s, Vienna offered him some honorary titles.

The Jewish "problem" continued to fester even in a city whose Jewish population numbered only 5,000 after the war and had increased to 9,000 by 1948, a number that has not grown since. The Viennese had always been anti-Semitic, of course, but Nazi rule had legitimized their feelings and Auschwitz had not really changed them.

The foreign office, at least, realized that something would have to be done about coming to terms with the Holocaust. In August 1945 the department's secretary general, drafted a memorandum outlining the problem and what to do about it.[14] The document reflects the author's anti-Semitic bias, but it was also prescient in laying out a position Austria should follow.

Jews control much of the world's media and dominate international finance, it argued, and therefore play a disproportionate role in global foreign policy. America and England were friendly to Jews, and "not for nothing has one therefore called Jewry the fifth world power that destroyed Hitler Germany." Austria, therefore, should avoid any action that would pit world Jewry—and world public opinion—against it. Something would have to be done about returning Jewish assets, but this was not easy, given Austria's desperate economic situation. Nor could Jews be given preferential treatment over Hitler's Christian victims lest that trigger a new wave of anti-Semitism.

The memo went on to cite international laws that complicated settling Jewish claims, but conceded that the Allies would ignore them and insist on generous reparations. The Allies did just that. But over the years wily Austrian bureaucrats threw enough monkey wrenches into the works to leave the British and Americans frustrated and stymied until they gave up. Cabinet discussions and public opinion polls during the early postwar years, moreover, made it abundantly clear just how anti-Semitic the Austrians remained, and how little interest they had in bringing Jews back—even when they realized that they would need them to speed reconstruction.

Polls the Americans conducted in the late 1940s showed that more than 40 percent of the Viennese felt that their "unfriendly" attitude toward Jews was due to race, Jewish failure to belong, and to "the fact that Jews only want to cheat Christians." The polls also found that the same 40 percent said Jews didn't want to work, were parasites operating on the black market, and exhibited "provocative" behavior. Nor was this a passing phenomenon. In 1973 the Austrian news magazine *profil* conducted a similar poll and found that 24 percent had "strong" anti-Semitic feelings, while 46 percent had "weak" anti-Semitic tendencies, while only 30 percent had none. An astonishing 35 percent opposed Christian-Jewish marriage.

In a cabinet session on January 14, 1947, the ministers complained that Austria was becoming the target of a concerted Jewish campaign to smear it as anti-Semitic (162–70). Foreign Minister Karl Gruber, concerned over reports of Austrian anti-Semitism appearing in foreign media, suggested an official government clarification explaining the "real" Austrian position toward Jews, in other words, a very benevolent one. It was a hard sell. The cabinet basically branded all such accusations as "lies, lies, lies"—not enough to quiet criticism abroad.

Chancellor Figl's ambivalent remarks that day confirmed the critics' point, even though his anti-Nazi credentials were impeccable. He had twice been sent to a concentration camp, but he told his colleagues: "The Jews just want to get rich quick. A Jew in Bad Gastein [a summer resort] told the mayor he had made 120,000 schillings, and owned four suits and six pairs of shoes. He says Austrians just don't understand business." The truth is, the chancellor continued, that "no other nation is as tolerant as we are (163)."

The issue did not go away, and as the years passed the cabinet became much blunter. When U.S. demands for creation of a special fund to help impoverished Jews who had returned to Austria were discussed on November 9, 1948, one minister huffed, "I don't know just how one race is supposed to get special privileges. Others who did not leave are not getting benefits, but the Jews are supposed to."

Interior minister Oskar Helmer was even harsher. He granted that the problem could not be shoved onto the Germans and that Austrians must bear part of the cost. "But everywhere I look I see signs of Jewish expansion—among doctors and in business and especially in Vienna. So you can't do a separate program. The matter is political. The Nazis too lost everything in 1945 and we now see NS college and university graduates working in construction. We no longer live in 1945. I'm for putting this thing off for as long as possible. There are people who will understand that. The Jews themselves will understand because they know that so many people are against them. We should simply tell them that we will see what we can do (196–97)."

The proposal was duly rejected because the government couldn't finance it. Figl suggested not bringing it before parliament to avoid domestic and foreign policy problems. "We can't afford a public no," Figl added. "We'll just say we're in the middle of budget talks (198)." That night Figl went to the IKG to give a speech commemorating the tenth anniversary of the Kristallnacht. It dripped empathy with Jewish suffering, stressed shared values, and called for working together to make Austria better. Ten days later an outraged Kultusgemeinde called a public meeting to protest new obstacles to government help. It did no good.

By 1948 the vigorous prosecution of Nazi war criminals the Allies had demanded was over. For two years after the end of the war top Nazis were tried before Peoples Courts, and a number of the worst offenders were hanged. Blaschke was given six years for Aryanizing a villa, and many others were jailed. But a signal of change ahead came in 1947 when Schuschnigg's foreign minister, Guido Schmidt, was put on trial for high treason and was acquitted. After that, many others who should have been executed or given long prison sentences were treated much more gently in Austrian courts, a fact that did not boost the nation's image abroad.[15]

But at home both Socialists and the People's Party realized that their electoral future was tied to the number of Nazis each one could attract. Figl had won an absolute majority in the December 1945 elections but had agreed to a three-party coalition. The Communists had dropped out of the government in 1947, leaving the two major parties in uneasy cohabitation. New elections were due in 1949. The half million or so members of the NSDAP had been stripped of civil rights including the right to vote. But Left and Right were sure the ban could not last and persuaded the Allies to let them lift it. They even permitted formation of a new party—the League of Independents (*Verband der Unabhänigen* or VdU)—who fielded candidates in the 1949 election and won 10 percent of the vote and sixteen seats in parliament. In the campaign the VdU denied the existence of an Austrian nation and argued that Austrians must belong to the German cultural and popular communities. A network of laws existed to prohibit outright Nazi activities, and they were enforced so that the VdU's rhetoric was often elliptical but easy for the initiated to understand. The Nazi return to civil society had been cleared.

This was the Vienna of the *Third Man*, of life among the ruins, the beginnings of the Cold War and rising East–West tensions. The city was divided into four occupation zones with the American districts—the seventh, eighth, ninth, seventeenth, eighteenth, and nineteenth—the most desirable to live in because they were the safest and had the most resources. The Russians occupied the most territory, but their realm stretched on the other side of the canal and of the Danube. Downtown the Russians ran only the fourth district. The inner city was split with each occupying power in control for one month at a time and the "Four Men in a Jeep"—the MPs of all the occupiers—in charge of security. It was known as the International Zone and through the 1940s and early '50s was the nexus of Cold War espionage. It was one of Vienna's most publicized postwar roles, and the only one that gave the city some international prominence.

But little of the spy glamour spread across the city itself. For most people life was drab and uncertain and often without much direction. The Vienna that emerged from war and Nazi rule had little in common with the vibrant city between the wars. My father, who loved Vienna beyond reason, returned from the United States in 1947 to a job at the American-run newspaper *Wiener Kurier*, thanks to a letter from an American general. (The Socialists, for whom he had been a key editor before 1934, refused to take him back since they had no room for "Austro-Fascists." My father's crime: he had stayed until 1938 before leaving.) He was happy to be home, but appalled by what he found.

"The city was familiar and close by," he wrote months later.

> The people were distant and foreign. They had become so strange, the people in the beloved, beautiful, old city of my fathers. And they still had the same names— Seidl, Pitzinger, Wokurka, Koslowski, Salieri, and Bolgar. No Veilchenfeld or Blau. But they were no longer Seidl and Wokurka, they were only called that. Nordic creatures, reduced and crumpled as if they had all gone through a delousing facility, populated the creaking streetcars. In Alpine costumes of creaking leather with the Hitler filth pasted under every second nose, standardized according to the norms of the office for racial purity. The women full-bosomed as the yard-stick of the BDM required, designed to bear children and more children. With all the grace of female elephants they plowed through the crowds. What's more, these Alpine-Nordic creatures spoke a foreign language from which the magic of the Viennese dialect had totally disappeared, the dialect in which the tangy sweetness of Middle High German had so often been alive. Snarling Prussianisms punctuated every sentence. Words borrowed from the Hebrew had disappeared and everywhere people spoke a pompous and stilted speech in which pieces of rude dialect struck like a fist in the eye.
>
> Closer inspection showed that they were no longer Nazis but somehow hankered for Adolf's times before the bombs fell. They were vague. They lived in the present and in a nebulous future without Jews and with Wiener Schnitzel. The majority were opportunists interested in the here and now. Only the old still loved the city. Baldur von Schirach's homunculi loved only themselves. Seven years of Hitler had atomized everything.[16]

After the 1949 elections the economic situation began to improve. The schilling had replaced the Reichsmark as the country's currency. UNRRA food shipments began to arrive in quantity and eased shortages. Most important, from 1948 to 1952 a billion dollars worth of Marshall Plan money began to flow into Austria, most of it to the Allied zones including Vienna, but none into the Soviet-occupied territories, exacerbating the economic split between the regions. Nevertheless, it was the largest infusion of new capital into the country ever. As a result, new factories were built and existing plants, like the Hermann Göring works in Linz, now called VOEST, expanded and modernized. Hydroelectric power was tapped with several mammoth projects completed by the mid-1950s. New power reserves allowed electrification of the railroads. In 1949

Austria's GDP exceeded prewar levels for the first time. The global boom that accompanied the Korean war helped boost output still further.[17]

Labor peace was assured through a series of wage-price agreements and stabilization pacts between unions and management. The Socialists still cursed the Austro-Fascists but the heat was gone from the rhetoric. Austria was becoming a semicorporate state based on the alliance between the enemies of the 1934 Austrian civil war, who carved up the perks of office to the point where you couldn't become a streetcar conductor without a party membership book. It was an alliance that allowed budgetary compromises needed to keep the economy on an even keel, even in recessionary times. Exports grew and not only in the "taste" industries that had been the Austrian prewar staple. Steel, electronics, mining, auto assembly and automotive parts, specialized machinery, and eventually arms production all became key elements in the economic mix.

Banking perked up. The capital market took on new life and as it did, so did the stock exchange. New credits flowed into all aspects of economic and social life—energy, investments, housing, even loans to complete reconstruction of the Opera and to help rebuild destroyed churches. Faith in the currency was restored. Funds flowed into banks and other savings institutions, boosting deposits in 1955 from 1.3 billion schillings ($52 million at the then exchange rate of 25:1) to 7.1 billion ($369 million).

1955 was a crucial year, the culmination of a decade's efforts to end the Allied occupation. A "state treaty" (rather than a peace treaty since Austria had no legal existence during the war) was concluded among Austria and the big four—the United States, Great Britain, France, and the Soviet Union—allowing foreign minister Leopold Figl to step out on the balcony of the Belvedere palace on May 15, hold up the document to the multitude gathered below, and announce "Austria is free." Behind him, smiling benignly, stood the other foreign ministers—John Foster Dulles, Harold Macmillan, Antoine Pinay, and Vyacheslav Molotov.

Negotiations had taken a long time, time in which Austria had become a pawn in the gathering Cold War. A first meeting had been held in London in 1947 and got nowhere. Stalin wasn't about to make any concessions. Hope rose two years later when Russia dropped support of Yugoslav claims on Austrian territory. But complex issues remained unresolved. Moscow had confiscated German assets in the Soviet zone and merged them into a large industrial enterprise called USIA, which it was not about to give up. In foreign policy Stalin offered to "neutralize" a united Germany, an offer the Allies rejected. Instead they pushed West Germany into NATO, thus complicating Austria's hopes for a treaty that might have been achieved within the context of a neutralized Germany. Stalin's death in 1953 provided new impetus and raised new problems that illustrated Austria's role as a pawn. Molotov linked Austria with the then unresolved Trieste issue—it was finally settled in 1954 when the city, a pawn between Yugoslavia and Italy, was returned to Italy. Next, the Russians suggested signing a treaty that would allow them to station troops in Austria. The Allies refused, but were more receptive to proposals for neutralizing Austria itself. In April 1955 an Austrian delegation went to Moscow and hammered out the details—no membership in military pacts, eternal neutrality, economic concessions on the USIA combine. The last Allied soldier left Vienna on October 25, 1955.

Now the economy really took off. From 1955 to 1960 the GDP grew 30 percent, industrial output by 35 percent. State-owned industry shared in the boom, almost tripling production in 1960 over 1949 totals.

American generosity helped as leftover funds from the European Recovery Program—the official name of the Marshall Plan—poured into the economically deprived East in a successful effort to bring the region up to the levels of the western provinces. In all, Austria received more per capita Marshall Plan aid than any other country in Europe.[18] Thus with American help, Austria, in the 1960s, became modestly prosperous. Certainly most people fared better economically than they had done since the monarchy, and not everybody had profited from economic growth back then. More and more consumer goods trickled down the economic ladder. (In 1962, as an example, our cleaning lady told my wife that we really didn't need to have blocks of ice delivered. "You know, Frau Doktor," she said, "I have this little box at home you plug into a socket and it keeps food cold. It even makes ice." My wife, raised in American deep-freeze plenty, grew apoplectic.) VW Beetles and Renault Dauphines began to replace Italian motor scooters. Gas-powered hot water heaters transformed cold water flats.

Tourism became a key element of economic growth. Its foreign exchange earnings regularly covered Austria's balance of payments deficit and revenues boomed even more as the Viennese learned to merchandise their history, specifically that of the House of Habsburg. The emperor Franz Josef's portrait was everywhere, as was that of his wife Sissi. Pastry was glorified; Mozart was made into a confectionery. Sacher's Hotel and Demel's pastry shop fought a legal war over the "original" Sachertorte, the glazed chocolate cake made with marmalade, and sales of both cakes flourished amid the publicity. The horses of the Spanish Riding School were cast in porcelain and sold in every curio shop. Lanz on Kärntnerstrasse sold embroidered leather shorts and darling dirndls to American tourists and their children. The Opera, the Philharmonic, and the Vienna Boys Choir attracted millions of tourists and their dollars and deutsch marks.

The new prosperity, however, had little impact politically, culturally, or intellectually. When Julius Raab, a member of Schuschnigg's last cabinet and a leading member of the fascist militia of the 1930s, replaced Figl as chancellor in 1953 democracy began to fade. Laws were made by the two parties in power with parliament a rubber stamp instead of a deliberative body. Renner's dream of party-style democracy had been achieved at the cost of leaving the rank and file in limbo. Increasingly over the years most Austrians felt disenfranchised, believing their votes would change nothing. Still, growing wealth helped many overcome their doubts. So did the burial of the past.[19]

The initial split between Socialists and Catholics over how much guilt Austria should burden for its part in the Nazi war and slaughter machine had long been healed. By the late 1940s they had agreed to hide behind the 1943 Moscow declaration that had called Austria the first victim of Hitlerite aggression. The declaration had also said that Austria was responsible for taking part in the war at the side of Nazi Germany, and that it would have to make some contribution to its own liberation. Responsibility, however, was not on the Austrian agenda, and over the years the government and the people went all out to duck it. They were victims and they had fought for their own liberation—the role of the Resistance was played up far beyond its actual accomplishments, accomplishments limited by the people's failure to support the anti-Nazi battle. Victimhood became an Austrian mantra. "We didn't know anything about concentration camps, believe me," my childhood friend Tony Zembsch repeated over and over in so many of our conversations across half a century.

Over time, victimhood became martyrdom—Austrians learned to emphasize how they had suffered under the Nazis. And gradually they persuaded the victors—and the rest of the world—that this living lie was the truth. The myth lasted for forty years, a time in which Vienna became the "isle of the blessed," impervious to the winds of change blowing across the world. The upheavals of the 1960s, from the free speech movement at Berkley to the 1968 riots in Paris and Berlin, barely made a dent.

The postwar culture boom soon fizzled. Most of the cultural magazines like *Der Plan* had to stop publication by the late 1940s. Those that survived, like the *Tagebuch*, a monthly, were reduced to small circulations and smaller influence. Painters struggled. Even those untainted by any Nazi associations found modern art difficult. The concept of "degeneracy" had rooted itself in the Viennese mind, and it would take decades to eradicate. Postwar architecture was a disaster. The new city buildings resembled nothing so much as slabs of Swiss cheese.[20] The architects who had built communal housing in the 1920s and early '30s were dead, had not been asked back, or had refused to return. Those with a modern outlook were not wanted by city fathers who pleaded poverty as an excuse for not producing anything better, ignoring that during Vienna's desperate poverty after the Great War, when there was no Marshall Plan money to help rebuild, the city had produced landmark architecture.

At the Burgtheater, Lothar Müthel resigned in April 1945 as director, more or less on orders of the Russians who wanted all Nazi theater directors out, the more or less untainted in.[21] They intended to relaunch high culture only weeks after the shooting stopped. Raul Aslan, the "grand seigneur" of the Burg, took Müthel's place. With its tradition-encrusted house on the Ringstrasse in ruins, the Burg opened at the Ronacher, a cavernous theater that in the past had housed variety shows. Early plays were retreads from the Nazi era, but gradually Aslan transformed the theater and took it into what theater historians now call a golden age. But Aslan was sixty years old and in poor health and therefore could only be an interim director.

So the man in charge of government-owned theaters, Dr. Egon Hilbert, began to look for somebody outside Austria who could bring the wind of the great world back to Vienna. He ran through a number of candidates, Jews and non-Jews, all of whom had the right credentials but either were afraid of Vienna's legendary "night of the long knives" in cultural affairs, or were —like Ernst Lothar, the former director of the Josefstadt, who had come home in an American uniform—rejected by the ensemble. In 1948 Hilbert finally persuaded Josef Gielen, who had mounted plays at the Burg before the war and who was a German Aryan married to a Jew, to return from his Buenos Aires exile.

Gielen lasted an amazing six years. Working with a solid cadre of directors unbrushed by brown paint—Leopold Lindtberg had worked in Zurich, Berthold Viertel in London and in United States—he brought the larger world of Western drama to Vienna and pushed the Burg into the forefront of German theater, indeed even to global prominence. But he too fell victim to Viennese artistic intrigue and lost his job as director. Hilbert, his patron and a concentration camp survivor, was shipped to Rome and replaced by a Catholic bureaucrat, while Adolf Rott, a man with a Nazi past, was made director. Predictably, quality nose-dived, even though Gielen continued to direct plays at the Burg.

At the Opera conductor Karl Böhm, an enthusiastic Nazi with close ties to Goebbels, was bounced from his job in April 1945 and replaced by Franz Salmhofer, a forty-five-year-old jack-of-all-musical-trades, who ran the opera—now housed in the Theater an der Wien, where *Fidelio* was first performed in the early 1800s—until 1954. There was no golden age in Salmhofer's regime. Two of his own operas graced the billboard of new works in the 1940s. The Austrian exiles and "degenerate" moderns were rarely heard. True, Alban Berg's *Wozzek* was first performed in Vienna after the war in 1952, but it was not until 1960 that the Berlin opera brought Schönberg's *Moses and Aaron* to a Vienna stage.

The great conductors like Böhm, Furtwängler, and Herbert von Karajan were quickly denazified, allowed to dominate the city's musical life, and to become Vienna's sometime cultural ambassadors in the West. When, as a United Press correspondent, I asked Karajan in Washington in 1956 why he didn't play more modern music he told me in some detail of the plans he had for the Vienna Opera, which he was then taking over. (The Austrians were always good at avoiding unpleasant questions.) The Vienna clients of the United Press splashed my interview across page one—this was news, modern music was not.

The Opera and the Burg reopened in traditional splendor in 1955 with *Fidelio* and *King Ottokar* as the opening works—solidly classical, bound to tradition—and everybody cheered Beethoven's liberation music and Grillparzer's ode to Austria. Both houses had been rebuilt just as traditionally with not a modern stitch on their new clothes. The Opera's great curtain was designed by Professor Rudolf Eisenmenger, a

Nazi favorite and a specialist in stamp design.[22] Down the line in the arts, conservative tradition reasserted itself, and down the line cultural interests faded along with the money to pay for innovation. Cultural budgets were high, certainly by American standards, but many in the arts considered them inadequate. And most of the money went to blowing incense on tradition and not on pushing Vienna into the modern world. Of course the open-minded audience was gone, not only the exiled and murdered Jews but also the upper middle class who had remained and become impoverished by war and age, with many now living on inadequate pensions, and thus unable to attend and support the performing arts. The working class of the 1920s and '30s, once hungry for culture, had lost its appetite. By the mid-1960s most of labor had moved into an amorphous lower middle class, more eager for the material joys of consumerism than for artistic ones.[23]

One result was a bad case of the doldrums. Vienna had become a deeply provincial city that the Cold War had left on the margins. The Iron Curtain began less than fifty miles from Vienna's outskirts, and whatever role it had played in the espionage wars of the *Third Man* era had withered once the occupying powers left. Intellectually it was a bland place, with none of the sense of adventure that had marked the twenties and thirties, and no sense of mission that could take its place.

On a national level the coalition between the "reds"—the Social Democrats—and the "blacks"—the People's Party—continued for another eleven years after the last Allied soldier left the country. It provided for economic growth and domestic stability, but over the years the tension between the two parties increased, especially squabbles over who got what job when elections brought small shifts in the number of seats each party held in parliament. Thus after the May 1959 elections, the socialists demanded and received the foreign ministry portfolio for the first time. But by the mid-1960s twenty years of coalition government had begun to take its toll. And in 1966 the People's Party won an absolute majority. The Socialists went into opposition, with time to ponder its future; specifically, foreign minister Bruno Kreisky began to think about running for the party leadership.

He had returned to Vienna from his Swedish exile for the first time in 1945 and gone at once to the foreign office to offer his services in rebuilding Austria. Gruber was delighted. Kreisky was a trifecta—lawyer, Jew, and Social Democrat—and Gruber hired him on the spot. But he had not counted on Schärf's opposition. The vice-chancellor wanted no part of someone who had been a radical Socialist youth leader.[24] So Kreisky went back to Stockholm as an Austrian diplomat. He returned in 1951 and eight years later was named foreign minister.

Now Kreisky was torn. The party will never elect a Jew, he told Inge Santner, the Vienna correspondent of *Der Spiegel*, when she suggested that he run for the top party job.[25] He ran and he won. In the 1970 elections he won again and made the Socialists the largest party—not a majority but close. He formed a minority government and a year later won an absolute majority, triumphs he repeated in 1975 and 1979.

Kreisky was a complex man given to reaching much farther than he could grasp as a small nation's leader. His record, therefore, is at best mixed. He pushed Austria into the twentieth century. He reformed criminal law so that adultery, homosexuality, and "insulting the honor of an official" were no longer punishable offenses.[26] For the left-liberal elite Kreisky's rule was a golden era. Jobs were plentiful. The economy boomed, but so did the nation's debt, which had been near zero when he took over. And the country's mood became upbeat over what many saw as long overdue modernization.

On the other side of the ledger, Kreisky pursued controversial policies at home and abroad. He had long been cozy with Nazis, had denied his own Jewishness, and plumped hard for letting the sleeping dogs of the past lie dormant. His relations with Israel, already awful because of his Mideast initiatives, worsened. He was the first Western statesman to deal with Yasser Arafat. He took the Arab side whenever he could.

He stepped down in 1983 when the Socialists lost their absolute majority, leaving as one legacy the "United Nations" city he built on the far side of the Danube in hopes of turning Vienna into the third UN headquarters after New York and Geneva. It would house the Atomic Energy Agency and UNIDO, the industrial development organization. He persuaded OPEC to set up headquarters in Vienna and hoped other international organizations would follow, although few did. Still, he had succeeded in flinging the city onto the far side of the river, paving the way for urban expansion in decades to come, and giving Vienna a shot at international substance (even if it never quite managed to capitalize on it).

Another legacy was less positive: Kreisky left the past where it had been for so long—buried. The Viennese did not have to confront what they had done, let alone accept responsibility for it. Instead, they could continue the myth of victimhood even though by the 1980s it was as frayed as an overwashed pair of underwear. It showed the first signs of tearing in 1985 when the Freedom Party's minister of defense—the Socialists had formed a coalition with the FPÖ after Kreisky stepped down—met a convicted Nazi war criminal on the Nazi's return from an Italian prison. The picture of their handshake went around the world and put the country and the city's unsavory past on front pages worldwide.[27]

More importantly, it triggered an investigation into the past of former UN Secretary General Kurt Waldheim, who was preparing to run for president of Austria. Edgar Bronfman, president of the World Jewish Congress, paid for the research that led to accusations that Waldheim, who had served in the Balkans as a Wehrmacht officer, was guilty of war crimes. Austrians were furious at the international inquiry: the Jews were at it again. The non-Jewish Austrians closed ranks, and in May 1986 Waldheim won hands down. The campaign was marred by some anti-Semitism, which Waldheim's treatment as a pariah in the international community—he was barred from entering the United States, for example—only exacerbated.

Cracks in society widened when a group of younger Austrian historians, annoyed by the failure of their elders in academia to confront the past, began to dig deep and publish unvarnished accounts of what had happened under NS rule, and how much its fragments remained part and parcel of the Austrian—and especially the Viennese—character. The findings angered many in Vienna who had long ago buried the past, but it made others confront their history honestly for the first time.

Franz Vranitzky, a Socialist former banker and finance minister, became chancellor in 1986, leading the resumption of a black-red coalition after a twenty-year hiatus. A man of style and character, he tried hard to make Austria once again respectable internationally and he made some headway. In a 1991 speech to parliament he acknowledged Austria's role as Hitler's helpmate. "We cannot escape our moral responsibility," he said, and promised to help those not considered in previous restitution. Two years later he repeated the message to an audience at Hebrew University in Jerusalem and noted in addition the cultural debt Austria owed to Vienna's Jews. It was not a moment to equal Willy Brandt falling to his knees at the memorial for the Jewish ghetto in Warsaw in 1970, but it was at least something. And given the obstacles Vranitzky faced it was perhaps more than that.

The Waldheim presidency had thwarted any chance the chancellor might have had of playing a role in softening the collapse of Yugoslavia next door, while the rise of a young Carinthian lawyer named Jörg Haider as head of the FPÖ limited his effectiveness at home and abroad. Haider championed right-wing politics with a strong Nazi strain, and his verve, energy, and media savvy—he was and is the best TV performer in Austrian politics—pushed his party up the electoral ladder. By the mid-nineties he was a clear threat to Austrian democracy.

In the 1999 elections the Socialists remained the largest party, but Haider had surged past the People's Party with more than 25 percent of the vote. So instead of resuming "red-black," People's Party leader Wolfgang Schüssel engineered a right-wing coalition with the Freedom Party, which had become much more extreme under Haider than it had been when the Socialists took them into the government in 1983. An outraged European Union imposed diplomatic sanctions against Austria. Again the Austrians closed ranks, and again they felt victimized and resentful of foreign criticism. The new government had a majority in parliament. It had been formed according to the democratic rules of the game. And, most important, Haider was not a member of the government. So why the fuss?

Opposition Socialists and pro-environment Green Party took to the streets, mostly in Vienna in massive but peaceful demonstrations against the new government that became institutionalized. Protesters gathered once a week for almost a year, and although they grew much smaller over time, a year of demonstrations is a substantial protest—and proof that some Austrians, at least, shared the EU's alarm over Haider's political surge. By 2002 Haider's antics—visits to Libya and to Saddam Hussein in Baghdad, the mouthing of Nazi slogans and veiled attacks on international Jewry, among other missteps—had disgusted enough of the electorate for the Freedom Party to lose badly in that November's election.

Chancellor Schüssel spent two months negotiating with Socialists, greens, and Haider before reaching agreement to continue his People's Party coalition with the FPÖ. By 2004 government policies had begun to erode some freedoms using the tested Communist salami tactics of one slice of freedom at a time—media intimidation, threats against opposition politicians including unsubstantiated charges of treason, curbing freedoms of the universities, changes in the judicial system, including scrapping juvenile courts.

Anti-Semitism, which the Waldheim affair had rekindled, reached the point where it was again socially acceptable. Haider and others, for example, use the code phrase "the East Coast" when they mean Jews, while even relatively liberal people are convinced the American media is a Jewish conspiracy. One example in the summer of 2003 did little to burnish the city's damaged image on this issue.[28] The Kultusgemeinde asked the government for help to finance its activities, arguing it had run out of money. For years the IKG had paid its bills through sale of returned real estate but now could no longer do so. Extra protection of Jewish installations was expensive. They had been attacked in the past and police protection was clearly inadequate. Schüssel dismissed the request with a contemptuous "I'm not paying for a bunch of broken down Mossad agents."[29] Eventually, after another burst of unfavorable publicity, the government came across with some of the needed funds. The controversy had generated so much anti-Semitic e-mail to the media that *Der Standard* refused to print hate messages from readers.

The fall of the Berlin wall and the end of Communism should have given Vienna a new lease on life, an opportunity to become once again what it had been under the monarchy—the focus of the Danube countries, the center of commerce, an engine of economic growth, and a hub for the new technologies, everything, in short, to which Baldur von Schirach had aspired for the city he once ruled. But Vienna missed the boat. It lacked the energy, the drive, the direction, and as a result the Southeast, the Northeast, Poland, and the Baltics turned to another center—Berlin. Since the 1990s a reunified Germany has been the dominant force in the region.

The Viennese salvaged some banking and retail business, and they are among the area's largest investors. But they failed to put enough people in each of the new countries who could have solidified their companies' position and allowed them to grow. "The Viennese don't like to leave home," Oskar Bronner, editor and publisher of *Der Standard*, told me. "They go to Hungary to get laid, to get drunk, and to fix their teeth. Sex, booze, and dentistry are cheaper." The lost opportunity of capturing new markets and assuring growth does not seem to bother the Viennese very much. They have been an "island of the blessed" for so long that they truly believe nothing can happen to them. Over the decades the city has grown rich, a combination of many factors dating back to

Marshall Plan aid but also rooted in prudent investment, industrial growth, a stress on exports, technological innovation, and the ability to shift with the demands of the times; but not, however, the ability to run ahead of them.

The city is one of the best administered in Europe, if not the world. Public transportation is a dream. Subway trains come every three or four minutes, lines have been expanded across the Danube so that the river will actually flow through the city, and living and working on the far side are becoming accepted and fashionable. Ecology is a civic priority. Buses run on methane tanks located on their roofs. Modern architecture has blossomed—to some extent thanks to a refugee architect who returned in 1965 from New Zealand. Ernst Plischke was thirty-five when he left Austria but had already built some of the most innovative housing of the 1930s. When he returned, official Vienna took little notice with commissions few and far between. So he taught a generation of new architects who have since seeded Vienna with interesting and innovative buildings, creating a skyline that complements the old architecture rather than destroying it.[30] A new museum quarter was built into the old imperial stables to house the kind of modern art that was disdained well into the seventies.

The city has learned to merchandise its past with a blatant hucksterism that Madison Avenue might envy. At first it was only the city's imperial splendor. But over time the lost Vienna moved into the tourist spotlight. For years a plaque high on the wall at Berggasse 19 told anyone who could read that far up that Sigmund Freud had once lived here. Freud was not popular in Vienna, even after the war. I wrote a thesis at the University of Vienna on "Understanding Modern Art" but was told by Hubert Rohracher, the head of the psychology department, that Freud had no place in my work.

That attitude changed as local authorities slowly realized that tourists were coming to Vienna not only to see the Breughels but to find traces of the genius who pried open man's subconscious. In 1971 Freud's apartment was turned into a museum, Kreisky attended the opening ceremonies, and Anna Freud sent the old door plaque, which read "Prof. Dr. Freud. 3–4" . . . it was as if Freud had never left.[31]

In 2003 an exhibit about the fate of the other Jews in Freud's building opened to the public with crocodile tears shed over the long delay in honoring those victims of the holocaust. The Vienna Philharmonic had grumbled about playing Mahler for decades until Leonard Bernstein bullied them into accepting the master as one of their own. (Outtakes of filmed rehearsals show Bernstein's fury at his musicians' failure to comprehend the composer's genius.) But then, after the war 40 percent of the orchestra had to be denazified.[32] Paradoxically, perhaps, Bernstein was the most popular foreign conductor the orchestra ever had.

Merchandising a past that was safely dead did not mean, however, inviting Jews or their descendants back to the city. Vienna has never made up the loss. For Jews were not only creative—they were patrons of the arts and sciences. They attended the performing arts, bought Klimt, Schiele, and Kokoschka when others purchased Nazi-style kitsch, and followed developments in science and philosophy. The kind of fruitful soil such citizens provided, which might have nourished a cultural reflowering, was never replaced. "About a thousand Jews returned after the war," Oskar Bronner, an Israel-born Jew, told me, "people like my father and my maternal grandfather. Today Vienna's Jewish community is made up of new immigrants, displaced persons like Simon Wiesenthal who drifted here and stayed, or my parents-in-law who came from Hungary in 1956."

Instead the children of the Viennese diaspora made their lives, and gave their talents, to other lands. Henry Anatole Grunwald played Mozart symphonies while writing *Time* cover stories and ended up as editor in chief of the Time-Life empire. He returned to Vienna only as U.S. ambassador to his homeland. Frank Grad taught law at Columbia. Both left Vienna in their teens. Lucian Freud became one of England's seminal painters. Frederic Morton, whose ties to Vienna remain close, wrote bestselling novels and nonfiction, slipping easily from his native Viennese into hospitable English. Erich Fried, one of the most important postwar poets in the German language, was never asked back from his London exile; after he died the University of Vienna bought his literary estate.

In 2000 Eric Kandel won a Nobel Prize for medicine. Born in Vienna in 1929 he had fled to New York at the age of ten. "The Viennese were the worst," he remembered in June of 2003 when he gave a lecture in his hometown. "Nobody, really nobody, helped us. Not even the children in my class would speak to me." Austrian President Thomas Klestil wanted to honor him after he won the Nobel Prize, but Kandel declined. "My Nobel Prize is not an Austrian prize, but an American, a Jewish-American one."[33]

Yet the attraction remains, the memory of what Vienna had been, a happy symbiosis of two cultures in which Jews flourished and accepted anti-Semitism as part of the bargain because the Viennese brand was still better than the pogroms in the Eastern shtetls from whence so many had come. In his book *Vienna and its Jews* George Berkley marvels that so many Viennese Jews—driven from their homes, humiliated, tortured— still hankered for the city that had so mistreated them. But life in Vienna had a sweetness and a joy that few other cities could match, and to some extent it has them still.

Today Vienna is a very pleasant place to live. The housing shortage is over. Food may be overrated—try finding a decent French restaurant— but it is not bad. The wine is good. The few cafés that survive still provide a clutch of foreign and domestic newspapers for the price of a cup of coffee—and endless time in which to sit and savor them. The Viennese believe their music and theaters are world class, which they are not, but their ready availability add to the city's charm.

Still, Hitler's legacy of provincialism has remained. Unless somebody like Jörg Haider rekindles Europe's fears of renascent Nazism or Fascism, Vienna looms small on Europe's political screen. The EU imposed sanctions on the pseudo-Fascist government precisely because Haider was an Austrian, and the memory of that other hysterical Austrian rabble-rouser was too strong to ignore.

Breaking stories at OPEC and the International Atomic Energy Agency (IAEA) sometimes bring American and other foreign correspondents to Vienna, but the city hardly qualifies as a major international capital. An NBC on-air correspondent signed of with "This is . . . reporting from Vienna, Austria." Nobody says "Brussels, Belgium" or even "Amsterdam, the Netherlands," or "Stockholm, Sweden." But newswise, Vienna needs to be identified.

During the Yugoslav wars Vienna was the staging area for media coverage, the hub where copy was received, rewritten, and transmitted. But the Vienna government, hobbled by Waldheim and Haider, played an insignificant role.

Normally, you have to look long and hard to find a Vienna dateline in the *New York Times* or the *Washington Post*. Indeed, a recent *Times* report highlighted Vienna's isolation. On August 3, 2003, Richard Bernstein wrote in the *New York Times* of "a sense of loss—a glorious past and a certain emptiness" in the city. "It is . . . museumlike, touristy, a bit dull, like an exhibit viewed through a glass case. It inspires the pathos of a place that was once at the center of the world and has been reduced to a lesser status."

And on February 21, 2004, *New York Times* critic Bernard Holland reviewed a Vienna Philharmonic concert at Carnegie Hall with its new conductor Seiji Ozawa under the headline "Ozawa Shows Off His New Band." Of the Philharmonic Holland wrote "Think of this orchestra as a walled city of moderate size. Inside those walls the repertory is limited but pursued with unusual penetration and spiritual energy. Think of Vienna as the same walled city in macrocosm, as a place preoccupied with its own psychic forces. For all the Viennese know, just outside those walls lies China." How much Hitler would have loved that review.

On CNN, Vienna doesn't make it very often in the weather report on major cities. Prague, Amsterdam, Brussels, Athens, and Stockholm do. By itself that's the final irrelevance.

The loss, for the most part, is spiritual. The scars of war have long been repaired. The stately buildings that gird Ringstrasse shine with new brilliance. Neo-Gothic City Hall, the Burgtheater and the Renaissance-style art museum have been newly washed and gleam in white and gray, illuminated at night, with the quality of the light changing with the sky— melancholy in November's drizzle, drenched in moon beams and halcyon lamps when the weather is clement. The Acropolis that serves as parliament is having the ramp redone and the statue of Pallas Athena regilded. Shower curtains cover the Opera to speed her cleansing. The equestrian statues of Prince Eugene of Savoy, who defeated Louis XIV at Blenheim, and Archduke Charles, the first general ever to vanquish Napoleon in battle—at Aspern in 1809—dominate the Heldenplatz. The images of past glories are everywhere.

But the images are not the reality. Politics in 2004 were smarmier than ever, mean-spirited, provincial, bereft of intellectual and cultural excellence. Haider may have lost the election in 2002, but he won again in Carinthia in 2004 to remain governor, using the platform of office to spew hate and venom—and always finding an eager media to magnify his fulminations. He demanded that a candidate for the European parliament lose his active and passive voting rights because he had supported EU sanctions against Austria in 2000 when the right-wing government was formed. His party demanded that a deputy who accused the government of "sorrow" over the demise of National Socialism, resign and perhaps face arrest. It also demanded that Socialist leader Alfred Gusenbauer resign because he had described the atmosphere in parliamentary debate as "pogromlike."

On June 7, 2004, Viennese historian Peter Hümer wrote in the anti-government newspaper *Der Standard* that "the outrage is greatest among those who owe their political rise and careers to the man (Haider) who considered National Socialism harmless, who praised the NS employment policy and the Waffen SS, and holds that concentration camps were detention centers. Some of these people still don't know if the Nazi defeat in 1945 was a liberation for Austria, who want to arrest anybody who dares criticize the government abroad, or at least take away his right to vote. . . ."

In fact, little has changed since two of Vienna's most provocative writers—Thomas Bernhard and Elfriede Jelinek—had scathingly criticized the city back in the late eighties.

Bernhard's play, *Heldenplatz*, was a slashing denunciation of everything Vienna stood for—and was so perceived, triggering a political ice storm with President Kurt Waldheim at the forefront: "I think this play is a gross insult of the Austrian people," he said, without having read the text or seen the play. Foreign Minister Alois Mock criticized public financing for this "global slander of Austria." (It had been performed at the state-subsidized Burgtheater.) Vienna's most powerful media magnate, Hans Dichand, editor and publisher of the *Kronenzeitung*, called it "an insult to the honor of Austria," and "a serious violation of the law." Fortunately, perhaps, Bernhard died before he could be arrested. He struck back at his critics from beyond the grave, however, by banning performance of his plays in Austria, but the executors of his will found a way around the ban and his plays are now everywhere. Vienna loves its critics, so long as they are dead.

Jelinek has left no chance unused to denounce her country and its capital. "I come from a beautiful land," she said in a speech in Cologne, "and its artists are allowed to live there" provided they don't criticize the country. Those who do "are not only encouraged to emigrate, they are driven out. . . I won't mention Jura Soyfer (a prominent young writer in the 1930s) who was murdered in a concentration camp, because that happened so long ago and has long been forgotten and above all forgiven because we are forgiven everything. . . . We are the most innocent and have always been the most innocent. We've even named a literary scholarship for Elias Canetti, so long as he stays away. Why, we'll even stage his plays at the Burgtheater—if they are not too long."[34]

When she won the Nobel Prize for literature in 2004 Jelink noted drily that the distinction was "no flower in Austria's buttonhole"—no matter how much local moguls tried to dress city and county in her honors. At that not everybody in Austria did. Letters to the editor were full of criticism at the leftward drill of the Nobel committee, denigrating the prize, and the "wrong choice" the Stockholm academy had made.

The city's culture in the twenty-first century is all in the past, and even its best and its brightest cannot break out into the wider world, and in truth probably don't want to. Provincialism provides a cozy comfort the city that was once on the knife edge of change does not want to abandon.

Notes

The most detailed account of the Anschluss is Dieter Wagner's *Ein Volk, Ein Reich, Ein Führer*, literally an hour-by-hour depiction of events and the leading actors in it. I have drawn on it for much of the color that threads through this chapter. Ulrich Eichstadt's *Von Dollfuss zu Hitler* is equally meticulous in its day by day account. *Fallen Bastions* remains in a class by itself—the most passionate, emotional account written with experienced events so fresh you can touch them. The Rashomon line that runs through many accounts with sharply differing details is a commonplace worth noting. Kristallnacht is one of the best-documented events of Hitler's rule in Vienna.

Throughout the text and the notes, the many references to newspapers have been abbreviated: VB (*Völkischer Beobachter*); NFP (*Neue Freie Presse*); NWT (*Neues Wiener Tagblatt*); KVB (*Kleines Volkblatt*); KKZ (*Kleine Kreiszeitung/The Little Paper*); NZZ (*Neue Zürcher Zeitung*).

Chapter 1

1. Wagner, *Ein Volk, Ein Reich, Ein Führer*, 15.
2. Andics, *Fünfzig Jahre Unseres Lebens*, 202.
3. Brook-Shepherd, *Anschluss*, 44–48.
4. Dr. Guido Schmidt's testimony at his treason trial, 1947, 60.
5. Ibid.
6. Steinbauer, *Ich war Verteidiger in Nürenberg*, 147.
7. Lothar, *Das Wunder des Überlebens*, 102–3.
8. *Foreign Relations of the United States*, 1938, vol. 1, 416.
9. Wagner, *Ein Volk*, 32.
10. *Neue Freie Presse*, March 1938.
11. Wagner, *Ein Volk*, 57.
12. Schausberger, *Der Griff nach Österreich*, 554.
13. Neuman, *Arthur Seyss-Inquart*, 86.
14. Schmidl, *Der "Anschluss" Österreichs*, 131.
15. Zernatto, *Die Wahrheit über Österreich*, 283–84.
16. Nuremberg, Documents of the International Military Tribunal (IMT), 1946.
17. Ibid.
18. Drimmel, *Vom Kanzlermord zum Anschluss*, 408ff.
19. Gedye, *Fallen Bastions*, 287.

20. Lennhoff, *The Last Five Hours of Austria.*
21. Zernatto, *Die Wahrheit über Österreich*, 302–3.
22. Wagner, *Ein Volk*, 149.
23. Brook-Shepherd, 166–67.
24. The transcripts are recorded in several books, often slightly divergent. See Thomas Chorherr, *Anatomie eines Jahres* (Vienna: Überreuter, 1987), 146ff.; Andics has a slightly different version, see 310ff. The most comprehensive transcript is in *Der Hochverratsprozess gegen Dr. Guido Schmidt vor dem Wiener Volksgericht* (Dr. Schmidt's testimony at his treason trial) (Vienna: Österreichische Staatsdruckerei, 1947), 60, 459ff.
25. Schuschnigg, *Ein Requiem*, 66–84.
26. Fritz Molden, conversations with author.
27. Kelfeit, *Ich kann nicht schweigen.*
28. Gerhard Bronner, conversation with author.
29. Felix Fuchs to author, May 9, 2001.
30. Gedye, *Fallen Bastions*, 294.
31. Ibid., 295.
32. Zuckmayer, *A Part of Myself*, 50.
33. Zweig, *The World of Yesterday*, 405–6.
34. Wagner, *Ein Volk*, 191.
35. Ibid., 212–13.
36. *NFP*, March 15, 1938, 1.
37. Technician at the Austrian Film Museum to the author, May 21, 2001.
38. *NFP*, March 16, 1938, 1.
39. Ibid.
40. Ibid.
41. *NFP*, March 17, 1938.

Chapter 2

1. Andics, *Fünfzig Jahre*, 8.
2. Vajda, *Felix Austria*, 571.
3. *NFP*, October 22, 1918.
4. Vajda, *Felix Austria*, 573.
5. Brook-Shepherd, *Austrian Odyssey*, 75.
6. Legend has it that during the Crusades, Duke Leopold V's white tunic and breeches had turned blood red after a day of slaughter on the walls of a Saracen town, but that his white belt had been untouched. The Duke left the Crusades, the legend claims, when Richard Lion-heart, who had spent the day in a cowardly sulk, sent his men swarming up the wall that evening to pull down the banner of the exhausted Austrians and claim victory for himself. Leopold bided his time, and when Richard rode home through the Duke's territory he had the king arrested. Leopold held him for ransom and won a shower of silver for his release.
7. Andics, *Fünfzig Jahre*, 15.
8. Brook-Shepherd, *Austrian Odyssey*, 81.
9. Luza, *Austro-German Relations*, 10.
10. The Treaty of Trianon was signed on June 4, 1920, but it was not until December 23 that the Allies formally asked Hungary to cede the disputed territory. The em-

peror Charles's unsuccessful attempt to retain the crown of Hungary in the spring
of 1921 delayed the transfer. The Allies finally set August 27, 1921, for the restoration but when the Austrians crossed the frontier on the 29th, they ran into
gunfire from Hungarian troops. Renewed Allied pressure finally settled the issue.

11. Braunthal, *The Tragedy of Austria*.
12. Leser, ed., *Das Geistige Leben Wiens in der Zwischenkriegszeit* (The spiritual and
    intellectual life of Vienna between the wars), 216ff. The book contains a series of
    lectures held in Vienna in May–June 1980.
13. Braunthal, *The Tragedy of Austria*.
14. Gedye, *Fallen Bastions*, 52.
15. The account of Austrian politics from Seipel's resignation to Dollfuss's murder in
    1934 is based on Brook-Shepherd, *Austrian Odyssey* and *Dollfuss*; Andics, *Fünfzig
    Jahre*; Gedye, *Fallen Bastions*; Drimmel, *Vom Kanzlermord zum Anschluss*; Reimann,
    Zu Gross für Österreich.
16. Andics, *Fünfzig Jahre*, 292, n5.
17. Gedye, *Fallen Bastions*, 125–26.
18. The text of the constitution can be found in the Internet at http://www.verfassungen.
    de/at/oesterreichs34.
19. Gedye, *Fallen Bastions*, 152–53.
20. Andics, *Fünfzig Jahre*, 279.
21. Molden, *Fepolinski und Waschlapski*.

Chapter 3

1. Smelser et al., *Die Braune Elite*, 51–66.
2. Sündermann was twenty-seven when he became Bürckel's flack. He died in 1972,
   having spent his postwar life writing a clutch of books defending the Third Reich,
   casting doubt on the Holocaust, and pushing extreme right-wing causes. Eher,
   the publisher of his book *Die Grenze Fallen*, was the official Nazi party publishing
   house.
3. Austrian state archive. Bürckels addendum, 44,
4. Foreign Relations of the United States, 1938, vol. 1, 439.
5. Safrian, *Eichmann und seine Gehilfen*, 36.
6. Botz, *Nationalsozialismus in Wien*, 181.
7. Maximilian Liebman, "Vom Appeasement zum Widerstand" in *1938, Anatomie
   eines Jahres*, ed. Thomas Chorherr, 311–56; Reimann, *Innitzer*, 92–120; Liebman,
   Theodor Innitzer.
8. Franz von Papen, *Der Wahrheit eine Gasse* (Innsbruck: List, 1952). Cited in
   Reimann, *Innitzer*, 93–94.
9. *Völkischer Beobachter*, March 27, 1938. Göring's two-hour election speech in the
   Nordwestbahnhalle was given on March 26, 1938.
10. *VB*, March 22, 1938.
11. Botz, *Nationalsozialismus in Wien*, 154–58.
12. *VB*, *NFP*, March 28, 1938.
13. *VB*, March 26, 1938.
14. *NFP*, March 27, 1938.
15. *VB*, *NFP*, April 1, 1938.

16. Botz, *Nationalsozialismus in Wien*, 171.
17. *VB*, April 10, 1938.
18. Botz, *Nationalsozialismus in Wien*, 172.
19. Recordings of Hitler's speeches are kept at the Phonotek on Vienna's Gumpen-dorferstrasse. Equipment is modern, and listening sessions are free.
20. Beppo (mid-1950s) and Bronner (2001), conversations with the author.
21. Kelfeit, *Ich kann nicht schweigen*, 17.
22. Zuckmayer, *A Part of Myself*, 48.
23. *Jüdische Schicksale, Berichte von Verfolgten*, 145.
24. Kampelmacher, *In die Emigration*. Kampelmacher fled to Holland where he be-came an eminent scientist with dozens of books on salmonella, veterinary medi-cine, and the like to his credit.
25. Safrian, *Eichmann und seine Gehilfen*, 37.
26. Ibid., 37–38. Policy toward the Jews was much more radical in Vienna than in Altreich cities with large Jewish populations, like Berlin. Jews there were not un-der the kind of pressure to leave that was put on Viennese Jews. Indeed, Eichmann's Vienna model would be copied in the Altreich so that the situation of German Jews worsened only after these policies were put in place in Vienna. That is one reason why so many later prominent German Jews like Henry Kissinger and Max Frankel left Germany after Hitler came to power.
27. Hennings, *Heimat Burgtheater*, 11, 21.
28. Lothar, *Das Wunder des Überlebens*, 110, 114–15.
29. *NFP*, April 16, 1938.
30. Talos et al., *NS Herrschaft in Österreich*, 451–54.
31. *Jüdische Schicksale*, 284.
32. Brigitte Lichtenberger-Fenz, "Es läuft alles in geordneten Bahnen," in *NS Herrschaft in Österreich*, 549.
33. Weibel and Stadler, eds., *Vertreibung der Vernunft*, 20–24; Heiss, *Willfährige Wissenschaft*.
34. *VB*, April 21, 1938.
35. Ibid., April 24, 1938.
36. Pfeifer, *Die Ostmark, Neugestaltung und Eingliederung*, 82. Cited in Luza, 81, n61.

Chapter 4

1. *VB*, April 26, 1938.
2. *NFP*, *VB*, May 7, 1938.
3. Sündermann, *Die Grenze Fallen*.
4. Encyclopedia of the City of Vienna.
5. Austrian National Bank statement, December 26, 2001.
6. *VB*, May 27, 1938, 1.
7. Botz, *Nationalsozialismus in Wien*, 331.
8. Luza, *Austro-German Relations in the Anschluss Era*, 220.
9. Walzer and Templ, *Unser Wien*, 123.
10. Ibid., 46ff.
11. Ibid., 44, 53.
12. *NFP*, *VB*, June 16, 1938.

13. Hennings, *Heimat Burgtheater.*
14. Safrian, *Eichmann und seine Gehilfen*, 39.
15. Kelfeit, *Ich kann nicht schweigen.* Internet Google version, 2nd item, 8.
16. Safrian, *Eichmann und seine Gehilfen*, 41–45.
17. *Neues Wiener Tagblatt (NWT)*, August 19, 1938, 1 (noon edition).
18. Pictures of the show were published in the *VB* on May 29, 1938, two months before the exhibition opened, clearly to whet the appetites of the potential viewers.
19. *VB*, September 1, 1938.
20. Reimann, *Innitzer*, 161.
21. *VB*, September, 27, 1938. (Headline is printed in red.)
22. *VB*, September, 28, 1938.
23. Innitzer's letter was sent from his country retreat in Kranichberg on September 10, 1939. A copy is in the Austrian state archives.
24. Reimann, *Innitzer*, 205.
25. Wolfgang Müller-Hartburg gives an eyewitness account of preparing the demonstration and its aftermath in 1938 in Chorherr, ed., *Anatomie eines Jahres.* The chapter is titled "Weitersagen: am 7. Oktober im Dom," 374–81. Reimann's version in *Innitzer* is on 206–11.
26. *VB*, October 14, 1938. The newspaper gave the story an eight-column banner headline on page 1: "Bürckel's Reckoning with Clerical Agitators—only one man rules here, the Austrian Adolf Hitler."
27. *VB*, October 13, 1938.
28. Botz, *Wien vom Anschluss zum Krieg*, 398.
29. Hermann Graml, *Der 9. November, 1938*, "Reichskristallnacht." This is a sixty-four-page brochure published by Schriftenreihe der Bundeszentrale für Heimatdienst, Bonn, 1956.
30. The report Hauptsturmführer Trittner sent to his superiors at the SS section Danube several days after the pogrom. See Gold, *Geschichte der Juden in Wien*, 94–95.
31. Andics, *Die Juden in Wien.*
32. Gold, *Geschichte der Juden in Wien*, 90–92.
33. Ibid., 93.
34. Rosenkranz, *Verfolgung und Selbstbehauptung*, 159.
35. *Jüdische Schicksale, Berichte von Verfolgten*, 230–35.
36. Krist, *Vertreibungsschicksale*, 59–85.
37. Kampelmacher, *In die Emigration.*
38. Gold, *Geschichte der Juden in Wien*, 94–95.
39. *Dokumente zum Novemberpogrom in Wien, aus Widerstand und Verfolgung in Wien, 1934–45.* These are documents on the November pogrom in Vienna. They are in a "documentation" titled "Resistance and Persecution in Vienna, 1934–1945," published by archives of the Austrian resistance in Vienna in 1984.
40. T. Friedman, ed., *Die Kristallnacht, 9. November 1938.* International Military Tribunal (Nuremberg), vol. 28, 524ff.

Chapter 5

1. Fränkel, ed., *The Jews of Austria.*
2. Tietze, *Die Juden Wiens.* My account of Jews in Vienna is largely based on Tietze's book, long considered a standard text on the subject.

3. In the United States, for example, it was the Credit Mobiliere affair.
4. Siegfried Weyr, *Die Wiener*, 10.
5. www.payer/de/fremd/mach and www.neundorf.de/Mach/mach
6. Spiel, *Vienna's Golden Autumn*, 126.
7. Ibid.
8. Ibid., 66ff.
9. See http://www.Bernstein-berlin-de/schule_und_schüler/bernstein/e_wien.htm
10. Spiel, *Vienna's Golden Autumn*, 163.
11. Leser, ed., *Das Geistige Leben Wiens*.
12. Friedrich Hacker in Leser, ed., *Das Geistige Leben Wiens*, 138ff.
13. Jahoda, Lazarsfeld, Zeisel, *Die Arbeitslosen von Marienthal*. A Suhrkamp edition was published in 1975.
14. Stadler, *The Vienna Circle*.
15. Leser, ed., *Das Geistige Leben Wiens*.

Chapter 6

1. Hans Kann, conversation with author.
2. Krist, *Vertreibungsschicksale*, 85.
3. Michael Kehlmann, conversation with author.
4. Austrian state archives (Österreichisches Staatsarchiv), Bürckel/Materie, 0.394 Unbearbeitete Gesuchs von Juden.
5. *NFP*, November 13, 1938, 1.
6. *NFP*, November 16, 1938.
7. The Ley speech was covered in all of the city's major media, from the *VB* to the *Kleines Volksblatt* (*KVB*).
8. Botz, *Wien vom Anschluss zum Krieg*, 272.
9. *NFP*, November 27, 1938.
10. Botz, *Wien*, 272.
11. *NFP*, December 12, 1938.
12. *VB, NFP, NWT*, January 1–2, 1939; Chorherr, *1938, Anatomie eines Jahres*, 412. Kraft durch Freude (KdF) was an organization of the German labor front (DAF) that handled recreational activities for German workers.
13. *NFP, NWT, KVB, Das Kleine Blatt, Neues Wiener Journal*, January 24–31, 1939.
14. Amann wrote Bürckel a six-page letter on January 14, 1939, from his office in Munich explaining why he needed to shut down the *NFP*. Earlier, on November 1, 1938, he had sent Hitler a five-page memo documenting his case with facts and figures. Rafelsberger's letter of protest was sent on February 1, 1939, too late to have any impact. The letters are stored in the Austrian state archives, Bürckel/Materie 2N40.
15. Luza, *Austro-German Relations in the Anschluss Era*, 110–13; Botz, *Wien*, 413–24.
16. Botz, *Wien*, 422.
17. Ruth Matteas, "Fasching in Wien" (Ph.D. diss., University of Vienna 1991); *VB* February 4, 1939.
18. *NWT* evening edition, February 22, 1939.
19. *KVB*, January 29, 1939.
20. *VB*, March 1, 1939.

21. *KVB*, March 5, 1939, 19; VB, June 8, 1939.
22. *VB*, March 4, 1939, eight-column banner headline, 1.
23. *VB*, March 25, 1939.
24. The letter is in Bürckel/Materie, 1939. On April 18, the Gestapo sent a copy to the Gau propaganda office with the notation that the writer of the anonymous letter could not be found.
25. The *NWT*'s headline put a brave face on the event: "The Führer's Triumphal Entry into Vienna, Endless Jubilation for the Augmenter of the Reich" ran the arrival headline, while his departure was rolled back to p. 7 with "Vienna Takes Leave of the Führer."
26. *VB*, April 21, 1939.
27. Luza, *Austro-German Relations*, 231–45; Botz, *Wien*, 429–37; VB, KVB, NWT, April 22, 1939. *NWT* ran an explanatory commentary on p. 6 the next day.
28. *VB*, May 4, 1939. In the same issue Dr. Walter Schmitt, a leading *VB* editor, wrote a commentary on the reorganization titled "Vienna's New Face." Over the next week, *KVB* and *NWT* published additional "explanatory" articles. On May 11, Bürckel himself followed up with a "programmatic" speech at city hall in which he reiterated the reform's central point "The party commands the state."
29. *KVB*, May 8, 1939.
30. Hausner, conversation with the author.
31. Goebbels's speech is cited in Evelyn Schreiner, "NS Kulturpolitik in Wien, 1938–45" (Ph.D. diss., University of Vienna, 1980), 195–97.
32. The scene is described, among others, in Walter Thomas, *Bis der Vorhang Fiel* (Dortmund: Schwalvenberg, 1947).
33. A contemporary photograph can be found in Pohanka, *Stadt unter dem Hakenkreuz*, 98.
34. Entry in Goebbels's diary, June 12, 1939.
35. The Vienna records of the IKG for January 1939, held at IKG offices in Seitenstettengasse, Vienna 1.
36. A précis of Gildemeester activities can be found on the Web site of the Historiker Kommission report at www.Historikerkommission.gv.at/forschungprojekte. d_arisierung. The commission spent three years investigating Nazi plunder and lagging Austrian restoration.Wu-memo, Ausgabe 20/00, notes, February 3, 2002, has an essay by Peter Berger that covers that topic. It is published by the Wirtschaftsuniversität (Economic University) in Vienna.
37. *Jüdische Schicksale*, 276–79.
38. Hans Kann, conversation with author.
39. Michael Kehlman, conversation with author.
40. Erich Lessing, conversation with author.
41. *Jüdische Schicksale*, 273–76.
42. Botz, *Wien*, 408–11.
43. Austrian state archives. The "Bericht" is signed Dr. E/Ni.
44. Austrian state archives. Mitteilungen zur Weltanschaulichen Lage, Sonderausgabe, May 1939. Ein Jahr Entkonfessionalisierung der Ostmark. Box 2500; Reimann, *Innitzer*, 206.
45. Reimann, *Innitzer*, 215.
46. *VB*, May 5, 1939, "Kirchenbeiträge in der Ostmark."
47. Reimann, *Innitzer*, 215.

48. Austrian state archives. *Denkschrift über die Frage einer zu errichtenden Südosthandelsstelle*, July 14, 1939.
49. Botz, *Wien*, 408.
50. The report is in the Bundesarchiv, Berlin, and is marked "Geheim! (secret)," N6.
51. Correspondence is in the Austrian state archives.
52. Ibid.
53. Ibid.
54. Molden, conversation with author.
55. Molden, *Fepolinski und Waschlapski*, 110–11.
56. Luza, *The Resistance in Austria*, 45.
57. Botz, *Wien*, 467.
58. The incidents are taken from *Widerstand und Verfolgung in Wien, 1934–45, eine Dokumentation*, vol. 2 (Vienna: Österreichischer Bundesverlag, 1984), 22–24, 44.
59. Luza, *The Resistance in Austria*, 43ff; Otto Molden, *Ruf des Gewissens* (Vienna: Herold Verlag, 1958).
60. *VB*, August 20, 1939.
61. Schöner, *Wiener Tagebuch*, 441–45.

Chapter 7

1. Schöner, *Wiener Tagebuch*, 441
2. *VB*, *NWT*, and *KVB* carried these items during September–October 1939.
3. *VB*, October 26, 1939.
4. *VB*, September 8, 1939.
5. *VB*, September 1, 1939.
6. *VB*, October 16, 1939, 3.
7. Luza, *Austro-German Relations*, 264ff.
8. Luza's account of the Fitzhum affair in his *Austro-German Relations*, 268–74; Martin Todok's report and other background documents are in the SS files at the Berlin Document Center, U.S. Archives in College Park, Md.
9. Fitzhum would die in a traffic accident near Vienna in January 1945.
10. *Jüdische Schicksale*, 164.
11. Rabinovici, *Instanzen der Ohnmacht*, 196.
12. *Jüdische Schicksale*, 164–70.
13. Ibid.
14. Rabinovici, *Instanzen der Ohnmacht*, 207, citing Safrian, "Vertreibung und Ermordung."
15. Safrian, *Eichmann und seine Gehilfen*, 79.
16. Ibid., 81.
17. *Jüdische Schicksale*, 165.
18. Rabinovici, *Instanzen der Ohnmacht*, 217.
19. Most of these items were published widely in Vienna newspapers, but their appearance in the *VB* gave them official cachet. The newspaper was the voice of the party.
20. *VB*, November 2, 1939.
21. Schreiner, "NS Kulturpolitik in Wien, 1938–45," 83–94.

22. *Österreichische Tragödie* (An Austrian Tragedy, a play in eleven scenes, freely adapted from historical themes) by Rudolf Örtel (Berlin: Langen-G. Mueller, 1938).
23. Bettauer, *Die Stadt ohne Juden.*
24. The Bürckel speech was given front-page treatment in the *VB*, March 4, 1940, and major display in the other media. They all stressed Bürckel's new role as cultural czar of Vienna.
25. "Die Ostmärkische Wirtschaft 2 Jahre in der Grossdeutschen Wirtschaft," RP Karl Barth, April 10, 1940.
26. Luza, *Austrian-German Relations*, 276.
27. *VB*, January 11, 1940; March 13–14, 1940; April 20, 1940.
28. On January 11, 1940, Gau economic advisor Walter Rafelsberger included a "Sonderbericht" or special report, in his weekly economic summary that he submitted to Bürckel. Titled "Die Lage am Kapitalmarkt" (situation on the capital market), written by "Direktor einer Wiener Grossbank" (the president of a large Vienna bank), it expressed concern about financing the war effort.
29. The Rafelsberger reports are in the Austrian state archives. Bürckel/Materie.
30. Karl Stadler, *Österreich 1938–45, im Spiegel der NS Akten*, quoted in Hirt, *Österreich: 50 Jahre Republik*, 107.
31. Reimann, *Innitzer*, 249–53; Luza, *The Resistance in Austria*, 71–72. Otto Molden, *Ruf des Gewissens.*
32. Luza, *The Resistance in Austria*, 100–110.
33. Luza, *The Resistance in Austria*, 49–55; Andics, *Fünfzig Jahre*, 377–82; Otto Molden, *Ruf des Gewissens*; Biron, *Die Letzte Beichte.*
34. Hennings, *Heimat Burgtheater.*
35. Why Hartmann acted as he did has never been clarified, except, perhaps, by his need for self-aggrandizement. He had a complicated family life. His parents opposed his acting career which never took off. He may have felt that joining Roman Scholz's group would give him added cachet. Accounts of his relationship with the Gestapo differ. At least one claims the Gestapo threatened him with prison if he did not turn informer; others maintain he did indeed have solid ties with the Nazis. Certainly he did after his betrayal. It is, however, unlikely that he did it for the money or that he knew he would get such a large amount.
36. Felix Fuchs, Fritz Molden, conversations with the author.
37. Schirach, *Ich glaubte an Hitler*, 263–66.
38. Henriette von Schirach, *Der Preis der Herrlichkeit*, 204.

Chapter 8

1. The *VB*, August 11, 1940, gave the ceremonies blanket coverage, spreading it across half the paper with an enormous, eight-column banner across the front page that read: "Schirach: No Promises, Work!" It also printed full texts of the major speeches.
2. More than Bürckel, Schirach sought and got blanket press coverage of all his activities, no matter how small or insignificant. He even had his press office issue a "chronicle" of his daily activities as reflected in the media: "Reichsleiter Baldur von Schirachs Tätigkeit als Reichsstatthalter, Chronik der Pressemeldungen mit Sach und Namenregister, bearbeitet von Richard Libiger. Vienna, 1942."

3. *VB*, August 15, 1940. The paper's chief cultural editor and drama observer Wilhelm Antropp wrote a lengthy appreciation of the Ballhausplatz and its role in Austrian history, unusual for the *VB*, which tended to ignore any Austrian concept.
4. This memo can be found in the Schirach file at the Austrian state archives.
5. *VB*, August 29, 30, and 31, 1940, gave the meetings extensive coverage, including the pomp and circumstance.
6. The *VB* editorial, August 29, 1940, noted that the meeting "proved once more what an important political function the city had to fulfill in the Greater German Reich . . . Vienna's much proven mediator role once again came into play."
7. Lang, *Der Hitlerjunge*, 291–93.
8. Aktennotiz für den Reichsleiter, dated August 24, 1940, and signed Adam. Austrian state archives: Schirach.
9. *VB*, September 2, 1940.
10. *VB*, November 20–21, 1940; *KVB*, November 21, 1940.
11. *NWT*, November 20, 1940.
12. *VB*, September 7, 1940.
13. *KVB*, December 8, 1940, 1.
14. *VB*, October 8, 1940.
15. Safrian, *Eichmann und seine Gehilfen*, 96.
16. Letter from the chief of Hitler's chancellery to Schirach, dated December 3, 1940. Cited in Schirach.
17. Henriette von Schirach reportedly said, "Then we might as well live in a museum" (Lang, *Der Hitlerjunge*, 273).
18. Schirach's early biography is laced through the four major books on his career: Lang, 17–22; B. v. Schirach, 7–17; H.v. Schirach; and Wortmann. See bibliography.
19. H. v. Schirach, *Preis der Herrlichkeit*, 192.
20. Schirach, *Ich glaubte an Hitler*, 268.
21. See Thomas [Anderman], *Bis der Vorhang Fiel*. This book is the best account of Schirach's cultural policies and of the cultural scene in Vienna during his tenure. Written when memories were still fresh, it has the immediacy of recent experience. Thomas does give his narrative an occasional twist (he was a member of the Nazi party although he claims in the book not to have been), and he writes a little bit as if the Gestapo were still at his back. By and large, however, other accounts back up his version of events; so does his frequent appearance in Nazi media. Goebbels, in his diaries, often makes Thomas a target of often vicious attack.
22. Ibid.
23. Ibid., 35ff.
24. *NWT, VB, KVB*, September 19, 1940, 1–2.
25. *VB*, October 28, 1940.
26. *NWT*, September 29, 1940, Sunday supplement. Titled "Vienna—Refuge of the German soul," it had as a subtitle "about the wakeful and wise blood."
27. Kaufmann's acceptance speech was also published in the *VB*, October 28, 1940. His rhetoric was carefully targeted: "This city stands in the sign of youth. Sheathed in the mantle of an honorable tradition, she shines in all her charm and dignity, in her certainty to achieve a happy future."
28. The soccer riot, for that's what it was, played out in the Vienna media with *NWT* running a first story on November 18, 1940. It was objective and relatively low-key. But, on the 19th, political writers took over and criticism of the Viennese

audience became sharper, charging the public with unsportsmanlike conduct, close to rioting. A third story on the 20th gave the incident a political dimension; the rivalry between the Ostmark teams and those of the Altreich was becoming dangerous.

29. P. J. Goebbels, *The Goebbels Diaries 1939–1941*, trans. Fred Taylor (London: H. Hamilton, 1982), 155.

30. Weys, *Cabaret und Kabarett in Wien*, 64–74.

31. Lang, *Der Hitlerjunge*, 293.

32. *NWT*, December 18, 1940. The story is datelined Paris "from our own correspondent."

33. Both Lang and H. v. Schirach mentioned the missing heart in their books.

34. *NWT*, October 9, 1940, announced the festivities, which the Nazis liked to do in order to boost attendance, and then reported on the ceremonies on November 9, 1940.

35. On October 18, 1940, the *VB* reported on a rally where Dr. Leopold Tavs, the city councilor in charge of housing, spoke, while Thomas Kozich, a vice-mayor in charge of sports, and others addressed a crowd in a cinema in suburban Hinterbrühl.

36. Kozich's account can be found in the Austrian state archives B/1166:1.

37. *VB*, October 24, 1940.

38. Prawy, *Die Wiener Oper*.

39. Thomas, *Bis der Vorhang Fiel*.

40. This letter is in the Schirach file in the Austrian state archives, Kt. 24, 317.

41. Thomas, *Bis der Vorhang Fiel*.

42. *VB*, January 4, 1941.

43. The *NWT* printed the text of Schirach's speech in a front-page story on January 16, 1941. The *KVB* put the story on page 3, but it too printed the text, along with a picture of Nazi dignitaries in black civilian clothes laying wreaths at Grillparzer's statue in the Volksgarten. One of the Nazis has his hand raised in the Hitler salute.

44. Kaufmann memo to Schirach of August 20, 1940. Austrian state archives, Schirach file.

45. *VB*, November 3, 1940; *NWT*, November 20, 1940.

46. Kaufmann's memo to Goebbels on November 9, 1940 and his letter to Schirach in January 1941 are in the Austrian state archives, Schirach file, as are the other memos cited in this section.

47. Kudrnofsky, *Vom Dritten Reich zum Dritten Mann*.

48. *VB*, March 2, 1941. Four-column banner on page 1 replete with pictures of Hitler and the Bulgarian prime minister.

49. *VB*, March 3, 1941.

50. *VB*, March 14, 1941.

51. *VB*, March 28–April 7, 1941. The newspaper carried daily stories about growing Yugoslav atrocities against Germans, and about the collapse of King Peter's regime. The day of the German attack is played on page 1 but is not the lead story; that went to the growing toll of Allied shipping that fell victim to U-boat attacks.

52. These items are drawn from press reports—the *VB*, *NWT*, and *KVB*—over the spring and early summer of 1941, and from *Widerstand und Verfolgung in Wien, 1934–45*, vols. 2 and 3.

53. *VB*, August 22, 1941.
54. *Widerstand und Verfolgung in Wien*, vol. 3, 480.
55. Thomas, *Bis der Vorhang Fiel.*
56. Ibid.
57. The text of the speech is in the April 8, 1941 issue of the *VB*.
58. *KVB*, April 21, 1941.
59. Schirach, *Eröffnung der Ausstellung Wiener Kunst in Düsseldorf am 29. September, 1941. Zwei Reden zur deutschen Kunst.* (Opening of the exhibit Viennese Art in Düsseldorf on September 29, 1941. Two speeches on German art.) This slim volume in hard cover was published in Weimar, 1942, by the Gesellschaft der Bibliophilen. The Austrian National Library in Vienna has a copy. The *VB* gave the show respectful coverage, running a preview on September 7, and a three-column commentary on the event itself on September 28, 1941.
60. Wortmann, *Baldur von Schirach*, 200.
61. *VB*, October 16, 1941.
62. The *KVB* noted the demand for Mozart Week tickets on November 25, 1941.
63. Thomas, *Bis der Vorhang Fiel.*
64. The text of Schirach's Mozart speech was front page in both the *VB* and the *KVB*, November 29, 1941.
65. Goebbels's Mozart speech is in the Schirach file at the Austrian state archives.
66. Thomas, *Bis der Vorhang Fiel.*
67. This account of Jewish deportation is based on Rabinovici, Safrian, Berkley, and *Jüdische Schicksale.*
68. *Jüdische Schicksale*, 503.
69. Ibid., 507.
70. His story and the letter he wrote can be found in the Austrian state archives, SR28.
71. The documentation for Tyroler's fate are in the computer records of the Dokumentationszentrum des Österreichischen Widerstands (Documentation Center for the Austrian Resistance) in Vienna.
72. Dubrovic, *Veruntreute Geschichte*, 216–17.
73. Thomas, *Bis der Vorhang Fiel.*
74. The typewritten text, nine pages long, is in the Schirach file at the Austrian state archives.
75. Thomas gives the most detailed account of Hauptmann's stay in Vienna; it is also discussed in Henriette von Schirach's book and in Lang and Wortmann's biographies.
76. Thomas, *Bis der Vorhang Fiel.*
77. Ibid.
78. Goebbels's diary, May 30, 1942.
79. Ibid., June 6, 1942.
80. *Die Kulturveranstaltungen Wiens, Winterspielzeit 1942/43.* (Cultural events in Vienna during the winter season 1942/43), edited by cultural secretary-general Walter Thomas. The twenty-three page brochure is in the Austrian National Library, 747003-B.
81. *VB*, October 12, 1941.
82. Wortmann, *Baldur von Schirach*, 204.
83. Thomas, *Bis der Vorhang Fiel*, 209ff.

84. Dietrich Orlow, *The Nazis in the Balkans* (Pittsburgh: Univ. of Pittsburgh Press, 1968).

85. *VB*, June 13, 1941. The story ran on page 1 below the fold and as an adjunct to the lead: Romanian strongman General Antonescu's visit to Vienna.

86. *KVB*, February 6, 1942.

87. *KVB*, March 14, 1942.

88. See Lang, *Der Hitlerjunge*, 313–29; Wortmann, *Baldur von Schirach*, 208–13. Press coverage was ample but with little commentary.

89. Delivered on the Reichssender Wien, the Vienna station, on September 4, 1942, at 6:45 P.M.

90. Text in the Schirach file, box 53, Austrian state archives. It runs more than eight densely printed pages.

91. Thomas, *Bis der Vorhang Fiel*

92. *Südost Echo*, September 18, 1942. This was a German-language weekly that covered events in Southeast Europe.

93. Lang, *Der Hitlerjunge*, 327.

94. Schirach, *Ich glaubte an Hitler*, 288.

95. Thomas, *Bis der Vorhang Fiel.* Thomas cites the Schirach quote that dismissed him.

96. Lang, *Der Hitlerjunge*, 332. Goebbels's diary entry for March 18, 1943.

97. *VB*, January 14, 1943. Prawy, *Die Wiener Oper*, discusses these aspects of opera development.

98. Wortmann, *Baldur von Schirach*, 215.

99. The letter did not survive, Lang wrote in his Schirach biography, *Der Hitlerjunge*, which was based on long taped interviews after Schirach's release from Spandau.

100. The media campaign to get women into factories began in February 1943, culminating with Schirach's speech on the topic on March 6, 1943. *NWT*, March 7, 1943.

101. Schirach, *Ich glaubte an Hitler*, 289.

102. *NWT*, March 19, 1943.

103. *VB*, April 21, 1943.

104. Knopp, *Hitlers Helfer*, 147.

105. Schirach, *Ich glaubte an Hitler*, 290–91.

106. Wortmann, *Baldur von Schirach*, 216.

107. Schirach, *Ich glaubte an Hitler*, 293.

108. Lang, *Der Hitlerjunge*, 341–42.

Chapter 9

1. Neubauer, conversation with author.

2. Walter Fritz, "Propagandafilme der Wien-Film (1938–1945)," in *Macht, Literatur, Krieg: österreichische Literatur im Nationalsozialismus*, Uwe Bauer, ed., 341.

3. Lichtenecker, conversation with author.

4. Holl, conversation with author.

5. Traudl Lessing, conversation with author.

6. Inge Zembsch, conversation with author.

7. Neustädtle, conversation with author.

8. Czedik, *Diary*, 43, 53, 83.

9. The *NZZ* piece was unsigned, i.e., only by the letters *W.Jg.*
10. Kehlmann to author. Kehlmann would become a leading stage, film, and TV director after the war, who worked mostly in Germany, leaving Vienna around 1950 in disgust because of Nazi remnants in the country. He returned in the 1980s.
11. Kann, conversation with author.
12. *Jüdische Schicksale*, 180.
13. Ibid., 210.
14. Ibid., 195ff.
15. Rabinovici, *Instanzen der Ohnmacht*, 313ff.
16. Lang, *Der Hitlerjunge*, 333.
17. Ibid., 347.
18. Ibid., 349.
19. Luza, *Austro-German Relations*, 336ff.
20. *KVB*, June 2, 1943.
21. Neubauer, conversation with author.
22. Hilde Haider-Pregler, conversation with author. Dr. Pregler is professor of drama at the University of Vienna.
23. *VB*, October 24, 1943, has an account of how well KdF was treating foreign workers: soccer matches, boxing bouts, and other events for their exclusive entertainment.
24. *Polnische Zwangsarbeiter in Österreich* (Warsaw: PZÖ, 1998).
25. "Now's the Time, December 2000 Porgy und Bess im Rondell." This was a publicity paper put out to coincide with the opening of a new nightclub in the Rondell site, December 2000. The story was included as part of the new club's "history."
26. Dor, conversation with author.
27. *KVB*, October 1943.
28. *NWT*, July 7, 1944, and *NWT*, summer of 1944. "The Italian worker—musically cosseted."
29. *VB*, December 29, 1943.
30. Ulrich, *Der Luftkrieg über Österreich*, 8.
31. *VB*, August 14, 1943.
32. *VB*, February 8, 1944.
33. *VB*, April 18, 1944. The paper laid it on with a trowel: "Once again the people stood at the graves of the victims of the Anglo-American air gangsters. Bathed in the golden glow of the sun, the blood-red flags of the movement were lifted into the azure blue sky. . . . "
34. Andics, *Fünfzig Jahre*, 412–16.
35. Schärf, *Österreichs Erneuerung, 1945–55*.
36. Luza, *The Resistance in Austria*, 152ff.
37. In addition to Luza's book, resistance activities in 1943 are covered in the following books: F. Molden, *Die Feuer in der Nacht*; O. Molden, *Ruf des Gewissens*; and Becker, *Österreichs Freiheitskampf*.
38. The crime items are taken from 1943 and 1944 reports in the *KVB*, which ran the juiciest stories, and in the *VB* and *NWT*, which printed more sober accounts.
39. The Vienna media gave Blaschke's appointment and subsequent activities as mayor much greater coverage than Neubacher or Jung ever received. The *VB*, for example, devoted almost a full page on December 31, 1943, to a portrait of the new

mayor; *KVB*, for another, headlined its portrait of "Vienna's mayor, a fighter and a friend of the arts." Schirach, who disliked Blaschke, gritted his teeth and gave the warm speech he was expected to deliver.

40. Rebhann, *Die Braunen Jahre*, 230 ff.
41. Both the *KVB* and *VB* on June 11 and 12, 1944, went all out in honoring the composer. The noted theater historian, Joseph Gregor wrote an appreciation in the June 11 *VB* titled "Richard Strauss: his mission in our time."

Chapter 10

1. Ulrich, *Der Luftkrieg über Österreich*, 18. Ulrich cites a Wehrmacht report dated July 17, 1944.
2. On May 8, 1975, Hofrat Dr. Otto Schobesberger sent an account of the incident to city hall in response to a public appeal by then mayor Leopold Grätz for reminiscences, documents, diaries, etc., that rank and file Viennese may have had in the last months of the war. All these documents are kept in the city archives where they are once again in the process of being cataloged after the archives had been moved to a new location.
3. *VB*, July 9, 1944.
4. *KVB*, July 11, 1944.
5. Szokoll, *Die Rettung Wiens 1945*, 190–246. This is Szokoll's autobiography, and I have followed his eyewitness account, in addition to Andics's earlier *Fünfzig Jahre Unseres Lebens*, 416–19, and Jedlicka's *Der 20. Juli in Österreich*.
6. Szokoll, *Die Rettung Wiens 1945*, 194–96.
7. Ibid., 225.
8. Jedlicka, *Der 20. Juli in Österreich*, 61.
9. Dor, conversation with author.
10. *VB*, August 25, 1944. The paper devoted three pages to the edict in a Berlin dateline story. The *KVB* bannered the story on the front page and gave it most of page 2, unusual for the tabloid and indicative of how important the Nazis ranked the edict.
11. *NWT*, September 29, 1944.
12. Regius began his copious and detailed diaries in March 1944 and continued them past the end of the war. They are located in the Vienna city archives.
13. Schöner, *Wiener Tagebuch, 1944/45*. See also chap. 6.
14. Ibid., 25–27.
15. *KKZ (Kleine Kreiszeitung)*, September 12, 1944. It is now the only tabloid left in the city.
16. Schöner, *Wiener Tagebuch, 1944/45*, 54.
17. Ibid., 59.
18. Ulrich, *Der Luftkrieg über Österreich*, 21.
19. Schöner, *Wiener Tagebuch, 1944/45*, 65.
20. Hella Kinn's diary covers the last year of the war in vivid, eyewitness detail. In 1975 she sent it to the city archives in response to Mayor Grätz's call for personal end-of-the-war accounts.
21. Ulrich, *Der Luftkrieg über Österreich*.
22. Margaret Bajez's diary is in the Vienna city archives.

23. Rauchensteiner, *Der Krieg über Österreich 1945*.

24. Ulrich, *Der Luftkrieg über Österreich*, 26–27.

25. *NWT*, February 20, 1945.

26. Fiedelsberger gave an interview to a city hall official in response to Mayor Grätz's call for reminiscences of 1945. A transcript of the interview is in the city archives.

27. Ernst Andreas's diary. Vienna city archives, box 4, folder 204.

28. A copy of Kaltenbrunner's letter in the Bundesarchiv in Berlin. The notation says "Blitz SHDS 14.9.44, 0.100 hours."

29. Friedrichs's twenty-two-page report was written on his return to Munich on September 21, 1944. A copy is in the Bundesarchiv in Berlin.

30. *VB*, September 17, 1944. The piece, by F. A. Grumbach, is headlined "In the Name of the German People" and is illustrated with pictures of the judges and the accused. Both are trimmed to fit preconceived notions.

31. *VB*, October 21, 1944.

32. Schöner, *Wiener Tagebuch, 1944/45*, 59.

33. *NWT*, October 5, 1944. The story was given two inside columns—a decent placement but not a blaring one. Placement was important in the Third Reich; Goebbels left nothing to chance.

34. The *VB* and the *KKZ* reported on the session on September 7, 1944.

35. *NWT*, October 8, 1944.

36. Ibid., October 31, 1944.

37. *VB*, November 12, 1944; *VB* and *KKZ*, November 26, 1944.

38. *VB*, December 31, 1944.

39. Traudl Lessing worked in the bunker as a telephone operator and radio announcer. She also looked after a campsite for seventeen-year-old girls just outside the bunker, and thus had a front-row seat on what was going on.

40. Ringler kept a diary over the last few months of the war. He gave the manuscript to the city in the mid-1970s and then had it published in book form as *Illusion einer Jugend, Fahnen und das bittere Ende*.

41. Becker, *Österreichischer Freiheitskampf*, 16–21.

42. Luza, *The Resistance in Austria*, 161–77.

43. Molden, *Fepolinski und Waschlapski*, 457. Fritz Molden would later marry Allen Dulles's daughter.

Chapter 11

1. Adele Hufnagl's diaries begin on January 30, 1945, and continue into the weeks after the war. They are in the Vienna city archives.

2. Stephanie Bamer's diary is also in the city archives.

3. Schöner, *Wiener Tagebuch, 1944/45*, 95.

4. Ibid., 100.

5. Gosztony, *Endkampf an der Donau*, 212.

6. K. Stadler, *Österreich 1938–45 im Spiegel der NS Akten* (Vienna and Munich: Herold Verlag, 1966), 341, 401. Both Gosztony and Stadler cite different sections of the same SD report.

7. Gosztony, *Endkampf an der Donau*, 213.

8. Ibid., 231ff.

9. Schöner, *Wiener Tagebuch, 1944/45,* 108.
10. Ringler, *Illusion einer Jugend,* 148.
11. *NWT,* March 18, 1945.
12. Ulrich, *Der Luftkreig über Österreich.*
13. Gosztony, *Endkampf an der Donau,* 231–46.
14. *KKZ,* March 30, 1945, and more expansively, *NWT,* March 31, 1945.
15. Karl Stadler, *Österreich 1939–45 im Spiegel der NS Akten,* 401–3.
16. *VB,* April 3, 1945.
17. Rauchensteiner, *Der Krieg in Österreich 1945.* Here I follow his account of the battle.
18. Ringler, *Illusion einer Jugend.*
19. Szokoll, *Die Rettung Wiens 1945,* 283ff.
20. Käs, *Wien im Schicksalsjahr 1945,* 14ff. This is more brochure than a full-sized book; it has twenty-three pages.
21. Gosztony, *Endkampf an der Donau,* 250.
22. Rauchensteiner, *Der Krieg in Österreich 1945,* 416. Blaschke's testimony before the Peoples' Court in Vienna after the war is cited in Rauchensteiner's note on this page.
23. Wessely was killed a week later. Rauchensteiner, *Der Krieg in Österreich 1945,* 416.
24. Ringler describes the bizarre scene in his entry for April 6, 1945. *Illusion einer Jugend,* 168.
25. Knopp, *Hitlers Helfer,* 152.
26. Papers of the Historical Commission in the Vienna city archives.
27. Ibid.
28. Ibid.
29. Szokoll, *Die Rettung Wiens 1945,* 356.
30. Andics, *Fünfzig Jahre,* 455–59. He gives a compressed but coherent account of what happened.
31. Schärf, *April 1945 in Wien; Österreichs Erneuerung, 1945–1955.* Schärf's books are biased accounts of events leading to establishment of a provisional government, but they come from an eyewitness and a major political player.
32. Matejka, *Anregung ist alles,* 134.
33. Schöner, *Wiener Tagebuch, 1944/45,* 201–3.

Chapter 12

1. Schöner, *Wiener Tagebuch, 1944/45,* 340.
2. Molden, *Besetzer, Toren, Biedermänner,* 37.
3. Andics, *Fünfzig Jahre,* 522.
4. Schöner, *Wiener Tagebuch, 1944/45,* 250.
5. Knight, *Ich bin dafür die Sache,* 85ff. This book is a transcript of government deliberations about restitution to Nazi victims.
6. Ibid., 83–84.
7. Andics, *Fünfzig Jahre,* 489.
8. F. Molden, *Besetzer, Toren, Biedermänner,* 16.

9. Matejka, *Widerstand ist alles*, 189–200. Matejka did not write a chronological account, but it can be drawn from his anecdotal mish-mash.
10. Ibid., 195.
11. The letter was published in the magazine *Strom* (March 1946) and is reproduced in Gerhard Habarta, *Frühere Verhältnisse* (Vienna: Verlag der Apfel, 1996), 28.
12. Matejka, *Anregung ist alles*, 207.
13. Fritz Molden, conversation with author.
14. Heinrich Wildner, the secretary general of the foreign office, signed the memorandum, but it appears to have gone through several other drafts before Wildner put on the final polish. The text can be found in Knight, *Ich bin dafür die Sache*, 100–12; I cite (pages) in subsequent paragraphs of my text.
15. F. Molden, *Besetzer, Toren, Biedermänner*, 109.
16. Although written in 1947, my father's essay was not published until I persuaded Ilse Walter, the editor of an Austrian anthology titled *In diesem Land* (Vienna: Kremayer and Scheriau, 1992, 198–201) to include it.
17. Andics, *Fünfzig Jahre*, 587–92.
18. Pick, *Und welche Rolle spielt Österreich?*, 67.
19. Andics, *Fünfzig Jahre*, 593–600.
20. Ibid.
21. The following discussion of Vienna's postwar culture is based to some extent on the author's own experiences at the time and on two essays in *Zeit der Befreiung, Wiener Theater nach 1945*, eds. Hilde Haider-Pregler and Peter Rösser (Vienna: Picus Verlag, 1998): Hilde Haider-Pregler's "Das Burgtheater ist eine Idee," 84–122, and Nicole Metzger's "Leopold Lindtbergs erstes Jahrzehnt am Burgtheater," 123–41.
22. Andics, *Fünfzig Jahre*, 601.
23. Ibid.
24. Fritz Molden, conversation with author.
25. Santner, conversation with author.
26. As an example, and as late as 1969, the wife of a prominent Viennese painter had his pregnant mistress jailed for "disturbing her marriage."
27. Pick, *Und welche Rolle*.
28. *Der Standard* was the only paper in Vienna to cover the story in depth during the summer of 2003.
29. The quote made the Vienna rumor mills but was finally confirmed by *Standard* columnist Hans Rauscher.
30. On July 5, 2003, *Der Standard* ran a retrospective article about Plischke and his reception in Vienna.
31. Spiel, *Dämonie der Gemütlichkeit*, 83–85.
32. *Wiener Kurier*, 1946.
33. Eric Kandel, interview in *News Über Uns* (a Jewish Vienna newspaper), summer 2003.
34. Speech delivered in Cologne on February 12, 1986, on the occasion of Jelinek's receiving the Heinrich Böll Prize. It was reprinted in the weekly *Die Zeit* that year and in *Blauer Streusand. Friederike Mayrèocker*, edited by Barbara Alms (Frankfurt: Suhrkamp, 1987), 42–44.

Bibliography

Andics, Hellmut. *Fünfzig Jahre Unseres Lebens.* Vienna: Molden Verlag, 1968.

———. *Die Juden in Wien.* Munich: Bucher, 1988.

Becker, Hans. *Österreichs Freiheitskampf.* Vienna: Verlag der freien Union der Övp, 1946.

Berkley, George. *Vienna and its Jews, the Tragedy of Success.* Cambridge, Mass.: Abt Books, 1988

Bettauer, Hugo. *Die Stadt ohne Juden: ein Roman von Übermorgen.* Vienna: Gloriette Verlag, 1922.

Biron, Georg. *Die Letzte Beichte, Geschichte eines Verrats.* Vienna: Edition S, Verlag der österreichischen Staatsdruckerei, 1988.

Botz, Gerhard. *Wien vom Anschluss zum Krieg.* Vienna and Munich: Jugend & Volk, 1978. *Nationalsozialismus in Wien.* Vienna: Buchloe: DUO, 1988

Brook-Shepherd, Gordon. *Austrian Odyssey.* London: Macmillan and Co., 1957.

———. *Dollfuss.* London: Macmillan, 1961.

———. *Anschluss, The Rape of Austria.* London: Macmillan, 1963.

Braunthal, Julius. *The Tragedy of Austria.* London: Victor Gollancz, 1948.

Chorherr, Thomas, ed. *1938, Anatomie eines Jahres.* Vienna: Überreuter Verlag, 1987.

Czedik, Maria. Diary: *"Uns Fragt man nicht," Ein Tagebuch, 1941–1945.* Vienna: Jugend & Volk, 1988.

Danimann, Franz. *Finis Austriae, Österreich, März 1938.* Vienna, Munich, and Zurich: Europaverlag, 1978.

Drimmel, Heinrich. *Vom Kanzlermord zum Anschluss.* Vienna: Almathea, 1987.

Dubrovic, Milan. *Veruntreute Geschichte.* Vienna and Hamburg: Paul Zsolnay Verlag, 1985.

Dutch, Oswald. *Thus Died Austria.* London: Edward Arnold & Co., 1938.

Eichstädt, Ulrich. *Von Dollfuss zu Hitler, Geschichte des Anschlusses Österreich, 1933–1938.* Wiesbaden: Steiner, 1955.

Feichtlbauer, Hubert: *Der Fall Österreich. Nationalsozialismus, Rassismus: Eine notwendige Bilanz.* Vienna: Verlag Holzhausen, 2000.

Fränkel, Joseph, ed. *The Jews of Austria.* London: Vallentine, Mitchell, 1968.

Fuchs, Martin. *Showdown in Vienna, The Death of Austria.* New York: G. P. Putnam's Sons, 1939.

Gedye, G.E.R. *Fallen Bastions:The Central European Tragedy.* London: Victor Gollancz, 1939.

Gold, Hugo. *Geschichte der Juden in Wien. Ein Gedenkbuch.* Tel Aviv: Olamenu, 1966.

Gosztony, Peter. *Endkampf an der Donau.* Vienna: Molden Verlag, 1969.

Gruner, Wolf. *Zwangsarbeit und Verfolgung. Österreichische Juden im NS-Staat, 1938–1945.* Innsbruck-Vienna-Munich: Studien Verlag, 2000.

Heiss, Gernot. *Willfährige Wissenschaft, die Universität Wien, 1938–45.* Vienna: Verlag für Gesellschaftskritik, 1989.

Hennings, Fred. *Heimat Burgtheater.* Vol. 3. Vienna and Munich: Herold Verlag, 1979.

Hirt, Ferdinand. *Österreich: 50 Jahre Republik.* Vienna: Institut für Österreich Kunde, 1968.

Jahoda, Marie, Paul Lazarsfeld, Hans Zeisel. *Die Arbeitslosen von Marienthal.* 2nd ed. Bonn: Verlag für Demoskopie, 1960.

Jedlicka, Ludwig. *Der 20. Juli in Österreich.* Vienna: Herold, 1965.

Jüdische Schicksale, Berichte von Verfolgten. Dokumentationsarchiv des österreichischen Widerstands. Vienna: Österreichischer Bundesverlag, 1992.

Käs, Ferdinand. *Wien in Schicksalsjahr 1945.* Vienna: Europa Verlag, 1965.

Kampelmacher, E. H. *In die Emigration.* Vienna: Jugend & Volk, 1988.

Kelfeit, Chas. *Ich kann nicht schweigen.* Vienna: Jugend & Volk, 1988.

Klusacek, Christine, and Herbert Steiner. *Dokumentation zur Österreichischen Zeitgeschichte, 1938–1945.* Vienna and Munich: Jugend & Volk, 1971.

Knight, Robert. *Ich bin dafür die Sache in die Länge zu ziehen: Die Wortprotokolle der österreichischen Bundesregierung, 1945–52.* Frankfurt am Main: Athenaeum Verlag, 1988.

Knopp, Guido. *Hitlers Helfer.* Munich: C. Bertelsmann Verlag, 1998.

Krist, Martin. *Vertreibungsschicksale.* Vienna: Turia & Kant, 2001.

Kudrnofsky, Wolfgang. *Vom Dritten Reich zum Dritten Mann.* Vienna: Molden Verlag, 1973.

Lang, Joachim. *Der Hitlerjunge.* Hamburg: Rasch & Roehring, 1988.

Lennhoff, Eugen. *The Last Five Hours of Austria.* New York: Frederick A. Stokes, 1938.

Leser, Norbert, ed. *Das Geistige Leben Wiens in der Zwischenkriegszeit* (The spiritual and intellectual life of Vienna between the wars). Vienna: Österreichischer Bundesverlag, 1981.

Libiger, Richard, ed. "*Reichsleiter Baldur von Schirach. Tätigkeit als Reichsstatthalter und Gauleiter in Wien, August 1940–November 1942.* (Gau press office report on Schirach's activities in Vienna from August 1940–November 1942). Vienna: Gaupresseamt-Archiv, 1942, Mimeographed.

Liebman, Maximilian. *Theodor Innitzer und der Anschluss Österreichs.* Graz: Styria Verlag, 1988.

Lothar, Ernst. *Das Wunder des Überlebens; Erinnerungen und Erlebnisse.* Hamburg: Paul Zsolnay, 1960.

Luza, Radomir. *Austro-German Relations in the Anschluss Era.* Princeton: Princeton University Press, 1975.

———. *The Resistance in Austria, 1938–1945.* Minneapolis: University of Minnesota Press, 1984.

Matejka, Viktor. *Widerstand ist alles: Notizen eines Unorthodoxen.* Vienna: Löcker Verlag, 1984.

———. *Anregung ist alles.* Vienna: Löcker Verlag, 1991.

Matteas, Ruth. "Fasching in Wien." Ph.D. diss., University of Vienna, 1991.

Molden, Fritz. *Fepolinski und Waschlapski auf dem berstenden Stern.* Vienna: Molden Verlag, 1976.

————. *Besetzer, Toren, Biedermänner.* Vienna: Molden Verlag, 1980.

————. *Die Feuer in der Nacht.* Vienna and Munich: Amalthea, 1988.

Molden, Otto. *Ruf des Gewissens.* Vienna: Herold Verlag, 1958.

Moser, Jonny. *Die Judenverfolgung in Österreich, 1938–45.* Vienna: Europa Verlag, 1966.

Neuman, H. J. *Arthur Seyss-Inquart.* Graz: Styria Verlag, 1970.

Papen, Franz von. *Der Wahrheit eine Gasse.* Innsbruck: List, 1952.

Pfeifer, Helfried. *Die Ostmark, Neugestaltung und Eingliederung.* Vienna: Staatsdruckerei, 1941.

Pick, Hella. *Und welche Rolle spielt Österreich?* Vienna: Kremayer & Scheriau, 1999.

Pohanka, Reinhard. *Stadt unter dem Hakenkreuz.* Vienna: Picus Verlag, 1996.

Prawy, Marcel. *Die Wiener Oper, Geschichte und Geschichten.* 2nd ed. Vienna: Molden Verlag, 1978.

Rabinovici, Doron. *Instanzen der Ohnmacht, Wien 1938–1945.* Frankfurt: Jüdischer Verlag, 2000.

Rauchensteiner, Manfried. *Der Krieg in Österreich 1945.* Vienna: Bundesverlag, 1984.

Rebhann, Fritz M. *Die Braunen Jahre, Wien 1938–45.* Vienna: Edition Atelier, 1995.

Reimann, Viktor. *Innitzer: Kardinal zwischen Hitler und Rom.* Vienna: Molden Verlag, 1967.

————. *Zu Gross für Österreich.* Vienna: Molden Verlag, 1968.

Ringler, Ralf Roland. *Illusion einer Jugend, Fahnen und das bittere Ende.* St. Pölten and Vienna: Niederösterreichisches Pressehaus, 1977.

Rosenkranz, Herbert. "The Anschluss and the Tragedy of Austrian Jewry, 1934–45." In *The Jews of Austria: Essays on their life, history and destruction*, ed. by Josef Fränkel. London: Valentine, Mitchell, 1967.

————. *Reichskristallnacht, 9. November 1938 in Österreich.* Vienna, Frankfurt, Zurich: Europa Verlag, 1968.

————. *Verfolgung und Selbstbehauptung, die Juden in Österreich, 1938–45.* Vienna and Munich: Herold Verlag, 1978.

Safrian, Hans. *Eichmann und seine Gehilfen.* Frankfurt am Main: Fischer Taschenbuch Verlag, 1995.

Schärf, Adolf. *April 1945 in Wien.* Vienna: Wiener Volksbuchhandlung, 1948.

————. *Österreichs Erneuerung, 1945–55.* Vienna: Wiener Volksbuch, 1995, 1960.

Schausberger, Norbert. *Der Griff nach Österreich, der "Anschluss."* Vienna and Munich: Jugend & Volk, 1988.

————. *Mobilisierung und Einsatz fremdländischer Arbeitskräfte während des zweiten Weltkriegs in Österreich*, Vienna, 1970.

Schirach, Baldur von. *Ich glaubte an Hitler.* Hamburg: Mosaik Verlag, 1967.

————. *Eröffnung der Ausstellung Wiener Kunst in Düsseldorf am 29. September 1941. Zwei Reden zur deutschen Kunst* (Opening of the exhibit Viennese art in Düsseldorf on September 29,1941. Two speeches on German art.). Weimar: Gesellschaft der Bibliophilen, 1942.

Schirach, Henriette von. *Der Preis der Herrlichkeit.* Wiesbaden: Lines Verlag, 1956.

Schmidl, Erwin. *Der "Anschluss" Österreichs, der deutsche Einmarsch 1938.* Bonn: Bernard & Gräfe, 1994.

Schmidt, Guido. Testimony at his treason trial. (*Der Hochverratsprozess gegen Dr. Guido Schmidt vor dem Wiener Volksgericht. Die gerichtliche Protokolle.*) Vienna: Österreichische Staatsdruckerei, 1947.

Schöner, Josef. *Wiener Tagebuch, 1944/45*. Ed. by Eva-Maria Csaky, Franz Matscher, and Gerald Stourzh. Vienna and Cologne: Böhlau Verlag, 1992.

Schreiner, Evelyn. "NS Kulturpolitik in Wien, 1938–45." Ph.D. diss., University of Vienna, 1980.

Schuschnigg, Kurt von. *Ein Requiem in Rot-Weiss-Rot*. Vienna: Almathea Verlag, 1978.

———. *Im Kampf gegen Hitler, Überwindung der Anschlussidee*. Vienna: Molden Verlag, 1969. Reprint, Vienna: Almathea Verlag, 1988.

Smelser, Ronald, et al., eds. *Die Braune Elite*. Vol 2. Darmstadt: Wissenschaftliche Buchgesellschaft, 1999.

Spiel, Hilde. *Vienna's Golden Autumn*. London: Weidenfeld & Nicholson, 1987. The German edition is *Glanz und Untergang*, Wien 1866–1938. Munich: Paul List Verlag, 1987.

———. *Dämonie der Gemütlichkeit*. Munich: Paul List Verlag, 1991.

Stadler, Friedrich. *The Vienna Circle*. Vienna: Springer Verlag, 2001.

Stadler, Karl. *Österreich 1939–45 im Spiegel der NS Akten*. Vienna and Munich: Herold Verlag, 1966.

Steinbauer, Gustav. *Ich war Verteidiger in Nürenberg*. Klagenfurt: E. Kaiser Verlag, 1950.

Steiner, Herbert. *Zum tode verurteilt. Österreicher gegen Hitler. Eine Dokumentation*. Vienna: Europa Verlag, 1964.

Sündermann, Helmut. *Die Grenzen Fallen, von der Ostmark ins Sudetenland*. Munich: Eher, 1939.

Szokoll, Carl. *Die Rettung Wiens 1945*. Vienna: Amalthea, Molden Verlag, 2001.

Talos, Emerich, et al. *NS Herrschaft in Österreich, Ein Handbuch*. Vienna: Österreichischer Bundesverlag, 2000.

Thomas, Walter [Wilhelm Anderman]. *Bis der Vorhang Fiel*. Dortmund: Schwalvenberg, 1947.

Tietze, Hans. *Die Juden Wiens*. Vienna: Edition Atelier, 1987.

Ulrich, Johann. *Der Luftkrieg über Österreich*. Vienna: Österreichische Bundesverlag, 1986.

Vajda, Stephan. *Felix Austria, Eine Geschichte Österreichs*. Vienna: Überreuter Verlag, 1980.

Wien 1938. Catalog for an exhibit at the Historical Museum of the City of Vienna, March 11–June 30, 1988. Vienna: Österreichischer Bundesverlag, 1988.

Wagner, Dieter, and Gerhard Tomkowitz. *Ein Volk, Ein Reich, Ein Führer: Der Anschluss Österreichs*. Munich: Piper, 1968.

Walzer, Tina, and Stephan Templ. *Unser Wien, "Arisierung" auf österreichisch*. Berlin: Aufbau Verlag, 2001.

Weibel, Peter, and Friedrich Stadler, eds. *Vertreibung der Vernunft (The Cultural Exodus from Austria)*. Vienna: Löcker Verlag, 1993.

Weinzierl, Erika. *Zu Wenig Gerechte, Österreicher und Judenverfolgung, 1938–45*. Graz, Vienna, Cologne: Styria Verlag, 1985.

Weinberger, Lois. *Tatsachen, Begegnungen und Gespräche*. Vienna: Österreichischer Verlag, 1948.

Weyr, Siegfried. *Die Wiener*. Vienna: Paul Zsolney Verlag, 1972.

Weys, Rudolf. *Cabaret und Kabarett in Wien*. Vienna and Munich: Jugend & Volk, 1970.

Widerstand und Verfolgung in Wien, 1934–45, Eine Dokumentation. Vienna: Dokumentationsarchiv des Österreichischen Widerstands, 1984.

Wortmann, Michael. *Baldur von Schirach, Adolf Hitler's Jugendführer*. Cologne: Böhlau, 1982.

Zernatto, Guido. *Die Wahrheit über Österreich*. New York and Toronto: Longmans, Green, Alliance Book Corp., 1939.

Zuckmayer, Carl. *A Part of Myself, Portrait of an Epoch*. Trans. by Richard and Clara Winston. New York: Harcourt, Brace Jovanovich, 1970.

Zweig, Stefan. *The World of Yesterday*. Lincoln: University of Nebraska Press, 1964.

Index

black market, 175–76, 195, 232, 264, 292
blackouts, 150, 151, 186
Blaschke, Hanns: appointment, 246–47, 259, 332;
  cultural policies, 81–82, 130, 252; defense of
  Vienna, 275, 279–80; on Fasching celebration,
  129; opposition to, 260; on Prussians, 215; on
  Thomas's art exhibit, 212; war crimes sentence,
  300; wartime governance, 262–63
Bloch-Bauer, Adele, 113
Bock, Fedor von, 8, 34
Bock, Fritz, 29
Bohemia, 42, 133, 142
Böhm, Karl, 220, 247, 307
bolshevism, 232–33
Bormann, Martin, 176, 213, 217–18, 221, 223, 236,
  259, 275
Born, Ludger, 166, 235
Botz, Gerhard, 73
Brahms, Johannes, 111
Brandt, Willy, 310
Braun, Eva, 179, 222, 223, 256
Braunthal, Julius, 48, 49, 51, 52, 55
Brecht, Bertold, 121
Brenner Pass, 56
bridges, 277, 284, 285
British Council for German Jewry, 138
Broch, Hermann, 117, 296
Brockdorff-Rantzau, Ulrich von, 46
Bronfman, Edgar, 310
Bronner, Gerhard, 25, 76, 78, 94
Bronner, Oskar, 312
Brook-Shepherd, Gordon, 18
brown shirts, 98, 157–58. See also SA
  (Sturmabteilung)
Bruckner, Anton, 4, 209
Brunner, Alois, 204, 205, 206, 208
Brunner, Anton, 204, 206, 235
Buchenwald, 155
Budapest, Hungary, 44, 108, 268, 272
Bühler, Charlotte, 111, 119
Bulgaria, 143, 174
Bumballa, Raul, 286–87
Bünau, Rudolf von, 276
bunkers, 265–66
Bürckel, Josef, 62–85; Anschluss event, 34; battles
  with colleagues, 144–45, 152–54, 187; Catholic
  church and, 64–66, 97–98, 99–101, 141, 143; cul-
  tural policies, 158–62, 172, 173, 179, 180, 185,
  188; death of, 294; dismissal of, 170, 171; economic issues, 88–90, 131, 143–44, 186; Globocnik
  and, 128; Jews and, 93, 95, 106–7, 123–24; labor
  and, 66–68; Ostmark laws, 134–35; plebiscite, 70–
  75; propaganda, 127; role and goals, 62–63, 84–
  85, 87, 96–97, 128, 150
Burgenland, 47, 51
Burgtheater: attendance, 226; An Austrian Tragedy
  at, 159; Bürckel's plans for, 160; defense of
  Vienna, 270, 280; Hauptmann week, 210; Hitler
  at, 137; leadership of, 92, 306–7; modern status
  of, 316, 317; Nazi control of, 80–81; propaganda
  role of, 225
buses, 313

cabarets, 184–85
Café Landtmann, 253
Canetti, Elias, 318
capitalism, 116
capital punishment, 195–96, 239, 245, 264, 275
Carinthia, 45, 46, 47, 134
Carnap, Rudolf, 120

Castagnola, Camilla, 126
Catholics and Catholicism: Anschluss event, 25; on
  Austrian independence, 242; on cremation option, 263; culture of Vienna and, 58; Jewish conversions to, 139; Nazi pressure on, 141–42;
  resistance among, 145–47, 165–69, 244; Socialists
  and, 305; status of, 57; youth of, 168–69
censorship, 92, 121, 197
Central Office for Jewish Emigration, 141
Cermak, Josef, 245
Chamberlain, Neville, 21, 99
charities, 157
Charles I, 39, 41, 44–45
Charles V, 108
chemical factories, 274
child mortality, 49
Christian Socials: elections of 1930, 53; Heimwehr
  and, 58; influence of, 115; 1919 elections, 43; ori-
  gins, 44; People's Party and, 290; post-Great War
  politics, 46, 47, 51; support for, 54
Christian trade unions, 243
Christmas, 263–64
churches, 64–66, 97, 99–102, 303
Churchill, Sir Winston, 220–21
Ciano, Galeazzo, 173, 216
Cicognani, Amleto, 65
circuses, 251
City Hall, 316
City Hall Park, 253
City Without Jews (Bettauer), 159–60
civil rights, 109
civil services, 256
civil war, 1, 3, 9, 10, 17, 52, 55, 56
Clericals, 15
Cold War, 303–4
communication services, 286
Communists: activism of, 166; Anschluss event, 16,
  36; Austrian Resistance and, 278; Bürckel on, 66;
  death penalty for, 245; departure of, 301; end of
  Communism, 312; post–Great War politics, 46;
  putsch (1918), 41–42; in Vienna, 287, 290
concentration camps, 124, 205, 206, 289, 293, 305
concert halls, 251
Concordat (agreement), 64–65
congresses, 252
conscription, 45, 146, 150, 151, 244
constitution, 56, 288
corpses, 286
correspondence from Jews, 123–24
cost of living, 292
courier services, 267
courts, 87, 232, 245, 261, 311
Creditanstalt (Austrian bank), 53
crime, 36, 95, 96, 101, 103, 195–97, 245–46, 286
criminal justice, 261, 309
criticism, ban on, 227
Croatia, 42, 108, 273
"crooked cross" or "Krukenkreuz," 9–10
Csokor, Franz Theodor, 121
"cuckoo" alarm, 255
cultural scene of Vienna: audiences of, 308; Berlin
  compared to, 69, 125, 130, 135, 136, 180, 191,
  192, 202, 212, 223; under Blaschke, 130; under
  Bürckel, 158–62; under Goebbels, 219–20, 251–
  52; Hitler's birthday, 247; under Matejka, 296–98;
  postwar status, 305, 306–8; under Schirach, 172,
  179–81, 197, 198–202, 209. See also music; opera;
  theater
currency, 47, 263–64, 302, 303
cynicism of the Viennese, 75